Contemporary Irish Literature

Transforming Tradition

WITHDRAW

Christina Hunt Mahony

St. Martin's Press
New York

ISBN 0-312-15871-8 (cloth)
ISBN 0-312-21901-6 (paper)

Library of Congress Cataloging-in-Publication Data

Mahony, Christina Hunt, 1949-
   Contemporary Irish literature : transforming tradition / Christina
Hunt Mahony.
      p.   cm.
   Includes bibliographical references and index.
   ISBN 0-312-15871-8
   1. English literature--Irish authors--History and criticism.
2. Irish literature--20th century--History and criticism.
3. Ireland--Intellectual life--20th century. 4. Influence
(Literary, artistic, etc.) 5. Ireland--In literature. I. Title.
PR8753.M34   1998
820.9'9417'09045--dc21   98-42864
                                                             CIP

Design by Acme Art, Inc.

First edition: November, 1998
10 9 8 7 6 5 4 3 2

This book is dedicated to my beloved father,
George Hunt

CONTENTS

ACKNOWLEDGMENTS

Many people have helped in the making of this book.

I would like to thank the staffs of the National Library of Ireland and of the Library of Trinity College, Dublin for invaluable assistance in answering queries and locating material. Thanks also to Kate Slattery and Michael Moloney of the Embassy of Ireland, to Janet McIver of the Northern Ireland Bureau, and to Carmel McGill formerly Northern Ireland Cultural Exchange Officer, British Council, all in Washington, D.C.

For their insightful reading of drafts of the book, I must thank Nicholas Grene, Maurice Harmon, Turlough Johnston, and George O'Brien.

Additional help in the form of productive discussion, useful information, practical advice, and, most important, needed support was provided by personal and professional friends and family members here and abroad— Sebastian Barry, Ann Belzner, James Blake, Kathleen Constable, Daniel Dempski, Nuala Ní Dhomhnaill, Roy Foster, Adrian Frazier, Clare Gill, Patricia Haberstroh, Rüdiger Imhof, Elizabeth Malcolm, Patrick Mason, Kevin MacAleese, Fintan O'Toole, Coílín Owens, Richard Pine, Tamara Prince, Daniel Reardon, Ruth Sherry, Bruce Stewart, Roland Viger, Patricia Wheeler, and my students past and present.

Essential clerical support came from Andrea Barnes, Kate Fenton, Rita Gdula, Maureen MacAleer, Molly O'Leary, and Jennifer Quigley, all in Washington; and from Geraldine Mangan in Dublin.

Ms. Rhoda McGuinness graciously provided permission to reproduce her sister's work as the cover art; and David Britton expedited and facilitated that decision—to them both my great thanks.

Maura Burnett at St. Martin's Press provided cheerful and patient editorial expertise, and often a good laugh to lighten the load.

Special thanks and an enormous debt of gratitude is owed to Amy Haywood Dorr for unflagging and intelligent editorial assistance.

To my daughter, Nora, and my husband, Bob, whose culinary skills improved noticeably during the three years this book was being written, I offer my loving thanks.

Finally, thanks to my father to whom this book is dedicated. First in his choice of wife, and later in his championing of his daughters, he was a feminist long before I knew what the word meant.

Permissions

John Montague

Lines from "Hag of Beare," "Grafted Tongue," "All Legendary Obstacles," "That Room," and "Tracks" from *Collected Poems* by John Montague are reprinted with the permission of Wake Forest University Press for North American rights and The Gallery Press for U.K. rights.

Paul Muldoon

Lines from "Incantata," "Meeting the British" and "7 Middagh St." by Paul Muldoon are reprinted with the permission of Wake Forest University Press and Farrar, Straus & Giroux, Inc. for North American rights and The Gallery Press for U.K. rights.

Lines from "As for the Quince" from *Pharaoh's Daughter* by Nuala Ní Dhomhnaill trans. by Paul Muldoon are reprinted with the permission of Wake Forest University Press for North American rights and The Gallery Press for U.K. rights.

Lines from "Immram" from *Why Brownlee Left* by Paul Muldoon are reprinted with the permission of Wake Forest University Press for North American rights and The Gallery Press for U.K. rights.

Lines from "Immram" from *The Astrakhan Cloak* by Nuala Ní Dhomhnaill trans. by Paul Muldoon are reprinted with the permission of Wake Forest University Press for North American rights and The Gallery Press for U.K. rights.

Richard Murphy

Lines from "Seals at High Island" from *High Island* by Richard Murphy and published by Harper & Row are reprinted with the permission of the author.

Lines from "Beehive Cell" from *The Price of Stone* by Richard Murphy are reprinted with the permission of Wake Forest University Press for North American rights and The Gallery Press for U.K. rights.

Nuala Ní Dhomhnaill

Lines from "The Mermaid," "A Poem for Melissa," "Feeding a Child," "Labasheedy," and "Mo Mhíle Stór" by Nuala Ní Dhomhnaill are reprinted with the permission of Wake Forest University Press for North American rights and The Gallery Press for U.K. rights.

Introduction

This book was written to respond to a growing interest in the vibrant cultural atmosphere in Ireland today. Not only is Ireland enjoying a level of unprecedented economic prosperity, moving as it has to take its place among European nations, but the artistic climate seems particularly favorable to fostering notable achievement in a variety of disciplines. Film studies and production, new to the country, flourish. Ireland's traditional music, sometimes blended with elements of pop/rock and often availing of new technology, has found a worldwide audience. Visual artists, fashion designers, and architects have moved out from Ireland to establish reputations in London, New York, and continental Europe. Similarly, today's writers in Ireland are producing an impressive body of work that gains daily in critical and popular acclaim. From Seamus Heaney's recent Nobel Prize for Poetry to the sweep of recent Irish Tony Awards in New York, Irish writers' timely and modern responses to the changes in the world around them carry with them the resonances of the recent and ancient past, and are cast in expressive and evocative language which reverberates throughout the English-speaking world and often equally well in translation.

Contemporary Irish Literature: Transforming Tradition is an attempt, then, to provide insight into the world of Irish writers today, and for those new to that world, to illuminate the subject matter and the themes which inspire them today.

Contemporary Irish poetry has been enjoying such a flowering, second only to that experienced a century ago in the Irish Literary Renaissance itself, that the reader is hard-pressed to know where to begin. Any discussion of modern and contemporary Irish poetry must, however, begin with W. B. Yeats and with his continuing influence on the generations of Irish poets that have followed him.

William Butler Yeats, born in 1865, came to maturity in an era, the 1880s, when Ireland became focused on regaining its political independence from Britain. They were turbulent times, politically and culturally; and Irish people began to link the demands of political nationalism with an emerging cultural nationalism. W. B. Yeats, a young man with a budding career, seized on this idea of cultural nationalism and purposely set out to create the Irish Literary Revival. However, his position in Irish society as a member of its Protestant minority made him an unlikely spokesman for an emerging national consciousness.

Although Yeats' own primary focus in this revival was to be on drama, and on the establishment of a national theatre (which eventually evolved into the Abbey Theatre), he was also active in many political organizations interested in reviving the Irish language and knowledge of Ireland's ancient saga literature. Yeats' multifaceted undertaking was successful in that he was able to create a new cultural identity for his country and its people, even if that identity is sometimes criticized as being artificially conceived and imposed. Ireland, as constructed or reconstructed in Yeats' imagination, *became* a place untouched by the corruption of modernity, a country in touch with the magical and supernatural world, a place of heightened spirituality and harmony with nature. The ancient, the heroic, and the timeless were emphasized—the progressive, the bourgeois, and the timely were rejected as being symptomatic of the negative traits of the modern age.

Yeats' own poetry, the power and poignancy of which far surpassed the political and dramatic aims of his revival plans, bridges the gap from late Victorian, fin de siècle, and somewhat decadent verse to the sinewy, post-Christian poetry which came into being in English in the period between Europe's two major world wars. The poet who ostensibly rejected the modern certainly grappled with its problems and ultimately contributed greatly to our lasting definitions of Modernism as an artistic mode.

Yeats' power and pervasiveness as an artist is felt throughout the English-speaking world, but nowhere is his dominance felt more strongly than in the Ireland he left behind after his death in 1939. Irish poets, exhorted by the great master to "learn your trade / Sing whatever is well-made" in one of his last poems, "Under Ben Bulben," have continued to write to Yeats, around Yeats, and, in some cases, despite him.

Perhaps the generation that immediately followed Yeats could be viewed as most benefiting from his influence, but it was an influence that could be overpowering. The three major voices in the years to come—those of Austin Clarke, Patrick Kavanagh, and later Louis MacNeice—emerged from different regions and backgrounds, none quite like Yeats' world. Austin Clarke, a Dubliner and a Catholic, shared more culturally and socially with James Joyce than he did with Yeats, but unlike Joyce and like Yeats, he began his career with a desire to illuminate Ireland's heroic past. With a thorough knowledge of the Irish language that Yeats lacked, Clarke wrote prose romances, translations, and original verse that featured not only Ireland's ancient and pagan times, but also the Celtic Romanesque period of Ireland's Christian heritage. This high period of Irish monasticism, with its emphasis on the preservation of learning and a reverence for the transmission of culture through a religious lens, was for Clarke Ireland's Golden Age. But Clarke, who lived and wrote well into old age, lived in a modern and rapidly changing Ireland, whose ethos began to rankle after its independence was achieved. The tendency of modern Irish Catholicism toward repressive and puritanical views, which had earlier dismayed the Protestant Yeats, became the subject of some of Clarke's most memorable, and at times bitter, poetry. Clarke's courage and unflinchingly direct assaults on this New Ireland could also take the form of intense self-scrutiny, even touching on such taboo subjects as mental break-down, marital infidelity, and loss of faith in a modern world.

Patrick Kavanagh, Austin Clarke's contemporary, shared Clarke's Catholic heritage but little else. Coming from a subsistence farm in Co. Monaghan, Kavanagh rejected the idealization of rural, agrarian landscape and the myth of an ennobled peasantry so crucial to Yeats' revival manifesto. Kavanagh, who had perforce worked the land, rejected that way of life early and castigated its brutalizing effects on the body and, most importantly, the spirit. Kavanagh, who literally walked across most of the country to embark on a literary career in Dublin, became an urban modern man but was never entirely assimilated into the world of the literati he found there. Uniquely situated between two Irelands, Kavanagh's poetry displays tension and a keen sense of irony.

Both Austin Clarke and Patrick Kavanagh have acknowledged disci-ples still writing in Ireland today. And although Yeats' masterful poetic corpus and his linguistic brilliance still remain the foremost poetic influence sixty years after his death, the influence of Clarke and Kavanagh is, in a sense that is not merely chronological, more immediate. It is in Clarke and Kavanagh's respective responses to Yeats, both fundamentally negative, that today's Irish writers find ways of coping with the burden of the literary past.

Louis MacNeice's influence on today's poets in Ireland has only recently begun to be recognized both by those writers and the critical establishment. The son of a Church of Ireland clergyman, MacNeice was educated in England and described himself as "banned forever from the candles of the Irish poor." But although Oxford and later work in London (for years with the BBC) removed him physically from Ireland, MacNeice's Irishness reverberates throughout his poetic career. Born in Belfast, with roots in Connaught in the west of Ireland, MacNeice, especially in later life, returned to Ireland regularly to find inspiration and to write. Although his poetic reputation and personal friendships allied him with W. H. Auden and the thirties poets who had the Spanish Civil War, World War II, and the modern industrialized world as their focus, MacNeice's necessary distancing as an Irishman distinguishes him from his English colleagues. Today in Northern Ireland MacNeice's very modern poetry—urban, traveled, and constantly aware of Irish-English tensions and anomalies—provides a rich source of influence for young poets seeking to explain, escape from, or engage in the troubled ongoing political reality of present-day Ulster.

From the idyllic recreated memories of Yeats' childhood in Sligo, written from the perspective of a young man in London and found in his early "The Lake Isle of Innisfree," to his postmodern "The Second Coming," an apocalyptic vision of the future in the wake of world war—Yeats has left a poetic legacy to Irish writers that is vast in its range. Yeats' poetry of Ireland's past, ingeniously combined with Greek mythology, his interest in Eastern religions and the occult, and his admiration for the Italian renaissance, gives way to Clarke's reverence for Irish monasticism. This reverence is tempered in turn with a keen sense of the bawdy and with irreverence for the indigenous ethos. Clarke later made frustrated attempts to expose modern Ireland's cultural deprivation as a result of that same enlightened and exuberant Christianity gone sour and hampered by a superimposed Victorian sensibility that lingered well into the twentieth century. Similarly Kavanagh's dispelling of complacencies, rural and urban, also insinuates itself into the Irish literary continuum. Clarke and Kavanagh's personal poetic visions of, and arguments with, the Ireland of their times are then echoed by MacNeice. His voice, often literally broadcast from Britain, is a sophisticated worldly response to his era that seeks solutions in Irish origins.

Another and very different poet with Belfast origins was MacNeice's contemporary John Hewitt. Hewitt, with the exception of a 15-year hiatus working as a curator in Coventry, remained in Northern Ireland, and his work has always been associated strongly with the region. Influenced himself by the writings of Methodist and Presbyterian thinkers, Hewitt wrote about, and in the dialect associated with, Ulster Protestantism. His work has in turn influenced the generation of poets now writing in Northern Ireland, many of whom openly acknowledge their literary debt to him. Hewitt attempts to define Protestant identity in Northern Ireland through verse that espouses the virtues of independent conscience and a certain rigor in matters of work and of morality. Although very much an urban man, he has a surprisingly large body of nature poetry, which retains a high level of sustained dignity in that he rarely succumbs to city folks' temptation to consider themselves part of the natural environment which they, in fact, only visit. John Hewitt's lasting poetic influence can be appreciated by the appearance of a recent *Collected Poems*, and the existence for the past decade of the John Hewitt Summer School in Co. Antrim, which attracts an extremely impressive range of critics, scholars, writers, and students.

Poets Denis Devlin and Brian Coffey, contemporaries of Kavanagh and MacNeice, were friends and collaborators, and both men spent much of their adult lives outside Ireland. Each was influenced by periods spent in Paris. Devlin became a diplomat, while Coffey earned a Ph.D. in Philosophy and became in turn a university professor in that discipline in the United States, and a math teacher in secondary school in England. Because of their multidisciplinary backgrounds and their long absences from Ireland, their immediate influence on subsequent generations of Irish poets was limited. However, their espousal, to different degrees, of European Christian thought and its history, and their internationalist perspective as writers, opened up Irish poetry beyond the parameters set by Yeats' generation and questioned by subsequent groups of poets who remained at home.

Thus when the elder generation of Irish poets today began their writing careers, they had a wealth of modern Irish poetry, written in English and well-known and published, on which to draw for initial inspiration. Not all of their influences were Irish, of course. Writers like Richard Murphy, Thomas Kinsella, and John Montague, all highly educated and broadly traveled men, could and did incorporate their knowledge of English, American, and continental poetry into their own work. But their responses to and uses of their Irish poetic forebears' work are complex and continuing. As Ireland changes, so, of course, does its poetry. The accrual of poetic referents, of historical, political, and mythological markers and symbols, and of linguistic echoes, both in English and Irish, inform the writing of poetry in Ireland today. In addition, because of Ireland's relatively small size and population, Irish poets do not write in seclusion or in any sense in a vacuum. Ireland also boasts a large poetry-reading public, often as influenced by the immediate poetic past as are its poets. In Ireland contemporary poetry is regularly featured in daily newspapers and on broadcast media, thus making poetry a more culturally integrated phenomenon than it is, for instance, in North America. In this context, the reader new to contemporary Irish poetry must become and remain aware of its immediate antecedents. As poets like Seamus Heaney, Thomas Kinsella, and Derek Mahon are influenced, so, in turn, do their respective and well-known bodies of work inform that of such younger writers as Paul Durcan and Paul·Muldoon. As older women poets such as Eavan Boland have had to struggle to find a voice in a poetic history that has been nearly exclusively male, so do their voices find more recent echoes in those of Medbh McGuckian and Paula Meehan. That there is such a burgeoning growth of new and excellent poetry in Ireland is testimony to the wealth of poetic sources on which new poets can draw, but it is also, of course, even greater evidence of the artistic talent, imagination, and intelligence of these fine craftsmen.

When introducing the broad and varied subject of contemporary Irish poetry to the reader outside Ireland, one must be wary of giving too much prominence to a poet or group of poets by virtue of placing them first or last on a long roster of distinguished names, or by grouping poets in a way that seems exclusivist or provincial. The reader should understand that this introduction does tend to favor chronology, but not slavishly. It is important to emphasize also that, as in any "contemporary" array of artists, those writers who are in terms of the more mundane professions considered to be of "retirement" age will be writing with long careers behind them, and will of necessity be drawn to very different subject matter and will have very different perspectives from that of their junior colleagues who are just beginning poetic careers. The older poet in 1990s Ireland knows, remembers, and lives in a different Ireland from those who are 30 or 40 years younger than he or she is. It is a different ethos, where ideological and political goalposts are set in different places in the broad field of consciousness. Grievances with institutions have been replaced (not necessarily resolved); remembered joys, once culturally predominant, can seem nostalgic. The older Irish poet remembers and writes lyrics to catch the anxiety and joy of awkward country dances at which a young man might consider an evening to be an exhilarating success if he put his arm around a young girl's shoulder and was permitted to see her to her door. He or she would have difficulty relating to the ennui and dissatisfaction experienced by the young poet writing today in an era of casual sex, unisex dressing, and AIDS awareness. And, as the emotional landscape has altered so radically and so quickly in Ireland, so has, of course, the topographical landscape and many of the man-made features superimposed upon it.

Some of Ireland's established poets, though well-known in Ireland, are less frequently read by a younger readership and less likely to be because some have not published much in recent years. Their not being included here has also to do with lack of accessibility. The reader new to contemporary Irish poetry should, however, actively seek out the work of poets like Pearse Hutchinson, whose most recent collection, *Barnsley Main Seam*, was widely acclaimed by critics. The multilingual Hutchinson, an accomplished translator of Catalan and Portuguese, has written award-winning poetry both in Irish and in English that projects an awareness that extends well beyond Ireland, and is internationalist in its politicization. Yet there is an innate Irishness in this poetry which, like so much of the poetry of those who followed Hutchinson, is concerned with the traumatic loss of the Irish language, and its effect on the national psyche. Hutchinson, an influential figure in Dublin poetry circles, has also been an editor of *Cyphers*, one of Ireland's many small, independent poetry magazines.

The phenomenon of the literary magazine figures also in the career of Dublin-born poet James Liddy, a barrister, who edited *Arena* and served on the board of *Poetry Ireland*. Liddy, now living and working many years in the United States at the University of Wisconsin at Milwaukee, is the author of more than ten volumes of verse. His translations from the French and the Irish, and his original poems in English, are witty and musical in the strongest Gaelic tradition.

James Liddy's Northern Irish contemporary, James Simmons, displays musical talent in combination with his poetry. But perhaps Simmons' most lasting and selfless contribution to Irish letters may be his founding of the influential political and cultural magazine *The Honest Ulsterman*, and his position as literary editor of Belfast's esteemed *Linenhall Review*. The poet now also runs a writing program for apprentice poets in Donegal, called "The Poet's House." Simmons' own poetry, very accessible to the novice poetry reader, is marked by a sustained wry humor, ironic distancing, and celebration of the sensual.

Another poet with a high visibility in Ireland, and one who has held influential positions peripheral to the world of poetry, is Anthony Cronin, who has also counseled various *Taoisigh* (Prime Ministers) of the Republic of Ireland on cultural matters. Cronin, whose literary companions in the fifties included the indefatigable Brendan Behan, is also the author of *Dead as Door Nails*, an autobiographical glimpse at the Bohemian life of Dublin in that era.

Poet Robert Greacen, born in Derry in 1920, has had a long, distinguished career as a poet, beginning with his three volumes published in the forties. Greacen's writing career has been varied and he has compiled an Ulster anthology, *Northern Harvest*, and *Contemporary Irish Poetry* with Valentin Iremonger. The appearance of *A Garland for Captain Fox* in 1975 marked his return to poetry, and this late flowering has now produced four additional volumes, including his recent *Collected Poems*. Much of Greacen's writing in the past two decades has focused, understandably, on the violence in Northern Ireland. His poetry not only decries this violence, but it also makes an attempt to understand its causes.

Another *Collected Poems* that caps a long and distinguished career of an Ulster poet appeared the following year when Roy McFadden's long-awaited volume was launched. McFadden, who has remained true to nonconformist principles, has eschewed public acclaim and denies the validity of poet as performer. Like Greacen, now a man in his seventies, McFadden has seen the development of more than one generation of poets in Northern Ireland, and was publishing *before* questions of national identity and diversity of cultural tradition became the preoccupation of writers there. McFadden, an urban poet, has rejected pastoral myths of Ireland, and his poetry insists upon engagement with people and the reality of the quotidian life, as is befitting a man who has always earned his living as a solicitor.

Limerick-born Desmond O'Grady, yet another accomplished transla-tor and a widely traveled poet, was much influenced as a young writer by Ezra Pound, who befriended O'Grady in the sixties. Although thus influ-enced, then, by the demands of Modernism and by imagist dicta, his own poetry retains a largesse, a grandeur, that is considerably more flamboyant than that of most of his contemporaries.

The midlands poet John Ennis writes of Irish country life with a lyricism that does not give way to sentimentality. His meticulous recreation of the daily rhythms of cattle fairs and the cyclical work of the small farm has much the same clear eye for the effects of strain and boredom as does the work of Patrick Kavanagh, and much the same realization of a world rapidly disappearing as that of Seamus Heaney. Another thematic interest is the poet's concern for the place of the returned or failed seminarian in Irish life. Although there is much modern literature in Ireland that features the priest or the failed priest, it is rare enough to have the subject explored by one who has undergone the experience himself.

Poet Eithne Strong, who is enjoying something of a renaissance of her poetic reputation, is a woman who was writing and publishing poetry at a time when few women were doing so. For many years the wife of one of Dublin's most prominent psychoanalysts, Ms. Strong is the mother of many children, and writes poems that examine and evaluate women as dutiful daughters, as eager and pliable young wives, and as burdened and/or con-tented mothers. She has also written several verse collections in Irish, a collection of short stories, and a novel.

Strong has been described recently in a book on Irish women poets as:

A woman and a writer able to transform what she calls the "chaos" of domestic life into poetry that insists on the values of home and family, love and forgiveness. It is a poetry that challenges us to confront the harsh realities of modern life, to look at what we are, and to understand that chaos is not restricted to domestic life.[1]

In addition to poets like those discussed briefly above, there is another group of poets in Ireland whose work in areas peripheral to creative endeavor is perhaps better known both in Ireland and abroad. Among the best known of these poets is Peter Fallon, the publisher of so many of the poets discussed in this volume. Fallon, who began the Gallery Press while still an undergraduate at Trinity College, can boast a long and distinguished line of poets whom he has helped to bring to prominence in the more than quarter century he has been publishing. A glance at the bibliography which follows this study will prove the point quickly. Fallon, whose own volumes of verse include *The Speaking Stones*, *Winter Work*, and *The News and Weather*, gracefully recreates the ordinary rhythms of conversation and of daily life.

Seamus Deane, professor of English and Keough Professor of Irish Studies at Notre Dame, comes to creative writing by another allied route and one that is common in Ireland. His poetry collections include *Gradual Wars*, *Rumours*, and *History Lessons*, and his autobiographical novel, *Reading in the Dark* (see chapter 3) appeared in 1996. Deane's reputation, however, is based primarily on his work as one of Ireland's most prominent literary critics. Two of his critical efforts, *A Short History of Irish Literature*, and a collection of essays on cultural nationalism, *Celtic Revivals*, are key texts for the student of Irish Studies. His recent compilation and editing of the impressive and essential (though controversial) three-volume *Field Day Anthology of Irish Writing* is a monumental undertaking and a lasting achievement.

Seamus Deane's poetry is tied closely and emotively to the poet's working-class Derry origins. Figures of young boys populate the poems, recalling the poet as youth, and intensity of family feeling pervades the verse. This is a poetry informed by lifelong political convictions and awareness of the ramifications of economic reality on people's lives. It draws forth an eloquence from the poet/scholar, as is evident in this passage from "Return," in which the persona returns by train to his blighted home town:

> Every valley glows with pain
> As we run like a current through:
> Then the memories darken again.
> In this Irish past I dwell

Like sound implicit in a bell.

Literary critic and Oxford don Tom Paulin has published both poetry and plays. Like Seamus Deane, Paulin has been a director of the Field Day Theatre Company, also discussed subsequently in this volume. He has published several very well-regarded volumes of poetry and is himself the subject of considerable critical appraisal. Paulin, although not born in Belfast, was reared there and considers the city to be his home. He is grouped with Northern Irish poets who evince a social and political consciousness that can, at times, inform their finest work while making complex demands upon the aesthetic priorities of the artist. Paulin's own major poetic influence is Auden, exhibiting as his work does a modern muscularity. More recent efforts of Paulin's have been accused of projecting utopian ideas. However, his fine long poem *The Book of Juniper*, utopian in situation and resolve, is fantastically peopled with the survivors of two armies of juniper-bearers who metaphorically represent Ireland's two warring cultures. It is a work of lasting achievement and one that can be added to the substantial body of creative work to have emerged from the Northern Irish conflict, and one that will remain long after, one would hope, that conflict is resolved.

In Ireland today there are many younger and maturing poets, and their number continues to grow. Many are published and have developing reputations among other writers, critics and readers. Their work should, and will, be included on university syllabi and in the contemporary Irish canon, eventually extending into the world of the Irish diaspora and English speakers in general. Although now their work is available outside Ireland only irregularly or in limited anthology selections, they are worth watching and waiting for. Among these poets several make more pressing claims for recognition than others.

Several of these poets, including Eamon Grennan and Micheal O'Siadhail, give occasional poetry readings in North America. Eamon Grennan, a poet and critic who has taught for many years at Vassar, has a growing body of work that focuses on familial and marital love. Micheal O'Siadhail , an Irish language scholar of distinction, has published poetry in Irish in the past. He writes now exclusively in English. *Hail! Madame Jazz*, published in 1992, includes translations of O'Siadhail's poems in Irish. O'Siadhail's recent poetry is pervaded by instances of communication gaps, linguistic or cultural, and searches for the means to overcome estrangement.

Gerald Dawe from Belfast and Theo Dorgan from Cork are both poets who have also run literary magazines and done great service compiling and editing books on contemporary poetry. Dawe is at present engaged in writing a biography of singer Van Morrison. Dorgan and Máirín Ní Dhonnchadha have edited a seminal collection of essays, *Revising the Rising*, that reject attempts at revisionist interpretation of the national myth.

Poet Denis O'Driscoll is respected in Ireland for his poetic translations and his services as amanuensis and facilitator for other poets. His own work is now maturing and its atmospheric language is acquiring a patina very much its own. Similarly Paula Meehan, who has been publishing for two decades, has in recent work acquired the poetic maturity necessary to project her own voice.

Finally, poet Peter Sirr is the director of the Irish Writers' Centre, one of Dublin's premiere venues for literary events—readings, workshops, and exhibitions. Sirr, born in Waterford City and now a resident of Dublin, has very much an urban voice, an attribute he considers more important to an understanding of his poetry than any overt association with Irishness or national identity. His poetry, which avoids authoritarian verse structures, operates in a post-Catholic environment that has been thus far more often the sphere of prose fiction in Ireland today.

Contemporary Irish poetry, then, has taken different roads, as the selections studied in this book will indicate. And, although the poetry emerging from Northern Ireland has perhaps attracted proportionately more critical attention, especially outside Ireland, the Republic could never be described as lacking or lagging behind in poetic talent. Today's Irish poets interrogate definitions of Irishness, explore regionalism, investigate the position of religion in their lives and in their communities. They also desire love, of all kinds, and wish to understand what that love is, and what it requires of them and us. Lastly, Irish poets in our era have a keen sense of themselves as citizens of a wider world beyond Ireland's boundaries. They bring their unique linguistic gift to this wider world so that we may relish it.

Drama in Ireland today is enjoying a flowering unknown since the Irish Literary Revival of a century ago. Although in the intervening hundred years there has always been notable, and often great, drama emerging from that small part of the world's stage, the sheer number and quality of playwrights working in Ireland today is unprecedented.

The dramatic movement of the Literary Revival, conceived by W. B. Yeats and his patron and fellow playwright Lady Gregory, and by J. M. Synge (author of *Riders to the Sea* and *Playboy of the Western World*, two acknowledged masterpieces of the twentieth-century repertoire), was unique because it sought to *establish* a dramatic tradition in Ireland. Although it did not have an indigenous dramatic history in the sense that such a tradition is usually perceived, Ireland had, of course, a native tradition of storytelling. Conducted mostly in the Irish language by *seanchaí* (storytellers), who were usually male, the tradition evolved from its origin as entertainment at simple family or local gatherings or feast days. The *seanchaí* tradition was of necessity dramatic, highlighting as it did the art of the monologist. Storytelling, however, is not overtly interactive and as such represents only one small part of dramatic tradition. Ireland also had something of a mumming tradition, associated with feast days (such as the Wren Boys who paraded from house to house on St. Stephen's Day, December 26, rather like the North American trick-or-treaters on Halloween. Wren Boys sing a set song about the death of a wren, a pre-Christian sacrificial ritual in origin, but one still observed, if only symbolically, in some parts of the country). But many other mumming rituals, like the presence of the formal theatre in Ireland, are relatively recent importations of English tradition into Ireland.

In the eighteenth century Dublin was "the second city of the British Empire" and had a strong theatrical presence. Irish playwrights like Sheridan and Farquhar went to London to forge their reputations, and there wrote plays in the English style. These would then return to play to fashionable houses in the Irish capital. In the nineteenth century such migratory patterns continued. Dion Boucicault (author of *The Colleen Bawn* and *The Shaughraun*), Bram Stoker (best known, not as a theatre man, but as the author of the novel *Dracula*), G. B. Shaw, and Oscar Wilde continued the tradition, along with an impressive assortment of Irish actor-managers, actresses, directors, and theatrical entrepreneurs who made their mark, always, in London first.

So when Yeats and his colleagues in the west of Ireland gathered at the home of fledgling playwright Edward Martyn, the idea of building an Irish theatrical tradition was a revolutionary one. However, this was not conceived as some sort of theatre of the people. What those who were invited to participate in the initial planning stages of the Irish Literary Theatre (which would become the Abbey Theatre) shared was an elitism by birth and/or artistic inclination that carried over into their conceptualizing of an ideal theatre. Theirs was a vision of an aesthetic theatre of rarified sensibility, something that would function as a corrective to the worst excesses and shortcomings of the rather bankrupt English theatre of the age. Melodrama and farce would give way in Ireland to serious and poetic drama that it was felt best conveyed the indigenous ethos.

Yeats' dramatic philosophy is not a matter of conjecture, as he articulated it fully in his prose writings and letters. Although he gained his primary reputation as a poet, he wrote plays and/or was engaged in theatre throughout his entire career. And, it was arguably in the theatre that the Literary Renaissance made its most lasting mark.

Yeats' plays are of several types, but his developing aesthetic favored plays that revivified Irish heroic myth. His Cuchulain Cycle of five plays, written over the course of his writing life, indicates a growing emotional complexity and a representation of heroism that evolved to accommodate the changing mores of more than three decades. Yeats also experimented with and borrowed from French symbolist drama and the esoteric Japanese Noh tradition. His Noh plays, a cycle that intersects the Cuchulain Cycle, include such visually arresting and experimental short plays as *At the Hawk's Well* and *The Only Jealousy of Emer*. These and others make use of elaborate masks, minimalist sets, dance, and ritual chant in combination. Finally, although Yeats did write plays in prose, his first love for stage language was verse, which he believed he could bring back permanently and integrally into the English-speaking theatre. This aim was not achieved, but many of Yeats' verse plays remain in the theatrical repertoire in Ireland and elsewhere.

Lady Isabella Augusta Gregory, Yeats' patron and collaborator in the writing of the famed polemical play *Cathleen ni Houlihan*, contributed scores of popular plays to the Abbey repertoire. Mostly "peasant" plays that were in turn tragic, comic, and tragicomic, Lady Gregory's dramas were not given to Yeats' elevated language, but were written exclusively in prose and often in dialect. And although she produced translations or versions of heroic sagas, Lady Gregory's plays were not populated with epic figures. Not surprisingly her plays had a broad appeal, and could be counted upon to fill the theatre.

John Millington Synge joined Yeats' dramatic enterprise several years after it began, and emerged the inarguably greatest dramatist associated with the movement. Prose spoken by peasants in Synge's plays is unlike any dialogue written by Lady Gregory, and can be said to be as poetic as anything written in verse by Yeats. The heroic in Synge is found in the marginalized and outcast—beggars, tramps, aged widows, and would-be murderers. Apart from Synge's two masterpieces, his dramatic corpus only includes four plays, three of which are set in his beloved Wicklow and display an intimacy and fondness for the county's countryside and people. His final dramatic effort before his untimely death, *Deirdre of the Sorrows* was his sole foray into myth and the aristocratic. The play was finished after Synge's death by Yeats, who had written his own version of the tale of the doomed young queen.

What did emerge eventually from the Abbey Theatre was a dramatic tradition not nearly as esoteric as that imagined by its founders, although one somewhat closer to Lady Gregory's preferred model. The Abbey, with its subsequent decades of realistic country kitchen dramas, became a national and a popular theatre in a way that nearly defied its founders, but was espoused by the populace as national theatre must be. Subsequent generations produced playwrights Sean O'Casey, Lennox Robinson, Padraic Colum, Brendan Behan, and Denis Johnston, all of whom achieved degrees of success with audiences outside Ireland.

The unique position of Samuel Beckett in Irish dramatic history has in recent years not only been acknowledged, but is no longer considered to be debatable. His is an anomalous influence, however, or so it might seem at first, because all of his plays were written in French. Beckett's enormous existential corpus, influenced initially by Yeats' later experimental plays, has in turn informed the work of living Irish dramatists as varied as Tom Murphy, Frank McGuinness, and Marina Carr. Beckett's subject matter and settings are never identifiably Irish in any appreciable way, but his theatrical voice often can be when the plays are heard and seen in English-language productions. His own favorite interpreter was the great Dublin actor Jack MacGowran, and Peter O'Toole was a famed interpreter of his best-known work, *Waiting for Godot*. As such recent critical works like Anthony Roche's *Contemporary Irish Drama* (significantly subtitled "From Beckett to Mc Guinness") argue, a thorough understanding of Beckett enriches our appreciation of all Irish drama of worth that has been written since.

In the last 20 years there has been an astounding quantity and quality of theatrical talent emerging from Ireland to take its place on the stages of the English-speaking world. Beyond these triumphs great interest is now also being shown in Irish drama in non–English speaking countries. Like contemporary poetry, contemporary Irish drama is busily being translated into an array of continental languages. Two recent examples of such international successes would include the Gate Theatre's production of 19 of Samuel Beckett's plays as part of the Lincoln Center Festival in New York in 1996, and the inclusion of plays by Brian Friel and Sebastian Barry in "Imaginaire L'Irlandais," held at various venues throughout France in the same year.

Theatre in today's Ireland is varied, not only in subject matter, but in venue. Dublin still provides the greatest range of potential for an emerging playwright, offering as it does not only the resources of the Abbey itself, but of its studio space, the basement Peacock Theatre. Here Irish language, experimental, and one-act plays are usually staged. In addition the Gate Theatre, founded in 1928, and long the domain of famed actor-directors Mícheál MacLiammóir and Hilton Edwards and playwrights Lord and Lady Longford, continues to flourish and is not bound by the constraints of being a national theatre confined largely to Irish work. Dublin also houses the

Gaiety Theatre, which like the Abbey can boast its own acting school, and the Olympia, another large old house, and a fixture in the memories of theatre-going Dubliners for generations. The Project is a combined theatre and exhibition space in Dublin's Temple Bar, an area of urban renewal with an emphasis on culture.

There are, of course, many more theatrical spaces in Dublin and outlying areas, but perhaps more important is the flowering of smaller companies like Rough Magic and Barabbas, which perform at a variety of venues like the City Arts Centre, another multi-use space. Playwright Paul Mercier's Passion Machine is another small company acquiring an impressive reputation. Other central Dublin theatrical undertakings of distinction occur at the Samuel Beckett Centre for Drama and Theatre Studies in Trinity College, which offers undergraduate and graduate degrees and makes use of the college's several stages, especially The Samuel Beckett Theatre. In addition to venues and companies of distinction, Dublin also boasts an annual International Theatre Festival, held since 1957. The festival attracts major British and European companies, as well as showcasing native drama, and now includes a children's and fringe festival.

But theatre in Ireland is not merely theatre in Dublin by any means. In Belfast the Lyric Theatre, founded in 1951 by Mary and Pearse O'Malley and originally named the Lyric Players Theatre, provides a showcase for the many new playwrights emerging in Northern Ireland. Experimental companies like the now defunct Charabanc, a woman's cooperative effort, and Dubbeljoint, have more recently appeared in response to the growing numbers of playwrights to emerge locally.

Nearly 30 years after the Lyric Theatre opened in Belfast, a small company, Field Day, was founded in Derry. Unlike the Lyric, which was originally governed by Yeatsian principles, Field Day sought to alter completely theatre in Ireland. Founded by playwright Brian Friel and actor Stephen Rea, Field Day's board soon included Seamus Heaney, Seamus Deane, Thomas Kilroy, David Hammond, and Tom Paulin. From its base in beleaguered Ulster, the directors of Field Day sought to offer an alternative to Irish people, an alternative they called "the fifth province of the mind." This imaginative region would operate beyond the borders and boundaries of geopolitics and institutionalized religion. Many of the plays commissioned by Field Day, or first performed under its auspices, are examined in some detail in the drama chapter that follows. Field Day's success was remarkable in the number of theatrical projects of distinction it undertook. Now it looks as though Field Day's future may be more one that is confined to publishing ventures. Its impressive three-volume *Field Day Anthology of Irish*

Writing was preceded and followed by series of trenchant pamphlets on a range of cultural issues, and now Field Day is undertaking a series of book-length studies of similar issues.

Galway, the most westerly of Ireland's major cities, boasts the impressive Druid Theatre Company, which moved to new performing space in 1996, although it had many successes to its credit under cramped conditions for the first 21 years of its life. Founded by director Garry Hynes (who also served for a time as the Abbey's artistic director), and actors Mick Lally and Marie Mullen, Druid specialized at first in restaging classics of the Literary Revival and plays in Irish. It has since mounted definitive first productions of plays by Tom Murphy and younger play-wrights Vincent Woods and Billy Roche. More recently the award-winning and constantly inventive bilingual street-theatre troupe, Macnas, has mounted annual spectaculars as part of the Galway Arts Festival, which is becoming one of the premier artistic events of the Irish summer season.

In Cork, the Granary Theatre, near University College, Cork, and the larger and more established Cork Opera House provide, respectively, both intimate and popular spaces for visiting productions. In smaller provincial cities, too, the modern theatre tradition thrives at places like the Hawk's Well Theatre in Sligo (named after one of W. B. Yeats' Noh dramas) and the Watergate Theatre in Kilkenny. Similarly, smaller and often quite innovative companies are based in smaller cities—like Bickerstaffe, named after an eighteenth-century Irish playwright and also based in Kilkenny, and Galloglass, in Clonmel, Co. Tipperary—continue to enrich a theatrical continuum that is old enough to be considered a tradition, but young enough to encourage constant self-interrogation.

Theatre in Ireland is multifaceted. Amateur dramatic societies and playwriting competitions flourish countrywide. Youth theatre burgeons. There are companies like Second Age in Dublin and Graffiti in Cork that mount productions specifically geared, respectively, to secondary and pri-mary school age children. Even radio drama, not generally available in this era to North American audiences, flourishes both north and south of the border on BBC Ulster and Radio Eireann respectively.

The dramatists studied in chapter 2 include some whose names are well known in North America, like Brian Friel, and some who are relatively little known, like Thomas Kilroy. Those whose plays are examined here in detail have been chosen not only because of their sustained dramatic achievement, but also, quite practically, because their work is available in print, and might be available in North American productions.

The playwrights in this chapter also include some lesser known, younger, and less-staged playwrights in an attempt to enlarge the canon of contemporary Irish drama abroad. Such a gesture, however, is fated to sins of omission. Some of the most exciting theatre in Ireland today, for instance, operates outside the parameters of set text and confounds the hierarchical concept of a single author. These are ad-libbed texts, devised ex tempore and occurring in somewhat altered form, and often collaborative efforts. Perhaps the two exemplars of this innovative approach are the productions of the lamented Charabanc, and also those like *True Lines* and *Double Helix*, which were directed by John Crowley, but devised by an ensemble of players for Bickerstaffe. These examples of contemporary drama are not usually available other than in the theatre, and often only fleetingly.

An excellent example of a recent Irish theatrical experience that would not be suitable for discussion here, but for different reasons, is playwright and actor Donal O'Kelly's play *Catalpa*. Like his earlier *Asylum! Asylum!* and *Bat the Father Rabbit the Son*, *Catalpa* is a one-man show. O'Kelly undertakes an astounding 26 roles in this play, including that of a seagull, a ship, and the Statue of Liberty. Its equally basic props— "a table, a chair, a bed, and a trunk . . . a bowl, a pair of boots, salt and pepper shakers, a towel, a box of matches, a chain, a silk bedspread, a gauze curtain"—are used to transform the action and the set. Such a play must be seen not read; in fact, reading its "dialogue" from the page is a thoroughly frustrating experience for the reader unable to see a production.

The selection of dramatists provided in this book, however, does represent a mix of all ages, regions, and orientations. Their plays, whether set in remote rural areas or in the modern urban world, represent Ireland as it has been in the past, how it has changed, and what it is today. Each playwright included in this study seems to be acutely aware of the Irish need for continual self-assessment. Each helps to clarify the ongoing process of fine-tuning Irish national identity against Britishness, Americanness, Euro-peanness, foreignness, or otherness. What emerges is unique, challenging, often contradictory, and sometimes highly mercurial. The plays are often language plays that invest a great deal in linguistic games of the constructive, informative, or merely frivolous kind. Telling their stories as they do, these plays connect today's Irish experience with timeless narratives of the past. They deal not only with themes of love, death, and family life, but also with damaging lack of communication, the aesthetic and creative experience, and the ambiguous position of faith in a postmodern world. In short, contempo-rary Irish theatre is a vital undertaking alive to the rhythms of our modern lives and eager to transform life into a lasting art that is true to its human origin, but also transcendent. Today's Irish theatre has accomplished this difficult objective with a grace and sleight-of-hand that can only make us admire the magic of it all.

Whether or not it is a misconception on the part of others, Irishness is and has been associated with the poetic. This is a view the Irish maintain of themselves, too. Linguistic facility and artistry is held to be a special talent of the Irish, and although like all other generalizations based on nationality it is a suspect notion, it is certainly one that persists. Similarly in the last century, since the establishment of the Abbey Theatre, and the modern theatrical tradition it inspired, Ireland has come to be associated with dramatic talent. As a result, from the time of the Literary Renaissance, Irish men and women who have chosen to write not poetry or plays, but to use prose as their medium of artistic expression, have worked in a tradition that has been considered less developed and certainly one that has been less touted.

Also, although happily today many excellent Irish publishers thrive, until recently the Irish publishing industry has been quite small, and most Irish authors of *all* types have had to go to Britain or elsewhere to find publishers. Writers of fiction found this requirement to be particularly true, and, often for longer than did poets and dramatists. The type of fiction by Irish writers that found its way into print was then subject to the tastes and requirements of editors outside Ireland, and in turn this influenced the kind of prose Irish writers produced.

Perhaps the most famous modern Irishman to find his metier in prose and to be published abroad was James Joyce, who began by publishing poems, but then moved to the short story and wrote a play. Finally, Joyce progressed to the novel—a form he was to master and then supercede.

Joyce's sole volume of short stories, *Dubliners*, defines and introduces modern Irish prose, and stands nearly a century after publication as one of the finest examples of modernist short prose in the English language. Similarly Joyce's aesthetic novel of the growth of a young man to maturity, and his cultural awakening, *A Portrait of the Artist as a Young Man*, remains one of the most fully achieved novels of its type, the bildungsroman[2], in the English language.

For these two works Joyce had models in English, and in the continental languages with which he was familiar, but he had no Irish models for either. That in this regard, as in many others, Joyce emerges as innovator is not at all surprising. That he, in turn, stands as the model for so much Irish fiction to follow is no more surprising.

Joyce's *Ulysses* is considered by some to be the ultimate revenge of the metropolitan colonial, by appropriating the English novel, fracturing it, and rendering it irrelevant. A day in the life of two Dublin men, *Ulysses* is a celebration of Irishness and humanity and an artistic tour de force. In its pages Joyce revels in exhibiting every stylistic device in the history of English and other literatures, and in classic rhetoric. The highly experimental quality of the book could be, and was, daunting for writers who followed Joyce, but it was also liberating, especially for Irish writers. Joyce followed this masterwork with the publication of *Finnegans Wake*, which continues and intensifies his use of stream of consciousness, or internal monologue, as a narrative technique. *Finnegans Wake*, also set entirely in the city of Joyce's birth, emphasizes the male and female principles in all of life. *The Wake* is a Freudian interpretation of how the process of sleep allows for dreaming, which releases imaginative capacity and frees the mind from linear constraints. Perhaps most important to an understanding of Joyce's influence and the literary past in modern Irish prose fiction, however, is a reminder that unlike his first two major works, *Ulysses* and *Finnegans Wake* are essentially comic works.

Samuel Beckett, who served as an assistant to Joyce in the late 1920s, wrote four influential "Irish" novels early in his career though he is much better known as a dramatist. *Murphy* is a Cartesian comedy set in London. Its eponymous hero, an Irishman, works in a lunatic asylum, and eventually dies in a fire. The novel contains many burlesque characters whom Beckett uses to lampoon the pieties of the Literary Renaissance.

A later trilogy in prose—*Molloy*, *Malone Dies*, and *The Unnameable*—uses a disjointed narrative structure to reflect the discontinuity of modernity. *Molloy* is a somewhat surreal tale that, with its use of bicycles and policemen, anticipates the work of Flann O'Brien. Characterized by it emphasis on loss, forgetfulness, amnesia, loss of direction, and physical decay, the novel is existential, and, to a degree, nihilist. The second novel of the trilogy, *Malone Dies*, published in French in the same year as *Molloy*, shares a skepticism about the validity of *any* narrative that is the essence of much contemporary critical theory. The characters in *Malone Dies* are nearly all aged, decrepit, grotesque, or a combination of the same.

The final volume of Beckett's unnamed trilogy is *The Unnameable*. Here narrative has been severely reduced, issuing as it does from a disembodied voice that belongs to someone who wishes not to speak at all. The novel is preoccupied with physical deformity and scatological references. With its negative awareness of language, *The Unnameable* does much to deconstruct the novel it purports to be.

Beckett's fiction, which issues from an Irish tradition that includes the writings of Jonathan Swift and Laurence Sterne in the eighteenth century, questions givens—time, historic continuum, the validity of nationalism, the necessity for religion, and the purpose of philosophical inquiry. The author's deft comic talent for dialogue and for the inevitability of human frailty leavens Beckett's otherwise inconsolably grim view of our world. It has been emphasized, though, that rarely (and certainly not in these novels) does Beckett ever write without a grain of hope.

Another writer with direct autobiographical connections to Joyce was James Stephens. Stephens was a prolific poet, novelist, short story writer, and translator. His best known fiction includes two novels, *The Charwoman's Daughter* and *The Crock of Gold*, and *Here Are Ladies*, a collection of rather Joycean short stories.

The Charwoman's Daughter exhibits Stephens' skill at portraying the female psyche, and the novel also takes place in the Dublin tenements that were often Stephens' imaginative source. Although Stephens' prose is often humorous, his social conscience when dealing with poverty is always a strong force. Like Beckett, Stephens is wary of rabid patriotism, and can take, at times, a distanced view of the excesses of the Gaelic Revival. His *Crock of Gold* uses Irish myth and folklore both positively and negatively, insisting on the validity of its often ribald humor, but overlaying it with Nietzschean principles of society and the self that are not found in the original mythological stories. *The Crock of Gold* accomplishes the aim of releasing Irish saga literature from the constraints of its great Victorian translators who, in their era, deflected the pagan power of myth with a decidedly Christian message. The influence of Stephens is seen most directly in the work of Austin Clarke's prose romances and in the novels of Flann O'Brien in the next generation.

Flann O'Brien is a literary name little known outside Ireland. One of the many pen names of Brian O'Nolan, a civil servant in Dublin, Flann O'Brien is the author of several novels that border on the fantastic. The most famous of these, *At Swim-Two-Birds*, comically combines Irish history, mythology, and popular culture in a book about a man who is writing a book about a man who is writing a book, and whose characters undermine their creators' authority. O'Brien's *The Third Policeman* grapples comically and surrealistically with atomic theory, a relatively new concept when the novel was written. The policemen in the novel ride bicycles so often that it is conjectured that they are in danger of exchanging so many molecules with the inert bikes that they may become bikes themselves. *The Dalkey Archive* uses characters and constructs from *The Third Policeman*, including its atomic-theory motif, but with a post- Hiroshima awareness.

Ireland's short story writers since Joyce have achieved distinction and world wide recognition. Chief among these are Frank O'Connor (pseudonym of Michael O'Donovan) and his contemporary and fellow Corkman, Sean O'Faolain (who was born John Phelan, the English form of his name). These men, when young, shared formative influences. Each was taught by the charismatic ideologue, Daniel Corkery, who helped to imbue them with a strong sense of national identity and a love of the Irish language. Each, perhaps as a result of Corkery's influence, was also an active participant in Ireland's struggle for independence. O'Connor and O'Faolain, whose works are by no means identical, wrote about an Ireland in a state of transition. In O'Connor, urban poverty is examined in light of its differences from rural poverty. The author also captures families and communities in the process of trading the Irish language for that of English as the primary language of the home and the *lingua franca* of the marketplace. O'Connor's most poignant stories focus on such change in the ethos and sensibility, as well as language.

O'Faolain, whose thematic concerns overlapped those of O'Connor in places, also displays a talent for recording changes in such areas of Irish life as religious belief and social mores. His would-be urban sophisticates might engage in adulterous affairs, often out of loneliness, but they are guilt-ridden in a society that still maintains very strong strictures against such behavior. O'Faolain also edited the influential magazine *The Bell*, which showcased new Irish writing and provided an open forum for cultural debate.

A contemporary of O'Connor and O'Faolain, Liam O'Flaherty was a native of the Aran Islands and wrote short stories that seem, in comparison, to have been written in a timeless rural reality. O'Flaherty's peasants deal with matters of survival and primal human traits—greed, sacrifice, love, hate, and lust. His stories also detail a knowing and loving relationship with Irish topography and its flora and fauna.

O'Flaherty's talent, however, was not confined to the rural, nor to the short story. His novel *The Informer* deals with gritty urban terrorism. Another novel, *Skerritt*, has as its central concern a struggle over personal freedom between a teacher and a priest that nearly destroys their community. Still another work, an historical novel, *Famine*, is set in the 1840s and bitterly and graphically portrays the wholesale suffering and destruction experienced by a broad swathe of the Irish population during the famine years.

Women prose writers of distinction became prominent in Ireland in the period from the 1920s to the 1960s. Foremost in international reputation among them is Elizabeth Bowen, the Anglo-Irish writer from Co. Cork who spent most of her adult life in London and Oxford. Bowen's classic Big House novel, *The Last September,* both relies upon and revivifies the Big House trope of nineteenth-century fiction, which depicted life on Ireland's largely Protestant-owned country estates. The world of the Big House was often like that of a small town, and as such it was a microcosm of the greater world. The Big House novel delineates social and class distinctions, and emphasizes religious differences and the social and political fall out from such different sets of beliefs. Mainly, however, the Big House novel, and Bowen's *The Last September* is no exception, charts the disintegrative process of a house, an estate, falling gradually to ruin through neglect, impoverishment, or, significantly, poor marital choices. The disintegration in these novels is also meant to mirror the erosion of power of the Anglo-Irish ruling class since the beginning of the nineteenth century, and the decline of prominent families. Perhaps the finest examples of this genre were penned by cousins Edith Somerville and Violet Martin, who wrote as Somerville and Ross, and whose Big House novel, *The Real Charlotte,* remains the finest example of the genre.

Elizabeth Bowen also wrote a number of Irish short stories of distinction, some of which emerge from another nineteenth-century Irish tradition—the gothic tale. Here her Anglo-Irish forebears, writers of ghostly prose, include Sheridan Le Fanu, Bram Stoker, and Oscar Wilde. Bowen's voice, however, is distinctly her own and one that is capable of seemingly contradictory elements. A childless woman, Bowen exhibited an uncanny talent to enter the world of children, particularly that of adolescent girls. Though a writer who never considered herself to be anything other than Irish, Bowen also wrote perhaps the definitive English novel of World War II London—*The Heat of the Day.*

Elizabeth Bowen's friend of many years, the writer Molly Keane (born Mary Nesta Skrine in 1904, with the later pseudonym M. J. Farrell), wrote of the world Bowen presented in *The Last September.* Instead of the poignant and tenuous prose that Bowen employs to convey the predicament of the Big House inhabitants, Keane turns a comic and, at times, sardonic eye on the same group. Keane's early novels were published under her pseudonym largely because it was her own class and extended family she was lampooning in such novels as *Mad Puppetstown* (1931) and *Two Days in Aragon* (1941). Her later novels, a flowering of distinction after a 20-year hiatus, appeared under her own name, as in maturity she had greater confidence as a writer and as a person. One of these novels, *Good Behaviour* (1981), has appeared recently as a television drama. Molly Keane died in 1996, an author who had belatedly achieved the recognition she deserved.

Kate O'Brien wrote from the other side of Ireland, geographically, and in other important ways, about an Ireland very different from Molly Keane's. Keane recounted the lives and loves of Protestant farmers based in Co. Kildare, Ireland's horse-breeding capital. O'Brien, the Limerick-born daughter of a successful Catholic horse dealer, emerged from the Irish middle class not much represented in Irish fiction since Joyce. O'Brien, like earlier writers of Big House fiction who map a family's fortune through generations, in *Without My Cloak* maps a Catholic family's attainment of wealth and social cachet, plus the personal price that may be required for such advancement.

O'Brien's other distinct contributions to modern Irish fiction include her European outlook, most notably captured in her well known novel *Mary Lavelle*, a female coming-of-age novel set largely in Spain, but also quite charmingly in a little-read novel, *As Music and Splendour*, in which two unlikely Irish heroines become opera divas in turn-of-the-century Italy. O'Brien also dared in both the European novels mentioned above, and, notoriously, in *The Land of Spices*, to portray homosexual love, for which her work was censored.

Mary Lavin, a University College Dublin graduate like Kate O'Brien before her, is remembered as one of Ireland's great short story writers and a precursor of feminist writers in Ireland. A widow from a young age, with children to rear, Mary Lavin's life as a writer was never easy. Her style, which is epiphanic, thrives on domestic detail, and her stories concern themselves intensely with the complexities of interpersonal relationships. Lavin also wrote novels, but her ear for disjointed, but revelatory, dialogue, and her talent for capturing the fleeting, illuminative moment, are particularly suited to shorter prose pieces.

The prose writers whose work is introduced in this book range from those whose writing has been in the Irish canon for decades to those who have enjoyed popular success, perhaps with first novels, only within the last few years. Emphasis was placed not only on the availability of the novels and volumes of stories, but also on subject matter. While it is distorting and confining to label writers or their work by nationality to the exclusion of other considerations, that is ostensibly the brief of this book. Therefore, decisions like that of excluding Irish-born novelist Brian Moore, long a resident in the United States, and whose subject matter has not recently been identifiably Irish, were not taken lightly nor arbitrarily. Moore's early novels such as *The Lonely Passion of Judith Hearne*, *The Feast of Luypercal*, and *The Emperor of Ice-Cream*, all published in the 1950s to considerable notice, certainly influenced writers to come. Also, Moore's considerable success in having his work adapted for both the small and the big screen have given Irish fiction international visibility for a long time.

Some prose writers whose work is excluded from this study have changed genre. Thomas Kilroy, whose plays are discussed in detail in the drama chapter, was also the author of one major novel, *The Big Chapel*. One of the most important books to emerge from Ireland in the seventies, *The Big Chapel*, was historically based, and dealt squarely with sectarianism.

Writer Desmond Hogan is best known for his two major works, *Diamonds at the Bottom of the Sea*, a collection of stories, and *A Curious Street*, a somewhat surreal novel. Hogan's style is narratively experimental and multilayered. In the last 15 years Hogan seems to have gone beyond fiction as a genre, or traded it for the travel essay/autobiographical memoir that novelist Aidan Higgins has espoused too.

German/Irish writer Hugo Hamilton has not acquired a large readership outside Ireland, but this Dublin-based writer has a lyrical and evocative style that he can adapt to, it seems, nearly any setting. Hamilton's fiction, set both in Ireland and abroad, explores and at times explodes layers of incongruity in modern life. The author of three novels, Hamilton's recent short story collection, *Dublin Where the Palm Trees Grow*, is as eclectic and surreal as its title suggests.

There are, as remarked above, several newly emergent voices included in this study, and they are representative of their type and generation. The lesbian fiction of Emma Donoghue, discussed in this book, would not in a sense have been possible without the pioneering work of Mary Dorcey, whose *A Noise from the Woodshed* is a seminal collection of this genre.

The travel writing, journalism, and fiction of Joe O'Connor (who is Sinead O'Connor's younger brother) is acquiring a large following in Ireland. *Desperados* and *Cowboys and Indians* are violent, funny, unflinching works of fiction observed with a sharp, but, at times, jaundiced eye and conveyed in a unique voice.

Northern Irish writers have come to the world's attention in the last three decades, in part and unfortunately because of the ongoing violence in their homeland. Novelist Glenn Patterson writes about his Belfast in *Burning Your Own* and *Fat Lad* (a mnemonic device used by school children to identify the six counties that comprise Northern Ireland) with a wit that is affecting and with an insight into the world of the child that is at times reminiscent of Roddy Doyle's Dublin and its children.

Eoin McNamee's novel *Resurrection Man* was a bestseller and has been made into a major film. Like so much recent Irish fiction north and south of the border, the novel investigates violence and the mind that thrives on hatred. McNamee, like many of the writers mentioned above, continues to attract a growing readership in North America and in Britain, as well as in Ireland.

Fiction in Ireland may have begun the century as the poor relation of the Irish Literary Renaissance, but it has not remained so. Modernization and Europeanization have been factors, of course, in the increased popularity of prose fiction that is homebred. But a storytelling tradition that is ancient is also largely responsible for the magical or revelatory tales recent Irish novelists and other prose writers have been telling us. That contemporary writing trends worldwide not only allow but at times demand that writers abandon the linear narrative and blur the historically sacred boundaries between the real and the imagined has been a fortuitous development that favors the Irish writer. As a member of a society that favors a good story over boring accuracy, that applauds the hyperbolic, and that values the virtues of being a good audience as well as a good storyteller, the Irish writer of prose today has found his or her welcome and deserved reader.

Contemporary Irish Literature: Transforming Tradtion is intended as an introduction to a wealth of this writing. It is hoped that those new to Irish literature, especially those living outside Ireland, will find guidance and some illumination within these pages. The student, as well as the general reader, will find new names here, and will also be able to learn more about authors who are already familiar.

CHAPTER ONE

Irish Poetry For
Our Age

Poet **Richard Murphy** was born in 1927, and is one of the most senior of poets writing today who continues to exhibit his lyric gift in recent and impressive collections. Richard Murphy was born into the Big House of the Anglo-Irish gentry in Co. Galway, a status to which poet W. B. Yeats merely aspired in his verse and life. He was educated at Canterbury, Oxford, and the Sorbonne and has taught in Crete and in the United States. A friend of noted poets Ted Hughes, Sylvia Plath, Theodore Roethke, and Louis MacNeice, Murphy has emotional markers that can often seem to be set in the recent past, but that can and do resonate with current concerns and a very contemporary sensibility.

Murphy's thematic concerns in his long poetic career have, of course, evolved with time, but some factors remain constant. The poet's position as a member of the Anglo-Irish ascendancy, a formerly elite and powerful minority in Ireland, continues to be examined. Also, Murphy's emotional distancing from the world of his diplomat father, a British colonial-government official in what is now Sri Lanka, makes his investigation of marginalization and postcolonial attitudes most timely.

Other thematic elements that reverberate throughout his corpus are his close personal association with the landscape of the west of Ireland, and especially that of its seacoast and offshore islands. This loving scrutiny of the wild and lonely places of Ireland, which produce in the poet both great calm and great yearning, stands in contrast to Murphy's affinity for poetry that celebrates that which is man-made—fine buildings, estates, hand-hewn boats, and lovingly restored cottages. Finally, Murphy's love of the natural world and his admiration for the skill of others who could tame or improve upon nature is also informed by his keen sense of Irish history. He thus exercises his skill at lengthy narrative poetry to display his knowledge and understanding of often controversial or tragic historical events.

Richard Murphy's reputation as a poet in Ireland is also based firmly on the consummate, and sometimes ostentatious, skill with which he uses words. His poems will often feature a word excavated lovingly from the lexicon. The word is then presented for exhibition, demanding our concentration and unstinting admiration. Words like "grapnel," "dewlap," "schist," "foetiferous," "succursal," "ithyphallic," "obelize," and "unvermicullated" challenge and astound the reader new to Murphy. One must accommodate not only to the specialized vocabulary within the poems intrinsic to the world of the sea, boats, and fishermen that Murphy so thoroughly inhabits ("dabs," "flukes," "coracle"), but also to the natural world of the flora, fauna, wildflower meadow, and cultivated garden ("asphodel," "chough," "pergola"). Similarly, lush and evocative word usage strengthens, rather than simply decorates, Murphy's Irish historical poems ("rapparees," "cuirass").

Murphy's two early collections, *Sailing to an Island* (1963) and *High Island* (1974), exhibit exquisite lyrical accomplishment. In "Seals at High Island" the poet/persona is the awed observer at the mating ritual of a bull and a cow seal in a nearby cove:

> She opens her fierce mouth like a scarlet flower
> Full of white seed; she holds it open long
> At the sunburst in the music of their loving;
> And cries a little.

Each of these maritime collections of Murphy's is set in the west of Ireland where he lived and restored an old sailboat specific to the locality. "The Last Galway Hooker" is a personalized history of the boat that displays both the poet's lyrical and narrative talents. This narrative mode finds fuller expression in his rendering of "The Cleggan Disaster" and "Pat Cloherty's Version of *The Maisie*," both poetic retellings of actual shipwrecks that are worthy successors to such famous shipwreck poems in the English tradition as Gerard Manley Hopkins' "The Wreck of the Deutschland" and John Masefield's seafaring poems of this century.

Perhaps Richard Murphy's most important poetic accomplishment, however, has no connection with the sea and, although finely structured

itself, is not overtly nor otherwise about buildings. "The Battle of Aughrim"
is a detailed account, told in various voices, of perhaps the definitive battle
of the Williamite War, waged in 1691, shortly after the more notorious
Battle of the Boyne.[1] The plain of Aughrim, located near Athlone in the
center of the country, is still open, tilled land. Visitors to the American Civil
War battlefield in Antietam will have experienced the eerie sensation of
nearly being able to envision the combatants on those farming and grazing
fields in Maryland, an experience quite vividly possible at Aughrim.

Richard Murphy's imaginative account of the battle considers the
implications of the Battle of Aughrim in Irish history and culture, especially
as it related to his own family. For James II's defeat at Aughrim paved the
way for Protestant dominance for at least two more centuries in Ireland. In
his poem Murphy underscores the irony, though his case is not unique, of
having had forebears fighting on both sides of the battle. The poem, divided
into four parts, "Now," "Before," "During," and "After," relies heavily on
documented history, with the Irish patriot Patrick Sarsfield being usurped
in James' army by an ineffectual French commander, St. Ruth, who died in
the battle. Sarsfield, forced to lead the retreat of the Irish forces, fled Ireland
shortly after the battle for France, as one of Ireland's famed Wild Geese—
Catholic gentry forced to resettle on the Continent in friendly Catholic
countries because of the limitation of their rights under the eventual Protestant rule of William and Mary.

"The Battle of Aughrim" is constructed in an assortment of meters and
rhymes. For instance, its opening poem, "On Battle Hill," is in iambic
pentameter quatrains with an alternating rhyme scheme that makes frequent
use of feminine and half or near-rhymes. A later poem, also in "Now," uses
the much more insistent four-beat iambic line in heavily-rhymed couplets,
which bring home the sinister effect of the huge lambeg drums still used in
Northern Ireland by members of the Orange Order to commemorate the
Protestant victory on July 12, 1691, at Aughrim.

Richard Murphy's treatment of this historical event of enormous
significance is composed at an ironic distance, and with a skill and a
sensibility suitable to the gravity of the task he has undertaken. The structure
of the poem is provided by the historical events themselves. Such structure
is of prime poetic concern to Murphy, who like many in previous generations
who went on to contribute a body of impressive poetry in English, was
rigorously trained in the highly structured requirements of classical poetry.
This structural awareness, which in Murphy is as strong as it would be to an
architect or an archaeologist attempting to retrieve and reconstruct structures of delicate, ancient beauty, is best showcased in his recent collection

The Price of Stone (1990), a construct of 50 sonnets, many of which are concerned intensively or ironically with the act of building. Each poem features a structure—a lead-mine chimney, a boys' reformatory, a castle in the west of Ireland, or the womb from which his son emerged. Most of the sonnets are composed in the "voice" of the structure itself, rather than one of its human or animal inhabitants. *The Price of Stone*, published to acclaim when Murphy was in his sixties, ensures that his poetic concerns continue to be contemporary, including as it does poems about teenage pregnancy, and the itinerant or "traveler" culture of Ireland's native, nomadic people. The volume also addresses illegitimacy, juvenile delinquency, and a homosexual encounter in a public restroom. The reader can also find in this collection the more traditional fare of the sonnet—the emptiness of a friend's cottage after his death, or the simple significance of neolithic and early Christian ruins that housed religious ceremonies in both Ireland's pagan and Christian past.

His "Beehive Cell," quoted in its entirety below, is an impressive example of language and form in harmonious conjunction. Together they capture the essential, pared-down, timeless, and nearly inviolable nature of this primitive structure, standing in a barren spot thousands of years after it was built. It is a poem that exhibits the technical intricacy and lyrical accomplishment that continue to inform Murphy's verse.

> There's no comfort inside me, only a small
> Hart's-tongue sprouting square, with pyramidal headroom
> For one man alone kneeling down: a smell
> of peregrine mutes and eremitical boredom.
>
> Once in my thirteen hundred years on this barren
> Island, have I felt a woman giving birth,
> On her own in my spinal cerebellic souterrain,
> to a living child, as she knelt on earth.
>
> She crawled under my lintel that purgatorial night
> Her menfold marooned her out of their coracle
> to pick dillisk and sloke. What hand brought a light
> With angelica root for the pain of her miracle?
>
> Three days she throve in me, suckling the child,
> Doing all she had to do, the sea going wild.

The contrasting phrases "pyramidal headroom," with its multisyllabic and upward motion, and "one man alone kneeling down," with its abrupt and lowly movement, encapsulate the hermit's aim—to elevate his thoughts to God while abasing himself on the earth's clay in prayer.

Similarly the stasis of the "peregrine mutes" and "eremitical boredom" conveyed in formal, Latinate diction, allows for the contrasting beginning of the next stanza "Once . . . have I felt a woman giving birth." The essential nature of the woman's task stands in simple relief to the high-minded, cerebral undertaking of the monks. Murphy then insinuates the Irishness of the ancient scene by beginning in his third quatrain to use specific and local vocabulary. A "coracle" is a small fishing boat; "dillisk" and "sloke" are two types of edible seaward gathered by women as a cash crop. The final couplet exhibits perfect closure—mother and child, earth and sea, all given life by the recurring "ing" verb forms in "suckling," "Doing," and "going."

John Montague was born in 1928 in New York. *The Planter and the Gael* (1970) is a selection of poems by Montague and John Hewitt, a poet of distinction from Co. Antrim who died in 1987. *The Planter and the Gael* concerns the same two tribal groups who fought in the Battle of Aughrim, although there are only a few battle poems here, and a few bearing witness to conflicts in the greater world outside Ireland. Montague, whose family, like Hewitt's, comes from north of the border (Co. Tyrone), is also the author of "The Rough Field," a long poem rather like "The Battle of Aughrim" in its use of a variety of metrical and formal poetic structures in the many smaller poems that comprise the whole. "The rough field" is the English translation of "Garvaghey," the name of the townland in which Montague was reared by his paternal aunts and grandmother, after being sent back to them in Ireland at the age of three. (Montague's parents remained for a time in New York where they were rather unsuccessful immigrants. His mother eventually returned home to her own family.) "The Rough Field," composed of ten sections plus epilogue, was published originally in an illustrated edition that made excellent use of sixteenth-century Irish woodcuts depicting primitive and often ghoulish battle scenes. But perhaps its most striking feature is that it contains a wealth of typographical experiments and makes innovative use of interspersing blocks of relevant quotes from historical documents with some highly autobiographical poems. Thus, for instance, in Part I, "Home Again," a poem that gives the poet's detailed account of a journey by bus from urban and grimy Belfast to the rural bleakness of Garvaghey, occupies the left margin of the page with wide gaps between its stanzas. Hugging the right margin in smaller print appear passages from an ancient travelogue by Lord Mountjoy as he traversed Ulster to inspect his lands near Omagh, Co. Tyrone, and quoted here verbatim.[2] But past and present also merge in a poem like "Lament for the O'Neills," in which Montague chooses to title his poem with the traditional word "lament" (or *caoine* in Irish) for a song to honor the dead. The poem makes excellent use of the half rhyme, as when the poet describes the fiddler's instrument as being made of "rosewood" with his bow "rosined" for play. Montague then immediately follows "bow" with "angle" and "elbow" to join near and exact rhymes in close proximity and to mimic the required angular posture of the fiddler. "Lament for the O'Neills" ends with a rendering in verse of the fiddler's musical portrait of the Flight of the Earls, the traumatic national event that also closes Richard Murphy's "The Battle of Aughrim."

Perhaps because Montague was born outside Ireland, he had, in a sense, to return to claim his birthright and his connection with his extended family and parish.[3] Many of Montague's most successfully realized earlier lyrics recreate an often affectionate, but not hagiographic, group portrait of the conduits of a fragile tradition, particularly the elderly inhabitants of Garvaghey and environs who gave credence to the maxim "it takes a village to raise a child." His much anthologized "Like Dolmens Round my Child-hood, the Old People" recreates a rural Ireland now largely threatened, with a seven-line stanza dedicated to each eccentric or outcast—the O'Neill family, all blind, living on the mountainside; Maggie Owens, animal lover, whose affinity with beasts gained her the traditional title of witch; Billy Eagleson, who defied a tribal taboo and married a Catholic. The poem owes much to the realism of Patrick Kavanagh of nearby Co. Monaghan, especially his "The Great Hunger," which focuses on the old, the celibate and the lonely. It rejects the romanticism of a Yeats, whose reverential attitude toward "Ancient Ireland" is roundly scoffed at by Montague in a direct reference in this poem.

Although not purely reverential in his use of the aged as subject matter for his poems, Montague's continued interest in the old, particularly old women, has produced several fine poems. Woman as traditional keeper of culture figures largely in his corpus, as does woman as crone, often giving the hint of supernatural power. Montague melds the sad reality of the aged spinster/virgin village outcast, powerless with no children or man in old age, with the wary respect paid the *cailleagh* (or hag), the witch figure of Irish lore.

"The Sean Bhean Bhocht" is one of Montague's best known "hag" poems, which bears the famous name of the "poor old woman" of lore who pleads with her sons to fight to save her land (Ireland) and often appears in the form of a beautiful young woman so as to lure young men into battle. Montague's poor old woman is merely a local storyteller, and owes much to Joyce's countryman with "rheumy" eyes whose knowledge of ancient practice and superstition both frightens and intrigues the young Stephen Dedalus in *A Portrait of the Artist as a Young Man*. In a similar vein, Montague's "The Hag of Beare" relates the ninth-century tale of one of Ireland's best known *cailli* (or hags):

> I am the Hag of Beare,
> Fine petticoats I used to wear,
> Today, gaunt with poverty,
> I hunt for rags to cover me.
> These arms, now bony, thin
> And useless to younger men,
> Once caressed with skill
> The limbs of princes!

Less mythic, but equally terrifying and witchlike to the poet as a child, is the woman in "The Wild Dog Rose," described now by the returning poet as "a moving nest / of shawls and rags, . . ." and the victim of an attempted assault by a local man. But she remains virginal, like the Blessed Virgin, with whom she is somewhat identified in the poem through the medium of the wild dog rose, a flower associated with Christian, specifically crucifixion, iconography.

The uncle for whom John Montague was named is the subject of the beautifully crafted poem "The Country Fiddler," in which the poet likens his artistic gift to that of the accomplished musician, and considers his talent to be a legacy. Montague's father receives a very different treatment from his son, especially since as an emigrant he has deprived his son of his true legacy—tradition. Bitter, sad poems like "The Cage" ("My father, the least happy / man I have known.") and "Last Journey," in which father and son are remembered traveling *away* from their home, bear witness to a conflicted poet in middle age still seeking continuity with the past in order to forge a coherent modern self-image. The poignancy of this conflict is captured best when the mature poet confronts his father, "A small sad man," disembarking from a transatlantic liner at Cobh in Co. Cork. When they stop en route home to hear Montague delivering a prerecorded reading on the radio, the over-anxious poet awaits his father's "Well done," uttered, as the title conveys, "At Last."

Montague's return to his native land also gave rise to another kind of repossession of his Irish legacy. An opportunity to learn the Irish language that had been denied to his immediate forebears becomes very important to him. Poems such as "A Lost Tradition," which contains the line *"Tá an Ghaeilge againn arís. . . ."* (We have the Irish again), map the linguistic reclamation process from the last of the elderly Irish speakers in the parish to the young poet / persona just beginning to learn his native tongue. "A Grafted Tongue" pursues a similar theme and uses a similar chronological telescoping mechanism. The poem conflates the struggling boy trying to learn Irish, with an imagined nineteenth-century Irish child being punished in school for having insufficient knowledge of the English language. Another poem "The Answer," dedicated to the English literary critic Christopher Ricks, presents a more subtle approach to the bilingual nature of Irish racial consciousness, as experienced by Montague. The two men lose their way in a remote area of Co. Kerry and Montague is directed, in Irish, by a courteous old woman. When asked by the English-speaking Ricks "What did she say?," Montague is unable or unwilling to force himself to make the translation and wordlessly points the way. If he were to translate the woman's words into English, it would not, after all, be what she said.

Irish history, family history, and the Irish language are not, by any means, Montague's sole lyrical interest. An accomplished love poet, Montague has produced a number of lyrics that are alternately delicate, poignant, sensual and, at times, effaced. "All Legendary Obstacles" and "That Room" both relate the anxiety and tenuousness inherent in love affairs. In the first poem the poet / lover, edgy in a California railway station, is finally reunited with his love:

> At midnight you came, pale
> above the negro porter's lamp.
> I was too blind with rain
> And doubt to speak, but . . .

As pained as is the greeting, the farewell that is retailed in the second poem offers no solace, however temporary, no kiss, however tentative:

> Side by side on the narrow bed
> We lay, like chained giants,
> Tasting each other's tears, in terror
> of the news which left little to hide . . .

John Montague's poems detailing his long or short-term relationships with women can also depict, aptly, not only the agony of the thwarted commitment, but also physical immediacy. Whether by the inclusion of a red slap mark on a lover's face, or in a poem vividly given over entirely to the poet's venting his sexual jealousy, Montague's love poems suggest at times a level of passion capable of including the brutal. Such passion is also present in his poems about the inequities of Irish history, and in particular, his resentment at having been "given up" by his parents at a very young age.

Regardless of his subject, John Montague is perhaps at his best as a poet when he is composing within the rigors of the very short (i.e. two or three beat) metrical line. The economy of syllable, of modifier, of phrase, is favored by a poet who has had to fight to overmaster a speech impediment. Thus "dumbness" is itself often, in part, the subject of his poems, as in this excerpt from "The Grafted Tongue," which tracks the halting process of learning a new language:

> to slur and stumble
> In shame
> the altered syllables
> of your own name.

John Montague's search for an apt method of expression that reflects the terse nature of his Northern Irish forbears and his own limitations, and his discovery and development of a skill in writing that harkens to the musical prowess of past members of the Montague family, is elegantly and succinctly rendered in such efforts as "The Grafted Tongue." Not all his poems are beautiful, in a tame and conventional sense, nor are they all meant to be lyrical; but Montague's best work exhibits rigorous craftsmanship and a verbal surety that is cause for our admiration.

Thomas Kinsella is a poet whose career is often linked with that of John Montague. They are contemporaries and each came to the poetic fore with first collections in the late 1950s. Forty years later Kinsella and Montague are artists who have developed very differently. Although both poets identified with the new mode of Irish internationalism in their early careers, the telling differences of personal biography, accumulated influences, and sources of continuing inspiration have caused a major divergence in their respective art. Perhaps the major distinction between the sources of cultural identification and fonts of inspiration for these two very different poets is that one is a countryman in upbringing, the other a city dweller.

Thomas Kinsella was reared in inner-city Dublin as part of an extended family, living quite close to aunts, uncles, and grandparents. John Paul Kinsella, the poet's father, was a cooper, or barrelmaker, in Guinness's brewery in an era when the dark stout was transported in wooden barrels. The Kinsella family, of cobblers, barge captains, and a parade of other colorful eccentric types, lived in a city where children often died of tuberculosis, and death in childbirth was a common occurrence in women who experienced numerous pregnancies. Kinsella's Dublin is a vibrant but sometimes frightening place, alive with an awareness of local history. Kinsella is the bearer of a legacy that is grittier than that of many Irishmen and may not fall easily into the imaginative frame at first constructed by the casual reader of Irish literature who has been in a sense conditioned to think of Ireland as bucolic. But Kinsella's Ireland, his Dublin, is that of Joyce, Brendan Behan, and Flann O'Brien in prose, and O'Casey on the stage.

Thomas Kinsella is a poet for whom incident, landscape, and interaction with others serve in the verse only as a means of gaining additional, more accurate, and more telling information about the self. Irish history, the use or non-use of the Irish language, the economic shortcomings of Irish and European Union governmental programs, the place of the Catholic Church in Irish public life, the role of the poet in the modern world, and, in particular, modern Ireland—all these are subjects at times for Kinsella's poems, but only on the entry level of consciousness. For in Kinsella all roads lead to an investigation of the moral and essential self in a post-Freudian, postnuclear world that offers the poet few consolations.

Kinsella's first four major poetic collections, all published in the decade from 1958 to 1968, cemented his poetic reputation in Ireland and in Britain. *Another September*, the first, casts a cold and dry eye on the process by which humans choose to mate and eventually marry—a formidable personal commitment for the poet. Its title poem could be said to be an anti-epithalamion (see Michael Longley's "Epithalamion," published a decade later). A postcoital poem, "Another September" is composed in three octets, the first of which moves from stillness at dawn and the lovers' contentment to a sinister range of natural imagery that threatens that achieved emotion. The next stanza moves imaginatively and warily into a domesticated future, and in the final octet a hallucinatory sequence stresses the poet's fear of the loss of individuality at the hands of armed shadowy "female" figures of Justice and Truth.

Truth is also featured in "Baggot St. Deserta," a poem from the same period and collection. Here the poet is alone and isolated in an attic room in the early hours of the morning—one of many solitary self-examinations Kinsella has published over the years. "Baggot St. Deserta" finds the poet/ narrator stationary, something that will become an anomaly in Kinsella's poems of this kind. The poet, consoled to some degree by ". . . the mathematic passion of a cello suite," is acutely aware of the presence of the river Liffey nearby and its progression to the sea and the world beyond Ireland. The Joycean models here are resonant and purposeful. Joyce's Stephen Dedalus chose exile as his only means to access the creative spirit; here Kinsella, resolutely remaining at home, at least for the time being, enters a brotherhood of poetic forebears by becoming overtly intertextual with W. B. Yeats' great poem "Easter 1916." In Kinsella, however, it is the sacrifice of "Versing" that can make, not a stone , but "A virtuoso of the heart." The poem ends artfully with a metaphor of arcing stars mimicked by the poet's final act of flicking his lit cigarette butt out the window—a fleeting, flaming connection between poet and cosmos.

Downstream, Kinsella's second collection, features "A Country Walk." One of the poet's peripatetic pieces, the poem is set during the day, and begins irritably, misogynistically, but quite comically, with the line:

> Sick of the piercing company of women
> I swing the gate shut—with a furious sigh.

The poet walks out of the town, passing familiar landmarks and making the reader aware how close town and country could be near his venue, Enniscorthy, Co. Wexford, 30 years ago. By the third stanza the poet encounters cattle, and empty autumnal fields by stanza four. As is true of many of Kinsella's poems, "A Country Walk" exhibits an intricate sense of local history as the poet sees a ford of the river Slaney that triggers a reverie of many such sites crucial to Irish history.[4] The strategic nature of the site provokes memories of violence, but it is also a dividing point where decisions must be made—a threshold to cross over.

Downstream opens with a discursive, jocular prologue of rhymed couplets that is purposely both intertextual with Yeats and tongue-in-cheek. However, it serves the much more serious purpose of recording the difference between the trappings of the poet and what a poet really is. The use of such abstractions as Laziness, Discipline, Error, Routine, and Futility suggest the often-conflicting and self-imposed demands made upon the writer.

The title poem of the collection is, like "A Country Walk," situated on a river, but not on its bank. Here the poet and a companion sail the River Nore to Durrow in Co. Laois.[5] The journey is metrically and imagistically measured and lush, to reflect the river's languid flow and the beauty of its flora and fauna. Kinsella's travelers discuss poetry en route, and the poet's persona has a copy of Ezra Pound's Cantos zipped into his jacket. This direct reference to a poetic forebear is mirrored in the poem by the intermittent presence of very Yeatsian and mythological swans. "Downstream" is a formal poem that places the persona in the context of the literary and historical past. As day turns to night on the river the poem becomes a rumination on the horrors of recent history—a local death under mysterious circumstances leads to a consideration of the horrors of the concentration-camp extermi-nations of World War II. The narrator turns in relief "Toward gentle Durrow" and the past—"An acre of abstract love and vanished skills." Although the remainder of the journey is not undertaken without a certain trepidation, the return of the emblematic and tranquil swan and the looming "wall of ancient stone," their destination, brings the poem to a close that achieves a degree of deserved peace after a mental and physical ordeal. "Downstream" ends, however, leaving the pair "Searching the darkness for a landing place," which suggests that such journeys are never-ending.

Wormwood and Nightwalker and Other Poems, published in rapid succes-sion in 1966 and 1968, are comprised of intensely subjective poems with a Jungian interest in dreams, a horror of the pitfalls of domesticity gone wrong, and a very keen sense of the capricious nature of illness and death. Most of these are night or break-of-dawn poems that explore the dark night of the soul or shudder in the cold reality of dawn. The title poem in Nightwalker and Other Poems, Kinsella's longest poem as a younger poet, is a cerebral and somewhat labyrinthine ramble set at midnight. The poem expresses Kinsella's dissatisfaction with the complacency he sees as being at the root of the New Ireland of the post-Treaty, post-Partition years after 1922. This is, after all, "his" Ireland, in which as a Catholic he holds a civil-service position that would not have been his in an earlier era. Kinsella focuses, rather like MacNeice in his famous long poem of 1939, "Autumn Journal," on the treachery and violence that underlay the founding of the modern Irish state. "Nightwalker," constructed in three parts, is composed loosely in blank verse and uses a variety of type faces, ersatz newspaper headlines, and other refracted paraphernalia of the modern world to convey the poet's sensibility and his angst. Indirect and irreverent Yeatsian referents litter the text and display the dissatisfaction common to the generation after political upheaval. Direct references to George Bernard Shaw, the Taoiseach (Prime Minister) of the day, and a seemingly incon-gruous, but apt, linking of the two female icons of two formidable powers—the Catholic Virgin Mary and the British Queen Victoria—place the poem in the troubled present of the poet's imagination. The poem ends, forlornly, with a dubious revelation on the part of the narrator as he continues to wander alone, a twentieth-century Everyman—"I think this is the Sea of Disappointment."

In 1970, Kinsella took up a post at Temple University. His poetic "output" continued to flow, but the poetry that emerged was different; it was more introspective and less given to narrative conjunctions or lyricality which would dilute the findings of the self-examination the poet had set for himself. *Notes from the Land of the Dead* (1972) is a collection of 18 short lyrics that features touchstones of the Dublin landscape: "Irwin Street," "Ely Place," "The Liffey Hill." One of the most often anthologized pieces from this collection is the brilliantly realized yet still somewhat enigmatic "Hen Woman." The poem relates, in a four-page sequence, the events of an instant. A woman is carrying a hen that is, unknown to her, laying an egg as she carries it. The egg, a perfect symbol of brand-new and self-contained life, falls "Through what seemed a whole year," and smashes onto a grating through which it disappears completely. The poet, having earlier warily identified the condition of the self, his self, with the capricious fate of the egg, is brought out of his desolate reverie by the more pragmatic reaction of the farm wife who simply laughs and says "It's all the one," meaning it doesn't matter. Her existential response aids the poet in redirecting his conclusion to a more positive belief in the simplicity of our world.

The Poetry of Thomas Kinsella, a critical introduction to the poet published by Maurice Harmon in 1974, regards Kinsella as a poet who "does more than express horror and disappointment" with the modern world. Harmon argues that "the basis of his response is a sense of possibility and expectation."[6] More recent commentators focus upon Kinsella's creative demand that the individual must make cogent response to his immediate world and to the world at large. Thomas H. Jackson in *The Whole Matter* argues that "One of the major convictions of his poetry is that a seamless continuity links persons, events, books, political events, and the levels of the individual self."[7] Brian John, writing the following year, describes the complexities of Kinsella's creative achievement thus:

> The search for structure to encompass meaning, whether within the self, the world of time and space, or the creative act itself, is compelling and necessary, even if, in the last resort, it must remain incomplete.[8]

The unadorned and often raw quality of emotion portrayed in Kinsella's work reveals the essential self, regardless of the pain involved for both writer and reader. This approach differs from that of many of his contemporaries, and often leaves Kinsella in an unhappy minority. Where Kinsella can, and does, find shared subject with his fellow Irish poets is when he focuses fully or partially on the creative act itself, and also on the struggle involved in not only successfully completing that act, but in doing so while maintaining the requisite level of personal integrity.

In 1972 Kinsella returned to the long poem with "Butcher's Dozen," which commemorates the death of 13 Catholics killed by members of the British Army in January of that year (a fourteenth man died subsequently).[9] The day has acquired the name "Bloody Sunday," and Kinsella's poem is specifically a response to the official Widgery Tribunal of Inquiry, which exonerated the soldiers.[10] He is one of the very few writers from the Republic who has directly addressed the Northern conflict in his verse.

"Butcher's Dozen" is constructed in jarring, heavily rhymed iambic quadrameter couplets that insist on the narrative, or storytelling, aspect of the poem. Although it is not written in ballad meter, the poem has the timeless quality of the best folk narrative, easily remembered and passed on:

> A month passed. Yet there remained
> A murder smell that stung and stained.

The victims of the violence, rising from the dead, identify and differentiate themselves as people. Then Kinsella accuses "England," in a direct address, of shameful acts and an even more offensively shameful cover-up of those acts. The poem continues, offering an aggrieved recitation of British injustice in Ireland, religious prejudice, and mutual ignorance and suspicion.

Since the volume *Butcher's Dozen*, Thomas Kinsella's poetry of the last two decades has often been published first under his own imprint, the Peppercanister Press. Peppercanister pamphlets have included *One*, which contains many tribute poems to family members, and *The Messenger*, a long poem about the poet's father. *The Messenger* is a tribute poem, albeit at times one that expresses regret that his father's life outlasted his vitality. The son's personal loss is palpable within this poem, which also conveys a strong sense of the previous generation as curators of an Irish traditional past that is becoming far too tenuous in the modern world. Kinsella writes of loss of future, of tradition, and even of manhood:

> It is more than mere Loss
> (your tomb image
> drips and blackens, my leaden root
> curled on your lap).

A 1987 collection, *St. Catherine's Clock*, continues Kinsella's exploration of family relationships and local ties. The poems move in time from the eighteenth century to the early twentieth century of Kinsella's boyhood. Thus Irish history, especially very specific events of Dublin history, including the execution of Robert Emmet, intermingle with key events of Kinsella family history as remembered by the poet from his youth. Subjects chosen for thoughtful illustration in the poems emerge from the art of the period, including engravings by George Cruikshank. Among these is a controversially comic rendering of a "simian" and subservient Irish race surrounding the coach of Lord Kilwarden, a liberal magistrate murdered in the 1803 Rising, along with his nephew, a clergyman.[11] More palatable to Kinsella and to Irish tastes, both then and now, are the beautifully proportioned engravings by James Malton of Dublin's fine eighteenth-century architecture, which depict a more refined, or at least benign, version of Irish life in the capital city. Kinsella's "1792, James Malton, del." is Breugelesque in its fondness for capturing ordinary life—"a couple of mongrels/ worrying the genitals out of each other"—and recalls the "innocent horse scratching its lazy behind" in W. H. Auden's great poem "The Musée des Beaux Arts," which was in turn inspired by Breugel's painting "The Flight of Icarus." This myth, so important to Joyce and central to an understanding of his Stephen Dedalus character, strengthens the chain of influence in Kinsella's work. The poem closes with a reference to Bow Street, depicted in the Malton engraving and, coincidentally but significantly, the street where the poet's grandparents lived.

Another poem in St. Catherine's Clock directly inspired by another visual work of art is "From a non-contemporary nationalist artist's impression" (probably a nineteenth-century painting found reproduced in a book or a reproduction commonly found in Dublin homes in Kinsella's youth. This painting or "impression" is not identified.) Here the horror and immediacy of the lurid method of the patriot Robert Emmet's death is captured by the poet as it was by the artist, as Emmet's degraded and dismembered body has:

> fallen into a grove of redcoats
> mounted with their rumps
> toward a horrified populace.

Not all the poems in St. Catherine's Clock are as self-consciously artistic as those discussed above. Kinsella's long poem "1938," recalling the year when he was ten years old, is a distinctly "homely" poem which, with its opening quatrain:

> two red-and-black matched silky-decorated
> tin boxes out of India

fit beside each other behind her
up on the tea shelf, behind her head.

announces a Joycean debt that students who have read *A Portrait of the Artist* will find reminiscent of young Stephen Dedalus' description of his "Aunt" Dante Riordan's pair of matching hairbrushes. The interaction of the young boy with the elderly female kin, here Kinsella and his Aunt Gertie, is similarly mysterious and somewhat daunting to the innocent boy in each case. "1938" is a highly descriptive poem which evokes the wonder-world of big Aunt Gertie's and little Uncle Ned's shop, brainy Aunt Bridie, family spats, domestic smells, and wealthy alien cousins, all from the viewpoint of the poet as a boy when ". . . the security of love / found a place in my marrow." "1938," the final year before World War II, which would change so much in European life (even in Ireland, although Éire remained neutral during the war), contains one of the three references made to time within *St. Catherine's Clock* that mimic chiming during the progression of the poem. Like many other poems that mark the eve of war, "1938," although written many years later, conveys in retrospect the ominousness of threatened change. The boy/narrator necessarily moves from innocence to the experience that age will bring—or from the point of view of the adult poet—that age has indeed brought.

If 1938 is a watershed year in Thomas Kinsella's poetic memory, 1939 is also an important year in any study of contemporary Irish literature, as it is the year of poet Seamus Heaney's birth.

Seamus Heaney is by far the best-known of contemporary Irish poets. In 1995 he was awarded the Nobel Prize for Literature. Indeed, not since his compatriot Yeats, an earlier Nobel winner, has there been a poet in the English language so widely read and highly regarded within his own lifetime. Here is a writer who has made the difficult transition from critical praise to popular readership. It is perhaps the mark of Heaney's broad appeal that some critical assessment is now geared to quibbling with this popular appeal.

Heaney was born and reared on a farm in the townland of Mossbawn in Co. Derry. The eldest of nine siblings, he was sent to St. Columb's College in Derry, a boarding school, for his secondary education. From St. Columb's, Heaney proceeded to Queen's University in Belfast, where he studied English literature. He has worked as a secondary schoolteacher and university lecturer in Northern Ireland, the Republic of Ireland, and America, where he held the Boylston Chair of Rhetoric and Oratory at Harvard University, and is now the Ralph Waldo Emerson Poet in residence there.

For three years he was also Professor of Poetry at Oxford, one of the highest honors awarded to a poet in the English language.

But the English language is not Seamus Heaney's only language; the poet's body of work includes subtle translations of ancient Irish poetry into resonant and sprightly English for his era. His *Sweeney Astray* is a distinguished version of a much-translated and much-loved tale of a cursed king condemned never to touch the ground, but to fly from limb to limb of the trees like a bird— a curse placed upon him by a saint who objected to the king's disrespectful attitude toward him and the Church. Although Seamus Heaney has also written an accomplished play, *The Cure at Troy*, based on the legend of Philoctetes from *The Odyssey*, and four well-wrought books of essays (*Preoccupations*, *The Government of the Tongue*, *The Place of Writing*, and *The Redress of Poetry*), his literary reputation is based securely on his large and impressive poetic achievement. His early collections, *Death of a Naturalist*, *Wintering Out*, *Door Into the Dark*, and *North*, locate and solidify Heaney's topography—the bogland and farming country of south Derry, not far from Ireland's internal border. Themes which are closely tied with family and community, specifically farmwork, its rhythm, skill, and efficiency, are explored and re-explored. He interrogates Irish heritage, exposed layer by layer in a poetic excavation of the bog as storehouse of Irish racial memory and history. Heaney, as the title of his first collection implies, has a keen eye for nature, and recalls the awakening and subsequent "death" of his interest in nature in childhood. In the title poem the poet as child recalls a squeamish encounter with frog spawn, with its capacity for producing abundant life from a mass with little visual appeal. This anomaly, and the poet's recapturing his temporary childhood rejection of "life" in its grosser forms, is the beginning of a lifelong process of growth that is reflected in a long poetic career that is still very much showing signs of increased nuance and complexity.

Heaney's most anthologized poem remains "Digging," the first poem in his first published collection. Its investigative, familial, and tribal aim recurs often throughout *Death of a Naturalist*—a downward delving into tradition. The purpose of this delving, though, is self-discovery with an insistence on continuity. "Digging" begins with an image of the poet holding his pen "snug as a gun." This blunt, effective reworking of the notion of the writer's tool as weapon is quickly sidelined into a detailed description of his father digging potatoes, and the remembered family tale of his grandfather's expertise at digging turf for fuel for the winter. The poet's final couplet gives his own work a place in family history—he will dig with his pen.

From this affirming poem, *Death of a Naturalist*, as its title implies, goes on to explore the tension and interaction between the living and the dead in such poems as the title poem, already mentioned, and "The Early Purges," an equally vivid childhood memory of a neighbor drowning kittens, a common practice for controlling the cat population on farms. The boy is frightened by the violence of the act, repeated by the neighbor, Dan Taggart, who also traps and shoots other animals and prepares them for eating. The poem, moving rapidly from innocence to experience, comes to the realistic conclusion that "living displaces false sentiments." The child's exposure to the reality of death among the barnyard animals strengthens him for the later death of a young brother mourned in "Mid-Term Break." This crisis in the Heaney family also serves to introduce the vulnerability of Heaney's father, seen weeping for the first time by his son. This moment, when his father is glimpsed in other than his usual assured and strong paternal role, will be traced for years in Heaney's poetry, even after his father's death years later. "Follower" fuses both views of this father. The father is "An expert" as he plows a field with the young boy following him, but in the conclusion, telescoped to the present, the adult son has metaphorically reversed the leading role with his father in old age.

Death of a Naturalist moves from the world of men and their work, and Heaney's admiration for them, to his courtship of the woman who became his wife. "Poem" and "Honeymoon Flight" map the initial shyness and trepidation the couple experiences, through a growing mutual need and heightening of sensibility, to the exhilaration of a new marriage literally ascending beyond the limitations of the world and its gravity.

Door Into the Dark and *Wintering Out*, Heaney's second and third collections, both feature Heaney's continuing interest in the world of work—mostly male work and manual work. *Door Into the Dark* is remarkable in this respect, providing glimpses of unlicensed bulls being hired to sire cows ("The Outlaw"), a young boy's primal encounter with the gaping cavern of the local forge and its near-mythic blacksmith ("The Forge"), and an awed respect for the local thatcher who seems to turn straw into gold ("The Thatcher"). This lyric mythologizing of the mundane is often marked by a vibrant sense of rhythm, which mirrors the rhythmic necessity of much manual labor done seemingly effortlessly and well.

Door Into the Dark also contains the controversial and much anthologized poem "Requiem for the Croppies." A vivid and violent sonnet for the nineteenth-century nationalist disinherited sons of farmers, the poem commemorates their rising in Co. Wexford in the famed Battle of Vinegar Hill in 1798:

> The hillside blushed, soaked in our broken wave.
> They buried us without shroud or coffin

And in August the barley grew up out of the grave.

The fields of men turning into fields of thriving crops is an old literary trope, but Heaney rings a change on it by having the croppies, who are on the run, appear at the poem's beginning with the same uncooked barley in their pockets—their only meager ration for the journey. "Requiem for the Croppies," written just before the beginnings of sectarian strife in Northern Ireland, is a poem Heaney stopped reading in public after the Troubles began, a controversial decision over which much ink was spilled at the time. Irish journalist Fintan O'Toole, writing an appreciation of Heaney on his being awarded the Nobel Prize, assessed Heaney's complex relationship to his poem as follows:

> Only someone deeply embedded within the Catholic nationalist tribe could have written "Requiem for the Croppies." But only someone acutely aware of the need to escape that tribal pull could have decided to stop reading it.[12]

"A Lough Neagh Sequence" is a set of five closely related poems dedicated to the men who fish the lough (lake) for a living. Sections of this sequential poem focus on the native eel of Heaney's region and the primal ooze in which it thrives, and on similarly imbedded worms, hunted at night as bait. From this liminal ooze, *Door into the Dark* then progresses to an earthier conclusion, concentrating next not on the lough but on the "Shoreline," one of Heaney's many such liminal places, so favored in early Celtic mythology, where one element or time meets another. These are places where a magical interplay of opposing forces can occur.

"Bogland" examines the porous life-giving peat bogs of Ireland that have provided essential fuel for hundreds of years, and that act as excellent preservatives for the artifacts of Irish history. This mummifying quality of the bog will be one of Heaney's preoccupations in the following collection, *Wintering Out;* and it is here in his career that Heaney begins his rather Yeatsian habit of closing one collection with a poem that will announce a central concern in his following collection.

Wintering Out, however, apart from its bog poems, contains a very important cluster of poems on language that address the crucial debate in Irish letters on the place and the value of the Irish language in contemporary Irish life. "Anahorish," "Toome," "Broagh," "Traditions," and "The Wool Trade" deal directly with language and its function in daily communication. Many other poems in this collection deal obliquely with "languages" or alternate modes of communication. Heaney differentiates between the harsher consonantal qualities of the English language and the softer vowel richness of Irish. He combines vowel richness and its ancient origins with references to the early Irish mound dwellers with their subterranean warren-like dwellings. Heaney's language poems also distance and differentiate between "us" and "them"—only the locals know the Irish pronunciation of topographical features (like "broagh," which has a seeming final consonantal cluster that is really an aspirated vowel.) The written, the modern, and the new in Heaney is not equal to the ancient and the oral. He even begins "The Wool Trade" with the famous musings of Joyce's Stephen Dedalus in *A Portrait of the Artist as a Young Man*, who queries the fairness of an Englishman's versus an Irishman's right to use, and ability to use, the English language. This cluster of poems focuses on a subject to which Heaney will return throughout his career.

Perhaps the most crucial tie to the Irish past in *Wintering Out* comes in "The Tollund Man," a poem set in an unlikely spot at the end of the Jutland peninsula in Denmark. "The Tollund Man," Heaney's eerie poem about one of a number of mummified bodies found in bogs in Denmark, is the subject of a fascinating book by P. V. Glob, *The Bog People*, which caught the poet's imagination. "The Tollund Man," "Naked except for / The cap, noose and girdle," is imagined as a migrant laborer and the victim of ritual sacrifice, linking him with all times and places—a recognition of human imperfection and frailty.

In 1973 Heaney's collection *North* solidified his already growing poetic reputation as he continued to explore the layers of historical artifacts found buried in the Irish bog and in the Irish past. "Viking Dublin: Trial Pieces," a six-part poem, concentrates upon the controversial archaeological finds of Viking origin along the River Liffey in Dublin. The site became the subject of strife between preservationists and municipal officials wishing to build civic offices there. Heaney's poem links key skeletal words such as "jawbone," "rib," "bone," "spined," "vertebrae," and "skulls" in an attempt to connect present with past. These are, in turn, linked to the skeletal ribbed remains of the Vikings' vessels that invaded Dublin bay. These trial pieces do no more than to posit a connection between them and the disconnected bits of our history we can know, an incomplete jig-saw puzzle. The poem urges us to be open to investigating and adjusting our understanding of the past to increase our understanding of ourselves:

> And now we reach in
> for shards of the vertebrae
> The ribs of hurdle,
> The mother-wet caches—

The poems that follow "Viking Dublin: Trial Pieces"—including "The Digging Skeleton," "Bone Dreams," "Come to the Bower," "Bog Queen," "The Grauballe Man," "Punishment," "Strange Fruit," and "Kinship"—are all subterranean explorations that exhume the past with a good deal of emphasis on anatomical and forensic realism, an odd blending of the mortal and the immortal.

Perhaps the most evocative of these bog poems, however, is "Punishment," in which Heaney reconstructs from her mummified state the physical beauty of a young girl—"you were flaxen-haired, / undernourished, and your / tar-black face was beautiful." His linking of this ancient seductress/victim with the young Catholic women in contemporary Northern Ireland who routinely had their heads shaved, and were tarred and feathered for consorting with British soldiers stationed there, suggests a sexuality that plays on the oppressor/oppressed relationship between Britain and Ireland and between men and women. Thus, "Punishment" opens the possibility for the powerful poem "Act of Union" to articulate the same themes in full. For "Act of Union" fuses a figurative male rape of a female dependent with her equally metaphoric impregnation. The fetus, male, will continue in the next generation the damage already visited upon the female body, representative of a dependent Ireland. The title puns knowingly, and with resonance for Irish people, on the 1800 Act of Parliament that abolished the independent Irish Parliament in Dublin and was largely responsible for more than a century of negligent misrule of Ireland by neighboring Britain.

Part II of *North* is the most overtly political group of poems Seamus Heaney has published. Among others, "Singing School," with its epigraphs (which include an excerpt from Wordsworth's *The Prelude*), sets up a dichotomy of place and orientation that is transformed into an Irish context by the poet. The poem's title is borrowed from a line of Yeats' well-known "Sailing to Byzantium." "The Ministry of Fear," Part I of "Singing School," is dedicated to Seamus Deane, a contemporary and also a Northern Irish Catholic. A bitter poem, and somewhat aggrieved, "The Ministry of Fear" is addressed to a fellow sufferer who has lived with the sting of inherent discrimination.

At a different remove, "Summer, 1969" explores the tangential relationship of art to politics when the poet is feeling guilty about his distance from Northern Ireland's problems until he visits the Prado, Madrid's art museum, and views Spanish painter Goya's rendering of war. After this revelation the closing two segments of "Singing School"—"Fosterage" and "Exposure"—leave the political arena and concentrate on the art and vocation of the writer and its imperatives.

In 1979 *Field Work*, Heaney's fifth collection, was published. The collection continues, as its title implies, an interest from which Heaney has derived structure and meaning for his life—the realm of agricultural work. Kaleidoscopically displayed, work is glimpsed in patterned fragments. A girl carrying "a basketful of new potatoes, / Three tight green cabbages, and carrots / With the tops and mould still fresh on them" (*Triptych 1*, "After a Killing"); "rights-of-way, fields, cattle in my keeping / Tractors hitched to buckrakes in open sheds / Silos" ("The Toome Road"); and "Haycocks and hind quarters, talkers in byres" ("The Stand at Lough Beg")—all these are background presences in poems not ostensibly "about" farm work. The poems often contrast idyllic agragarian memory with the political reality of the day and its complex modern resonances. These disparate gleams of two realities are perhaps best interrelated in "The Singer's House," in which the poet hears local folk songs that conjure for him salt mines and farm kitchens, and his link with the past is reaffirmed in the final line, "We still believe what we hear."

"Glanmore Sonnets," a sequence of ten, are poems composed in the Co. Wicklow retreat to which Heaney and his family moved in the summer of 1972 after his decision to leave Northern Ireland. The sonnet sequence is lush and gives the impression of heavy growth typical of the green, hilly Wicklow landscape. However, unlike Heaney's own Co. Derry, with its farmers and others who make up a village community, Heaney's Wicklow is populated nearly exclusively by plants, birds, and animals. The only "voice," other than the poet's, that is heard on occasion, is his wife's, and the tension of displacement from home is audible in their exchanges. This period in Wicklow, so important to the development of the poet *qua* poet, was one of major domestic readjustment, a fact that Heaney has acknowledged in more recent interviews. Tension turns to bitterness and accusation in "An Afterwards," in which the poet does not speak himself, but allows his wife to vent her spleen at first in a tirade against all poets whom she would place "in the ninth circle" (or the lowest part) of Dante's *Inferno*.

The deceptively named poetic title sequence "Field Work" is a four-part poem of rediscovery in which husband and wife become lovers as if for the first time. The four sections are united by a metaphorical repetition of the territorial notion of "marking." The poet misremembers the whereabouts of his wife's vaccination mark and later marks or stains her "to perfection" with a currant blossom and with mold, while on an idyllic walk through the woods. This basic interplay of bodies as familiar, distant, and then familiar again, signals a deserved peace and reconciliation.

Heaney's 1984 collection, *Station Island*, is constructed in three parts—a series of varied and impressive short lyrics, followed by the long title poem, and, finally, "Sweeney Redivivus" (Sweeney Among the Living Again). The last section consists of related lyrics on the Sweeney myth from Heaney's Ulster, the subject also of his translation *Sweeney Astray*.

Station Island is a powerful collection that gives clear indication of the sweep of Heaney's maturing talent. The opening lyrics would form an impressive collection on their own. "Shelf Life" is a serial poem of six parts, which focuses minute attention on primitive and mundane objects made of granite, iron, and pewter. Here an iron, a plate, a spike, and even an incongruous snowshoe, shine in their essential clarity of form and function. Other lyrics feature simple objects similarly sanctified and clarified, such as in "A Hazel Stick for Catherine Ann," "A Kite for Michael and Christopher"—objects linked emotionally and seamlessly to Heaney's children and their individual personalities and talents. These are rare glimpses into intimate moments with the poet's family, including newly relaxed poems about his wife—the conjugal familiarity, the joy of many years, distilled in-jokes, and shared minor pleasures. "La Toilette" racily compares his wife's white bathrobe covering her body—that she was taught as a child to regard as the Temple of the Holy Ghost—with the white drape, or *vellum*, used to cover the chalice for Mass.

"Station Island" is an important poem. It is essential to the reader's comprehension of Heaney's lifelong poetic intention and accomplishment. As a postmodern poem, "Station Island" represents a poet's apologia for his subject matter, his style, his choice of career, and his use of the past in his art, all couched within the metaphor of pilgrimage.

The poem is set on Station Island in Lough Derg, Co. Donegal, a site of ancient religious devotions that predate Christian Ireland.[13] Heaney, a skeptic, but not irreverent, embarks upon the pilgrimage in an attempt to understand his past. As he does so, the experience becomes vaguely hallucinatory: as the night and the cold and the hunger penetrate his consciousness, the poet encounters multiple figures from the personal, historical or, literary past. Each figure challenges a tenet of his personal belief system.

Simon Sweeney, a neighbor long dead, is followed by the author William Carleton, a nineteenth-century Catholic writer from Northern Ireland who turned Protestant because it was a pragmatic career choice. These ghosts jostle with Heaney's grandmother, who, like many of her time, is given to Marian devotions. Her memory returns to Heaney "among bead clicks" on Station Island. He is also "visited" by a young priest whose unctuousness on visits home had struck the poet in the past as being a sign of self-conscious religiosity. In "Station Island" the priest returns, disembodied, to accuse the poet of a similar fault. The priest is followed by former schoolmasters, comic in their disappointment with life, poet Patrick

Kavanagh, and childhood sweethearts, transmuted into imagined beauties lusted for in adolescence.

But by Section VII of "Station Island," which is composed in 12 sections, the memories and the ghosts become more pressing, recent, and informing. A friend ambushed by gunmen during the Troubles in Northern Ireland and remembered for his "athlete's cleanliness," is now manifest as "the perfect, clean, unthinkable victim." Section VIII, which relates closely to the preceding section, is a poem of a type known as a palinode—a poem that argues with, or takes issue with, an earlier poem. Here Heaney takes issue with "The Strand at Lough Beg," an earlier poem on the death of a cousin, Colum McCartney. The poet's self-accusation begins not with McCartney and his death, however, but with another death (or a dying) that the poet believes he was unequal to. This was a very different death of a friend who lived to be only 32 years old. Heaney's final visit to the hospital is marked by silence and awkwardness. The ghost of this friend transforms itself midway through Section VIII into the resurrected form of McCartney, who accuses Heaney of a "literary" treatment of his bloody death that failed to register the brutality of the act:

> The Protestant who shot me through the head
> I accuse directly, but indirectly, you . . .

Here Heaney's choice of multiple monosyllabic words in the first line quoted is blunt—its sound mirroring the sense of the dead man's accusation. The emphatic *J'accuse* of the following line leaves no doubt of the posture of the narrator, who alternates between assuming the voice of the poet and acting as his tormentor. This self-accusation continues in Section IX, becoming at times self-loathing. Heaney uses the adjectives "biddable" and "unforthcoming" to characterize tribal faults in Northern Ireland, which he acknowledges as his own traits, and ones that he had earlier admired in verse.

It is the final section of "Station Island," in which James Joyce appears and enters into acerbic dialogue with the poet, that is its most illuminative. Here Heaney is writing lines in which, ostensibly, Joyce tells Heaney what his obligations and priorities as a writer are or should be. Of course, this is an authorial sleight-of-hand that evokes the authoritative Joyce to justify Heaney's own aesthetic requirements. But the thematic imperative of "Station Island"—to commit, to engage, and to articulate, is reiterated here:

> You lose more of yourself than you redeem
> doing the decent thing.

From the sublimity of dialogue with one of the great masters of modern literature in "Station Island" Heaney proceeds to open his next volume, *The Haw Lantern*, with an attempt to recover the very beginnings of his love of letters in "Alphabets." The poem traces the growth of the mind, rather as Joyce did in *A Portrait of the Artist as a Young Man*, from preliterate infancy through the rudiments of forming letters and numbers. There is a homeliness to this poem in its rural markers. A "Y" is a forked stick, a "2" a swan's neck and back. An "A" is composed of "Two rafters and a cross tie."

The central poetic sequence in *The Haw Lantern*, in both the structural and thematic sense, is "Clearances," written to honor the memory of Heaney's mother. Here an appreciation of her simple work well done is highlighted, as had been the work of men previously in Heaney's corpus. The poet comfortably slots into roles usually assigned to daughters, as he recalls folding sheets cold from the clothesline, and peeling potatoes alone with his mother in moments of silent tranquility. At one point he contrasts this silence and intimacy to the scene at her deathbed, where the parish priest "Went hammer and tongs at the prayers for the dying," and where there were many mourners present.

The poet and his mother's different, but oddly similar, reactions to language and its challenges is the ostensible subject of "Clearances 4." His mother, he claims, habitually feigned ignorance of foreign words and phrases. The poet, returned home, betrays his learning by similarly affecting the accent of his youth. Neither wishes to be singled out in an Ulster culture that frowns on nonconformity. This betrayal by silence is a recurring theme in Heaney, with the poet often caught in vacillation between admiring and condemning the typifying trait of his kinsmen.

Perhaps the most poignant, then, of the "Clearances" sequence, occurs in section 7, where his taciturn father participates in a verbal fantasy to comfort his dying wife when he re-enacts their courtship rituals of many years earlier. Here Heaney's diction, punctuation, and syntax are simplicity itself in his recreation of a cherished moment:

> She could not hear but we were overjoyed.
> He called her good and girl. Then she was dead,

The "Clearances" of the title emerge as central at the end of this poem—spaces illuminated after the death of his mother, which he and his siblings tacitly understand are to be filled by them, the next generation, as the cycle of life and death continues.

Two poems in *The Haw Lantern*—"From the Frontier of Writing" and "From the Republic of Conscience"—share the convention of fusing the timelessness of the ideological and the aesthetic with the contemporary local geopolitical specific. The frightening and isolated experience of being stopped by a border patrol is likened to the lone experience of writing in the first poem. The second poem recreates that other notably isolating and alienating of modern experiences—arriving in a foreign and hostile airport with "No porters. No interpreter. No taxi." Each is an attempt to explain the utter loneliness of the personal examination of one's conscience. The extent to which this is the most individual of experiences is brilliantly illuminated in section II of "From the Republic of Conscience," in which Heaney sketches a grotesque looking-glass world of alternative social behavior and symbols, only to return, relieved, to his home turf. The poem is unusual in Heaney's corpus to this point in that it toys with the surreal, which surfaces again at the end of this volume in poems similarly titled, like "From the Canton of Expectation." The latter bewilderingly records the rapidity of social change that has occurred in Ireland since Heaney's childhood. Such poems contrast the kinetic demands of nationalization and political action required by the transition to the modern, with the more static and traditional qualities of religious belief and contemplation.

The Haw Lantern closes, significantly, with "The Disappearing Island," a short lyric that signals the subject and the overriding symbolic crux of Heaney's next volume, *Seeing Things*. The disappearing island, a natural phenomenon and also a feature significant in Celtic myth, is, significantly, the central focus of Brian Friel's recent play *Wonderful Tennessee* (see drama chapter). In *Seeing Things*, especially in its short second section of lyrics sparingly entitled "Lightenings," "Settings," "Crossings," and "Squarings," Heaney pares experience to essentials.

In section viii of "Lightenings" Heaney explores most directly his new central metaphor—a vision of a mythical ship.[14] One of its heavenly crewmen climbed over the side and down a rope to earth, despite the earth's atmosphere nearly "drowning" his heavenly body. Heaney, the fearful nonswimmer, has procured an airborne boat from myth, and used once again the mingling of two elements—air and earth—while inferring a third, water. Thus he creates the illuminating moment that is sought by all artists. The final lyric in "Squarings," section xviii, confirms this aim and Heaney's firmness of purpose, and eclipses the divide between faith and revelation:

> Strange how things in the offing, once they're sensed,
> Convert to things foreknown;

And how what's come upon is manifest
Only in light of what has been gone through.

When *The Spirit Level* was first published in 1996, it was noted that this
was a volume marked by travel, in fact a rather heavily vehicular volume.[17]
In addition to an imaginary rail journey, Heaney's protagonists drive their
tractors into Derry (his brother Hugh in "Keeping Going"), drive coal lorries
("Two Lorries"), have flown to Manhattan, California, and back home to
Ireland ("Flight Path"), take the train to Belfast (also "Flight Path"), and
abandon motorbikes in order to go fishing ("The Gravel Walks"). Perhaps
more notable in this collection is the amount of walking and running, and
the number of references to feet that occur. The feet are literally of the sort
we use for walking, but feet are, of course, also a unit of measure, the two
originally closely related. Perhaps more to the point, the foot is a unit of
measure in a poem, a metrical unit. "Poet's Chair," dedicated to sculptor
Carolyn Mulholland, combines a predominant stone motif, strong reverber-
ations of Yeats' "Lapis Lazuli" (also about a stone carving) and "Sailing to
Byzantium," and the heavily repeated use of the word foot:

  catsfoot, goatfoot, big soft splay-foot too.

The prefix "trans" is used prominently in this collection and supports
the poet's vehicular metaphor. Since to "translate" literally means to cross
over, we return to Heaney's familiar mining of the energy found in liminal-
ity—threshold places where one crosses over. There are several doorsteps
or thresholds to be found in *The Spirit Level*, and as they are crossed over the
personae become literally or figuratively airborne or liberated.
    The liberation of travel and movement has a complementary but more
somber metaphoric alliance with all the ash imagery in *The Spirit Level*. The
ashes offer an ephemeral counterbalance to the weightiness of all the stone
imagery already indicated, while being the traditional imagistic reminder of
mortality ("ashes to ashes, dust to dust"). Even in the use of "ashplant," a
name common in Ireland for a walking stick made from an ash tree, Heaney's
"The Strand" plays knowingly with the mortal and the immortal. His father's
ashplant makes a trail on the strand, or beach, that no tide can eradicate
from the poet's memory.
    To conclude, the central focus of *The Spirit Level* is a long poem,
"Mycenae Lookout," which has as its ostensible subject the uneasy peace
that ensued after the Trojan war. The parallels to Northern Ireland after the
short-lived IRA cease-fire of 1994 are apparent, especially as the cease-fire

had been abandoned by the time the collection was published (and has since been renewed and violated in turn). The poem opens with a nightmarish vision recounted by a lone watchman too brutalized by war to adjust to peace. Here and elsewhere in the volume, Heaney uses powerful and blunt language to indicate his conviction that there are no easy transitions to peace, that it will be difficult, again, to cross over.

Seamus Heaney's corpus is an impressive one for any poet in any age, and his personal accomplishment as an artist has earned him his international reputation. It has been suggested, however, that the sheer power of that reputation has indirectly taken a toll on the careers of his contemporaries in Northern Ireland. It could, perhaps, be argued more effectively, however, that Heaney's fame has helped to shine an artistic spotlight on Ulster writers and Irish artists of all kinds. The following two poets, Michael Longley and Derek Mahon have, in any case, also acquitted themselves as artists, like Seamus Heaney and others, in a way that defies the tiny parameters of their native province.

Michael Longley is a friend and contemporary of Seamus Heaney's, born in Belfast in 1939. He published his first collection of poems, *No Continuing City*, in 1969. Longley's corpus is not large—until recently it consisted only of four additional volumes (*An Exploded View* [1973], *Man Lying on a Wall* [1976], *Echo Gate* [1979], and *Poems 1963 – 83* [1985], which contained a section of new poems). The poet was able only recently to give up his full-time job with the Northern Ireland Arts Council, where he was employed for 20 years. Recently, however, Longley's poetic gifts have flowered, and two collections have been published in four years— *Gorse Fires* (1991) and *The Ghost Orchid* (1995). Longley is also distinct in another way from many of his contemporaries in that, with the exception of an occasional foray into the critical essay, and a short collection of autobiographical prose pieces (*Tuppenny Stung* [1995]), he has not pub- lished in other creative genres. His gift is truly a lyrical one, and although many lyric poets find their powers receding in middle or old age, Longley is fortunate to be experiencing a renewal or an intensification of lyric inspiration.

Like Louis MacNeice, another poet with Belfast connections of the generation before him, Michael Longley earned his college degree in Classics. This training is shown to advantage not only in the metric and structure of his verse, but also in Longley's intimacy and ease with the emotively powerful and timeless tales retold by the great Latin and Greek poets and dramatists. These have recently become his overt subject matter, aptly fused with the truculent realities of the political instability of his native city. To start with a very recent poem, and then work through a poetic career marked by its early successes and the restraint and discipline of the true artist, Michael Longley's "Ceasefire" was published in *The Irish Times* almost immediately after the announcement of the IRA cease-fire of August 1994, and is quoted here in full:

> Put in mind of his own father and moved to tears
> Achilles took him by the hand and pushed the old king
> Gently away, but Priam curled up at his feet and
> Wept with him until their sadness filled the building.
>
> Taking Hector's corpse into his own hands Achilles
> Made sure it was washed and, for the old king's sake,
> Laid out in uniform, ready for Priam to carry
> Wrapped like a present home to Troy at daybreak.
>
> When they had eaten together, it pleased them both
> To stare at each other's beauty as lovers might,
> Achilles built like a god, Priam good-looking still
> And full of conversation, who earlier had sighed:
>
> 'I get down on my knees and do what must be done
> And kiss Achilles' hand, the killer of my son.'

The poignant simplicity of its final couplet; its rendering of the unfortunate timelessness of the human urge to slaughter; its yoking of the Trojan myth to the nearly mythic tragedy of Northern Irish life; and its grave joy in the similarly recurring human capacity for forgiveness, makes "Ceasefire" one of the many gems of Longley's long career.

Classical forms both have underlaid the structure and often become the subject of Longley's finest poetic efforts since his was an emerging voice. "Epithalamion," published in the sixties, is a traditional wedding song in the mode of Spenser in English. Here the male persona functions dually as groom and troubadour, unlike in the original Greek versions, in which male members of the wedding party composed and sang love songs to serenade the lovers and to encourage fertility. Longley's wedding song traditionally allies the lovers with both nature and with royalty, and plays extensively with light and dark imagery to create an isolated and perfect night world of love threatened by the inevitable, mundane return of day:

These are the small hours when
Moths by their fatal appetite
That brings them tapping to get in,
Are steered along the night
To where one window catches light.

Who hazard all to be
Where we, the only two it seems,
Inhabit so delightfully
A room it bursts its seams
And spills on to the lawn in beams, . . .

"Epithalamion" could be said to begin for Longley a career of domestic poetry. Family—wife, father, mother, nanny, twin brother, grandmother, cousins, aunts, uncles, and children- figures regularly in his collections; but one of the richest relationships explored, over and over, is that with his father.

Peter Longley settled in Belfast after being mustered out of the British Army after World War I, and then served again in World War II. Longley's portraits of his father are remarkably domesticated for poems written by a man for a man. Poems like "The Linen Workers" and "The Third Light" associate the aging, ailing figure of Peter Longley with the touching accoutrements of ordinary, middle-aged, middle-class life—cigarette butts, dentures in a glass, glasses of sherry, a favorite newspaper. Longley senior died of testicular cancer, and during his final illness he was nursed by his son. The father's life, his illness, and his death continue to be the subjects of poems for more than 25 years, whereas only quite recently has the poet begun to grapple with ambivalent feelings about his late mother. The poet takes his cue once again from the Homeric tale of the return of Odysseus to Ithaca, where he is recognized because of a birthmark, and not by his mother but by his beloved nurse. Thus "Eurycleia" begins with the rather ominous and sad line "I began like Odysseus by loving the wrong woman," to introduce the extent of the break in the natural maternal bond. Clearly Longley's primary familial attachment, then, is to his father, and poems about his father's extended family figure prominently as a result. Here the palpable longing for continuity is apparent immediately to the reader, as it is to the poet's clairvoyant paternal English grandmother in "Second Sight." The poet imagines her looking right through him as he enters her home in England. "Second Sight" also includes reference to aunts and uncles who fulfill the mythological function of directing the poet/hero in the quest for his past.

His father's siblings function similarly in "In a Mississauga Garden" set in the North Carolina that was the home of several of these aunts and uncles.

Michael Longley's poetry is often most admired, especially by other poets, for its economy and clarity of image. Rather than having experimented with the long poem, as we have seen many of his contemporaries in Ireland have done, Longley favors the serial poem, a long poem made up of several short, related lyrics, a form more favored by modernists. His serial poems, though they are fewer in number than his shorter lyrics, are modernist often both in their subject matter and in their disjointed but quintessential linking of each part with the other.[16] Thus Longley's "Words for Jazz Perhaps," with its knowingly updated nod to Yeats' "Words for Music Perhaps," salutes four giants of the jazz world—Fats Waller, Bud Freeman, Bessie Smith, and Bix Biederbecke—and revels in the foreignness represented by these artistic missionaries to the Northern Europe from the distant and exotic American south. "Lares," "A Nativity," "Letters," "Carrigskeewaun," and "Doctor Jazz" are all serial poems with sections either titled or numbered. The last is inspired by Jelly Roll Morton, Billie Holiday, and other jazz greats.

"Carrigskeewaun" is the name of the mountain that dominates the part of Co. Mayo where Longley keeps a cottage. The poem, more closely integrated than some of his other serial poems, consists of five sections named for topographical or simple man-made features (i.e. "The Mountain," "The Path"). The poem's persona, glimpsed as husband and father, is in acute harmony with the variety and tenuousness of the natural world he describes. His voice calling the children, footprints disappearing from the sand, the sun setting on the lake—all are fleeting, but recurring and reassuring to the poet. Each is also an excellently suited subject for his serial format, which exhibits the combined skill of the finely honed short lyric and the structural demands of the longer poem relieved of its more traditional uninterrupted narrative.

Mayo, southwest of the border from Belfast, is Longley's source of alternative rural imagining. In "The West," "In Mayo," "Mayo Monologues" (another serial poem), and "Detour," Longley gives himself over to a strong naturalist impulse and a longing to merge with the place and its ethos. In "Detour," this urge is carried to the extent of imagining, or indeed planning, details of his own funeral cortege proceeding through the streets of the town. The funeral goes nearly unnoticed, except for the subdued habit of Irish country people of doffing their hats, standing still, and making the sign of the cross—silent signs of respect for the dead.

But the classics and, increasingly, Northern Ireland and its tribal upheavals, pull strongest on Longley's imagination. Recently *Gorse Fires* made conspicuous and renewed use of Greek myth, particularly favoring excerpts from the Odyssey. *The Ghost Orchid* continues to reinforce Longley's imaginative nexus with the Latin and Greek in such poems as "After Horace," "Baucis & Philemon," "Phoenix," "Poseidon," "Phemios and Medon," and others that display a disarming, modern, and antiheroic interpretation of their prototypes. But there are also poems like "Ceasefire," which elevate the actions of mankind today into the heroic realm.

Lately Longley's talent for the domesticated topic has found a new dimension in an unlikely subject—the continued strife in his home province of Ulster. Longley juxtaposes the mundane lives of Ulster's victims with the horror of sudden death in poems like "The Ice Cream Man," in which the shopkeeper who sold ice cream to the Longley children becomes yet another hapless victim in the sectarian tragedy. In "Wounds," a bus-conductor victim wears comfy carpet slippers; his wife is clumsily consoled by an abashed young British soldier mumbling "Sorry, Missus." "Wreaths" is a commemoration of another shopkeeper's death, and that of ten linen workers, whose place of death the poet visited. The persona in "Wreaths" is rendered most indignant by the sight of the workers' personal belongings strewn along the road—"spectacles, / Wallets, small change, and a set of dentures . . . ," a desecration of their privacy and humanity.

In *Ghost Orchid* the domestic Longley continues to choose bijou subjects for controlled poetic examination that at times approaches apotheosis. Longley's willingness to explore a feminine element in this collection has been noted by reviewers, especially as it appears in "A Gift of Boxes" and "A Flowering," which explores the eventual androgynous nature of old age. But *Ghost Orchid* also contains some celebratory or overtly phallic poems that seem a release for Longley, similar to Yeats' poems of maturity. "Poseidon," "Mr. 10 ½," and "Massive Lovers" are differing examples of the poet's ability to cope with masculine insecurities, which he disposes of quite artfully in "Mr. 10 ½", a poem about Robert Mapplethorpe's photographic art, in particular his genital self-portraiture.

Treatment of the Mapplethorpe controversy apart, however, it must be said that Michael Longley is much more likely to derive inspiration from the natural world than from the art world. There is, however, a tradition in Irish poetry, as there is in the poetry of other Anglophone and European countries, of writing poetry that takes as its imaginative starting point a man-made work of art.

Derek Mahon is such a poet. Born in 1941, Mahon also came to prominence in the sixties in Belfast, like Heaney and Longley. His first collection, *Night-Crossings* (1968), dedicated to Michael and Edna Longley, begins with another artistic, here a literary, form of tribute that helps to place the poet's work simultaneously inside and outside an Irish tradition. "In Carrowdore Church-yard," subtitled "at the grave of Louis MacNeice," announces Mahon's funda-mental artistic debt to a poet whose "Irishness" was in question for many years. "In Carrowdore Churchyard" is a crucial document in our understanding of a poet sensitive to multiple and complex influences, yet one who always steers wide of the risk of obeisance. The scene, on bleak high ground in late winter, is projected into the coming spring, credited with "Igniting flowers" in the landscape. Diction associated with the best of MacNeice, a poet of unfailingly exquisite word choice that surprises but rings true, is respectfully "placed" in this tribute poem. Mahon's "reticent trees," and his play of hard against soft, which is MacNeice's trademark metaphor for the contradictions of Irish life; his inclusion of "the bombed-out town" in reference to MacNeice's wartime London and Mahon's Belfast—all perform ably the task Mahon has undertak-en. This is an artfully constructed tribute poem, fragile but strong, which exhibits the best of his own poetic skill.

In "Glengormley" modern, antiheroic triads—"man / who has tamed the terrier, trimmed the hedge / And grasped the principle of the watering can" are Mahon's territory (Mahon grew up in Glengormley), inherited literarily from MacNeice. The yawning chasm of suburban middle-class complacency, the surface order of modern life, is juxtaposed to Ireland's heroic past, and, in some cases, found wanting. The poem's resolve, however, firmly places the poet in this middle-class present, and not with the degree of deprecation we might expect. Mahon's is not a mode that rejects the modern, although it can spot its shortcomings and articulate them in a way that the modern reader can recognize with sudden shock or with glum assent.

Mahon's poetry which is placed, or which takes its inspiration from, abroad is plentiful in his corpus; but the poet's Northern Irish and Protestant heritage is no less powerfully depicted. "Homecoming" is a semiphoric recording of jet lag and the cold reappraisal of home which is often forced upon the reluctant returned émigré—"behold / this is the way / The world grows old." It refutes coldly, clearly, and emphatically Eliot's modernist dictum in "Little Gidding" ("We shall not cease from exploration /And the end of all our exploring / Will be to arrive where we started / And know the place for the first time."). Instead Mahon's is a postwar consciousness that differs from Eliot's in its degree of resignation:

> We cannot start
> at this late date
> with a pure heart,

> or having seen
> the pictures plain
> be ever innocent again.

Mahon's Irish or "home" poems are not at all confined to Belfast, nor to Northern Ireland, but also reflect his travels. "Beyond Howth Head," a long poem published separately in 1970, is set in Ireland, but projects, or even bilocates, at times beyond Ireland's perimeters, as its title suggests.[17] Mahon begins the poem on the far-off and imagined western coast of Ireland with a prevailing westerly wind moving east across the country he proceeds to chart. Even though the wind blows west to east, in Mahon's second stanza he imagines an even more westerly source for this connective wind, on the far side of the Atlantic, "from Long Island or Cape Cod." "Beyond Howth Head" then continues to link the Irish diaspora and the Anglophone world through the invisible airborne power of BBC radio waves "with a pounding pen from Cheltenham or Inishmaan"—the urban British and rural Irish poles of those islands. The poem, composed in tight quadrametric octets of heavily rhymed couplets, is in the tradition of the poetic letter. It exhibits a casual awareness of geopolitical reality in 1970 outside Ireland (the CIA in Cambodia); and its use of familiar brand names, and its linking the literary-historical past with its present reality (these are references to Hamlet, Edmund Spenser, Beckett, Yeats, and Milton's "Lycidas"), cross deftly with references to Belfast's bombs and Norman Mailer's novel *Armies of the Night*. Thus "Beyond Howth Head," when it was published, presaged a major talent and a distinctive voice with traditional links that Mahon has striven ever since to develop and maintain.

Derek Mahon's love poems, like his poems that return him home on a real or imaginative plane, are carefully placed within each of his collections. In Mahon's work private loves often intermingle with and provoke thoughts of a more public or philosophical nature. But poems such as "Two Songs" are simple, crystalline distillations of remembered love that capture its fragmentary and lasting impressions—"your bright shadow / puts out its shadow, daylight, . . ." Mahon also borrows with assurance from Irish-language love poetry, although he is not trained in it, with phrases that resonate through Irish folk memory—"My love like the sloe- / blossom on a black thorn bush." This dark image, in contrast with the whiteness of the snow on which it lies, etches the vivid, playful, and voluptuous nature of the male and female dichotomy fused in fleeting harmony.

The semiphoric and the quintessential have become Derek Mahon's mode, an imagist inheritance typified in his well-known poem "A Disused Shed in Co. Wexford," published in the volume *The Snow Party* (1975). The poem explores isolated things and the empty spaces that surround and define them. Blossoming mushrooms in the shed have been anthropomorphically "waiting for us," to be discovered in their darkness. The poet, his "light meter and relaxed itinerary," leads a postmodern photographic safari in an endangered and exotic land. The purpose is to "shed" light, even if the light is dangerous, on the silent victims of history. The otherworldly quality of "A Disused Shed in Co. Wexford," in which mushrooms are capable of desire, perspiration, and insomnia, is a marvel of sustained poetic insight. Like a crystal balanced on a fine edge, the poem's shape projects a shadow that does not resemble its form at rest. Because the language of victimization, holocaust, and war is so exhausted, Mahon refracts our perception through that of a lowly fungus, making us value that perception as much as our own supposedly more evolved view of the world.

"A Kensington Notebook," a long poem composed in compressed lines to replicate jottings, offers the reader an insight into a host of his literary forebears—Irish, English, American, and French. Kensington, an area of London long known for its literary associations, was home to many writers including Mahon. "South Lodge," the name of the house where the early twentieth-century novelist Ford Maddox Ford lived, is the first venue in the poem. "A Kensington Notebook," however, also visits the American Henry James, the English D. H. Lawrence, the Irish Yeats, and many other artists, painters, and sculptors. It notes their unique contributions and weaves the philosophy and politics of their eras before focusing on the ephemeral quality of art, and questioning its purpose and its lasting effect. "A Kensington Notebook," then, is an apt exercise in fusion—of countries, disciplines, and eras. These talents are brought to bear even more effectively in another poem, "Courtyard in Delft." Here Mahon recreates for us, in words, a seventeenth-century Dutch domestic painting—"Immaculate," "House-proud," and "scrubbed." The poet helps to intensify the reader's perception of the painting by continuing in the poem's second stanza to remind us of what it is *not*, citing the voluptuous artistic flourishes of other eras and places. When he returns to the Netherlands of the seventeenth century, however, he executes a poetic sleight-of-hand. Suddenly we are propelled into the domestic interior of his childhood home, vividly recalled as he studies the painting:

I must be lying low in a room there,
A strange child with a taste for verse,

Here the artistic transformation is complete. The poet, claiming "I lived there as a boy," is absorbed into the canvas in a consummate imaginative act. Such an imaginative leap by a poet requires Eliot's "willing suspension of disbelief" over the limitations of time and place, and also figures as a recurring activity in the work of poet Paul Durcan, a study of whose poems follows.

Derek Mahon's 1992 *Selected Poems* closes, significantly, with the long poem "The Yaddo Letter,"[18] dedicated to his children, Rory and Katie, from whose mother he is now estranged. Composed in comic heroic couplets, the poem adopts a relentlessly informal tone (the children are addressed as "you guys"), and relies on a heavy end-rhyme scheme to maintain its comic tone, despite the seriousness of its message. The subject matter of "The Yaddo Letter" is really the poet's wistful memories of his children, now teenagers, in their younger years when the family lived together in London. His wish is to impart fatherly advice and exercise fatherly control over his children, although he is no longer a part of their daily lives. Intimate personal moments of regret, failure, and loneliness vie in this poem with word games. A composer named Gloria has her name followed in parentheses by *"in excelsis"*; the lyrics of a nineteenth-century Irish popular/folk song about lost love are interwoven into the text. Mahon becomes intertextual with Yeats and quotes Henry James in an attempt to fuse the personal and the professional, once again.

"The Globe in North Carolina" is one of Derek Mahon's best-known and most anthologized poems. It is a poem that emerges from an old literary tradition, the night poem, in which the isolated poet is working at his craft, cut off from the rhythms of daily life. As is frequently (but not always) the case in such poems, here the poet is also further dislocated by being thousands of miles from home and from his beloved. From the physical prop and impetus of a globe that he spins in his hands, the poet's thoughts glide from sunset on the eastern coast of North America, as the darkness travels west to the mountains. The poem, in artlessly rhymed couplets ("coniferous haze" / "anglepoise," "motor courts" / "kitsch resorts"), becomes rapidly "global" or cosmic as the poet's mind's eye soars to a far perspective that alters strings of car headlights, which become "Lost meteorites in search of home." Again loneliness and a yearning for home are the dominant notes; but "The Globe in North Carolina" progresses beyond the personal to an envisioned loss of civilization in its entirety. America, with its vast expanse and penchant for constant change, can be an energizing concept in much of Mahon's work. Here it is bleak and pervaded by the knowledge of past civilizations once glorious and now gone:

> Who, in its halcyon days, imagined
> Carthage, a ballroom for the wind?

The poem closes with a stanza addressed to his lover sleeping several time zones away across the Atlantic, while the poet reluctantly returns to his writing, accompanied only by the mournful whistle of a passing train. "The Globe in North Carolina," like Yeats' "Meditation in Time of Civil War," Kinsella's "Baggot Street Deserta" and "Nightwalker," and MacNeice's poems on the eve of World War II, places a man in his time. The fear of change links his condition to that of men in similarly disjointed or jarringly changing times. Though the poem hardly derives comfort from this historic continuum, solace is derived from the personal—from his work and from his experience of love.

Derek Mahon's most recent volume, *The Hudson Letter* (1995), contains nearly all new work, unlike his *Selected Poems* of three years earlier. *The Hudson Letter*, as its name implies, is set largely in Mahon's temporarily adopted New York (lower Manhattan to be exact). It is comprised of four shorter poems and the longer epistolary form he used so effectively earlier in his career. Its opening lyric, set in the large east-coast Irish port of Dun Laoghaire, is significant in its choice of position for the poet/narrator, who sits nearly out on the sea at the far end of the town's Victorian pier. So, from its start, *The Hudson Letter* employs a distancing mechanism. "Noon at St. Michael's" also projects to an American lover at her home in Connecticut or walking in Manhattan:

When you walk down Fifth Avenue in your lavender suit,
Your pony eyes opaque, I am the man
beside you, and life is bright
with the finest and best.

The narrator, not centered in the place of his imagination, is also not the center of the poem. The poet imagines her "rereading Yeats in a feminist light," as he ends the poem; but he is thus also beginning the volume with the promise of experimenting with different perspectives and hitherto alien experiences, to which he will adapt his Irish and male consciousness.

The other shorter lyrics in *The Hudson Letter* seem disparate on first reading. "Pygmalion and Galetea" is a version of Ovid's famed story in *The Metamorphosis*; "An Orphan at the Door" is a translation from the Irish language of one of Nuala Ní Dhomhnaill's poems; "The Travel Section" is a version from the French of Jules LaForgue. Despite their differing sources, however, these poems share with "Noon at St. Michael's" common themes of displacement, loneliness, and lost love. Pygmalion creates a woman to love out of sheer loneliness, determination, and artistic skill. The unnamed female speaker in

Ní Dhomhnaill's poem peeks poignantly through a letter box into the home of her former lover. In the final poem, inspiration from the *New York Times* travel section provides the poet/narrator with a wild west home on the range that sounds convincing until the interjection of the telling lines:

> And if fond memories of the Place Vendome
> or the high hopes of my contemporaries
> Should tempt me into thoughts of going home . . .

Reinventing the self in a new venue is the stuff of daydreams, much harder to accomplish in real life. The deep loneliness of the poet forces him to grapple with his personal and professional failures or shortcomings, which will intrude again in the long title poem, "The Hudson Letter."

The eighteen sections of "The Hudson Letter" have real New York coordinates—the 10th St. Pier, St. Mark's Place, Chinatown, and many others. They are introduced by multiple epigrams that are quotations taken from a wide range of sources—from third-century Chinese writers to Schubert and Woody Allen. Such eclecticism is meant to mimic the cacophony of choice that is New York City, and that bewilders and excites all newcomers, like Mahon.

Like Joyce's *Ulysses*, the "Hudson Letter" is a peripatetic journey through an urban labyrinth that offers humor, irony, suspicion, isolation, revelation, and potential danger. Again like Joyce's novel, Mahon's serial poem has poems set at different times of the day, although it is not chronological. Mahon as immigrant links himself imaginatively in turn with an Irish serving-girl who arrived in Lower Manhattan a century earlier and who writes home to her mother on the Aran Islands; with English poet W. H. Auden, who lived in New York in the forties; and with John Butler Yeats (father of poet W. B. Yeats), whose journey to New York and refusal to return "home" disturbs Mahon's mind.

The final resolve of "The Hudson Letter" is clear. Set entirely in winter, the poem projects toward a spring of "primrose and gentian," in a final passage that is lyrically superb. Delicate and voluptuous lines like "the secret voice of nightingale and dolphin" follow not far after lines of equally impressive spare sensuousness—". . . a car slips into gear in a silent lane." Finally, however, Mahon's repeated and urgent "Take us in; take us in!" suggests where his allegiance and his heart, scarred by failure but hopeful of a new beginning, have led him.

Failure as subject matter, especially in the domestic arena, emerges time and again in Ireland in the generation of poets which includes Heaney,

Longley, and Mahon. Such failure, however, once understood, can often give rise to poetic and personal renewal.

Brendan Kennelly was born in Co. Kerry in 1936. In the preface to his 1969 *Selected Poems*, Kennelly seems to be attempting to elevate "failure," as the world calls it, to be the business of poetry and of poets. ". . . [w]hat is poetry? There have been many attempts to define it. . . . I see it basically as a celebration of human inadequacy and failure."[19] This manifesto, placed at the beginning of a volume that gathers the best of his first three published collections, may be misleading in its seeming negativity. Kennelly's poetry would instead be viewed by many Irish people as being uniquely buoyant and celebratory among that of his contemporaries. Along with producing his large corpus, which includes several original plays, dramatic versions of the classics, and an eclectic assortment of essays, Kennelly is also a well-known media personality in Ireland.

Kennelly's acclaim first came when he was a young man and newly appointed lecturer at Trinity College in Dublin. Early poems of note, such as "My Dark Fathers" and "Lislaughtin Abbey," solidified Kennelly's reputation when he was only in his twenties. When one examines a poem such as "My Dark Fathers," it is easy to understand the extent of his early recognition.

Occasioned by the poet's attendance at a lecture by Irish writer Frank O'Connor on the era of the Irish Famine in the 1840s, "My Dark Fathers" assesses the poet's own relationship to Irish history. For Kennelly, tradition was vividly reinforced orally in the Co. Kerry of his youth. An economically constructed poem of five octets with a strong alternating end rhyme, "My Dark Fathers" contrasts a prefamine pride and natural grace in the Irish peasant with the dehumanization that was the lot of the survivors. Kennelly also uses the raw material of historical reports of the time, which emphasized the overwhelming silence of the countryside. To recreate the mute despair of a country bereft of more than half of its population, Kennelly creates a poetic world in which music and dance are gone, forgotten. The darkness of pain, death, and shame so poignantly and unflinchingly examined in "My Dark Fathers" continues as the poet's focus in "The Blind Man," a study of marginalization. The blind man of the title, who "walk[s] the inner alleys night and day" and "move[s] down sidestreets of the marrowbone" is deprived of light. "Dark from birth," to him light is only an abstract imagining. In a traditional approach to the subject, which is authentic and durable, Kennelly has his blind man remind the reader that "vision is not simply seeing straight," and forces us to remember that illumination need not be visible to be real.

"Lislaughtin Abbey" is now the site of Brendan Kennelly's parents' graves, but when this poem was written, its associations for the poet were less intensely personal. The abbey's function as resting place for generations of the local dead of his village of Ballylongford and the surrounding area is the poet's initial subject. On another level, however, "Lislaughtin Abbey" functions as a near pantheistic celebration in which the human dead become one with nature—joining starlings, grass, and the waters of the River Shannon. Kennelly's conclusion alters our perception of life and death by emphasizing that it is we, the human living, who are temporarily outside this natural unity:

> Restless at the gate, I turn away
> Groping towards what can't be said
> And I know I know but little
> Of the birds, the river and the dead.

A contrasting fear of nature's violence is the subject of, but only the starting point, for Kennelly's "Dream of a Black Fox," the title poem of his third selection. The poem is a slightly surreal account of lovers sharing a dream vision of an outsized fox that challenges their conception of nature and of themselves. The woman's encounter with the fox is more timorous, but the male persona ultimately forfeits the right to challenge his demon, as the indifferent fox leaves him alone in the night with his unresolved thoughts:

> It might have taught me
> Mastery of myself,
> Dominion over death,
> But was content to leap
> With ease and majesty
> Across the valleys and the hills of sleep,

Brendan Kennelly, like others of his poetic generation, has also turned his hand to the long historically inspired poem. Kennelly's *Cromwell*, almost 150 pages in length and comprised of more than 250 very short poems, is, the poet tells us, "imagistic, not chronological." Its hero, comically named M. P. G. M. Buffún Esq., uses an ersatz Irish spelling to mask a synonym for a clown—who is also a lawyer! His fate in the poem is inextricably tied to that of Oliver Cromwell, a man and a name still loathed in Ireland for his violent anti-Catholic campaign in the mid-seventeenth century. (Cromwell's name in many parts of Ireland provokes a reaction similar to that reserved for Union Civil War General Sherman in the American South).

Cromwell's rhetoric is considerably more modern than that of most of Kennelly's poetry. Its accumulation of short lyrics, kaleidoscopically connected in thematic terms, produces an effect more self-consciously innovative than the Kennelly reader is accustomed to find. Perhaps the inclusion of one lyric in its entirety will begin to suggest the quirky, postmodern possibilities Kennelly toys with in this seemingly unlikely choice of subject. The speaker is Buffún, and the poem's first two lines pun on "put the knife in" (slang for "to torment" or "to tease") and also on being someone's "football" (someone to metaphorically kick around):

Coal-Dust
It was dear Mummy who put the knife in
First. For two years I'd been her football
And sometimes found myself in the coal-bin,
A succulent darkness that even now retains all
Its promises of tin-lidded security.
Not many men know the taste of coal at
Such an early age, but coal-dust was my
Original love. I lived with it
Even when in a fit worse than usual
Mum prodded my belly with the bread-knife
(Stainless Sheffield) an inch below my little button.
Nothing lethal, you understand. After all
These years, it's the scar I like most in life
And have grown to peek at with some affection.

The juxtaposition in *Cromwell* of comic diction and trivializing rhetoric with acts of cruelty and violence (here the emotional and physical abuse of a child by his mother), places in a stark light human capacity for inflicting pain and suffering on others. The poem's recurring concerns, however, are disparate. Several lyrics are absorbed by a need on the part of Buffún to search for his violent and unstable mother figure. This strange attachment, and his voyeuristic interest in the more private details of his birth, produce the same queasy reaction occasioned by the yoking of violence with frivolity mentioned above. Parts of *Cromwell* in this sense owe a debt to Laurence Sterne's *Tristram Shandy*.

Other parts of *Cromwell* explore the uneasy and continuing relationship between England and Ireland, here recorded in dialogue form by Big

Island and Little Island. They focus upon the legacy of resentment that remains in Ireland over the decision to allow Cromwell's soldiers the right to acquire Irish land in place of conventional payment. Here Kennelly brings a detailed reality to the poem in his listing family names and place-names near his birthplace that bear the legacy of this Cromwellian plantation, still vividly recalled in the locality, although it occurred over three centuries ago.

Perhaps a bit more typical of Kennelly's longer poems, however, are Rabelaisian poems like "Moloney Up and At It," a tale of prodigious amounts of drink and unfettered womanizing; or the quieter, more reflective "Island-man," with its title so similar to and resonant of one of the great masterpieces of Irish vernacular prose.[20] Kennelly's poem, unadorned, shares a timeless quality with the best of the traditional literature from the western islands. It reads, although composed in English, like a version or a translation of an earlier poem from the Irish. Here are Kennelly's opening stanzas:

> I will try to speak of the island
> As though
> My words were clear
> As a field of snow
>
> Covering the green centre, the dark edges,
> Patches of blue mud
> Cracking in summer into zigzag lines
> Suggesting the directions of my own blood.
>
> I hear the old men talk like prophets
> Of heaven and hell;
> When the tide is out I take in my hands
> An empty shell. . . .

Indeed Kennelly's poetic skill extends to, or may take inspiration from, translation. Like many of the poets in this volume, he has taken his turn to translate the work of contemporary Nuala Ní Dhomhnaill. Kennelly has also tried intermittently throughout his career to make poetry in the Irish language available and relevant to modern Irish Anglophone readers. Thus Kennelly has made a realistic transition from the Irish-speaking Kerry of his childhood to the increasingly urban and English-speaking reality of Ireland as it approaches the next century.

Michael Hartnett is a poet as closely associated with his rural origins as is Brendan Kennelly, and is also a Dublin resident of many years. The two poets are most unlike, however, in Hartnett's articulated reluctance to become a part of the academic establishment, which has at one time or another housed and fed so many poets.

Born in 1941 in Newcastle West in Co. Limerick, Hartnett is a gifted bilingual writer, in whom the tug of allegiances between languages and cultures became so strong that it occasioned his publishing a manifesto of sorts in 1978, entitled *A Farewell to English*. Although for years after Hartnett wrote only in Irish (his name appears as Mícheál Ó hAirtnéide in his Irish-language titles), the poet has begun again to use English as a language to communicate his art to a wider audience, including that outside Ireland. Hartnett began publishing poems as a teenager and has, with the exception of translation, not engaged in other forms of writing to any extent. He has, however, edited a literary magazine, *Arena*, and an anthology, *Choice*, the latter with poet and publisher Desmond Egan.

Hartnett's two-volume *Collected Poems*, published in 1985 and 1986, begins aptly with a prefatory poem, "Prisoners," which is followed by the first poem chosen from his earlier work, "Sickroom." "Prisoners" concerns lovers who live apart from the world either at his insistence or with her complicity. Caught in a never-never land suspended between the Celtic pagan and the Irish Christian worlds, the couple live a fevered, claustrophobic, sensual life informed by ancient ritual. Like so many of Hartnett's poems, "Prisoners" evokes a perfect, if impossible or destructive, world of intimacy, which the poet seeks and never seems to find or maintain. "Sickroom," again a rendering of claustrophobic intimacy, projects its own end as the sickroom visitor peels away convention as he looks at the dying person's medicines— "these are not roses beside you, nor are these grapes"—and projects the feared and unspoken end anticipated by both visitor and patient.

Fear, restlessness, an honesty given to occasional cruelty, and a genuine yearning for complete oneness with another who will become alienated or exhausted—these define the emotional framework of the Hartnett poem. Nowhere is this tendency more prominent than in poems that deal with the otherworld, or the mythological or the legendary past. In "Sulphur," Zeus anticipates the death and destruction of his chosen lover, whose human frailty cannot withstand his potency:

Fire will encase her
and unlace her

and undo her:
I will woo her
with my sulphur
and engulf her
with my fire: . . .

One of Hartnett's best-known poems is one of his many wake, or funereal, tribute poems. "For My Grandmother, Bridget Halpin" honors the woman who reared him, and through whom he maintained an intimate connection with the Irish language. A bereft poem, interestingly cast in English, "For My Grandmother, Bridget Halpin" recreates the old woman's solitary death and emphasizes the irony of her having bequeathed her land to someone who was childless. The remembered connection of the grand-mother with the natural world with which she was intimate gives some final, if incomplete, comfort:

You never saw . . .
The trees change a leaf:
and the red fur of a fox on
a quiet evening: and the long
birches falling down the hillside.

In 1987, in A Necklace of Wrens, Hartnett collected many of his poems in Irish and published them with English translations on facing pages. The collection makes more of the poet's work accessible to readers educated outside Ireland. The title poem ("An Muince Dreoilíní" in Irish) is, as its title suggests, composed of smaller gems. Four compact stanzas of four equally compact lines each, the poem captures an imagined moment in which a boy finds an empty wren's nest and lies very still in the meadow while the tiny birds perch, making a "feather necklet" around his neck. The idyllic scene of boy and nature, suspended in perfect harmony, is then jolted into another level of consciousness. Suddenly the birds' claws, as they take flight, pierce and scar the boy's neck. This rather Yeatsian juxtaposition of tranquil avian beauty with terrifying avian violence is bijou in all its accomplishments in English—artful, tight repetition, monosyllabic precision, and clarity, and its balance between action/inaction, human/animal, and delight/pain.

The sparseness and clarity so admirable in "A Necklace of Wrens" is often repeated and fully achieved in the volume. "Easpa Codlata," given here in English in full, is a poem that captures the desolation, defeat, and impossibility of its vexing subject:

Sleepless

The light flew
like a nettle-sting
into my pupils
in spite of my hands.
My eyes closed
but instead of repose
that light moved
within golden shoes
and galloped before
my sight.
My body alive with sleepy ants,
my mind alive with phantoms,
I was a restless couple wrestling with myself.

The heavy and intricate end and internal rhyme ("restless" and "wrestling")
is arresting, as is the inclusion of "sleepy" ants in contrast, but not aurally,
with the speaker.

A contemporary of Michael Hartnett's, **Eavan Boland** was born in Dublin in
1944, and is one of the few women whose poetry has become inarguably
canonical in today's Ireland. She is also one of only three women to be included
in the Contemporary Irish Poetry section of *The Field Day Anthology of Irish
Writing* (the others were Eiléan Ní Chuilleanáin and Medbh McGuckian).

Although Boland published her first volume of verse over 30 years ago
(*New Territory*, 1967) her poetic output for the next two decades was limited.
Domestic life made numerous claims upon this writer's time, but the years
since 1986 have been particularly fruitful for Boland. She has quite recently
achieved a large popular following in the United States, where she now reads
her work at such prestigious American poetry-reading venues as the Library
of Congress and the 92nd Street YMHA in New York.

Boland's poetry of the past decade is not only more prolific, it is a
poetry that has become politicized, perhaps of necessity. Boland is a poet
who always inhabited a female world—a later collection is titled *Night Feed*,
and its title poem is a rumination at dawn by a new mother suckling her
infant. She has belatedly ridden the crest of feminist-focused critical analysis
and the popularity of women's studies programs. She is no longer vaguely
apologetic for, nor unsure of, the validity of her suburban and domesticated
muse. Indeed such an imaginative dynamic has acquired a counter validity

that is now dominant in critical circles. Through all of these changes, and, of course, Ireland's rapid cultural changes (even more rapid for women, and for married women in particular), Boland's priorities as a poet have not so much altered as they have evolved. This evolutionary process has also operated on a larger scale, as Boland herself acknowledged in 1987, in that it is only recently that "women have moved from being the subjects and objects of Irish poems to being the authors of them."[21]

In *In Her Own Image*, published in 1980, are several poems Boland published with the Arlen House Press, a feminist press that she helped to launch and to nurture. Its first poem accosts the traditional female muse as an artifice of male imagining and/or as a traitor. In "Tirade for the Mimic Muse," this traditionally conjured female guide is berated first as a "slut," and then as "whore," "kind-hearted tart," and "ruthless bitch." Boland accuses the muse of having abandoned women and their travails in favor of becoming the darling of male poets.

A pair of poems that follow, "In Her Own Image" and "In His Own Image," ally themselves with the themes introduced in "Tirade for the Mimic Muse." However, both use mirror imagery to convey the "otherness" of men and women living in the close and prolonged proximity of marriage. Other titles in this volume—"Anorexic," "Mastectomy," and "Menses"—convey talismanic female fears, dangers, and limitations. The poems in *In Her Own Image* are composed in very short lines and are accompanied by line drawings that imply the presence of an elongated mirror in which the poet examines herself and her gender.

Published two years later, her next illustrated Arlen House volume, *Night Feed*, seems to proceed from *In Her Own Image*, past the shortcomings of the female life, to its pleasures and its fulfillment. This fulfillment is found, not surprisingly, in motherhood, especially in the title poem, in which the poet's persona learns, to her satisfaction, that "This is the best I can be."

Significantly, "Night Feed," addressed to a *female* infant, is almost ceremonial in its dawn setting. The calm and fully realized female maturity apparent in this poem continues with garden and seedling analogies of nurturing in "Before Spring," and with multiple renderings of the intimacy of mother and suckling child in "Energies," "Hymn," "Partings," and "Endings." In these poems there are none of the shortcomings or regrets there are in her poems that focus on suburbia. "Monotony" and "Woman in a Kitchen," decry the drabness of suburban Dublin life, and contain little of the snug warmth of the infant-focused poems. Each is startlingly devoid of color or comfort, and each decries the unsatisfying and isolated routine of modern domestic life.

Small wonder, then, that other poems in the collection, "The Woman Changes Her Skin" and "The Woman Turns Herself Into a Fish," feature transmogrification fantasies that turn nightmarish in "The Woman As Mummy's Head." This trio of poems deals differently, but equally directly, with the female reaction to the phenomenon of aging, in a poetically natural progression appropriate in a volume that examines growth and seasoned maturity.

Outside History (1990) could be viewed as a sublimated feminist title. The volume is divided into three sections that contain 35 poems. "Object Lessons," the first section, uses the word *object* in a literal sense, not just in the connotative sense in which one speaks of "object lessons." Here, every-day, domesticated objects, or objects which might have been everyday items in the past, are used in a manner similar to the way in which Seamus Heaney used them in *Seeing Things*. These objects in Boland's work accrue significance and manifest their essential nature as they are isolated, admired, and exalted. The first poem features "The Black Lace Fan My Mother Gave Me," which functions as its deceptively artless title. Although the poet conjures the world of the fan—her parents' courtship in Paris—the fan itself is acknowl-edged by the poet to have, within it, "the reticent, / clear patience of its element." In a final succinct metaphor the poet links the artifice that is the fan, this fading emblem of the love that would create her, with the natural "object" of a blackbird's wing in its "whole, full, flirtatious span. . . ."

The poems that follow "The Black Lace Fan My Mother Gave Me" are filled with such everyday objects. They are found in "The Rooms of Other Women Poets," in which the poet examines the personal belongings of other women writers to search for some objective link between herself and them. In "Object Lessons," the title poem, a humble coffee mug, belonging to the poet's mother, is smashed on the kitchen floor in a new house, presaging the mother's death. The mug is emblematic in that it, like the poem, tells a story—of a hunting scene with dogs in pursuit of a rabbit, "A thrush ready to sing."

In "The Shadow Doll" the poet uses the word "airless," as she did in "The Black Lace Fan My Mother Gave Me." In the latter poem the word seemed to convey not only the stifling heat of a Paris summer, but also the atmosphere of sexual tension and expectancy associated with courtship. In "The Shadow Doll" the word "airless" is used to compare the condition of the Victorian bridal doll in a dome of glass, to that of the real bride for which it was a model.

In Part II of *Outside History*, a sequence of poems begins with "Achill Woman." Set in a remote outpost of Co. Mayo on the west coast of Ireland, the poem's college-aged persona is studying for English-literature exams on the Courtier poets of the seventeenth century. This genre is known for its high degree of artificiality and is informed by the flattering language of the court. Its irrelevance to the young woman becomes apparent after a discussion with an old woman who is engaged in the primitive and timeless work of fetching water from a pump. Aristocratic English literary past and peasant Irish (or universal) present reality collide as the young woman falls into an exhausted sleep with these conflicting experiences "crying out their ironies."

The poetry of **Paul Durcan** (b. 1944) provides a transition between the work of the generation of Seamus Heaney, Thomas Kinsella, Brendan Kennelly, and their contemporaries, and that of younger generations of Irish poets. Chronologically and thematically, Durcan's writing shares much with the earlier group. However, certain features of language, an ingrained irreverence for convention, and the use of all aspects of popular culture mark Durcan as a herald of the shift in values that is emerging in Ireland today. Durcan's work, and that of Paul Muldoon, younger by seven years, is strangely and consistently polar, having one foot in the Ireland of tradition and another very firmly in the contemporary world. Durcan's poetry, written within Ireland, and Muldoon's, now largely written outside the country, sound a funky iconoclastic note that audiences outside of Ireland have come to expect in the novels of Roddy Doyle, in the lyrics of major Irish rock bands, and in the Irish experimental film corpus. Durcan's verse is populated by the unlikely and the impossible, from pre-Raphaelite beauties lifted from their canvases and imaginatively transported to the realm of L.A. biker gangs ("The Meeting on the Turret Stairs") to dancing naked security guards in Bewley's Oriental Cafe, a Dublin institution ("Bewley's Oriental Café— Westmoreland Street"). His readers must also allow themselves to experience the contrary tug in the direction of tradition that Durcan excels at conveying to a thoroughly modern readership, as in his poem "The Girl with the Keys To Pearse's Cottage:

> When I was sixteen I met a dark girl;
> Her dark hair was darker because her smile was so bright;
> She was the girl with the keys to Pearse's Cottage;
> And her name was Cait Killann.

This poem, from his early collection, O *Westport in the Light of Asia Minor*, closes with a touch of modern ambivalence, but is fundamentally loyal to the memory of 1916 hero Padraig Pearse, a figure of great reverence in Ireland. The girl, like the mythic Roisin Dubh (Dark Rosaleen) who represents Ireland, is, as is traditional, forced to emigrate. In Durcan's paraphrase of a folksong, "You have gone with your keys from your own native place." But unlike Durcan's poems that toy with the disparate worlds of Irish tradition and Irish modern reality, "The Girl with the Keys to Pearse's Cottage" exhibits little truly ironic distance from tradition on the part of the poet, a trait that is stronger in Durcan than much critical commentary acknowledges.

Paul Durcan's preferred poetic mode has been described as Whitmanesque. His lines are long and often do not conform to metrical convention. However, self-conscious and effective use of repetition and offbeat (in the literal and metrical sense) rhyme tend to strengthen his poetic forcefield. Perhaps the most distinctive signature of a Durcan poem is the nearly inevitable point at which realism is abandoned, if only temporarily, for the surreal or fantastic. "Dun Chaoin," his poem set in the Co. Kerry parish of that name, is an examination of belonging or of not belonging, so often explored in Durcan's work. Because Durcan is a Dubliner, with strong rural and republican roots in the Co. Mayo of his father, he has experienced the countryman's scorn for the city dweller (a "Dublin jackeen" is the pejorative term). In "Dun Chaoin" the poet/ narrator, alert against the possibility of being slighted, enjoys an unexpected shared moment of aesthetic appreciation with a Kerry barman, which leaves them both shaking with laughter. Durcan, not content to record the joint experience on a single plane, reinforces for the reader an instant of heightened consciousness by continuing thus:

> And as I looked up from the counter shaking my head
> The big man too was shaking his, birds and tears
> falling out of the rafters of his eyes.

The recreation here of the visual spectacle of dormant birds roused and fluttering from the rafters, surrealistically superimposed onto the natural phenomenon of the man's tears falling from under his heavy brow, mark this poem as springing from Paul Durcan's idiosyncratic bag of imagistic tricks. Durcan uses the bird metaphor to rescue the poem from its initially querulous and hesitant tone, encased in modern anger. It moves toward a liberated and confident close that harkens to Ireland's mythic past. The poet/narrator is rendered heroic in the end, as he leaves the pub secure in the worth the barman has discovered in him. Juxtaposition of unlikely diction and metaphor strengthens, then, rather than detracts from, Durcan's best efforts.

Two recent collections, *Crazy about Women* (1991) and *Give Me Your Hand* (1994), are fine, if quirky, gatherings of illustrations of paintings and sculptures from, respectively, Dublin's and London's national art galleries. Here, both obscure and well-known works of art are given the Durcan treatment. These analyses offer an off-the-wall perspective that only briefly become tangent with the artwork itself. Thus "The Levite and his Concubine at Gibeah," featuring a sixteenth-century domestic scene, occasions the poet's inserting himself, by name, into the poem. He then substitutes a contemporary suburban Dublin landlady for the owner of the house in the painting. Having compelled the initially confused or reluctant reader to accept the commonplace or local for the exotic of another country and era, Durcan then proceeds to accuse himself of postmarital indiscretions that cause him to be ejected from the world of the painting.

Cartoon appeals to Durcan. Physical humor vies with pun ("The Pieta's Over") and with advertising jingles, rock-song lyrics and titles, and tabloid headlines. These features lift Durcan's poetry out of Ireland and propel it into the world of American pop culture and its Euro equivalent. His poems are set, quirkily at times, but again and again, in the far-flung places to which he and members of his family have traveled during the 25 years since he began to publish. A list of such Durcan titles illustrates this point better than any additional description might—"Diarrhoea Attack at Party Headquarters in Leningrad," "The Berlin Wall Café," "The Paris-Berlin-Moscow Line," "Siabhra in Moscow." Amsterdam, Saskatoon, Tbilisi—all are places filled with the errant Irishmen of Durcan's imagination. Perhaps these are descendants of Louis MacNiece's Irishmen "who slouch around the world with a gesture and a brogue / And a faggot of useless memories."

At home Durcan's verse focuses more on failure, loss, and introspection. Two events that heavily inform his recent work in particular are the dissolution of his marriage and the death of his father. Nessa Durcan is the long-suffering ex-wife who is the focus of so many of Durcan's poems of the eighties, especially in *The Berlin Wall Café*, published after the Durcans' breakup. Nessa is apotheosized, cherished, commiserated with, and sorely missed. She is Durcan's icon of classic Irish beauty, her long red hair linking her to the flamingly redheaded Helen of Troy figure so beloved of W. B. Yeats and representative of *his* mortal beloved, Maud Gonne (see "In the Springtime of her Life my Love Cuts off her Hair" and "Nessa"). Both of these muse/ goddesses of modern Irish poetry also owe something to prehistoric Irish warrior queens of myth in their bravery, devotion, and mesmerizing beauty. Durcan adopts for his tribute poems to *his* Nessa (significantly the name of the mother of Ulster's greatest high king) an arch-Yeatsian mode in "She Mends an Ancient Wireless." He praises Nessa's ability to juggle job and home, to knit sweaters for her daughters, and do all the minor household repairs of which her poet/husband is incapable. He can also adopt the simple and abject tone of these lines from "Hymn to a Broken Marriage":

> . . . if I could put back the clock
> fifteen years to the cold March day of our wedding,
> I would wed you again and, if that marriage also broke
> I would wed you yet again, if it a third time . . .

The above lines also convey, in the Irish literary and oral collective memory, the resonances of early love poetry in Irish, with its tradition of hyperbole and repetition.

Nessa Durcan is a most unusual figure in modern English-language verse, in that Durcan has hardly an unkind word for her; and the reader is left with the firm opinion that if Durcan in mid-life is experiencing crisis and abandonment, it is somewhat his own doing. These poems are also unusual as a group in that he always uses his wife's real name, and relies on its use frequently. In "Nessa" and "Hymn to Nessa" and other poems she is not every woman, she is not protected with anonymity, nor is she given a poetic pseudonym.

In his 1987 collection, *Going Home to Russia*, Durcan begins to write about the recent death of his father, which became the focus of a later collection, *Daddy, Daddy* (1990). In "Hymn to my Father" Durcan continues to explore the closeness wished for, and the identification belatedly found, with a stern moralistic man, a judge, who was not easily affectionate. The poet admires his father's thoroughness, how he could make a place his own by having a bit of history to relate about each building or statue in his adopted Dublin. Turning a ramble in the city into a quest, Durcan warns his father's shade:

> If you turn to the right, you will lose your horse
> To the left, your head;
> If you go straight on, your life
> If you were me—which you are—
> Knight at the crossroads,

"Hymn to my Father" captures not only the traditional Oedipal wish to *be* the father, but also gives voice to many of Durcan's generation in Ireland who have watched tradition in their country eroding rapidly in their time. It is Durcan's generation that has begun to experience the vacuum and the modern doubt that is left in its place.

In "Going Home to Mayo, Winter 1949," Durcan asserts a childish innocence on the part of the narrator as the five-year-old persona asks his father, who is driving, to "pass out the moon." This superhuman request, made of a mortal man, is occasioned by an optical illusion that has become a game between father and son to pass the time in the car. The boy here is still young enough to believe in his father's omnipotence. Many years later that same son watches his father dying in a hospital while a nearby radio incongruously plays a Broadway version of Irish tradition, "How are Things in Glocca Morra?" Durcan's own title, simply "Glocca Morra," hints at bitter irony and inconsolate despair as his link with genuine tradition slips away:

> A source disappearing,
> Source of all that I am before my eyes disappearing,

It is worth noting that Paul Durcan, who is Dublin-reared and educated, was never really able to call himself a Dubliner on paper until after his father died in 1988. But Dubliner he is, and although there is in Ireland an urban writing tradition of considerable distinction, many Irish writers who were fundamentally urban dwellers continued to make their reputations in large part by writing about their rural origins or the past, not the urban reality of their day. Contemporary Irish writers like Thomas Kinsella and Paul Durcan thus continue, in a sense, to write against the grain of tradition as they write in an urban mode. Newer poems by Durcan have done just this, and done it successfully:

> The reading from the prophet (17:22–24)
> Was a piece about cedar trees in Israel
> (It's a long way from a tin of steak-and-kidney pie
> For Sunday lunch in a Dublin bed-sit
> To cedar trees in Israel).
> ("10:30 a.m. Mass, 16 June 1985," *The Berlin Wall Café*)

The poem, taking place on Father's Day, calls for Durcan to declare his fatherhood. So as one father of rural origin passes away, another urban father, the poet himself, is acknowledged. A new Dublin-based tradition is begun, legitimized by the poem's conscious borrowing from the Old Testament book of Ecclesiastes:

> . . . let the rest of us Praise these men our fathers.

Finally, Paul Durcan's ambivalent, but close, relationship to Catholicism forms the subject or the background of many of his poems. In his "Christ Bidding Farewell to his Mother," another painting chosen for *Crazy About Women*, the solemnity of the biblical occasion, depicted so somberly by the painter Gerard David, is subversively undermined by likening the sterile room in the painting to a disinfectant-scented veterinarian's waiting room. The Christ figure self-pityingly refers to his own role as adult son, with no clearly emerging mandate as yet, as a "Dogsbody." As with so many of his poems, however, "Christ Bidding Farewell to his Mother" is not fundamentally an irreligious poem. Nor is "Hopping Round Knock Shrine in the Falling Rain, 1958," which depicts a skeptical fourteen-year-old Durcan coming unexpectedly to glimpse "the potential of miracle," "the actuality of vision," while hampered by an injured leg and an aunt who was a fierce believer in the power of Marian devotions.

There are, thus, hints in Durcan's poetry of a postmodern sensibility vis-à-vis Ireland's sacred institutions, secular and religious. However, there is never a complete severing of links with the past, and only rarely is there the outright rejection of tradition by the poet necessary to inform a truly postmodern response.

Ciaran Carson is another poet with a sensibility that straddles two generations. Born in Belfast in 1948, Carson continues a modern lyric tradition reinforced strongly there in the decade or two before his career began. Carson's corpus of five volumes of award-winning poetry quickly earned the recognition of fellow writers and the reading public alike. Like James Simmons before him, Carson in his poetry readings often seeks to combine his musical skill with poetry, as they have traditionally been allied arts. Carson, with an awareness of bardic tradition, can mix current poems with traditional ballads, accompanying himself on guitar, or intermittently playing the tin whistle, and tying together the threads of this tradition.

Carson's early poems, which appear in *The New Estate* (1976), favor adaptations from Old Irish and include two companion poems about St. Ciaran, Carson's namesake. "St. Ciaran and the Birds" and "St. Ciaran's Island" explore the natural world, isolated both from the encroachment and the comfort of mankind, and the enforced silence that results from such isolation. The hermit Ciaran, whose iconography is akin to that of Francis of Assisi for gentleness and harmony with the lesser creatures, is, however, under a curse. The final couplet of "St. Ciaran and the Birds":

I will acclimatize.
My head will shrink in size.

echoes the rhyme and the physical threat Stephen Dedalus experiences in *A Portrait of the Artist*, "Pull out his eyes, Apologize." In each case the protagonist realizes that isolation is the necessary price the artist must pay for success and fulfillment.

The New Estate locates the poet Carson in the Northern Ireland of both past and present. Poems on weavers, bleach-greens for flax, and linen mills appear side by side with "The Bomb Disposal," a short poem that indicates the need for "deviations from the known route." Such deviation has been imposed for more than two decades on Belfast's residents, who, like Carson, are wary and whispering in a city with "its forbidden areas changing daily."

Carson's next published volume, *The Irish for No* (1987), begins with a poem, "Turn Again," which will also open his subsequent volume, *Belfast Confetti* (1989), and will be discussed as it relates to the later volume. Interestingly, *The Irish for No* also contains a poem entitled "Belfast Confetti," which does not appear in the volume of that name.

The Irish for No is divided into three parts, the first beginning with "Dresden," a poem named for a city obliterated by bombs in World War II. The obvious parallels between Dresden then and Belfast now provide the poet's imaginative crux in this lengthy poem of equally lengthy unrhymed lines. "Dresden," though poetic in form, is narrative in style, like some of Paul Durcan's work. "Judgement," the next poem in *The Irish for No*, is constructed similarly to "Dresden," but Carson's long yarn-spinning stanzas are alternated here with rhyming couplets that tell related stories in ballad form. In "Judgement," Carson brings Irish past and present together by having the narrative sections of the poem, which represent present-day dialogue in Northern Ireland, connect with traditional ballads in their relating of expectations, mistrials of justice, treachery, and bribery. This storytelling mode continues throughout Part I of *The Irish for No*, although Part II, introduced by "Belfast Confetti," ushers in a selection of shorter, more conventional lyrics, which still retain the long line featured in the earlier poems.

"Belfast Confetti" uses three quite different image patterns, all conveyed as being disrupted, to try to recreate for the reader in a linear fashion the very nonlinear experience of living through a bombing. The poet's persona, attempting to compose a poem, is distracted from his thoughts, which suddenly seem metaphorically just a jumble of "exclamation points," "broken type," and "question marks." He understands in a flash that it is not just his composition, but the composition of his city that is being shattered.

Using map imagery, which is central to "Turn Again," the persona projects a vision of a debris-strewn labyrinth where once there was order. The third set of images is provided by the military presence at the bomb site, another failed attempt at maintaining order. The total disorientation is fused in three questions, the first two often issued as a challenge at such crime scenes:

> What is
> My Name? Where am I coming from? Where am I going? . . .

The title poem of *The Irish for No* opens the final part of the collection. It is a free-associative meditation that reproduces quotidian Belfast life with a cosmic and timeless overlay. Carson's penchant for place-names, with their Joycean propensity to "fix" actions and words forever in our minds, is strongly observed in "The Irish for No." The poem's title is triggered by the realization that the current Ulster Bank advertising slogan—"The Bank That Likes to Say Yes"—is impossible to translate into the Irish language (Irish has no single word for "yes," nor does it for "no"). In the poem a reverie begins with an argument overheard between two teenagers, a boy and a girl. The boy has shimmied up the drainpipe and crawled in her casement window, evoking *Romeo and Juliet*, another story of sectarian strife. The poem then continues to turn on the irony of contrast between the famed Unionist slogan "Ulster Says No" and that of its largest bank, eager to overcome sectarian divide in pursuit of profit. Carson's mind then drifts sadly and inevitably to a recent sectarian death, perhaps a suicide. The poet finds comfort in word games involving snatches from his own poetry and that of others, particularly Seamus Heaney, before rubbing his eyes and focusing on a final, polar, unresolved image that locates his predicament:

> And the unfed cat with the ying-yang of a tennis ball,
> Debating whether *yes* is *no*.

Belfast Confetti uses as its title a slang term for the post-bomb debris that too often litters the streets of that city. In this volume long poems in verse and prose unearth the daily intimacies and tensions of contemporary Belfast life. These are placed in contrast with the achieved serenity of versions in English of Japanese haiku. "Turn Again" begins with a nineteenth-century map of the city that features planned buildings that were never built. The reader enters an imaginary domain that is a comfort in the bombed-out twentieth-century city, where real buildings that *did* exist also appear on maps, but not in reality. Using his old and frayed map, the peripatetic narrator notes with timely irony, "The Falls Road hangs by a thread," and ducks into a side-street in an attempt to alter history.

Mapping or tracing in this collection is a motif of which the reader should remain cognizant. In "Loaf" the young narrator, placed in a utilitarian job with a commercial bakery, provides a younger contrast to his coworker, who verbally maps the past while they clean away years of historical grime. The coating of flour that pervades the poem and the place provides an opportunity for each to trace his name on a window pane. This action occurs immediately after the seasoned worker asks the new man if he (the narrator) would remember him, and immediately before their names are removed in the process of cleaning. Tracing, mapping, and remembering can counteract the threat of the eradication of the physical. Similar emphasis is given to substances that have whiteness or pallor in common. In "Loaf" the poet recalls eating chalk, "Raw / Flour, oatmeal. Paper" as a child. In "Snow," the poem that follows "Loaf" in *Belfast Confetti*, not only snow, but "chalk," "milk," and "ivory" are found, along with the use of "pearl," "translucent," and "pallor," which bleach the interior landscape. Not all of *Belfast Confetti* is bleached of color, however, as its particolored title suggests. In fact, bright and unexpected color, joined with a wedding motif, pervades "All the Better to See You," a brilliantly achieved study in red. Passion and innocence vie in this poem, composed in the lengthy lines that are becoming Carson's signature. The poem culminates in a deranged vision of the persona as a painter of a surreal version of Little Red Riding Hood in which a bride and groom are found dead and curiously bloodied in a forest.

After "All the Better to See You," with its knowingness worthy of Bruno Bettelheim,[22] a poem such as "Queen's Gambit," although possessed of a brilliant palette of color itself, seems quite tame. Here the poet inserts color ingeniously with the synesthetic phrase "a gauzy, pinkish smell of / soap and sticking / Plaster." But the incident at the heart of "Queen's Gambit," taking place in front of the pharmacy that houses the soap and sticking plasters (band-aids), is a bomb disposal. The smells, colors, and textures of the minor pleasures of real life—"Pear's Soap, an orange-sepia zest of / coal-tar," "moiré light," "a Champagne telephone"—are threatened. Soon numbers, cold numbers, replace sensory experience. Carson plays with the religious and historical values of 6s or inverted 6s (9s) in the Irish consciousness—1916, 1690, and telephone numbers made up of such combinations. These permutations with numbers, especially their inversion or mirroring, move the poem toward its final ambiguous venue. The persona, looking in a mirror while having his hair cut, hears a convoluted tale of disguised identity and betrayal that was the terrorist attack presaged as the poem opened. The shorn

persona, in one of the numerous transformations, reincarnations, and alter-
ings of identity that litter this volume like confetti, walks away from the
scene ironically unburdened, a "new man."

Historical consciousness is also reinforced in *Belfast Confetti* by Carson's
inclusion of two unusually complementary documents—excerpts from critic
Walter Benjamin's autobiographical memoir *A Berlin Childhood Around the Turn
of The Century*, and from the *Ordinance of the Corporation of Belfast*, from 1678.
The former advocates losing oneself in a city in order to find oneself, an
undertaking in which the poet engages in most of the longer poems here.
The latter indicates that the chaos the poet encounters in his travels through
present-day Belfast had parallels of danger in the city's past. Thus there is a
tension and a foreboding that runs through *Belfast Confetti* and begins in
childhood memory. "Ambition" is a poem that is interspersed with clichéd
quotes from the narrator's (and presumably the poet's) father, which are
emblematic of his life and his relationship with his son. From the book's
dedication to Carson's father to its closing poem "Hamlet," in which a local
ghost (Hamlet's father?) cannot return to haunt the scene of many crimes
"Since the streets it haunted were abolished," *Belfast Confetti* seeks direction.
Carson attempts, often in vain, to hang on to tradition, in a bizarrely
ephemeral world that is all too real. His final resort to the cosmos, a guide
and a replacement for Belfast's missing geography, is both a beleaguered
prayer and an affirmation.

Belfast Confetti is a volume also characterized by reiteration or echoing.
This technique might involve a recurring image, like that of confetti, found
literally or figuratively, and often in unlikely places; or it might simply take
the form of a repeated word. "Barfly" features two gunmen firing warning
shots into The Arkle Inn, turning its lunchtime menu into confetti. "Jump
Leads," containing a slight echo of "All the Better to See You," closes with a
groom in a wedding photograph "spattered / with confetti." "Barfly" uses the
verb "punctuate" to indicate what happened to the bar's menu. This transforms into the title "Punctuation," which contains familiar "chalky diagrams
in geometry, rubbed out in the instant / They're sketched." "Punctuation"
even contains the word "echoes," a self-conscious effort on the part of the
poet to encourage the reader to track these linking words and images that
support his themes.

First Language (1993) in the case of Ciaran Carson is the Irish language.
There has been a very well-developed revival of the Irish language in West
Belfast, now considered an urban *gaeltacht*, or Irish-speaking area. Thus, the
opening poem in *First Language* is written in that first language, but is
ironically capped with a title in French, *"La Je-Ne-Sais-Quoi"* ("The I-Don't-

Know-What"). The second poem in *First Language* is called "Second Language" and is written in English, described in the poem's opening lines as "not being yet a language"—not a language yet for the poet. In this volume, language serves a metaphorical function similar to that of maps in *Belfast Confetti*—a means of communicating, of getting somewhere verbally. This volume also continues the use of color imagery, or simply color names. The effect is rather like adding a second coat of paint, which always gives resonance to its color. In "Second Language," the very young child/narrator, not yet fluent in English, hears bright English words exchanged in the air above his head like colored baubles—"Sienna consonants embedded with the vowels *alexandrite*, */emerald*, and *topaz*."

First Language, like *Belfast Confetti*, dwells in a world that is informed by contemporary urban folklore. Popular myth is explored but not debunked, as is the case in the work of some postmodern poets. Carson, although flippant at times, and perfectly capable of presenting in postmodern terms, differentiates his own experience and that of Belfast from the usual experience of much of the Anglophone world. Belfast, under siege of one sort or another for thirty years, has been prevented recently from evolving as most other English-speaking places have. Its tolerance for the trappings of the arriviste life projected from such centers as London, New York, and Los Angeles is limited. Belfast defines itself differently, and there is less alacrity to dump the beliefs and values of the immediate generations past when one has to live in such close proximity to these generations, and when one's life could be at risk on a daily basis. Thus when Carson dedicates a poem to "The Brain of Edward Carson," there is no snigger as he makes use of the metaphoric, phrenological, and anatomical methodology of Carson's era to attempt to define the tribalism that continues into his own age.[23] That the poet shares a surname, but not a cultural heritage, with the great lawyer and statesman of the opposing political camp, adds greatly to the irony of the poem.

Language or languages also figure largely in Carson's versions from the French and the Irish-language poetry rendered in this volume in English. "Drunk Boat," "Correspondences," and "The Albatross" derive from Baudelaire, the French Symbolist poet of the mid-nineteenth century; "Second Nature" from the verse of Seán Ó Riordáin, a twentieth-century vernacular poet from Co. Cork. Similarly music as language is the mechanism that connects "Bagpipe Music" and "The Ballad of HMS *Belfast*" to various linguistic tonalities of *First Language*. "Bagpipe Music" is the exact title of a much-anthologized poem by Louis MacNeice that purposely mimicked (and not overly reverently) the sound of the bagpipe for its meter. Carson's "Bagpipe Music" contains an imbedded reference to the earlier poem,

> Scrake nithery lou a mackie nice wee niece ah libralassie

in the recurring doggerel that gives tempo to the poem. The scene, possibly a traditional Twelfth of July celebration of the victory of King William of Orange at the Battle of the Boyne in 1690, is emblematic of Ulster's sectarian divide. The poem eventually gives way to the implied threat of violence presaged in its first line:

> He came lilting down the brae with a black thorn stick
> the thick of a shotgun.

"Bagpipe Music," in its imitation of the emptying of the bellows used to fill the pipes, shares long-winded phrases with "The Ballad of HMS *Belfast*," which, ballad-like, uses insistent end rhyme. This ballad is a sailor's shanty that charts an imaginative voyage to distant exotic realms, but is returned to the reality of present-day Belfast as the slumbering narrator awakens to remember he is on a prison ship moored in Belfast Lough.

Belfast present is Carson's premiere imaginative dwelling place in this volume. It is mythologized by two poems that are derived from Ovid's *Metamorphoses*. The tragedy of Hecuba, wife of Priam and Queen of Troy, plays itself out in this poem, with the grieving mother, bereft of all her children, asking,

> O gods, have you reserved
> some more for me?
> New funerals? New death?
> (Ovid: *Metamorphoses*, XIII, 439-575)

Anyone who has followed the years of tit-for-tat murders of one sectarian group against the other in Northern Ireland will have no difficulty in finding parallels with the story of the Trojan War, in this grieving and, eventually, politicized matriarch.

Carson continues the story of Troy's war in "Ovid: Metamorphoses, XIII, 576–619" with the tale of the memorial to Memnon, son of Aurora, the goddess of dawn. It is a reenactment of civil war played out annually in the sky by birds, a ritual too reminiscent of the annual Battle of the Boyne commemorations in Ulster to be overlooked or minimized.

Ciaran Carson's oeuvre is impressive in its variety of style and subject and in its simultaneously high degrees of cohesiveness of theme, setting, and language. The poet continues to define his place as a man, and as a writer, by means of employing Irish and ancient history and myth. That the mining of such sources can result in very different art can be seen by comparing Carson's work with one of his contemporaries, Eiléan Ní Chuilleanáin, whose city is located on the opposite end of the island, and whose use of history focuses on different periods and begins from a female perspective.

Eiléan Ní Chuilleanáin has taught for many years in the English Department at Trinity College in Dublin. She is, however, a native of Cork, where she was born in 1942. Ní Chuilleanáin has published since the sixties, but her first major volume, *Acts and Monuments*, was published in 1972.

One of the most predominant features of this collection is a gathering of poems that feature islands, water, and journeys by sea. As Ireland is an island surrounded by islands, the idea of isolation in seeming contiguity is a paradox that the Irish consciousness has often had to confront. Ní Chuilleanáin's "I Saw the Islands in a Ring Around Me" develops in the first of two stanzas the implied circular motif imbedded in the insular—circular islands, islands in a circle, a circular buoy, even a circular saw as a referent for the noise emitted by a boat on the bay. The poem's second half, also an octet, ties that circularity to that of a clock face, and thus potentially never-ending circularity is controlled. The pilot of the boat becomes the fulcrum, as though guiding the hands of the clock in their regular motions. Thus the poem's persona, as she views the pilot in silhouette, can fit him into the timely order she has created.

The urge to control or subsume the reality of islands as distinct and therefore potentially dangerous entities that threaten stability is continued in "More Islands." Here it is islands, not the treacherous seas that surround them, that are responsible for shipwreck, disaster, and death. "Ferryboat," set on one of the many ferries that ply between Ireland and Britain (both islands), continues to explore the persona's fear of, and respect for, the power of water. Being "at sea" is an idiomatic expression for loss or confusion, and this notion is explored playfully by the poet's linking the buying of tax-free goods to its legal basis—the passengers are between island nations, "officially nowhere."

This dislocation, or lack of metaphysical compass, is carried over into the next poem, "Survivors," which begins ominously, but in a manner one begins to associate with Ní Chuilleanáin:

> Where the loose wheel swings at the stern
> Of Noah's ark, I can see the man himself
> Death mask profile against a late sunrise
> Bleeding profusely from a wound in his throat.

The pilot, Noah, again silhouetted against the horizon, is dead and unable to lead the chosen and paired creatures to the new world they are to propagate. Cannibalism and blood sacrifice erupt, reminiscent of the "crimson tide" and "mere anarchy" that occur in Yeats' "The Second Coming." The persona enters into the poem and partakes of a life-saving ceremony, drinking blood in a ritualistic gesture that assures her survival. As calm descends, the final stanza of the poem opens onto a clairvoyant episode that reconnects the persona with the distant past—"before I was conceived." A salient feature of this period of imaginative un-history is that then the sea was immovable, and thus controlled, safe—"Nothing was able to move."

Such imagined tranquility in Ní Chuilleanáin's work seems destined not to last long. In "Second Voyage," a carefully constructed and beautifully realized poem, the poet recreates Odysseus' second voyage in Homer. The great hero's long, hostile relationship with the sea, a result of his angering the sea god Poseidon, becomes the subject of comic, exasperated diction:

> If there was a single
> Streak of decency in the waves now, they'd be ridged
> Pocked and dented with the battering they've had,
> And we could name them as Adam named the beasts.

In Ní Chuilleanáin's work, as in nature, man may be Lord of the animals on the earth, but the sea always has the power to overmaster him. The poem closes with the beleaguered and exhausted Odysseus trying to calm himself by recalling domesticated uses of water—"The sugarstick of water clattering into the kettle," for instance.

Danger from water in this collection is omnipresent—"Antediluvian" contains within its title the inherent threat of the sea. Even the title poem, which would suggest no connections with the sea, is a postdiluvian undertaking. As "Antediluvian," and with it the volume, closes, the staying power of the earth—unmoving and comfortably predictable—reasserts itself as the volume draws gradually to a more positive close.

Three years after *Acts and Monuments*, Ní Chuilleanáin's second major collection, *Sites of Ambush*, appeared. A more varied and ambitious collection, it also contains poems that again emerge from Homer and that also rely on sea and water imagery. *Sites of Ambush*, however, draws more immediately and closely from Irish history and from the poet's travels abroad. Also featured in this collection is Ní Chuilleanáin's extensive knowledge of late medieval and Renaissance literature in English and its conventions. "The Lady's Tower" co-opts the tower, a masculine image of power, isolation, and creativity, and one certainly resonant for Irish readers familiar with Yeats' Norman tower and Joyce's Martello Tower. Ní Chuilleanáin's tower, however, is also resonant of a lady's bower from the courtly tradition of English literature. Derelict, but inhabited by a lone female persona who focuses on its kitchen, the tower is the site of forlorn domestic tasks performed to keep it a loving and domesticated place against the incursions of the natural world, the dictates of history, or the passing of time.

In "At the Back Door of the Union," Ní Chuilleanáin moves to a familiar nineteenth-century Irish scene of the death of a mother and child in a poorhouse. The scene evokes memories of the years of the Irish Famine in the 1840s, but artfully synthesizes this iconography with that of the Christian nativity—"a new-laid star," and the poor "in groups like sheep and lambs." The gathered poor look inside the union, or poorhouse, to see the shrouded corpses of an old woman and a boy, an inversion of the young virgin mother and her divine son in swaddling clothes. This epiphanic moment, solemn and relying strongly on the solace of religious conventions, at the same time questions the promises of Christianity in the face of wholesale death and desolation.

"Site of Ambush" brings Ní Chuilleanáin to the equally sobering reality of twentieth-century Irish history. Divided into two segments entitled "Reflections" and "Narration," the poem again uses water as an instrument of silent, but horrifying, death. The first stanza of "Narration" sets a tense scene of soldiers preparing for an encounter. With its consistent awareness of time ticking away and the presence of a nearby stream, the poem is intertextual with Yeats' "Easter 1916," actualizing his predominant metaphors. Ní Chuilleanáin's insertion of a deaf child into the site of an ambush, a boy carrying water to a well, adds a chilling reality to the scene. Even nature has abandoned the site in anticipation of the brutality to come—"the fields faded, like white mushrooms / Sheep remote under the wind," "the birds shoaled off the branches in fright."

The second stanza takes place after the ambush, and the truck full of soldiers, taking the child with it, is buried in the stream. The poem harkens back again to "Easter 1916," and Yeats' attempt to deromanticize war—"No, no, not night but death." Ní Chuilleanáin's soldiers, although they "slept like fading hay in waves," are made more overtly accusing in death as "their bodies / And words above their stillness hang from hooks / In skeins, like dark nets drying." The poem's close returns to time imagery, in the form of a watch belonging to one of the dead men that has floated to the surface. Ní Chuilleanáin enforces the temporality of all human undertaking and the precariousness and fragility of human life.

Ní Chuilleanáin's next collection, *The Rose Geranium* (1981), contains a serial poem of distinction entitled "Cork," the city in which she was reared. A poem containing within it thirteen individual poems, "Cork" features certain man-made landmarks that are emblematic of the city—a reclaimed island (in a city criss-crossed by the channeled tributaries of rivers), graveyards, the snug of one of Cork's timeless pubs, spires, shops (appropriate in an historically mercantile environment), and quays.

In addition, the pervasive presence of water is evident throughout the poem, and "Cork" captures the rather dizzying effect of a tiered city with many aged and listing buildings. Ní Chuilleanáin captures ordinary Cork lives like the shaft of light that illuminates a dark, old pub. Here the reader glimpses:

> A woman's head, bowed
> A glint on her forehead
> Obliquely seen leaning on the counter
> At the end of a vista of glasses
> And one damp towel.

The scene, poignant in its stasis, carries a sorrowful weight, made more louche by the figure being a woman, alone, and drinking in a pub in the daytime. The "one damp towel," however, puts an end to any tendency toward pathos as it domesticates and normalizes the scene at the same time.

The fifth poem in "Cork" continues a labyrinth metaphor begun in part 4, and is visually evocative of Cork's twisted, narrow streets and serpentine rivers. The persona, on a Sunday morning walk, encounters no human beings, but remarks their presence in their absence through a table laid for Sunday lunch, washing on the line, and lace curtains. The poem's final line—"We could be in any city"—universalizes the rather empty but comforting Sunday morning scene. Although we *could* be in any city, the persona and the poet are both well aware we are not.

Part ten of "Cork" is titled in the Irish language "Géarsmacht na mBradán," which means "strict control of salmon" in English. Here Ní Chuilleanáin playfully explores the wording of the notice. It is not the salmon, of course, that are controlled, but rather the fishing of them by local people.[24] The persona exchanges places with the shimmering fish, which emerges flashing and leaping into the alien element of the air, if only briefly. The fish itself, then, has escaped the "strict control" threatened by the sign above it.

From writing about her native Cork, Ní Chuilleanáin moves in *The Magdalene Sermon* (1990) to writing poems occasioned by the memories of women whose lives have literally or figuratively touched hers. In *"J'ai Mal a Nos Dents,"* a tribute poem to an aunt who spent most of her life on the continent, the poet recalls the aunt's years far away from her Cork home and her return there during World War II as an old nun evacuated from her convent. The interplay between French and English in the poem shows Sister Mary Antony's gradual immersion into and ejection from the life in France she had chosen. The poem's title, containing a comic grammatical error, obviously part of the family lore about the aunt and her French acculturation, familiarizes and humanizes what could otherwise have become hagiographic.

"The Promise," a poem of foreboding, illustrates a description of Ní Chuilleanáin's work made recently by Jonathan Allison, in a review of *The Magdalene Sermon*. Allison remarks that "Usually her poems encapsulate a telling scene from a larger untold narrative, and aptly many of the poems have titles like those of paintings."[25] With its nearly allegorical title, "The Promise" opens *in medias res*, both dramatically and lyrically:

> So a grave-thief
> Breathes deep and bristles, if
> A bare coin gleams
> Between pelvic rays,

The poet, en route to a sabbatical in Italy, is airborne, and as ill at ease in the air as she is on the sea. The poem, composed in varying stanzas, includes one in italics that acts as a dream sequence, and from which the above quote is taken. The dream is nightmarish, with visions of skeletons in gaping graves in an ancient setting. The remainder of the poem also has a skeletal quality, and the dichotomy of flesh and bone, wounds and healing, continues. The rattling of bottles of wine in the turbulence-tossed airplane brings the poet, with relief, to the comforting conclusion that anticipates the plane's safe landing.

In *The Brazen Serpent* (1994), Ní Chuilleanáin's most recent collection, traveling is also featured, specifically the poet's stay in Italy mentioned above. This sojourn was sought as a respite not long after the poet's sister had died, thus numerous poems in *The Brazen Serpent* concern her sister's final illness and death. "The Secret" and "A Witness" are angry poems in which Ní Chuilleanáin explores the phenomenon of "the family secret" and the damage it can cause individual members who carry its burdens. In "A Witness" the particular referent is her grandmother, Geraldine Plunkett Dillon. Mrs. Dillon participated in the 1916 Easter Rising and had one brother executed and two others imprisoned for their parts in the failed revolution. She lived into her nineties and was forced to assume the role of survivor in the national mythology. Ní Chuilleanáin draws parallels to this phenomenon and the "family secret." Custom demands the story of each be told only in part, perhaps, and always in an acceptable way that neither paints the dead in a negative light, nor disillusions the living.

Although this collection is called *A Brazen Serpent*, there is no individual poem that bears that title. Rather the title of the collection can be said to draw together many poems concerned with death and the seeking of redemption. The brazen serpent was an Old Testament icon believed to have curative power and was presented to the Israelites by Moses, who acted as an intermediary between them and God. Its New Testament equivalent is the crucifix, on which Christ, another intermediary between God and man, died in the ultimate redemptive, or curative, act.

Relics, holy places, female saints, and holy virgins populate *The Brazen Serpent*. The consolation of icon and ritual comforts the poet within these pages. Christian ritual is then in turn linked to the rituals of the writer. Finally religion and writing, and the inspiration each requires, are fused in Ní Chuilleanáin's image of hermit monks emerging from their cells in her closing poem, "Studying the Language." Although the author tells us this poem belongs in the earlier *The Magdalene Sermon*, its position as end piece of *The Brazen Serpent* ties the unifying thematic threads that bind her poems to each other and to the traditional craft of writing poetry in Ireland.[26] Ní Chuilleanáin's poetry, exhuming and incorporating the female role in these religious and aesthetic rituals, secures for herself and for Irish women writers to come a valued place in that tradition.

The cloistered environment of Eiléan Ní Chuilleanáin's most recent volume seems a far cry from the imaginative world of poet Paul Muldoon; but these writers, like other contemporaries, explore themes that intersect significantly at times. The examination of family secrets, the attempts to understand the death of friends and family, even the potentially uncomfortable connections between the demands of religious belief and the requirements of writing—all these are subjects for both poets, although Muldoon has moved his geographical and imaginative base to the New World.

Paul Muldoon was born in Co. Armagh in 1951. The poems from his first four collections, *New Weather* (1973), *Mules* (1977), *Why Brownlee Left* (1980), and *Quoof* (1983), have been gathered into his *Selected Poems 1968–1983*, published in 1986. In a sense, however, this gathering is quickly becoming less than entirely representative of his oeuvre, as Muldoon has experienced a flowering of inspiration in the last decade. Recent noteworthy efforts include major long poems such as *Madoc: A Mystery* (1990) and "Incantata," published in *The Annals of Chile* (1994). Another volume, *The Prince of the Quotidian*, was published the same year.

As indicated above, the most obvious biographical distinction between Muldoon and other Northern Irish poets is that, whereas the latter have the habit of taking up occasional teaching positions outside Ireland, Muldoon seems to have based himself "permanently" in the United States. He now teaches in the Creative Writing Program at Princeton University. Muldoon is also acquiring an American crossover reputation that is quite unusual among recent Irish writers. The distinction being made here is quite fundamental and directly affects the type of poetry being written. Whereas, for instance, Seamus Heaney has a high level of recognition among North American writers, readers of poetry, and students, his reputation is as an *Irish* poet. In contrast, Muldoon is sometimes now published first outside Ireland, is written about regularly in American poetry journals, and has generally joined the postmodern international ranks. Also, whereas others must derive all or most of their inspiration from Ireland (often requiring their physical presence in their own country), Muldoon seems to have a more portable muse.

Thus it seems a fruitful idea to begin looking at Muldoon's poetry at what might otherwise seem an odd juncture, with the publication of *Madoc*. It is his most thoroughgoing effort thus far to fuse his native and his acquired traditions, with particular reference to their early historical and cultural interstices.

Madoc: A Mystery has been called "baffling, clotted with the labor that produced it, a wild goose chase"; and critical opinion in Ireland and Britain seemed temporarily to concur that Muldoon had separated himself from his Irish influences, the literary markers that help to define contemporary Irish poetry and its unique voice.[27] *Madoc* may well illustrate the dangers inherent in the mixed marriage of Irish poetry and the American academy. Alternately it may be exploring that conjunction in order to expose its flaws and its inevitability, fixing on the nexus of the American and Irish colonial experience. The poem consists of nearly 250 individual poems bearing the names of major thinkers more or less in chronological order, from those who predate Pythagoras to major contemporary figures like Jacques Derrida and Julia Kristeva (both primarily linguistic critical theorists). A poem titled "Steven Hawking," the great Cambridge mathematician whose life and mind are threatened by a degenerative neurological disorder, closes *Madoc*. Significantly subtitled "A Mystery," *Madoc* is written largely in a contemporary, and vulgar, American idiom. Various American settings include the town of Ulster in northern Pennsylvania, giving the poet an opportunity to blend or intersperse bits of Irish history into what is essentially an American adventure. *Madoc* is populated by American historical figures like Thomas Jefferson, many Native American tribesmen, and a nearly edenic roll call of North American flora and fauna. These are all novel and exotic to the poet, as they must have been to the early English-speaking settlers of this part of the world in the late seventeenth century. This was also the period during which the similar plantation of Ulster (Northern Ireland) was undertaken by Scots. In this regard Muldoon differs from many European writers in his conceptualization of America. For Muldoon, modern America has a complex past. It is not a blank slate, nor the place of unlimited freedom other writers from abroad have traditionally conjured.

In *Madoc: A Mystery*, Muldoon imaginatively employs two early would-be explorers of America, Samuel Taylor Coleridge and Robert Southey,[28] his poetic forebears. It is Southey with whom Muldoon identifies. The poem is written in a jaunty irreverent manner that is oddly reminiscent of the voice of the late Irish poet Austin Clarke in his late comic verse play *The Impuritans*. Clarke's play is in turn based on American author Nathaniel Hawthorne's short story "Young Goodman Brown," a naif's journey from innocence to experience, which may have ironic autobiographical appeal for Muldoon.

Because *Madoc* is based on a voyage that in fact never took place, its levels of self-conscious artificiality are complex and numerous. Shifting perspectives, the kaleidoscoping of narratives, and a suspension of closure are all traits that characterize *Madoc*, a poem whose subtitle is crucial to our understanding of its author's intent. What *Madoc* shares with many of Muldoon's other long poems is its quest structure and theme, and a conscious duality. Its Welsh original also involved a legendary, perhaps historical, quest.

Madoc is also importantly a poem about colonization, and deals with elements of the imperial takeover of another land and people through violence, intermarriage, the repression of language, and the superimposition of foreign culture. The mysteriousness of the poem merges artfully in places with the colonization themes when characters disappear at times from the narrative, as do both Coleridge and his love, Sara Ficker. Such disappearances suggest their both having "gone native," the quintessential defeat of all imperialist aims, when colonizer privileges the culture of the colonized over his or her own.

Madoc: A Mystery is a very ambitious poem, and one that achieves partial success. As a device for the poet's coming to terms with and successfully incorporating New World tropes into his canon, *Madoc* succeeds and identifies new Muldoon territory that he will continue to mine for imaginative purposes from this point in his writing career.

A few years after *Madoc*, Muldoon's "Incantata" appeared. It is an elegy
to Mary Farl Powers, a young Irish sculptor whose untimely death from cancer
rocked Muldoon, her former lover, out of any newly acquired tendency for
opacity or pretension. Instead he returned to the range of poignancy and clear-
eyed human insight that informed his earlier poetry. "Incantata" captures well
the passionate, but inchoate, shared life of two young lovers not yet truly
formed as people, nor as artists, and charts the intermingled personal and
artistic development of each. Significant also is Muldoon's use of snatches of
the Irish-language endearments and lines from songs—to indicate this was an
Irish love, though operating very much in the modern, or postmodern, world
of Samuel Beckett's plays and Alexander Calder's mobiles (which influenced
Powers' work). "Incantata," composed in octets and using a repetitive structure
of phrases and clauses beginning with "of":

> Of the sparrows and finches in their bell of suet,
> of the bitter-sweet
> bottle of Calvados we felt obliged to open
> . . .
> of the priest of the parish
> who came enquiring about our 'status,' of the hedge clippers

is highly reminiscent at times in its diction and voice of the heady love poetry
of Louis MacNeice, whose "Flowers in the Interval" and segments of "Autumn
Journal" also captured lost love with immediacy and longing through the use
of incantatory repetition. Muldoon records precisely and quirkily the unique
intimacy of two people that can never be replicated in another pairing. Paul
Muldoon's recent long poems, then, indicate his range of literary interests
and recurring preoccupations; but to see how these emerged one must turn
to his earlier poetry.

Muldoon's first collection, *New Weather*, locates Muldoon geographically in the Moy valley where he was reared. The poet's anguished search
for his father in his corpus at times seems to be a projection of a literal
undertaking, although it is not. Rather the metaphorical implications of the
search engage the poet. The metaphorical expansions he will explore in his
later quest poems begin in such dreamscapes as that which occurs in "The
Waking Father," an imagined or remembered father/son idyll of a day
fishing. The poem is made more intimate and "real" by the use of the
colloquial word "spricklies" for minnows.[29] The gentle outing, evoked in the
poem's first stanza of five lines, turns to imagined violence and then fantasy,
as the poet substitutes piranhas for the spricklies. Eventually he transforms

a vision of his father, either dead or asleep, into that of a king. Although it is not uncommon for a child to imagine a dead or absent parent as an unquestionably superior person, the frequency with which Muldoon's father is conjured dead, but somehow elevated, demands the reader's continued focus even if the poem is not ostensibly about the father.

A related interest in breeding or generation, introduced early in Muldoon's career and maintained experimentally since, is his exploration of cross-species infertility with its oxymoronic "inbred" irony. In the title poem of *Mules*, Yeatsian in its desecratory fascination, Muldoon observes the telescoped conception and birth of a mule, the sterile offspring of the Muldoon's mare and a neighbor's donkey. Similarly Yeatsian are Muldoon's deliberate echoes of the famous sonnet "Leda and the Swan," which depicts another cross-species coupling, this time from Greek mythology. Yeats' poem marks the conception of Helen of Troy and Clytemnestra, two accursed women at the center of the legend of the fall of Troy. Muldoon's borrowing, more in Yeats' comic mode used in his play *The Herne's Egg*, merely notes the birth of a mule, nothing more. However, the poem celebrates this event by the use of a poetic detail in which the mule's placenta is likened to a parachute by which the mule, like a demigod, descends mysteriously to earth. Other unproductive pairings occur in another important poem in *Mules*. In "Armageddon, Armageddon," it seems everything and everyone is paired, even the title, to little ostensible final gain. This serial poem of seven three-stanza poems, usually of four or five lines, relies heavily on repetition. It is not, however, an unsubtle poem, weaving as it does the worlds of pre-Christian and Christian Ireland, just as it does the poet's Catholic youth in Northern Ireland with that of Protestant neighbors (including the "ghost" of poet W. R. "Bertie" Rodgers, who was a local Church of Ireland clergyman). "Armageddon, Armageddon" also features two brothers, a father "torn between his two ponies" (to be doubly interpreted on a literal or metaphorical level), and a mother "bent-double," all of which carry out in full the duality that informs the volume and seems to defy nature by failing to be generative.

Paul Muldoon is, as we have seen thus far, a poet compelled by structure and dependent upon its contrarily liberating limitations. He is also highly aware of the necessity of extending structuring as a principle from within the confines of a poem to the shaping of each collection, and the collections as they relate to each other. Thus it is not surprising that his third volume, *Why Brownlee Left*, and his fourth, *Quoof*, each contain 27 short lyrics that are followed by a postmodern rendering of a traditional long poetic form. *Why Brownlee Left* contains the mock-heroic voyage poem "Immram," which uses the Irish word for voyage as its title and the basis of its plot structure. *Quoof* closes with "The More a Man Has the More a Man Wants," which replicates or mimics the invasion literature of ancient Ireland.

Perhaps a reader's approach to Muldoon's anti-sagas should most logically be made via his lyrical accompaniments to each of them. In poems such as "The Boundary Commission" and "*Anseo*" (one of Muldoon's most anthologized poems), duality is again explored in the sense of unresolved contraries or dual-edged ironies. In "The Boundary Commission" the poet depicts a border town in Ireland with butcher and baker, on opposite sides of the street, finding themselves "in different states" (or different States). The reality and idiocy of geopolitical borders, with their arbitrary quality, prompts the poet to imagine a very Irish shower like a "wall of glass" that also divides the village. Literal divides reappear as psychological chasms in "*Anseo*." The Irish word, sung out by several generations of Irish schoolchildren, means "present" or as Muldoon writes "here, here and now." From this first spoken word of the Irish language Muldoon free-associates to a schoolfellow who was beaten into supposed submission by their schoolmaster only to turn up as a paramilitary on the other side of the border years later. The ironic and chilling link between oppressed past and terrorist/ liberator present is the "*Anseo*" he answers at drill to his paramilitary superiors.

Duality continues to inform this collection in Muldoon's title poem, in which Brownlee, another absent father-figure, leaves "two acres of barley" and ". . . his pair of black / Horses, the man and wife," and abandons his farm, to the mystification of his parish. Perhaps Brownlee transforms into the subject of "Immrama" (not to be confused with the long poem "Immram"), who not only escapes, but manages to travel far enough to reach Argentina, where Muldoon imagines him, as a betrayer, consorting with Nazis and fathering another family. Which atrocity is the greater, another duality in the balance, is left to the reader.

"Promises, Promises," like his earlier "Armageddon, Armageddon," echoes the single word of its title, but this time with the added irony that the repeated word is itself an idiomatic expression for betrayal. This poem is an introduction to the fund of New World images Muldoon will develop later in *Madoc* and other poems. Here his imaginative territory becomes the east coast of the United States in early colonial times. The internal structure of "Promises, Promises" intensifies the poem's duality, repeating as it does in a relatively short poem the first three lines of the first stanza in the first three lines of the third (and final) stanza. Significantly, the marijuana introduced in stanza one as the persona (Mary Jane), who lies "stretched out under the lean-to" in North Carolina, is transformed into a "warm, naked" woman "slender and shy" in a hallucinatory vision of the woman the persona has left behind in a London flat. This drug-induced quality surfaces slightly in *Why Brownlee Left*, but becomes a predominant feature of *Quoof*, which opens with "Gathering Mushrooms," a poem indebted for its primary inspiration to Derek Mahon's "A Disused Shed in Co. Wexford." In addition, a middle section of the poem, in which a father- figure harvests the mushrooms, is autobiographical in that Muldoon's father farmed mushrooms. It is also parodically Heaneyesque—one of many such instances in Muldoon's work.

In "The Gathering Mushrooms," hallucination is more allusive than participatory until the final stanza, which is spoken by a horse, perhaps Muldoon's prefiguring of the Brucephalos character in *Madoc*.[30] The poet's hallucinatory intention, however, is announced in the title of the following lyric in *Quoof*, aptly entitled "Trance." Here, in its Christmas Eve setting, the poet substitutes Nordic myth and ritual for the legend of Santa Claus and ends the poem with another horse image—a new rocking horse "unsteady on its legs" like a newborn foal.

Both of Muldoon's earlier long poems, "Immram" and "The More the Man Has The More a Man Wants," make use of his New World imagery—an imagery that relies on Native American lore and the kind of antic humor the reader has been introduced to in the work of Paul Durcan. Clichés are strung up by their heels: "Dressed to kill, or inflict a wound"; or ". . . I should have called the cops / Or called it a day . . ." Historical personages appear in unlikely places or in an incongruous historical context—Mr. and Mrs. Alfred Tennyson register as guests in a contemporary New York hotel overlooking Central Park. Prayers become updated mantras—"The Lord is my surf-board. I shall not want." The reader can be distracted by witticisms and verbal acrobatics, but Muldoon's purpose in "Immram" seems to be to construct, through these dream-like images, a father-figure and an identity for himself. The poem is in a sense a version of "The Voyage of Mael Duin" (Muldoon), from Ireland's ancient literature, and also the subject of a radio play by Louis MacNeice.[31] But "Immram," with its echoes of so many other Muldoon poems, provides continuity in his work in an artistic manner that in less sure hands would fail.

"The More a Man Has the More a Man Wants" features a hero, Gallogly. Soon, Muldoon introduces an incongruous, but by now somewhat familiar, Native American character who has landed at Belfast's Aldergrove Airport—an interchangeable tribesman who will surface again in the narrative. The poem, set largely in the grim reality of the inner-city, features a young girl, tarred and feathered, and is more than reminiscent of Seamus Heaney's poem "Punishment." Again parodies of Heaney's work, but also of others, seem at times to infest "The More a Man Has the More a Man Wants," a poem ultimately less successful than those in which the intertwining of things American with things Irish takes place in America. But "The More a Man Has the More a Man Wants," with its truncated ending of Belfast street dialogue ignorantly describing the horrific aftermath of a bomb-blast—a dismantled body—succeeds in capturing the numbing, surreal, and cyclically repetitive horror of terrorism in the postmodern world.

Muldoon's 1987 collection, *Meeting the British*, contains some of his most mature and autobiographical work, coming as it does soon after two informing events in the poet's life—his marriage and the death of his father. Many of the poems in *Meeting the British* were written during a stay on the remote Dingle Peninsula of Co. Kerry, and perhaps for that reason in part, there is a highly sustained magical element in the poems. "The Coney," which opens the volume, sets its tone by having for its title and one of its subjects a rabbit.[32] Muldoon's coney is reminiscent of the White Rabbit in *Alice in Wonderland*, and beckons the poet to join him in an "other" world. It mischievously attempts to lure the nonswimmer into the water, and inveigles him further by evoking the name of, and confusing the poet with, his father.

On a less magical note, however, several of the poems in *Meeting the British* examine the deterioration of the poet's relationship with Mary Farl Powers. "The Marriage of Strongbow and Aoife" uses an historical event of mythic significance to the Irish, the union of native Irish with conqueror, represented in an iconographic painting that hangs in The National Gallery of Art. The title poem of *Meeting the British*, rendered in succinct, uneven but rhymed couplets, returns to Muldoon's fascination with colonizer meeting those about to be conquered. "Meeting the British" captures the innocence-to-corruption arc that is too often the end result of such encounters. Narrated by a Native American, the poem projects an idyllic moment with ominous overtones:

> We met the British in the dead of winter
> The sky was lavender.

It then moves on to record details that place the poem during the French and Indian Wars, thus introducing conflict and the specter of death into an otherwise benign landscape. The poem's closing couplet,

> They gave us six fishhooks
> and two blankets embroidered with smallpox

is a chilling indictment of the European presence in this world, made more eerie by the use of the domesticated and dainty "embroidered" to introduce the deadly disease that would prove much more fatal even than warfare or imperial greed.

"7, Middagh Street" is the signature long poem that forms the second half of this volume. The title places the poem in a noted poetic and artistic venue of the earlier part of the century—a house in Brooklyn lived in and visited by W. H. Auden, British composer Benjamin Britten, the tenor Peter Pears, Louis MacNeice, American novelist Carson McCullers, stripper Gypsy Rose Lee, and others. The poem's seven parts are each titled with these speakers' names, but the poem is largely imbued with the presence of Auden, the presiding spirit of the house. Set during a Thanksgiving dinner, the poem harkens, of course, to early encounters between Native Americans and settlers of British origin. It brings together a different sort of native American with more recent, World War II – era British settlers also escaping conflict at home. The decision by Auden and others to sit out all or part of the war in New York was a highly controversial one. Muldoon combines this thematic thread of the artist's responsibility in society with its implicit connection between literature and politics. Using the reader's knowledge of Auden's great tribute poem to his Irish poetic forebear, "In Memory of W. B. Yeats," Muldoon interrogates one of the most disputed areas of cultural criticism in Ireland today. Turning inside out Yeats' self-searching (or self-aggrandizing) question from his poem of later life, "Man and the Echo,"

> Did that play of mine send out
> Certain men the English shot?

Muldoon asks—

> If Yeats had saved his pencil-lead
> Would certain men have stayed in bed?

The 1916 rising invoked here represents yet another ill-fated meeting with the British, and one that is a defining moment in the Irish national myth. Muldoon's question becomes the ultimate postmodern response that defies earlier parameters of inquiry set by the previous generation as it emerged from the colonial experience.

"7, Middagh Street" is a multiply allusive, highly intertextual poem written as a corona (or crown), the final line of each section being echoed in part or in full, or somehow carried over into, the succeeding section.

Thus, despite the varying metrical and stanzaic structures of the individual poems, "7, Middagh Street" sustains a high level of thematic and structural cohesion appropriate to the artistic cross-pollination that characterized life at that address.

After *Meeting the British*, Muldoon did not publish another major volume for seven years, and then he published two collections in 1994. When the reader considers that *The Prince of the Quotidian* and *The Annals of Chile* were both published in the same year, he might initially be perplexed by their disparity of content and tone. *The Prince of the Quotidian* is unlike any of Muldoon's other work—consisting of 31 short untitled anti-lyrics, the volume seems at first to be comprised of something like notes for poems, rather than poems themselves.

The Annals of Chile is a substantial volume of poems. A discussion of one of its long poems, "Incantata," opened this section on Muldoon's work. However, part two of *The Annals of Chile* consists of a single, very long (150-page) serial poem, "Yarrow," the name of a wildflower known to be invasive and possessed of medicinal qualities. "Yarrow" is a free-associative poem in which words or phrases from one short lyric will be echoed in a later one. The invasive, destructive, but quite beautiful, yarrow initially triggers in Muldoon's poem the sort of destructive, but necessary, changes in the history of the world's civilizations that W. B. Yeats envisioned in such poems as "The Second Coming." The phrase "All would be swept away" repeats the apocalyptic message, but "Yarrow," which has been described as "operatic" in structure, soon trades in the leitmotif of global devastation. It becomes clear that the yarrow plant is one of Muldoon's many linking mechanisms between the Old World of his childhood and youth and the New World of his maturity. Using the yarrow as an *aide-memoire* from his temporary vantage post in Newfoundland, he returns from the past and from exotic places to remember a typical domestic scene—his mother browsing through a seed catalogue, his father resting on a rake. Each is obliquely engaged in a germinative, gestative process. The poem also represents an attempt by the poet to come to terms with his mother's death and the death of her world. "Yarrow" soon abandons the natural for the technological and, employing the arrhythmic attraction of a remote-control device, Muldoon borrows chronological images from television and old movies to indicate the inchoate passing of time in human memory. These artificial images, mixed with the real images of childhood at home in Northern Ireland, converge with the poet's reconstruction of a destructive relationship with a woman named S___. Her nervous collapse is allied throughout "Yarrow" with the similarly disintegrative progression of the life of poet Sylvia Plath, which ended in suicide (as does S___'s life).

Repeated snatches of memory, invoked by the repeated phrases "All I remember" and "That was the year," vie for the poet's concentration and, indeed, the reader's. These phrases loosely encase another of Muldoon's voyage frameworks in which the time-traveling bard visits scenes of Irish myth, recent Irish history, and of European and American history, culled largely from video sources.

Paul Muldoon's postmodern tendency to the kaleidoscopic and arrhythmic are indications of the artist's need to pull against the natural urge toward order and harmony in art that we have been conditioned to antici-pate. Such conditioning can, of course, dull receptivity on the part of readers and can lead an artist to complacency, a fault that Muldoon avoids.

A similar unwillingness to take the reader where he or she anticipates going informs the work of Medbh McGuckian, a colleague of Muldoon's at Queen's University in Belfast. In the eighties she returned to her alma mater as its first female writer in residence.

Medbh McGuckian was born in Belfast in 1950. Her first volume of poems caused something of a stir in her hometown. But when *The Flower Master* appeared in 1982, early references to McGuckian's difficulty of access for readers appeared too. Kevin McEneaney, reviewing *The Flower Master* in the *Irish Literary Supplement*, found that "The sheer energy and intoxication of her inspired rhetoric tends in its choice of diction and dense imagery to obscure and create unnecessary confusions."[33] Indeed, charges of obscurity and confusion have haunted this poet's career, perhaps with some justification. Persistence, however, will unearth much that is illuminative, nearly revela-tory, in McGuckian's poetry.

The Flower Master can best be approached by understanding that flowers and gardening represent the predominant image patterns therein, and inform the poet's thematic assertions in individual poems and for the volume. That the volume is entitled *The Flower Master* suggests the concern with power also present, specifically the power balance that exists in all human sexual relations. The title of McGuckian's volume also suggests a nearly Victorian substitution of flora for the human fauna in the recurring sexual or sensual encounters portrayed here. In its title poem the poet's indeterminate first-person plural personae "Stroke the neck of daffodils / And make them throw their heads to the sun." The sensuality and arousal implied by the stroking, which is also rhythmic and ordered, compels the formerly passive and nodding blossoms to preen in what is a traditionally male symbolic presence.

Other recurrent metaphorical links in this volume include the related presence of seeds and seedlings, a phenomenon less confusing when the reader understands that McGuckian at the time was gestating herself. As a young wife, either pregnant, nursing a newborn, or with her very young children, the seed-nurturing and growth-imagery cycle was prominent in her consciousness.[34]

Similarly related to her personal circumstance as young mother and nurturer are the myriad of references, direct or veiled, to gray or grayness in this volume. Blurred boundaries, inclusivity, is seen by contemporary critical theorists and those who apply their theories, as quintessentially female, a trait repressed in the male western tradition. The division into black and white, clean- cut lines of demarcation in all aspects of life, is perceived as a male construct. McGuckian's grayness defies such hierarchical delineation.

As a collection, *The Flower Master* offers voluptuousness that can confound or escape interpreters. "The Chain Sleeper" is a languid study that is visual, tactile, and olfactory in its female sensuousness, while not overtly sexual:

> Unshameable this leggy girl who sleeps and sleeps
> In china duck-down, one breast bigger than the other.
> She dresses under her dressing gown, her fussy perfume
> Eating into all the storable floors of blue.

The irregularity of the girl's breasts, whether "real" or an optical illusion, adds rather than detracts from the torpor of the poem so deftly conveyed by the use of the word "Chain" in its title. Addiction, compulsion, obsession—all appear and reappear in *The Flower Master*, suggesting a loss of will or enchantment that is in itself always suggestive of sensuality. In "Tulips" the female persona admits:

> Touching the tulips was a shyness
> I had had for a long time.

This neurotic prohibition, self-imposed although ostensibly abstemious, is of course also provocative. Unexperienced voluptuousness awaits its chance when the tulips might be finally touched. The poem's close is, then, an inevitable progression through female sensuality to:

> The womanliness
> Of tulips with their bee-dark hearts.

In a similarly vivid language, "The Orchid Garden" features abnegation of will, or a certain sexual abasement that always hovers in McGuckian's verse:

> In my alpine house, the slavery I pay
> My willful gentians! exploring all their pleats
> And tucks as though they had something precious
> Deep inside, that beard of camel-hair
> In the throat.

The cold clarity and isolation implied by the use of "alpine" combines with the riotous color of the gentian. The narrator, the putative slave to the "willful" flower, is simultaneously involved in an act that is desecratory—perhaps a humiliation that is enjoyed.

Voluptuousness is not the only sensory experience conveyed in *The Flower Master*, where cold and isolation can also be explored in as much desolate detail as is the overripe. "The Long Engagement" begins with such a bereft scene:

> In my all-weather loneliness I am like a sparrow
> Picking left overs of rice in a mortar,

In "The Sofa" a purpose for such isolated and lonely experiences emerges, although it is not the only purpose. The poet/narrator details the writer's, and particularly the female writer's, dilemma. Her need for companionship and compassion is at odds with the requirement for solitary time to execute her craft:

> I was about to start writing
> At any moment; my mind was savagely made up,
> Like a serious sofa moved
> Under a north window.

In Medbh McGuckian's second major collection, *Venus and the Rain* (1984), the opening poem, entitled "Venus and the Sun," signals a series of anomalies and contraries in a volume that the author has recently asserted "nobody has ever liked."[35] *Venus and the Rain* records, in part, the poet's fragile but productive state of mind as she approached, experienced, and eventually healed from what would conventionally be termed a nervous breakdown.

Not surprisingly, however, in McGuckian's experience, as recorded in her verse, the conventionally negative becomes the metaphysically positive—barrenness turned to fecundity on the emotional plane.

Venus and the Rain is filled with poems that take place in, describe, or are at times defined by rooms, and especially the parts of rooms that are meant to allow egress—doors and windows. The tension created allows for a claustrophobia that is understandable in one who had been confined. Escape, however, is always a possibility in the poem, even if not fully realized. More placid, but ultimately more frightening in its implications, is the assertion,

> This house is the shell of a perfect marriage
> Someone has dug out completely;

This poem, ominously titled "The Villain," features McGuckian's permutating rooms, houses, and children that appear and reappear all throughout this volume. Browns have temporarily replaced the grays, and the more vivid colors of her other work. Brown, for McGuckian, though hardly a positive color, is a tint or hue in which one can experience illumination achieved only after experiencing darkness. Thus "coppery," "brass-studded," "raisin-colored," "fuscous," and "tan" convey the vagaries of emotion and the range of the poet's personal experience.

In 1988 *On Ballycastle Beach* was published, and a perfunctory glimpse at the titles of the poems it contains allows the reader to know that she or he is in McGuckian's poetic world—"My Brown Guest," "A Conversation Set to Flowers," "Little House, Big House," "Through the Round Window."

The reader who ventures to such poems as "Querencia," however, will observe the expansion of this territory by the seemingly contrary means of firmer delineation and exploration of the territory that is already hers.[36] A young woman; a house like a fastness of love, with bower-like windows; a time of emergence from "the apple-green shutters / Of sleep"—all of these suggest security or an idyll. The scene is shattered by the presence of a man, a lover, who disturbs the tranquility by "throwing stones in the water."

The isolation and illumination of household objects in McGuckian's work recurs intensified in *On Ballycastle Beach*, as do referents to painting and to hair. Often these two are linked in a visual web. "Blue Vase" is such a poem, and one that heralds its ripeness of language with the marvelous choice of "overblouse" as the second word in the poem, echoing as it does so subtly "Blue Vase" (pronounced here vaz not vase). The poem is an offering from bride or new mother to husband/lover:

My house is a small blue vase,
As difficult to give you as a present
from a trousseau or layette.

It is meant to be the quintessence of their love, shining "As a painting that gathers up /ˌthe light of the same astonishing hair."

Marconi's Cottage, published in 1991, is a book in which the poet addresses the conflicting demands of being a mother and an artist. But this is only one tension acknowledged in the volume.[37] As an island remote from the rest of Europe, Ireland was much affected by the invention of radio, still an invaluable link to those living on offshore islands and other remote areas. That McGuckian's volume might be transmitting mysterious messages, rather like those the radio seemingly magically receives, has been noted by reviewers. The implication is that a decoding process for comprehending McGuckian requires the reader to leave behind all ideas of preordained boundaries—male/female, instinctive/intellectual, the tacit/the articulated.[38]

McGuckian's work does not lend itself easily to paraphrase. Indeed the poet's most subtle work can be said to defy such treatment, an achievement the poet has striven for consistently. Perhaps the opening statement of the first poem in the collection—"View Without a Room"—will illustrate the commentator's, and the reader's, dilemma. The poem's title, misleading with its play on words, is a subversion of a cliché. The anticipatory reader is then challenged with:

My bones are painted two shades of red
Like the bones of a salmon.

Here meter, repetition, color imagery, assonance, and consonance unite in fluid yet concrete verse. As is true of so much of McGuckian's work, neither literal, periphrastic, nor metaphorical levels of meaning emerge upon first or even subsequent readings. An approach might more successfully be made to McGuckian's poetry if the reader returned to his knowledge of the seventeenth- century metaphysical poets' use of conceit, or extended metaphor, as a possibility to be explored.[39] Such metaphor resides in the cerebral rather than sensual realm, at least initially, and is often not immediately pleasing, nor apparent. The conceit, though harder work, is ultimately more satisfying, both intellectually and emotively, for both writer and reader alike, as its intellectual origin can expand to accommodate the individuated emotive experience we each seek as readers.

There is a recurring nexus of weather, winter, and rain with an intrusive male presence in these poems. The female personae of "Dear Rain," "The Lion Tamer," "Brothers and Uncles," "A Small Piece of Wood," and other poems strive to maintain independence against the metaphorical inclemency of nature, against the intrusive nature of men, and against their own natural inclination to a sensual or sexual surrender that undermines the possibility of that desired freedom.

Another conceit running through *Marconi's Cottage* that can seem at first merely decorative, or at best imagistic, is that of costume. Archaic clothing references—material, stuff, milliner's plumes, and such festoon this volume. These trappings are flagrantly and definitively female—"pale frock and raspberry / Boots," "my youngest, speedwell blouse," "My dress was gun-metal grey, with a blow-away / Hem"—serve a dual function. They disguise, and thereby protect, the woman under threat from a man and from her own emotional weaknesses. They also introduce a discourse, or a code, that is incomprehensible to the male, and provide the female persona/poet with a new "secret" language with which she can explore herself and her world.

In "Charlotte's Delivery" the pulse-points of McGuckian's imaginative body are again felt. A poem about the birth of her daughter, "Charlotte's Delivery," connects winter imagery, clothing metaphors, and intrusive male-ness differently, but with the same original imprinting mechanism. Here the unassailable mother-child, particularly mother-daughter, bond informs the poem's two stanzas:

> In the wrecked hull of the fishing-boat
> Someone has planted a cypress under the ribs.

The threat to such permanence and security, possibly male, is introduced with the sinister use of the cypress, a symbol of mourning. The tree, a newly planted life form, is suggestive of growth and fertility within the abandoned skeleton of the boat. Its placement beneath the "ribs" of the boat makes it seem a gestative image. The contradictory association with death is McGuckian again exercising her poetic need to explore seeming contraries.

To return to McGuckian's use of color, "Breaking the Blue" and "Oval of a Girl" center on the poet's near obsessive and pervasive use of blue in her corpus. Blue is a multifaceted force in McGuckian's work—the color of the sea, domestic interiors, and waning daylight. Blue is, of course, Marian by association, and such devotions are historically female, tied in particular to the innocence of young girls. This association in McGuckian is both upheld and subverted. It occurs from her earliest work, but later it is apparent that blue is for McGuckian the color of clarity, purity, and unassailable mystery. In "Breaking the Blue" the "other" is addressed or accused thus:

> You, who were the spaces between words in the act of reading,
> A color sewn on to color, break the blue.

Listen now to the echoing words, phrases, and images that appear in "Oval of a Girl," having gained in resonance since the early stages of McGuckian's career:

> . . . I am flooded
> By no ocean but a second you.
>
> Who might just as well have been water
> Breaking and mending with a dark little movement,
> A kind of forlorn frenzy leaking over into sound,
> For whose unpronounceable blue I am an ear.

The essential blueness here fills and is comprehended by a female vessel, the poet.

The title poem of the volume, "Marconi's Cottage," contains both the attempt to crystallize the essence of the ordinary evident in "The Blue Vase" and a backdrop of blue, the color of the essential experience of life. The isolated cottage, outlined against the sea and the horizon, is elevated, nearly deified:

> Maybe you are a god of sorts,
> Or a human star, lasting in spite of us
> Like a note propped against a bowl of flowers,
> Or a red shirt to wear against light blue.

In "Marconi's Cottage," and in its companion-piece, "Red Armchair," McGuckian seeks and finds harmony in the play of opposites. The note, handwritten or "man" made—art—stands in contrast to the natural merit of the flowers. The jaunty, self-conscious, and artistic adornment of the red shirt allies with "a red arboreal background / To the other's marine imagery," found in "The Red Armchair" in a room that "could also be the studio of two artists." What seems initially the intrusiveness of the red, a stain on the pristine purity of McGuckian's blue, is not only *not* intrusive, but essential.

It is the artist's signature, and the real experience of human life pressed against the abstract possibility of human aspiration.

McGuckian's most recent poems, gathered in *Captain Lavender* (1994), have a tactile and visual frame of reference apparent from the start of the volume and gathering in intensity throughout. "Porcelain Bells," "Cupboard with Painted Shop," "Ceramic and Wood for Bronze," "Still Life with Eggs"— her titles resonate fragility, texture, and appealing smoothness. In McGuckian, sensuality in encounters with simple objects, rarified by high levels of aesthetic apprehension, is quintessentially female in its particulars but Aristotelian in its stringency:

> You draw your fingers along the tablecloth
> of gold leaves on your black dress
> as if they were inhabiting an old shell,
>
> and its slow dark fruitful spring
> makes a plaster cast of the moon
> like no book that ever slid from me.

These lines, like those earlier in which McGuckian forestalls the temptation to touch the lush tulips, are vibrant with sensory pleasure. The final line given here, however, marks this as not only a poem composed in a unique voice, but one that puts an end to titillation by having this daydream halted by the suggestion of the movement of the sliding book.

Another recurring motif in *Captain Lavender* is a sense of visual distortion that can skew perspective and lead to optical illusion. "Still Life with Eggs" begins:

> You are almost kneeling, a diagonal shoreline
> between two harbours, in the house-fostered darkness.
> The tilt of your head reflects the arc
> of the tablecloth, the curve of the sea.

The poem warns readers *not* to rely on the usual methods of measuring, nor to take solace from the historical givens of time and space.

The poems in *Captain Lavender* also include several tribute poems to McGuckian's father, who died not long before its publication. "Elegy for an Irish Speaker" is one such poem that manifests, perhaps more starkly than any other creative work produced thus far in Ireland, just how strong an imprint remains on the Irish after having lost their native language. McGuckian's father was *not* an Irish speaker, but the poet is on record as saying that this fact was not as important to her as was writing a tribute that would link her father to the past and the heroic elements of Irish tradition. Such distancing from the facts of her father's life, in favor of honoring his spirit, results in the imaginative willing of her father to merge with herself . The poet engages in the following lines in a dialogue with Miss Death, his mistress, mother, and prison warden now:

> He breaks away from your womb
> to talk to me,
> he speaks so with my consciousness
> and not with words, he's in danger
> of becoming a poetess.

◆   ◆   ◆

Translation as a mode of discourse in contemporary Irish poetry is an integral part of the literary landscape. Seamus Heaney has translated major poets like Osip Mandelstam and Cszechlov Milosz. Hugh Maxton (pseudonym of critic W. J. McCormack) translates regularly from the work of Hungarian poets. We have seen translations and versions of Greek, Latin, and French poems by Michael Longley and Derek Mahon. There are many more examples. This fertile meeting of languages and ideas gives a broader European or global dimension to the work of living Irish poets.

This introduction to today's poets of Ireland deals only tangentially with the complex linguistic enterprise of translation, and only as translations or versions occur in published volumes along with original poems. As stated in the introduction, however, the sole exception will be to look at the work of poet Nuala Ní Dhomhnaill, who composes only in the Irish language, but who has undertaken translation into English herself. She has also attracted as translators of her work the finest of Irish poets, many of whom are discussed in this volume. As Ní Dhomhnaill's work in Irish is accessible to so few readers outside Ireland, we must deal with her work at a second remove, which is, of necessity, unsatisfactory. Given this limitation the reader can still access the work through works of art (translations) that are distinct artistic identities themselves. (A poem by Ní Dhomhnaill translated by Paul Muldoon is, strictly speaking, no longer merely a poem by Ní Dhomhnaill).

Perhaps it is best at this juncture to distinguish what poets *mean* when they term their work "translations" or "versions" (sometimes designated by terms like "after" or "from"—"after Baudelaire," "from the Irish of Nuala Ní Dhomhnaill").

A poetic translation is a concerted effort, preferably by a poet, to provide a poem in a second language that conveys as closely as possible the message of the poem in the original language, and also replicates the poem's technique. Thus unstinting effort is made to imitate the original poet's meter, scansion, diction, and imagery. This is a complex task, as languages vary in their structure, poetic forms, and requirements. (If the image is of eggs "sunny-side up"—a term understood in North American vernacular and used regularly in diners and coffee shops—a literal French equivalent, like "looking at the sun"—does not capture the essential nature of the idiom. It is too poetic, not gritty or off-hand enough for the circumstances). Translation requires, then, an intimate understanding of both languages—the language of the original poem, with its idiomatic, metrical, and historical imperatives, and an equally sound appreciation of the finer points of the language into which the poem is being translated. Often the finest translations are not verbatim, but a constant search for the idiomatic and linguistic parallel that will locate the essential quality of the poem. A translation by Medbh McGuckian of Nuala Ní Dhomhnaill's poem *"Toircheas 1"* is an excellent example of the best word in translation not being the exact equivalent. In Irish, Ní Dhomhnaill uses an image of a galleon in full sail to describe pregnancy in the poem, but because of the imperial connotations of the word "galleon" in English, which would interfere with the femaleness and the tranquility of the image, McGuckian substitutes a "treasure-laden cloud" that "sleepwalk(s)" across the sky for the placid image of the floating ship.[40]

A version of a poem is more free form, and is often undertaken by a poet with an affinity for a language in which he or she is conversant but not fluent. A version also implies a greater personal stake on the part of the poet who creates the version, a greater level of making the poem more his own or her own. Often personal interaction between poets bridges the gap. Michael Longley, who has written "Aubade, after Nuala Ní Dhomhnaill," does not pretend to fluency in Irish, but rather to an affinity with Ní Dhomhnaill herself, and with her poetry and her ideas. He has written, and wishes to write a poem of his own that deals similarly with subjects close to both their hearts. Translations or versions should not be considered superior or inferior; they are different. Their purpose is different, and what they effect is different—it isn't a matter of degree.

Nuala Ní Dhomhnaill was born in Lancashire in England in 1952 of Irish-speaking parents. She spent much of her childhood in Ventry, Co. Kerry with her maternal grandmother. There her knowledge of the Irish language intensified. Earlier in her career Ní Dhomhnaill wrote, published, and conducted poetry readings solely in the Irish language and exclusively for Irish-speaking audiences. Her commitment to the Irish language was, and remains, paramount. She still composes and thinks artistically in Irish only, and is committed to reclaiming Irish as a living language in contemporary life. But in 1986, when asked to read in Irish and in English translation for an American audience, which could not access her poetry, she agreed, with trepidation.[41] The experiment was successful, and the response was immediate. Now Ní Dhomhnaill conducts bi-lingual readings, and translations and versions of her work in English have proliferated.

It can also be posited, without perhaps stretching a point too far, that Ní Dhomhnaill's openness to various forms of translation (for which she has had to endure criticism from some Irish-language advocates) results largely from her being a *female* poet. She is remarkably receptive to interpretations of her work, welcoming collaborative enterprise. She is also surprisingly devoid of the jealous energy with which poets usually guard their work, opting instead for an eclectic input from others and their projections of her ideas. That her work is largely interpreted by men presents, however, a potential problem. A poem devised by a woman on a subject intimate with the female experience (childbirth, pregnancy, the relationship between mother and daughter, a tentative love affair between a female speaker and a male object of affection), and translated by a man will, of course, result in a complex balance of emotional stimuli and response. However, Ní Dhomhnaill's poetry has female translators too.

Perhaps the best entré into Ní Dhomhnaill's work for the non-Irish speaking reader can be achieved by being presented with two translations of the same Ní Dhomhnaill poem, executed by different poets. *"An Crann"* has been translated by Michael Hartnett as "The Tree," a transliteral title, and begins thus:

> A fairy woman came
> with a Black and Decker.
> She cut down my tree.
> I watched her like a fool
> Cut the branches off one by one.

Compare this with Paul Muldoon's "As for the Quince" which, as its title announces, seeks a slightly more original poetic rendering:

> There came this bright young thing
> with a Black & Decker

and cut down my quince-tree.
I stood with my mouth hanging open
while one by one
She trimmed off the branches.

Ní Dhomhnaill's original poem illustrates one of her signature traits—the commingling of the ancient and the contemporary in what seems, at first, a nearly surreal fashion. Thus she thrusts the "banshee" (or *bean sidhe*, fairy woman) of ancient Celtic belief and lore, into the do-it-yourself present of brand names, suburban gardens, and power tools. That the power tool, a destructive force here, is wielded by a woman, adds to the incongruity and startling freshness of the poem. Hartnett's translation concentrates on the simplicity and the timeliness of the diction used by Ní Dhomhnaill in Irish. It is quite different from the somewhat postmodern spin Paul Muldoon sees as essential to convey, not necessarily what the poem is saying, but what it is doing.

Subsequent stanzas, though again different in each translation, show even the reader in English the kind of linguistic acrobatics Ní Dhomhnaill can execute. (Irish is a language in which the rules and formal requirements and varieties of poetic forms are often more stringent than they are in English.) Hartnett writes:

"Oh," she said, "that's *very* interest*ing*."
with a stress on the "very"
and a ring from the "ing".

In a similar mode, but subtly different, is Muldoon's

"'O," says she, "that's very interesting?"
There was a stress on the "very".
She lingered over the "ing".

Each translation seeks to do poetic justice to Ní Dhomhnaill's internal rhyme *as gaeilge* (in Irish) which is at least visible to the English speaker:

Bhí *cling* leis an -*ing*.

Hartnett chooses the euphonic, musical "ring," as a means of making sound mirror sense. Muldoon's "lingered" also contains the "ing" sound, but instead of being onomatopoeic, contains within it the Latin root for both "tongue" and "language" (*lingus*).

Nuala Ní Dhomhnaill's *Selected Poems*, translated by Michael Hartnett, first appeared in 1988. In her introduction to the volume, Irish language poet Máire Mhac an tSaoi describes Ní Dhomhnaill's work, and her place in contemporary Irish culture thus:

> I can only express here a very humble gratitude because she has given
> voice to a world I thought had died, and because she has demonstrated
> its acute relevance to the world in which we live today.

Here again there is an immediate recognition of the fusing of the ancient and the modern in this poetry. Poet Mhac an tSaoi remembers the "dignity" of the Irish-speaking world of her childhood, and the timeless quality of Ní Dhomhnaill's verse awakens cultural memories for her, as it does for many Irish people today. The following is a discussion of a small, but representative, sampling of her work as rendered by Hartnett.

"Miscarriage Abroad" exists in an intimate female world. The female persona, far from home, experiences an early miscarriage. The poem is written at the time that *should* have been the child's birthday. The poem uses, as does much of Ní Dhomhnaill's poetry, vivid water imagery that gives a constant sense of motion to the poem. The end of the aborted pregnancy is the moment "the dykes broke"—a fearful and dangerous kind of movement. Later "white ribbons of tide" resemble infant clothing—a calmer, more rhythmic use of water. However, the poem gains in power from the evoking of folkloric/superstitious practices. Especially vivid is the closing image of the aggrieved woman, denied motherhood, who will not look upon a friend's newborn with her "evil eye." This superstition, that eye contact with a childless woman, or one who had lost a child, could injure or kill another woman's child, was prevalent in Ireland in one form or another until quite recently. Indeed, it probably survives to some degree to this day, as it does in other parts of the world.

"The Mermaid" echoes many of the imagistic patterns of "Miscarriage Abroad." Mermaids resurface time and again in Ní Dhomhnaill's work, as do tidal places, each of these images encompassing two seemingly disparate entities brought together in one body or at one time and place. The mermaid, of course, combines human and fish, and needs to dwell both in the sea and on land. The tides, which give rhythm to "The Mermaid," cover and uncover the earth (shoreline) with the opposing element of water. "The Mermaid," a poem that confronts compromise, deals directly with the consequences that follow actions or decisions:

> Not without pain
> have I landed:
> I broke
> The natural law.
> . . . . . .
> Believe you me
> it was love, not God,
> who gave the order.

In "Parthenogenesis" the human and the undersea realm meet again on the folkloric level. The poem is constructed like an oral tale, with a strong narrative and a prosodic style. The tale of a human woman who is unknowingly impregnated under water by a sea creature, and bears a "mer" child, is one of many Celtic legends that involve cross-species or changeling elements. It also borrows from the silkie legends that abound on the western shores of Ireland. Silkies were believed to be seal-like creatures with human characteristics, or the reverse.

The mother/child bond in Ní Dhomhnaill's work is a powerful and recurring presence in such poems as "Miscarriage Abroad," "Feeding a Child," and "Parthenogenesis." In "A Poem for Melissa" it is a young girl, not an infant, with whom the poet's maternal persona bonds. The poem relies for achieved effect on the contrast between the delicacy of the child and of the world the mother wishes to create for her, and the violence of protective emotion that arises at the thought of any damage coming to her:

> I will stand my body between the millstones
> in God's mills so you are not totally ground.

The violence of the Old Testament image, with all its retributive power, makes explicit within the poem the earlier implied depth of feeling. Similarly the veiled or de-fanged violence of another biblical image is neutralized by the poet:

> The ox would gambol with the wolf
> the child would play with the serpent
> the lion would lie down with the lamb

Elements of the magical or the supernatural inhabit nearly all of Ní Dhomhnaill's work. "Marvellous Grass" (the title poem of Ní Dhomhnaill's 1984 collection *Féar Suaithinseach*) is another poem that not only explores the power of superstition, but compounds the effect by placing the superstition within the framework of orthodox religious practice. The young female persona approaches a priest to receive communion and is shocked to recognize him as a former lover. The guilt-ridden priest drops the host—an act of desecration. The young woman takes to her bed with what would now be termed a psychosomatic illness of the sort that still baffles doctors and other healers. Only a redemptive act by the fallen priest will remedy the situation, one that will bring him to her bed again, but this time to her sick bed.

Even a poem like "Feeding a Child," which dwells in the very realistic and intimate realm of a mother suckling a newborn, uses Ní Dhomhnaill's familiar tidal imagery to carry the reader on rhythmic waves to magical lands beyond. These are liminal places where realistic boundaries are blurred. After this foray into folklore and the fairy tale (the poem uses lines from nursery rhymes like "fee-fi-fo-fum" and "you are my piggy / who went to market"), the author returns to defend her ideological base in a question asked of the "smiling and senseless" infant:

And who are the original patterns
of the heros and giants
if not me and you?

Heroes and giants, heroines and goddesses emerge in unlikely places in Ní Dhomhnaill's poetry. In "The Broken Doll" the banal modern sight of a naked plastic doll thrown down a well is an image of the detritus of contemporary life (often very apparent in rural Ireland where trash collection can be erratic). This image is commingled in the poet's mind with the holy wells of Ireland and the practices that accompany them. Here symbolic, fertile hazelnut trees and robins of legendary magical powers join a landscape crowded with animals who are mostly nocturnal. The child who has carelessly lost the little doll is, significantly, male. The doll transforms in Ní Dhomhnaill's final frightening image to Hamlet's dead love Ophelia, drowned by her own hand but driven by his neglect and betrayal. The poet thus brings together not only lore and legend, but also literature and the essence of male/female relationships, to an otherwise mundane scene.

That conventions in English and in Irish poetry can be quite different is well illustrated by Ní Dhomhnaill's poems "Labasheedy" and "*Mo Mhíle Stór.*"

(The first title is a place name in Co. Clare. It is the anglicized spelling of the Irish phrase that means "the silken bed." The second title is an endearment translating approximately to "my dearest darling.") "Mo Mhíle Stór," like "Marvellous Grass," has been translated by Seamus Heaney, although Heaney translates the latter poem as "Miraculous Grass." (See Ní Dhomhnaill's 1990 volume *Pharaoh's Daughter* to compare with Hartnett's version.) Each of these love poems emerges from a tradition that has, for the most part, not survived in English—the love poem composed by a woman to celebrate male beauty. "Labasheedy," borrowing also somewhat from the epithalamion tradition in English, is a bridal poem, but with a twist. Here the pure white silken skin, the voluminous hair, the "damp lips . . . sweet as sugar" all belong to the putative groom. As the poem draws to its voluptuous and metaphoric close the perfect fusion of male and female principles is accomplished, producing a seamlessly androgynous effect as female narrator projects her tribute to her man:

> I would pick a pair of flowers
> as pendant earrings
> to adorn you
> like a bride in shining clothes.

"Mo Mhíle Stór," using much the same conventions and diction as "Labasheedy," maps the progression of a love from its youthful onset, through prolonged separation, and tribulations, and loneliness, to a bittersweet sensual reunion after youth is gone:

> I covered you with honey
> and saw your hair
> was straight and grey.
>
> But still in my memory
> you are ringleted:

At times Ní Dhomhnaill chooses to delve directly, not into the supernatural, the superstitious, the legendary, or the folkloric, but into the task of interpreting myth. When she does, she does so bravely, and with a female angle of vision that insists upon at least partial reevaluation of that myth. "The Shan Van Vocht," a female myth-figure already discussed here as she is represented by John Montague, is the title and the subject of a poem written by Ní Dhomhnaill and translated by Ciaran Carson. The tone is antimythical instantly, questioning the claims of this (male-created?) female icon. The Shan Van Vocht is associated, not just with liberation, but with bloodshed and manipulation. The old woman of lore is conflated here with Queen Victoria, who sent "stricken youths . . . soldiering . . . in the White Man's Grave." Implied is the absorption into modern Irish renderings of myth, imperialist elements that the poet finds suspect and foreign to the indigenous Irish collective consciousness. The former "empress" is here a "cranky" inhabitant of a nursing home, "Jacketed to her wheelchair." The Shan Van Vocht is thus rendered elitist, old, and inconsequential. She is contrasted with the entrance of two young Irish working girls, servants in the nursing home. Their diminished prospects in modern Ireland are presented by the poet as the end result of the errors of the recent Irish historical past and those who reconstructed its myths.

A final look at Ní Dhomhnaill's interpretation of myth can be provided by reading her fourteen-part "Immram" (or voyage). The poem is translated by Paul Muldoon, who, as we have already seen, has written his own lengthy version of this staple of Irish saga literature. Ní Dhomhnaill's "Immram" concentrates upon a mythical voyage to the reappearing magical island of Hy-Breasil, a nirvana-like place of aspiration where the limitations of mankind do not prevail. Hy-Breasil offers coveted immortality to humans who venture there, although the price paid for such privilege is the impossibility of returning to the mortal world. Here the imaginative locale described by the poet lies off the Kerry coast beyond the Blasket Islands. The poet's trademark blending of the ancient, complete with stately and suitable diction:

> Your voice sounds
> like thunder
> o'er the foam.
> Magnificent
> and worshipful
> is its boom—

with the incongruously modern, provokes a response that is a combination of delight, humor, and enforced rumination. The mysterious disappearing island is demythologized by having its erratic appearance accompanied by imagined traffic jams and the imagined construction of a "Heritage Center." Here Irish myth would be interpreted not merely for tourists, but for Irish people who have lost this vital connection to their past. The exoticism of the saga, again lost to a media-weary modern Ireland, is recaptured by Ní Dhomhnaill through imbedded, incongruous, but delightful, tropical references:

It has a tropical look on occasion:
The first time its palms and banana-trees hove
into view of my telescope, it seemed to lie in the
Indian Ocean.

Nuala Ní Dhomhnaill, then, represents something of a unique phenomenon in modern Irish writing, a poet successfully functioning in two languages, while composing exclusively in one. She has opened the door to much redefinition of the creative act. That it should be the work of a woman that has caused this productive upheaval in Irish letters is of great significance, in the Irish language or in English.

The foregoing study of a selection of poems by a number of Ireland's leading poets is by no means exhaustive. In fact, in Ireland today there are many more poets publishing, and with considerable readership, than a study of this scope could ever adequately convey. The poets whose work was chosen to be written about in some detail here were chosen either because they are canonical, in Ireland, or in Irish Studies in North America and Britain (which is not quite the same thing), or because they are likely to become so.

Poetry in contemporary Ireland is a thriving art form. Not only are there more local publishing opportunities available to poets today, but various forms of governmental and privately sponsored arts subventions encourage poets, especially young poets. Also, the poetry reading as an institution, whether for an individual or a group, continues to attract a large following among Irish people and also among many foreign visitors who also travel to Ireland on cultural holidays. Poetry workshops and seminars for professional and amateur writers proliferate, as do university and community-based creative writing programs. Even daily newspapers continue to publish recent poetry on a regular basis.

Irish society in ancient times placed great value on and gave considerable political and social power to its poets. This is a tradition that has not remained intact in the modern world, but its legacy may still be traced in the high level of esteem that the Irish afford their poets. Irish poets in turn respond with a vitality and a rigor in pursuit of their craft that is worthy of their lineage.

CHAPTER TWO

New Ireland
On Stage

John B. Keane, perhaps Ireland's best-loved playwright, was born in 1928 in Listowel, Co. Kerry, where he still lives. Keane, who began his career through winning the amateur All-Ireland drama festival in 1959 with his play *Sive*, is an unapologetically popular and provincial voice in the theatre, something which was quite revolutionary in Ireland when he first appeared on the theatrical scene. Keane's plays, much more focused on character than language per se, emphasize quotidian dilemmas, some universal and some the particular focus of his farmers and small-town folk. Land ownership, marriage, inheritance, fertility, and integration into community life are his subjects. Keane also examines the role, positive and negative, that the Church has played in modern Irish life. Like many of his contemporaries Keane also grapples with the ever-present phenomenon of Irish emigration, especially in his oft-performed *Many Young Men of Twenty* (1962).

Keane's familiar, and at times sentimental, style can be deceiving. His *Big Maggie* (1969), which continues to be staged regularly in Ireland, England, and North America, is a forthright play about a woman freed to become an individual by the death of her husband. Keane's Maggie defies the conventions that would demand that she withdraw or seek a lesser place in her community. This defiance of convention also informs Keane's best-known work, *The Field*, which is known to North American audiences in its film version of 1990, starring Richard Harris as Bull McCabe. Although

McCabe's hunger for land is certainly conventional, his method of trying to obtain it is not, and is ultimately damaging in its obsession.

John B. Keane is the author of many nondramatic works. A prolific short story writer, he has also written a noted novel, *The Bodhran Makers* (1986). A recurring feature of all his work is his continual probing of Irish mores. Keane's contribution to contemporary Irish writing has been described thus:

> Keane tends to illuminate contemporary problems by a consideration of local customs and religious practices; often the received traditions and current values appear to be at war. The moral dilemma resulting from the dichotomy between modern life and traditional practices is the core of the playwright's social criticism.[1]

Hugh Leonard (pseudonym of John Byrne, b. 1926) is a popular dramatist in much the same way as John B. Keane, but with important differences. Whereas neither playwright writes of an up-to-the-minute, post–European Union Ireland, Leonard's Ireland is somewhat more modern. It is an urban Ireland in contrast to Keane's rural representation. Both writers share a tendency toward nostalgia and sentimentality, but in Leonard, perhaps more than in Keane, that natural inclination is kept in check by working-class urban wit and middle-class urban ennui.

Popularity should not be a disabling feature for a playwright, as drama is by its nature a very public art form. Hugh Leonard, whose name is well known because of the vast assortment of radio broadcasts he makes and television screenplays and journalism he writes, has often been accused of being a popular dramatist in the pejorative sense. His exclusion from *The Field Day Anthology* confirmed this accusation, but fails to acknowledge Leonard's degree of engagement with Irish and other audiences. Leonard's following in Ireland is immense and has been so for many years. He also enjoys a considerable reputation in Britain, where much of his television work is on view regularly. With several of his major plays and some film scripts, Leonard has extended his reputation to North America. The first stage version of *Da* won several Tony awards in New York in 1973, and was followed by the popular film version of the play, starring Barnard Hughes and Martin Sheen. Also in 1973, there appeared a successful first production of *The Au Pair Man* in New York, produced by Joseph Papp and starring Julie Harris and Charles Durning. These major theatrical successes, with an enviable assortment of directors and actors, suggest a substance to Leonard's material that is at times recognized by the critical establishment outside Ireland more readily than it is within Ireland.

Leonard's major overseas successes came, however, after years of writing plays and having them produced at home. One of the more noteworthy of these earlier efforts was *The Patrick Pearse Motel* (1968), one of Leonard's comic swipes at Dublin's newly emerging bourgeoisie. The characters Dermod and Grainne Gibbon (named for Irish mythology's famed pair of doomed lovers) live in affluent suburban Foxrock. Although outwardly the ideal couple, in truth Grainne is bored with her life and seeks to have an affair with James Usheen (Usheen, or Oisín, is also the name of a mythological hero), a television personality she knew in her youth. Counterpoint to Dermod and Grainne is played broadly by Dermod's business partner Fintan Kinnore and his wife Niamh (Niamh is Oisín's lover in mythology). The latter couple are older and less glamorous, and the comedy of their exchanges is heightened by Fintan's rather idiosyncratic view of female beauty that is at odds with that of everyone in the cast, and in the audience. The Patrick Pearse Motel is a new concern owned jointly by Dermod and Fintan, and takes its name from the hero of the 1916 Easter Rising—one of a string of motels in a chain, all named for patriots.

The plot of *The Patrick Pearse Motel* is farcical—mistaken identity and situations that are, or appear to be, sexually compromising recur predictably in a comic fashion. Verbal double-entendres and clever balletic blockings of characters, amounting nearly to choreography, abound. Leonard is deft in the dramatic management of characters, lines, and comic timing. There is also a high level of coincidence, such as Dermod's hiring as manageress of the motel one Venetia Manning, an Englishwoman and James Usheen's former mistress.

After having set up all the comic variations in Act I in Dermod and Grainne's home, Leonard uses the second half of the play to work the changes on the comedy at the motel, where all the characters assemble in Act II. The patriotic motif is dealt with comically throughout, as is adultery. The play is cast in a highly improbable mode, into which the audience enters, aware of its improbability. Leonard's writing, however, is always sufficiently tied to the real to allow the audience to identify with the characters and situation. One such tie to reality is his naming James Usheen's off-stage nemesis in the play Eamonn Andrews, a real Irish television personality of the time.

The Patrick Pearse Motel is the type of comedy with which Hugh Leonard became identified by Dublin audiences. It afforded the Irish an opportunity to laugh at themselves and to deal with themes formerly either held as taboo or only portrayed seriously. Although the play contains multiple comic references to religious observance and ecclesiastical annulment when marriages are threatened, Leonard's representation of residual Catholicism does not threaten the consciences of the characters. Similarly irreverent is his dismissive treatment of Irish nationalism, especially in the comic form of Hoolihan, the 1916 veteran who is night watchman at the very busy Patrick Pearse Motel. This skewering of conventional patriotism has its roots in Irish theatre as far back as O'Casey, but Leonard's comedy, especially in its representation of shifting sexual mores, is more than standard fare. It could be said to have extended the range of acceptable treatment of sensitive material in its era.

Hugh Leonard's *Da* is well known and widely-staged. In the play, Leonard's father-figure is made into an archetype by the consistent use of the familiar diminutive "Da." Da's real name, Nick Tynan, does not even appear in the cast list. It must be pieced together from the scraps of dialogue within the play, which also yield his history of daily subservience. Da's has been a colonial existence, a gardener for an Anglo-Irish family, and more recently for a Catholic family that has replaced them in the house where he works. Thus Leonard recreates the pattern of twentieth-century Irish history, and ushers in the possibility of the broader world of Charlie—Da's autobiographical playwright/son. Charlie lives in London and has returned to Ireland for Da's funeral. A contemporary of his creator, Charlie is an adult character in the play, but there is another character who is Charlie's childhood self at about age sixteen. This mechanism creates for the Irish audience the dual-son character that is also favored by playwright Brian Friel. The adult Charlie is filled with unanswered questions, which he addresses only now to the ghost of Da. The discourse has only one participant and the father cannot *hear* the son's impatient questions, which strive to connect generations and to reinforce tradition in the play.

Da's position in society, and as a man, has been compromised. He was obeisant to his unworthy employers and, at times, supremely wrong-headed. At one point, Charlie recalls, his father could only assert himself by attaching his hope for the future to Hitler, if for no other reason than that Hitler was *not* English.

Da is a version of the Ireland of his time, powerless and unable to focus his anger and energy in productive ways. He cannot acknowledge the connection between his lack of autonomy in the past and his present political naiveté. Charlie, the son of the New Ireland, has nothing at first but contempt for his father's weaknesses. Although not an Anglophile after all his years in London, Charlie can see somewhat objectively that his father, like his country, blames continued failure on forces outside himself, and does not change nor grow:

> Charlie: All those years you sat and looked into the fire, what went
> through your head? What did you think of? What thoughts? I never
> knew you to have a hope or a dream or say a half-wise thing.

This is fairly primitive betrayal—after all, the male elders staring into the
fire and gaining wisdom from the experience is a standard feature in many
societies. Here it is merely a comic cypher—an Irish joke.

Leonard uses the dramatic trope of having the son in this play initiate
the retelling of an idyllic memory of a father-son outing. Da and Charlie,
when Charlie is seven years old, take the dog for a walk along the cliff
overlooking Killiney Bay near their home. Their talk is the stuff of fairy tales,
couched in a real-life context. Charlie, who like his creator is an adopted
son, is told that his bogey-like *real* mother lives on a lightship in Dublin Bay
from which she is unable to escape. There will be, he is assured by Da, no
chance of her coming to take Charlie away—no absconding with their new
tradition. There is much talk of an imagined, rich future. These are ritualized
conversations, oft-repeated by father and son to the point of being memo-
rized. They too function like primal riddles of the tribe—because Da has
taught young Charlie not only the answers, but also the questions, something older Charlie may have forgotten or has chosen to ignore:

> Charlie: There's a ship. Is that it, da? Is that our ship coming in?
> Da: Where? No . . . no, son, that one's going out.
> Charlie: We'll be on the pig's back then, da, won't we?
> When we're rich.
> Da: We won't be too far off it.
> Charlie: And what'll we do?
> Da: Do?
> Charlie: When we win the Sweep.
> Da: We won't do a shaggin' hands turn.

Here, then, despite both his subservient role as a man in a newly modern
Ireland and his perceived failure to achieve wisdom, is a father whose
traditional paternal obligation as a father is actually being fulfilled. The play
also closes with the fixture of a legacy, here the return to Charlie of all the
money that he'd sent to his father to supplement Da's meager retirement.

In Leonard's work tradition, the past is not remote, nor is the past/
present link ever really broken. The past is a confusing and fused mass—like
the other part of Charlie's legacy, a bizarre sculpture of 29 pairs of eyeglasses
melted together during the great San Francisco earthquake, a ludicrous gift

from Da's previous employers. It is as impossible to extricate a single pair of glasses from this mass as it is to extricate Da, and his colonial experience, from the modern identity that Charlie will continue to develop after his father's death.

Audiences for the plays of John B. Keane, Bernard Farrell, and Hugh Leonard will understand that the world of Kerry farmers may seem very distant from that of middle-class, suburban Dublin, and it is. Playwright Bernard Farrell (b. 1941) writes his social comedies about a world very like Hugh Leonard's, but his critique of Irish society is in many ways quite similar to that of John B. Keane's. Each playwright focuses on the social ills affecting his group and perhaps overlooked by the authorities in the form of government and religion. When Farrell features the threat of unemployment (*All the Way Back*, 1985) and strikes (*All in Favour Said No!*, 1981), he writes at the core of his people's world, much as land and inheritance is at the center in Keane's world.

Bernard Farrell's earliest success, the frequently produced *I Do Not Like Thee, Doctor Fell* (1979), deals with the then-new and somewhat baffling phenomenon of the encounter group. His most recent hit, *Stella by Starlight* (1996), won the coveted Best Irish Play award at that year's Dublin Theatre Festival. Throughout his career Farrell has exhibited the deceptive facility of the comic writer who functions as social critic. His *The Last Apache Reunion* (1993) deals squarely with the personal appraisal that is demanded when one attends a class reunion. Such reunions, in life as in art, often the source of incongruous stories and tales of hilariously dashed expectations, can also force moments of clarity as we weigh the relative success, wealth, love, and happiness in our lives.

When Moses Met Marconi, first produced in 1983, was recently revived at Dublin's small Andrew's Lane Theatre. Inspired by the introduction of local radio in Ireland, the play deals deftly with such polarized subjects as small-town versus big-city life, women's choice of marriage and/or career, and the generation gap. Most importantly, however, the play examines the media's search for the right balance between providing entertainment and providing the information necessary for us to live as responsible, intelligent citizens who can make informed choices. Marconi, also a figure in Medbh McGuckian's poetry and in Brian Friel's *Dancing at Lughnasa*, has become an iconographic signifier for communication in Ireland. Farrell's title, with its strong biblical associations, contrasts old and new, but also "the law" with those whose job it is to disseminate the details of the law and to offer interpretations of same. Bernard Farrell's comedies take the purpose and the function of comedy in the theatre seriously and address such concerns. The playwright, aware that in the theatre he too is an interpreter of society for its members, undertakes that task with a fondness for human nature that makes us laugh, but with an integrity that substantiates his view that:

> . . . there is no such thing as the easy laugh, because you have to work for it.[2]

Brian Friel (b.1929) is another of the few living Irish playwrights whose reputation has crossed the Atlantic. Friel's appeal, however, is broader than Keane's and Leonard's, and extends well beyond Irish diaspora audiences. Although best known to recent audiences for being the author of *Dancing at Lughnasa*, Friel first came to prominence in America with such Broadway hits as *Philadelphia Here I Come!* (1964) and *The Loves of Cass Maguire* (1966). That these two plays of Friel's should resonate with North American audiences is not unusual in that each concerns the touchy subject of emigration. In fact, each features returned Irish émigrés, thereby acknowledging a complexity to the subject in our age. A full generation later, with *Lughnasa*, Friel mesmerized audiences with a tale that was not primarily focused on emigration, although some of its characters do emigrate from Friel's imaginative home base, Ballybeg (which literally translated from the Irish language means "small town"). In *Lughnasa* Friel charts the demise of a way of life in Ireland before World War II and during the first years of the struggling new entity that was the Irish Republic.

Friel's world, Ballybeg, is a world rapidly disappearing, or indeed largely gone. The innocence, isolation, unselfconscious eagerness, and faith exhibited by his characters are impossible in a world with a postmodern awareness. Even some of Friel's more recent plays, like *Wonderful Tennessee* or *Molly Sweeney*, which are set in an Ireland over a generation later than his earlier plays, do not fully acknowledge the angst associated with our world. They do display, however, a more modern sensibility that makes unquestioning faith improbable and unalloyed innocence a rarity. Therefore, although Friel as a writer has moved forward in his plays to approach the reality of modern Ireland, it can hardly be said that he grapples fully with contemporary issues. Rather Friel as a dramatist attempts to address problems that are timeless, and often does so in a manner that is freed from the limiting conditions of time and place.

Brian Friel's use of language on the stage is the subject of much recent critical attention both in Ireland and abroad. Although it would be unfair simply to label his corpus as consisting of "language plays," his work is highly dependent upon language to convey its message. Even vivid characterizations like those of the five Mundy sisters in *Dancing at Lughnasa* are overshadowed by the play's richness of language, particularly that of its reminiscing narrator. In Friel's *Translations* language *becomes* plot. For language in Friel is linked inextricably to memory. For the playwright, memory, whether individual or communal, defines us. Friel's language, poetic and highly evocative, is often intended to provoke, at least initially, a nostalgic reaction. His best use of language, however, is that which surpasses or checks the nostalgic impulse to question perceptions of reality past and present.

Like so many Irish writers before him, Brian Friel often uses music or references to songs or their lyrics to enhance his evocative words. In a manner reminiscent of Joyce, he can temporarily "freeze" a character in a time, place, or mood by bonding that character to a melody or lyric, often repeated. Gar O'Donnell's jivey lyrics of American pop tunes propel him toward his future in Philadelphia—their ephemeral and tantalizing quality contrast the sour predictability of his life in Ballybeg. The dance tunes emanating from the radio in *Dancing at Lughnasa* temporarily whisk Chris Mundy and her suitor Gerry away from the drab reality of their lives, as it did the night they conceived their son. The plaintive melodies played on the dying George's accordion underscore the tenuousness of life in *Wonderful Tennessee*.

Music in Friel, along with some verbalization of visual imagery, reminds us of the primary ties that bind—love and loyalty. Each of these—like the tune that won't go away or the paradoxically vivid visions that are experienced by the blind title character in *Molly Sweeney*—can confound reason in his characters, as they make decisions and live with their consequences.

Many of Brian Friel's plays also feature father-son pairings. Friel's fathers are intermittent or very distant characters, but very different from the considerably more aggressive and oppressive fathers with which the other playwrights of Friel's generation generally present us.

In *Philadelphia Here I Come!*, Friel offers us a dual-character son—Public Gar, and Private Gar (short for Gareth—Gareth O'Donnell), so that the character of the father, S. B. O'Donnell, is overmatched in this play before it even begins—one father, two sons. The play concerns the only child of an old widower (whose young wife has died in childbirth) and his decision to take advantage of an offer to emigrate to America. He even has an offer to be sponsored, housed, and more or less adopted by one of his maternal aunts and her husband, who live in the Philadelphia of the falsely triumphalist title. The play includes a crucial scene from the recent past in which the Americanized aunt and uncle make an appearance. This scene gives a rather grim underlay of reality to the wilder pipe dreams of American life Gar imagines in the privacy of his bedroom. His is an exotic America of "incinerators," "elevators," and "smooth operators," among whom, of course, Gar hopes to be numbered shortly. However, the America that is displayed on Friel's stage is somehow lacking this vitality. This failing is conveyed by the forlornly materialist and childless aunt, her pliant husband, and their true-blue American friend, Ben Burton. Burton has been brought to Ireland largely, it seems, to validate the couple's Americanness in the eyes of the villagers of Ballybeg, where the two were born. This America, Friel suggests, can only be as shallow and dissatisfying as the tragicomic trio on stage. In choosing to leave Ballybeg and go to Philadelphia, young Gar is rejecting his own father, and his home. He is also rejecting his homeland and his legacy as an Irishman—and to what purpose? Friel seems to ask. On the other hand S. B. O'Donnell, resolutely incommunicative throughout the play, like the stage Ulsterman he is, would not dream of asking his son to stay, nor would he even suggest that he might miss his son.

Significantly, the father's subconscious, unlike his son's in the play, is not articulated for the audience. One could suggest, however, that it is subtly displaced to the character of Madge, the housekeeper/surrogate-mother who acts as mediator between father and son in many instances. The monolithic and dour S. B. O'Donnell comes alive only when playing a completely predictable evening round of draughts (checkers) with the local Canon.[3] He represents for Friel the puritanical and often priest-led genera-tion of the immediate past in its negativity. However, the true past, tradition, is never something that Friel favors jettisoning. So, to provide a more positive and compelling link with this past, he creates a surrogate father, the conveyor of an older and worthier wisdom than that of the play's "real" father. The surrogate father in the play is the Master—Gar's old schoolmas-ter, whom Gar pities but respects. Master Boyle, a learned man, much damaged by drink, fulfills the function of father in metaphorical terms in the play. It is he, not S. B. O'Donnell, who confers a talisman on the young man as he embarks on his new life. In this case the gift is a rather touching, but perhaps unhelpful, book of Master Boyle's own poems. The Master also imparts the necessary words of wisdom or release required of a father to send his son into the world:

> Boyle: You're doing the right thing, of course. You'll never regret it. I gather it's a vast restless place that doesn't give a curse about the past; and that's the way things should be. Impermanence and anonymity— it offers great attractions. . . .

With this false advice, from this false father, Friel reinforces a theme that prevails throughout his dramatic corpus. For tradition in Friel is paramount; without it there is no continuity and without that continuity, we are nothing. Private Gar longs for a word from his taciturn father that will enable the son to change his stated plan of emigration, save face, and maintain traditional links. He also hungers for someone to tell him about his long-dead mother. Gar wishes that someone would supply the link, provide the memory, so that tradition can continue unbroken. Gar becomes yet another emigrant who could not remain confined by the definition of Irishness that was provided by the previous generation. He will now be forced to redefine himself, not by his Irishness, but in large part by his lack of it. He will become the next generation's returned Yank, defined as Irish outside Ireland, never quite Irish enough inside Ireland.

The father as a removed fixture, somehow unattainable, is reinforced in this play with another incident dependent upon shared memory. Gar recalls an idyllic summer's day of father and son fishing in a blue boat—the son wearing the father's hat, and the father singing. But the father claims no memory of the occasion in Friel's play, and this is an amnesia for which there is no forgiveness. It is the father's *duty* to remember, and to communicate memories to his son. Gar, his tradition completely severed, marches into the modern world, forced to leave his Irishness behind.

With *Faith Healer*, Brian Friel returns to Ballybeg, but only briefly and then tragically. The play was first performed, not in Ireland, but in New York, in 1979. That *Faith Healer* was premiered outside Ireland is somehow appropriate to this, the least ostensibly Irish of Friel's plays. The plot, such as it is, concerns the dubious career of Irish faith healer Frank Hardy. Frank has eked out a living for himself, his Irish wife Grace, and his cockney manager Teddy, by traveling to small Welsh and Scottish towns to work cures on desperately afflicted and gullible people. However, nationality and setting in this play are nearly immaterial, because its central conflict is a universal moral question much beyond such considerations.

Faith Healer consists of four parts (called parts, not acts). Each part is a monologue—the first and last by Frank, the second by Grace, the third by Teddy. The play is, then, intended to be a talking play, and one that is actually reinforced by stasis. Nothing happens as each character appears on a stage adorned with only a few chairs and a poster advertising Frank Hardy's curative powers. The text of the play is calculated in its repetitive structure, with each character retelling his or her version of several crucial events in the past and recent past. That memory, always such a powerful force in Friel's work, is fleeting and at times self-serving, is crucial to our understanding of the play and its individual characters. The events that are scrutinized and multiply interpreted for the audience include the death of Frank's mother, Grace's giving birth to a stillborn child in a remote Scottish village, Frank's curing of ten people on a single night in a Welsh village, and Frank's violent death at the hands of several young men in Ballybeg after his healing powers fail. Each of the characters, in monologue, manages partially to expose truths that are obscured or omitted by the others. Teddy reveals that Frank abandoned Grace while she was in labor and refused to discuss or acknowledge the stillbirth. Grace reveals that Frank's Part One monologue detailing his mother's death is, in fact, the story of the death of his beloved father with which he had difficulty coming to terms. Loyalties and interdependency among the three are reinterpreted again and again to reveal a complex web of human faith, failure, loyalty, and betrayal. Frank needs to remember himself as being importuned to heal people; Grace recalls that he often was compelled to force himself on people to reaffirm his power. Each says that the scratched recording that announced each of Frank's performances was a concession to the other's dubious taste.

None of the minor details of the play are of importance themselves, but the aggregate effect of the squalid hand-to-mouth existence that emerges is of great importance to our understanding of character and motive. Of particular relevance is the dedication of Teddy, who seems to have less at stake in the undertaking than either Frank or Grace. Frank has a genuine gift, however erratic it might be. Grace has a genuine love for, and need for, Frank. They are a pair linked by a poignant love that allows each of them to escape complete loneliness and isolation. But Teddy, a two-bit huckster who had previously promoted acts such as "Miss Mulatto and Her Pigeons" (a.k.a. Mary Brigid O'Donnell), seems to have little to gain from his association with Frank Hardy. Teddy's monologue even reveals indignities visited upon him by the pair in the past, such as their abandoning him after the night of the ten miracles to spend a night in a posh hotel as Christmas approaches. This part of Teddy's narrative is one of the few instances in which his relentless and often willfully blind optimism and positive thinking falters. It is a crucial glimpse of the reality of his situation, essential for his maintaining a rapport and sympathy with the audience that will rival that elicited by Frank and Grace.

Although the vagaries of memory are a central consideration in *Faith Healer*, the play is not *about* memory. Rather *Faith Healer* is a play about faith. Whether the faith is faith in God, a more encompassing religious faith, an acknowledgment of supernatural power for which Frank is merely a conduit, or a faith in the power of human love in the face of human frailty, is for the audience to decide.

The climactic scene in *Faith Healer* is introduced and approached in all three characters' monologues, but it is never illuminated until the end of the play, and then not fully. In Ballybeg Frank Hardy is confronted by a young man confined to a wheelchair after a construction accident in England. Accompanied by a phalanx of drunken friends, the crippled youth is representative of a disenfranchised generation in Ireland.

Frank Hardy goes to his death at the hands of these bitter young men, secure in some kind of faith that he will attain personal salvation. Frank's violent end is offered by Friel, not as a despairing suicidal plunge, but as proof that this life is a small part of what we are. Frank's death acknowledges the supernatural to which he had more access than most humans do in their lifetimes.

In its tripartite narration, *Faith Healer* is written in a form that Friel replicated in his recent play, *Molly Sweeney* (1995). In *Molly Sweeney* a blind woman, her well-intentioned but inept husband, and her patronizing doctor all relate the story of her "decision" to have an operation to restore her sight. The operation, a temporary success and ultimate failure, deprives her, finally, of more than her sight. The self-justification of each character's narrative, the explanation of motive, both selfish and selfless, is resonant of the monologic variations on the same theme woven so effectively in *Faith Healer*. *Molly Sweeney*, a play less successful than *Faith Healer* because ultimately less profound, focuses both on faith and on healing (in both the medical and religious senses). *Molly Sweeney*, however, fails even in its artful use of "visual" imagery to achieve the illumination, rendered with such simplicity, of Frank Hardy's act of faith.

Friel's *Translations* (1980) is as secure in its place in the modern Irish repertoire as is *Dancing at Lughnasa*, although it is not performed quite as often for foreign audiences. The play is something of an anomaly in that it aims to tell the story of the death of one language, Irish, and its gradual replacement by another, English. But the audience must also accept the notion that the majority of the characters, whom we hear speaking Friel's lines in English, are actually supposed to be conversing in Irish!

Translations has been a controversial play since its first performance. Friel readily admits he has made free with historical fact in order to posit a broader and putatively more important point. Set in 1833, the play focuses on the British government survey of Ireland that was intended to provide an accurate map of the country with uniform anglicized place-names. The arrival of Her Majesty's sappers (surveyors) sets off a chain of events from which the inhabitants never fully recover. It also heralds another major upheaval—the initiation of the new national school scheme that will replace Ireland's indigenous hedge-school system.[4]

Translations is a play nearly exclusively about language, and about language on many levels. That language is the prime means of identification of a people is crucial to our understanding of all the actions taken in the play. Indeed, from our first introduction to the character Sarah in the first scene of Act I, language is an issue, and one that can be discomfiting. Sarah, a young village girl, has been rendered mute by a traumatic experience. Manus, the son and assistant of the local hedge schoolmaster, Hugh, is attempting to help her regain her speech. As Sarah reclaims her speech, so shall she reclaim herself.

The other students of the hedge school attend with varying degrees of regularity and commitment, but are all adult and attend voluntarily. Their master, Hugh, is a learned and disappointed man—a recurring figure in Friel. He is also an alcoholic. The plot concerning the hedge school, its fortunes, and the dubious future of men like Hugh and Manus, coincides with the surveying plot in the person of Owen, Hugh's other son. Owen functions as the translator to the British surveying team. Translating in Friel does not have a positive, nor even a neutral, connotation in the play. Translating here is an act of treason. When Owen agrees to translate the names of rivers, town lands, promontories, and hillocks in his native place into the language of the occupying army, he commits, in the eyes of the villagers and eventually in his own eyes, an act of betrayal.

Translations also includes a subplot that involves an ill-fated love affair between Maire, a local young woman who is the eldest of a large family and destined for emigration, and Lieutenant Yolland, a soldier with an affinity for the Irish language, landscape, and people. The lyric heights to which Maire and Yolland climb is made poignant and delightfully comic to the knowing audience because neither can understand more than a word or two of the other's language. But the language of love triumphs, at least temporarily; and Friel makes us acutely aware both of the breadth and emotion conveyed by language and the other forms of communication humans can and do use to keep from becoming isolated.

Such isolation and loneliness seem to run like a threnody through *Translations* as Manus' love for Maire goes unrequited. Jimmy Jack, the 60-year-old bachelor "infant prodigy" of the school, becomes so enthralled by the world of antiquity that he actually thinks he is going to marry Pallas Athene, the daughter of Zeus. The widowed schoolmaster Hugh sees himself with both sons gone and the imminent closure of his school likely at the play's end.

There is a great deal of overt, even broad, comedy, especially in Acts I and II of *Translations*, in scenes involving Jimmy Jack, Maire, and the coltish characters, Doalty and Bridget. In Act III, however, after Yolland's murder by disgruntled locals, the play becomes serious, violent, and tragic. It also becomes much more openly political and politicized. Yolland's superior, as he threatens to kill all the livestock and level all the houses in the surrounding district unless the murderers are given up, ominously recites the new place-names of the locality in English. These are, in turn, translated back into Irish by Owen, which produces a chilling effect on stage as the villagers of Ballybeg learn their fate.

As *Translations* closes, Hugh, the character who at times acts as a mouthpiece for the playwright, articulates Friel's apologia:

> . . . that it is not the literal past, the "facts" of history, that shape us, but images of the past embodied in language.

That Friel comes down, ultimately, on the side of the myth of history is certain. It allies him with such Irish historians as the anti-revisionist Brendan Brandshaw and the revisionist literary critic Seamus Deane (note—the revisionist debate in Ireland has very different ideological referents in historical and literary spheres).[5] The myth of history, certainly a potent force in Ireland, can, of course, take many forms. In *Translations* its power is reinforced by the setting of the play in the heat of August, when the people of Ballybeg are unnerved by what they fear is "the sweet smell," which signaled devastating potato blight. This periodic curse culminated in the Great Famine of the 1840s, which reduced Ireland's population perhaps by as much as half through starvation, disease, and emigration. The Famine, which resonates so powerfully even today with English injustice and mis-management, is subtly tied here to the territorial mapping project of a decade earlier—two in a series of imperialist transgressions seen as having far-reaching consequences for Irish people.

Dancing at Lughnasa (1990) is Friel's celebrated and more recent rendering of life in Ballybeg. The small-town element is important in that it is not country life, but small-town life, that we must always remember is Friel's bailiwick. This milieu is little understood and sometimes dismissed by both city and country people alike.

In *Dancing at Lughnasa* Friel's father character, very unlike the dry, silent S. B. O'Donnell of *Philadelphia Here I Come!*, is the mercurial Welshman Gerry Evans. Gerry is another "type" of Irish father often featured in the literature of this and later generations of Irish writers—the absent or intermittent father (one thinks of John Montague's poetry, and of George O'Brien's prose trilogy of Waterford life, especially *The Village of Longing*, the first volume in that trilogy). Intermittent fathers are revered at times by their sons merely *because* of their intangibility, the unknowable quality of their lives elsewhere. Often the intermittent father is himself an emigrant, or a widower forced to leave a boy to be reared by others while he earns a living. In *Lughnasa*, however, Gerry makes infrequent appearances in Ballybeg for a very different reason. He is not married to the mother of his son Michael, the play's retrospective narrator.

In what might seem a strange accommodation for a rather remote village in Donegal in 1936, Gerry Evans, a traveling salesman, dancing master, and jack-of-all-trades, is the acknowledged father of a child by Chris. She is the youngest of five adult unmarried sisters who live together in what was their parents' home. The two other inhabitants of the house are both male. Michael is seven years old at the time of the play, although he narrates it as an adult. Jack, a priest, is his uncle, and the women's only brother. The circumstances of Michael's birth distinguish the Mundy family. Instead of his illegitimacy being covered up or denied, the child is accepted and cherished by what another Irish writer, Elizabeth Bowen, in *Seven Winters*, a memoir, has called "a committee of aunts." Michael's father's visits are anticipated by these aunts, if not with enthusiasm, then with surprising degrees of tolerance for the most part. Michael is the only member of the household who is also a member of the generation of the New Ireland, born after Irish independence. He represents the hope of an Irish future, not merely for his mother, but for an extended childless family. Young Michael's links with tradition are channeled nearly completely through *female* experience in his seven-year-old consciousness, but he is intrigued by another element of his inheritance that comes from the romantic, amusing, and un-Irish Gerry. Gerry promises at one point in the play to give his son a gift, a form of inheritance. The much-talked-of "manly" black bicycle, which could be viewed, of course, as a means of escape from Ballybeg, never materializes. Nor does Gerry ever make Michael his legitimate heir.

Gerry is an anachronism in many ways. Friel makes us aware that Ireland in the play is advancing, motorizing, and mechanizing, despite the sylvan de Valéra rhetoric of the day. But Gerry, a Welshman and an outsider, rides a bicycle to try to sell gramophones, a technology more or less already superceded by the radio, which is such an important prop in the play. This outdated and unsuccessful foreigner *has* no legacy for his illegitimate Irish son, and soon Gerry announces his romantic intentions to go to fight in the Spanish Civil War.

The modern world—the world of motor cars, radios, and the Spanish Civil War—impinges much more in *Dancing at Lughnasa* than it does in *Philadelphia Here I Come!*, although the earlier play has a more recent setting. Also the broadening chasm between the old world and the new is much more apparent in *Lughnasa*. Michael, as the adult narrator, views the lives of his mother, his come-day-go-day father, and his maiden aunts as one would fossils in amber. They are caught forever in his memory, which functions in this play, as in Friel's earlier drama, to serve tradition and link generations.

The tenuousness of such connections is reinforced in the play by Friel's use of another surrogate father. Father Jack, 25 years a missionary in the African jungle where he exclusively used the native language, has returned home unstable and nearly incapable of communicating in his own language with his own family and his own people. Father Jack thus *also* fails to transmit tradition to the boy Michael.

Dancing at Lughnasa, set at the end of the old Celtic calendar at the autumnal/harvest feast Lughnasa, is an apocalyptic play. The boy Michael, born in the same year as the playwright, observes the passing of the old order with a fond and often sentimentalized portrait of life with the five Mundy girls—efficient Kate, stern Agnes, irreverent Maggie, simple Rose, and innocent, but defeated, Chris. The run to nostalgia in the play is countered, however, by the gruesome end to which these women come. The realities of the New Ireland impinge, especially Ireland's economic war with Britain in the 1930s. Kate loses her teaching job, the only salary in the household. Agnes and Rose, after losing their piece-work in a local glove factory, emigrate to London where they die penniless. Jack never functions as a priest again and dies within a year of the play's setting. Gerry Evans does not oblige his son by dying a hero in Spain, which at least would have been something of a legacy. Instead he is disabled in the war, marries and has another family in Wales, and never tells Chris Mundy of their existence. The play closes with a highly evocative verbalized memory by Michael of the dancing referred to in the play's title, a scene the audience has already witnessed. Michael recalls the nearly primitive native dancing that temporarily overtakes the sisters during that Lughnasa season of 1936 and its links with pre-Christian Ireland. The memory of that dancing *is* his inheritance, his tradition.

Since his great international success with *Dancing at Lughnasa* Brian Friel has continued to produce new plays at a prodigious rate. Although his most recent plays have not enjoyed the same degree of popularity, nor the same critical focus and intensity, they are each noteworthy and may well pass into the contemporary Irish repertoire.

Wonderful Tennessee (1993) is a modern Irish suburban tale, cloaked in heavy classical allusion. An oddly balanced sestet of paired characters embarks upon, but never achieves, its goal—a journey to a mysterious island. The island, said to disappear from view, is resonant of both Greek and Irish mythological sources. The nonappearance of a boatman/driver, meant to transport the group to the island, also has primal associations with otherworld or supernatural myth, which is intensified by our awareness that one of the six, a musician, is dying. The play echoes Beckett's *Waiting for Godot* in its existentialist dialogue, its stasis, and its unrealized anticipation. *Wonderful Tennessee*, however, is ultimately not dramatically engaging, although the questions it asks and the subjects it raises are worthy of further investigation by the playwright and move Friel closer to postmodernism than he has yet been.

Brian Friel, a most productive, insightful, and seasoned spokesman for Irish Theatre, has given audiences delicate and provocative portraits of Irish life. His body of work, much more extensive than the selection discussed here, becomes canonical as it is written, an achievement that has the distinction of having both popular and professional approval. Friel's is a most prolific and lyrical talent. His lifelong relationship with the modern theatre indicates a dedication and conviction that is rare. His subject range is impressive, his interaction with contemporary events fitful but productive. Friel's belief in culture and tradition over history and politics is firmly convincing. His exploration of human frailty and emotion is unfailingly sympathetic, though purposeful and, finally, enriching for his audience.

Thomas Murphy, born in Tuam, Co. Galway in 1935, can rival any of Ireland's playwrights for the title of finest living dramatist. Less performed and read outside Ireland than some of his contemporaries, Murphy has had a history of considerable success in Britain, but has been considered not to "translate" well to North American stages, except for specialist Irish audiences.

Murphy's works ask hard questions and deliver hard answers. With the exception of *Famine*, his plays are set in the Ireland of Murphy's era or the early part of this century. Although the plays often make indirect or subtle use of Irish history, they are not overtly concerned either with history or with mythology. However, *Bailegangaire*, his notably and atypically female play, does derive directly from the folkloric in a blend of timeless and timely issues. Murphy's plays, despite their modern settings and liberation from the Irish propensity to reiterate its history in all its parts, are indeed very Irish in setting, linguistic turn, and thematic concerns. Deracination; the threat or reality of exile; ostracization within small communities; unfilled longings that seem at first merely romantic, but which are much more complex; questions of faith and belief; and the desire of man to strive for the fully realized life—all these are the playwright's thematic markers. Some of these themes resonate more strikingly in Ireland than they do in other parts of a world already too thoroughly postmodern to feel the tug of the orthodox and of past value systems, or to accord them continuing respect.

Kenneth Tynan was the preeminent London theatre critic of the period of Murphy's first major success, *A Whistle in the Dark* (1968). In a contemporary review of the play, he concentrated upon its implied and ongoing menacing quality:

> Thomas Murphy is the kind of playwright one would hate to meet in a dark theatre. I have always been obscurely frightened of loudly singing Irishmen, and of Irish debaters, who corrugating their brows and stubbing my chest with an index finger, beg me to prove them wrong, and am now convinced that I am scared of Irish dramatists as well.[6]

The play is about Michael Carney, who emigrates to England in an attempt to escape his limited prospects at home, but also to avoid the violence and abuse of his father, "Dada." His attempt is undermined when his boorish brothers and Dada follow him to Coventry.

Given that the general contemporary critical reaction to the play was so fundamentally racist, it merely confirmed that this is indeed a play about what it means to be a modern Irishman, albeit an Irishman born in a newly emergent state whose autonomy had been controlled from outside for a long time. The stunted personal growth of the five Carney brothers is testimony to that. But their inability to mature as men, as human beings, as brothers, has been much more immediately thwarted not by the evil effects of British imperialist rule, as some critics might contend, but by the stifling presence of their father, whose personal history rivals Nick Tynan's in *Da* for enforced or self-inflicted subservience. In Murphy's play, poverty, lack of opportunity, and the other social evils visited upon the Carneys (as representative of the Irish) in the past are not deflected with humor nor with nostalgia, as they are in Leonard or Friel. Instead they are manifested in their most damaging and destructive form—an entire family of men who in today's terminology would be quickly and emphatically labeled dysfunctional. That the tenor of the initial British critical reaction was that the family was dysfunctional merely *because* it was Irish was and is not surprising. Nor is the equally negative Irish critical response when the play opened at the Abbey less than a year later. The Irish response failed to acknowledge that fathers and sons like the Carneys *existed* in Ireland, and in the emigrant communities of England such as in Coventry. The British response failed to acknowledge recent British history as having any connection with the existence of Carneys either in Britain or in Ireland.

Michael Carney is distinguished from his brothers in two important ways. First off, he is married, and married to an Englishwoman, and secondly, he is "respectable," or striving to be so. But in his family's eyes Michael is not, like his brothers Hugo and Iggy, just another unfortunate emigrant forced to leave his fatherland. Instead Michael is considered by his family to be a traitor. Leaving home to earn a living is one thing, but assimilating is another. For his part Michael is eager to de-ghettoize. He is not a drunkard, a womanizer, nor a brawler. He has always found the requirements for being a *real* Carney—for which in their narrow definition we are supposed to read Real Irishman—too difficult and, at times, somewhat irrelevant. He views his brothers' and father's machismo routine as being one that is futile and self-defeating. This is an exhausted and outmoded form of Irishness that needs to be redefined:

> Harry: You're not a Paddy?
> Michael: We're all Paddies, and the British boys know it.
> Harry: So we can't disappoint them if that's what they think. Person'lly, I wouldn't disappoint them.
> Michael: You won't fit into a place that way.
> Harry: Hah? Who wants to?
> Michael: I do.
> Harry: You want to be a British Paddy?
> Michael: No. But a lot of it is up to a man himself to fit into a place. Otherwise he might as well stay at home.

Michael and Betty, who are newly married in the play, are as yet childless. As a result Michael is focusing his own hopes for the future, not on a son of his own, but on his youngest brother, Des. The struggle for Des, the Carney hope for the future, will end in his hideous, senseless, and accidental death by Michael's hand. Des' death is Murphy's powerful indictment of the warped grasp past definitions of Irishness can have on the present, or perhaps his belief in the futility of trying to escape from the past.

Murphy's Dada is one of the most truly malignant fathers ever to stalk an Irish stage. Dada is yet another failed middle-aged Irishman, unable or unwilling to hold a job. A blowhard, Dada, or Michael Carney Sr., is something of the evil twin of Captain Jack Boyle in O'Casey's *Juno and the*

Paycock. A descendant of Simon Dedalus, the father in Joyce's *A Portrait of The Artist*, Dada is "a praiser of his own past," and is just as much a coward as either of his literary forebears. This father, impotent with rage over what he sees as being the lot dealt to him in life, asserts his manhood and his paternity by encouraging his pugnacious sons to combat among themselves and with others. But Dada is ultimately a failed father. With no job himself, he has no place in the New Ireland. Despite his avowed patriotism and his smattering of the Irish language, he has no legacy but violence to pass on to his sons. That the tragedy of Des' death has not been caused by England, nor by the brother whose hand actually performed the act, is made quite clear by the playwright at the end of the play. Murphy's stage directions indicate that Dada be isolated on one side of the stage. His surviving four sons stare accusingly from the opposite side their rebuke to the Ireland of the immediate past—the failure of de Valéra's era and its policies to provide a future for them as Irishmen in a modern world.

Murphy's next theatrical success, written during this period but produced in 1975, was *The Sanctuary Lamp*. The play is not one of Murphy's larger repertory pieces but one that works within the intense confines of a small cast. This single-focus format will find additional severely controlled expression later in his playwriting career. Such tightly structured dramas as *The Gigli Concert* and *Bailegangaire* are, like *The Sanctuary Lamp*, each essentially interwoven monologues and dialogues for three actors. *The Sanctuary Lamp*, with four characters in its cast, is constructed in two acts. Its central character, Harry, is based in part on Jack Doyle, an Irish prizefighter and celebrity during Murphy's youth who died ignominiously in London.[7] It is noteworthy how this play and others by Murphy and his Irish contemporaries are influenced strongly by the voices heard and the visual images evoked while listening to the radio in childhood. Friel's *Dancing at Lughnasa*, Murphy's later *Gigli Concert*, and Thomas Kilroy's *Double Cross* also feature radio broadcasts as an integral part of their plots and of the imaginative lives of their characters.

The Sanctuary Lamp questions the Catholic belief that the presence of God is indicated by the burning flame of the sanctuary lamp. The play thus operates on the edges of a world that is both postmodern and slightly surreal. This is the world of the traveling circus, of Harry, a strong man, Francisco, a juggler, and Olga, a contortionist and the offstage wife. Harry's life is, we learn, destroyed by the dual loss of his daughter, who has died, and his wife, who has left him for his former best friend, Francisco (although only Francisco appears as a character in the play). Although Harry would like to exact revenge for the betrayal, he is strongly motivated to forgive. This latter urge is, he hopes, the requisite for his being forgiven for any responsibility he bears for his daughter's death. Murphy then inserts into this drama of conscience and self-examination a 16-year-old homeless girl, Maudie, who is also seeking refuge in the church and is destined to become Harry's surrogate daughter.

Murphy's stage directions for *The Sanctuary Lamp* indicate no details of venue other than "A church in a city." No country is named; but the play could be set in England, as both Harry and Maudie's speech indicates their working-class English origins. Francisco, despite his Latinate name, is Irish, and the only Catholic in what is a Catholic church. He seems no more convinced that God exists than does Harry. Only the young Maudie seems to harbor a naive and fundamentally anthropomorphic view of God, although Harry's speech can at times echo her tone. In speaking to Maudie of the sanctuary lamp itself and its significance, Harry says to the girl:

> Well, it's his spirit actually. They nabbed his spirit and they've got it
> in here. It's a mystery of course but that's what religion is. (She looks
> at him.) Personally, I think they should let him go but, there you are.

Later Harry's slightly blasphemous tone sharpens considerably:

> I've great respect for him, mind you
> . . .
> A very high regard. A veritable giant of a man, if you want my opinion,
> but between one thing and another, his sense is gone a little dim. And
> who would blame him? Locked up here at night, reclining—y'know?
> Reflecting his former glory.

The reclining (declining?) figure of God is for Murphy a flickering and passive presence. Superseded in a postmodern world, this god may still exude light, and therefore illumination, but it is merely a punning reflection.

As is true in nearly all of Murphy's plays for the stage, *The Sanctuary Lamp* contains the threat of violence throughout. Indeed, Harry finally punches Francisco, who incorrigibly has begun to lure Maudie as he had earlier lured Olga. Significantly, though, Harry's penknife, to which he refers and which the audience can *see* in *The Sanctuary Lamp*, is never used.

Late in the play Francisco reveals that Harry's wife Olga is dead of a drug overdose. The ranks of the dead are also swelled by references to both Maudie's dead mother and her dead baby, Stephen. As the play closes, however, loss and pain are replaced by forgiveness and reconciliation, signaled by Murphy's having the three—Maudie, Francisco, and Harry, all of whom have experienced bouts of guilty sleeplessness—fall asleep together *in* the confessional.

The Sanctuary Lamp also draws heavily on the Bible. Harry, the strong man who has lost his strength and regains it, resembles Samson. Francisco, in his repudiation of the old hierarchical structure of the established church, is certainly a prophet for the new—a John the Baptist figure, crying out unheeded in a cold postmodern desert of a world.

As the play closes, Harry and Francisco, the two reconciled warring parties, plan to depart together in the morning. They will explore two striking symbolic concepts, one introduced by each man. First, Harry evokes a Platonic vision of a sort—of a soul like a silhouette:

> And when you die it moves out into . . . slow-moving mists of space
> and time.

This metaphor, once established, continues with many modifications. The silhouette-souls are stacked:

> softly, like clouds in a corner of space where they must wait for a time.
> Until they are needed.

Eventually new souls act as seamless patches on old souls, creating the perfect union of souls to which mere mortals can only aspire.

Francisco, for his part, conjures a lush vision of limbo, a place in traditional Catholic belief for souls of the innocent unbaptized, between heaven and hell. Limbo is traditionally conceived as a limited fate, deprived of the presence of God. For Francisco it is a safe place beyond the whim of a capricious God, with:

> thousands and thousands of [other] fat babies sitting under the trees,
> gurgling and laughing and eating bananas. . . .

In Murphy's play the sanctuary lamp, as is required by Church injunction, is never extinguished. There may be the interrogation of God and his institutions by his characters. There may be the entry into blasphemous debate. But finally there is a humanism that replaces the vagaries and strictures of established religion. All of Murphy's characters seek forgiveness from God in the play. His power to forgive is reiterated in the text. However, ultimate forgiveness comes to humans from other humans. Maudie sees a vision of her dead mother, who is finally happy in the next life. The healing value of this vision frees her daughter to proceed with life. Similarly, in Harry and Francisco's mutual forgiveness there is liberation from the grasp of the dead and from stagnating inactivity. Even the play's penultimate speech, spoken by Francisco, confirms the replacement of faith in God, and the need for his forgiveness, with faith in man and in his own power to forgive:

> Oh my god I am heartily sorry for having offended Thee and I . . . See?
> I can't remember. I've beaten them.

This speech begins with the opening words of "The Act of Contrition," a prayer that Catholics say after having received absolution from the priest in the confessional. Francisco's having forgotten the rest of the prayer, a much-rehearsed mantra from a religious childhood, is a major step in achieving a postmodern sense of equilibrium in a world where God's solace may no longer be sufficient to man's needs.

Obsession is a postmodern subject. Its extremity intrigues the mind of an artist freed from the constraints of orthodox religious belief, and belief in progress as inevitable and essential. Obsession denies the efficacy of and requirement for moderation, and the respect for limits in traditional society. With no rules, or new rules, and the imperative to defy conventional views, the postmodern man is free to explore subjects viewed previously as taboo or unsavory.

In *The Gigli Concert* (1983) an Irish man (called simply The Man) is a "successful" business man who has made it in the world's terms, only to reject those terms or to see their profound limitations. His obsession, which seems bizarre to the audience as the play opens, is to be able to sing like the great early-twentieth-century Italian tenor, Beniamino Gigli.

In order to achieve his goal, the unnamed property developer places himself in the hands of an English "healer," J. P. W. King. An unfulfilled man himself, King recognizes and acknowledges his inadequacies in the face of the other man's need. Both utter an identical existential question in the play's opening scene:

> Christ, how am I going to get through today?

With this exact repetition, the ambiguity of their roles becomes quickly apparent, although one is ostensibly the healer while the other is in need of healing.

Quickly, The Man converts his desire to sing like Gigli into a belief that he *is* Gigli. He gives J. P. W. all the biographical details of Gigli's childhood as his own, a fact that J. P. W. does not fully understand at first. By the play's third scene, the extent of the destructiveness of The Man's obsession becomes apparent. His uncontrollable desire to recreate Gigli's achievement has soured his life to such an extent that it has unraveled his marriage and his relationship with his nine-year-old son.

In the following scene J. P. W.'s girlfriend, Mona, makes her first appearance. Although their initial "dialogue" on stage takes place in the intimacy of a double bed, two people less in touch with each other would be hard to imagine:

> Mona: You're not listening to me. (*He nods.*) I shouldn't have dropped
> in? (*He nods.*) You're bored now? (*He nods. She kicks him or whatever.*) I had
> to dash out—I'd promised to take my god-child to her ballet class—
> then back home And-I-Was-Ravenous. I ate three eggs, then two
> yoghurts and I was still hungry, wondering what I'll have now. And I
> thought I'll chance you. You're not listening to me!
>
> J. P. W.: I am. Well, I am going to see this thing through too.
>
> Mona: (*To herself.*) Oh my God.
>
> J. P. W.: He may even shoot me if I don't.
>
> Mona: Who?
>
> J. P. W.: Benimillo. A practical man, like my father . . . But this practical
> man is declaring that the romantic kingdom *is* of this world.
>
> Mona: And that's all you were doing last night, reading?

When The Man supplants Mona in this scene, the drinks flow and some domestic truths emerge. The Man guesses correctly that J. P. W. is not married, as he has said he is. Each man, then, has a fantasy that he needs, but J. P. W. is not abashed when his fantasy is discovered.

As an integral part of *The Gigli Concert* Murphy has inserted as a counterpoint, or form of harmony, to his dialogue a selection of recordings of Gigli singing. In this sense something of Gigli functions as a character in the play, particularly when the text of his aria is chosen to act as a commentary to the main text of the play.

As the situation of The Man worsens in the play, his wife takes his son away, and the two men have a bonding scene. We will see similar sessions occur in other work by Murphy, as well as in the work of Thomas Kilroy and Frank McGuinness. In *The Gigli Concert* sexual truths are exchanged by J. P. W. and The Man, but although they are often the stuff of painful revelation, in this play they are exposed freely and willingly. The most painful revelation each man eventually makes will be in a part of his life much more intimate than his sexuality. In this sense Murphy toys with the construct of the confessional sequence, exposing its banality.

The Man continues with the putative story of his own autobiography, not that of Gigli, and his need for fantasy begins to make itself apparent. Suffering a brutalized, fatherless childhood and ruled by a maniacal elder brother, The Man realized early that aesthetic deprivation deforms human experience. J. P. W.'s contrastingly benign childhood, complete with ineffectual father, is, in its own way, equally poignant:

> But fathers, you know? formal, straight backs, frowning, unsure of themselves. I think they feel a little spare, and that is a pity.

After the revelations of the night the desolate Man breaks down, embarrassing himself, as their next meeting proves. The Man, defensive and denying some of the revelations of the night before, antagonizes J. P. W. and calls him a charlatan. J. P. W. is aware of this truth before he is accused. He explains, however, the genuine extent to which he has gone to help The Man, whose obsession has begun to obsess him. As The Man later leaves, convinced he is cured by J. P. W., the play focuses on J. P. W., suicidal and alone without Mona, who has died of cancer. In an ironic scene just before the play's end, it is J.P.W. who realizes, or believes he has realized, The Man's aesthetic fantasy by singing "Tu Che A Dio Spiegasti L'Ali" from Donizetti's opera Lucia de Lammermoor.[8] The idea of realizing this dream, the accomplishment of his willing himself to achieve the seemingly impossible, provides J. P. W. with the will to live. With the dawn he leaves the place of his years of defeated despair. Though the achievement was not his goal, and though not witnessed nor able to be repeated, the attainment of this wonder sustains J. P. W., and, we are to believe, the human spirit.

The Gigli Concert, it should be noted, is basically a dialogic exposition between J. P. W. King and The Man. The presence of Mona as a third character, and one who is not a fully realized one, is problematic. Her tragic circumstances are not fully explored by Murphy, even in their relation to either J. P. W.'s or The Man's dilemma. Mona, childless and basically alone, is facing death, an existential dilemma of greater proportion and immediacy than that of either of the men. Murphy does not allow Mona full range to explore her dilemma, but she is not meant to be a throwaway or comic character, nor one who represents "the unexamined life." There is, perhaps, a higher degree of stoicism in Mona than in either

J. P. W. or The Man, rendered here to some slight degree poignant simply by not being articulated.

The female voice in *The Gigli Concert*, then, goes almost unheard. (Interestingly, when Gigli sings in the play, it is never in a love duet with a soprano, although such duets are frequent in tenor performances). The focus of the play, as in Murphy's earlier work, is male. One significant difference between *The Gigli Concert* and the playwright's other plays set in Ireland is that, for the most part, it is remarkably free of Irish context. Both this lack of detailed female characterization and of essential Irish referents stands in stark contrast to the probing investigation of the female psyche and the cultural configurations of a rapidly modernizing Ireland that inform his next major play, *Bailegangaire*.

As we have seen, obsession is explored to fruition in Murphy's work. In *Bailegangaire* obsession takes different forms, but retains the power ultimately to liberate Murphy's damaged characters. In this play Murphy explores dramatic territory new to him and alien to many male playwrights. The play is a three-hander for women, with the featured role of Mommo, a bed-ridden grandmother, along with Mary and Dolly, the granddaughters she has reared. It features Murphy's trademark, counterpointed monologue, used to effect in both *The Sanctuary Lamp* and in *The Gigli Concert*, but now expressed through a female consciousness.

As in so many of Murphy's plays, in *Bailegangaire* (1985) there is a subtext that is the crux to our comprehension of the characters' actions and motives, but that story is not fully revealed at first. Just as in *The Sanctuary Lamp* the audience needs to know of Olga's infidelity and death, so here in *Bailegangaire* the audience needs to hear Mommo's story. This is the story of how Bailegangaire, which means "the town without laughter," got its name. Mommo, one of the great roles for a mature woman in the contemporary Irish theatrical repertoire, was originated at the Druid Theatre in 1985 by Siobhán McKenna, an actress most closely associated with the Abbey Theatre, where she performed for many years.

The play, cast in two acts, is a static one. Except for one comic trip to relieve herself, Mommo is stationary in her bed, which dominates the living space of the main room—the country kitchen—of a three-roomed cottage. Although this is a cliched environment on the Irish stage, Tom Murphy has indicated in his initial stage directions his insistence that Mommo's cottage not be romanticized. Instead, Mommo's unwinding of her folkloric story, with its tragic end, is interspersed with contemporary elements that are meant to jar the audience's perception of traditional rural Irish life. It is 1984, and the stalwart Mary, a victim of economic reality in the west of Ireland, has returned home from years of nursing in England. Dolly, her younger sister, is an abandoned wife of sorts, also an identifiable type in modern Ireland where, until recently, divorce was prohibited. Dolly, liberated to a questionable degree, rides a motorbike, uses irreverent and abusive language, is promiscuous, and is pregnant by a man not her husband.

However, the tension in this static play is provided by Mary. Despite her defeatist demeanor and outdated ladylike mannerisms, Mary is doggedly attempting to prod her grandmother into articulating the repressed memory of a family tragedy that resulted in the death of her brother Tom. Dolly, although more overtly aggressive, does not aid Mary in this aim. Instead Dolly confuses the senile Mommo, frequently causing her to restart the tale from its beginning. Mommo's story focuses on a journey she and her husband, Seamus, made to a fair to sell goods. Their orphaned grandchildren, who lived with them, were small. Bad weather forces a stop in a strange village and Seamus is provoked into a "laughing contest" in the pub, where a local Seamus has a reputation for a fine laugh. Tempers flare and subside, and eventually all is resolved in a long night of celebration and drink, propelled by Mommo. On their late return to their cottage (the same cottage as in the action of the play) they learn that their grandson Tom was burned to death when the children tried to use paraffin (kerosene) to light a fire. Two days later the grandfather dies of grief and remorse, and Mommo, Dolly, and Mary survive, never to acknowledge the tragedy again.

Plotting in the tale within the play is complex, but *Bailegangaire* is much more a language and memory play than one of incident or character. There is a mesmerizing quality to the ritualized repetition of Mommo's story. It is not told to its devastating conclusion, but on a perpetual loop that excludes, until the end, revelation and closure. This effect is enhanced by the audience's growing understanding that Mommo's story is so oft-repeated, so intricately entwined with their lives, that both Dolly and Mary know it by heart. However, when they try to usurp, hurry, or alter the story, Mommo asserts her exclusive right to it. She also keeps command of the two younger women and of the stage by feigning lack of memory, by purposely or otherwise failing to "remember" who Mary is, and by treating her dismissively, like a servant. Mommo also reverts to childlike language, wheedling behavior, and other subversive acts to get her way and to maintain it.

With the disclosure at the end of the story, however, Murphy's characters experience the same kind of release experienced in *The Sanctuary Lamp* and elsewhere in his dramatic corpus. Mommo is, in a sense, free to die, her conscience as clear as it can be. Mommo's granddaughters, relieved of contrasting burdens, exchange predicaments, after being freed by mutual honesty. Dolly rids herself of the unwanted child whose illegitimacy would be known by all, and whose existence could wreck what remained of her marriage. Mary escapes the opposite burden of loneliness by agreeing to take Dolly's child and pretend it is her own. *Bailegangaire* closes with Mary stepping into the *mater familias* role just abdicated by Mommo. Her final speech suggests that the "story" of the child soon to be born—altered to accommodate the mores of Bailegangaire—may prove a necessary form of distorted autobiography similar to that which Mommo bore as her burden for so many years.

Tom Murphy's dramatic corpus is large, and as this discussion of a selection of his plays indicates, varied in treatment and situation. Though the author could be said to write the language plays so favored by today's Irish dramatists, to label them as such is to deny the full dramatic force of their intention and execution. The sustained tension and underlying polemic in each play links the playwright's developing craftsmanship. His achievement is moved onto a plane where ideas, and the language in which they are conveyed, are presented and argued. Murphy's felicitous, but unrelenting, dramatic structure demands that his audience leave the theatre questioning definitions of Irishness, manhood, faith, and love.

Thomas Kilroy was born in 1934 in Co. Kilkenny. He has taught at University College, Dublin, and been Professor of Modern English at University College, Galway, a post from which he resigned in 1989 to devote himself to writing full time.

After the success of his early novel, *The Big Chapel* (1971), Kilroy has worked mainly in dramatic media, writing for the stage and also for television and radio. He shares with Tom Murphy the trait of being little known as a dramatist outside Ireland, or certainly less well-known than the plays deserve.

Thomas Kilroy's roots in the Irish midlands and his years in the west of Ireland, where he continues to live, may appear at first somewhat at odds with the setting and subject matter of his first dramatic success, *The Death and Resurrection of Mr. Roche*, which is a decidedly Dublin play.

The Death and Resurrection of Mr. Roche (1969) has as its central incident a night of drinking by a group of aging "lads" that devolves into an episode of queer-bashing. The play borrows from folkloric sources such as Synge used in *The Shadow of the Glen*, and as Joyce appropriated also from the urban folk song for *Finnegans Wake*, and also from recitative Dublin party pieces such as "The Night Before Larry was Stretched." *The Death and Resurrection of Mr. Roche* exploits the convention of the presumed murder (or death) of the title character. Here a middle-aged homosexual's "death" occasions self-examination and reproach among the other five men. His "resurrection" provides the ironic jolt essential to the play's success.

The first of the play's three acts begins about 11:30 PM in the flat of Kelly, one of the drinking buddies who continue their night on the town after pub-closing time. The group consists at first of Kelly and three others. They are in their mid-thirties and have not met in two years. Only one of the men, Seamus, has married. Another, known only as "Doc," is a failed medical student. Myles, who completes the party, is something of a dandy. Later they are joined by Mr. Roche, who is in turn accompanied by Kevin, a young student already very ill from drinking.

Kelly, the drunkest of the friends, seems the most misogynistic and the most dependent on these stag gatherings. He has derailed suggested plans for after-hours entertainment, including a trip to a barbecue in the Dublin mountains or a dance in town. Either of these choices would, of course, have included women, the abstract subject of much speculation throughout. It would seem as though either plan would be more attractive to the group. Despite continuing references to the barbecue and the dance, though, only one of the men will eventually seek female company. In truth, as the ribald talk of the night continues, the audience begins to see that, as in Synge's *Playboy of the Western World*, "there's a great gap between a gallous story and a dirty deed." The men's macho talk of women is merely that—talk.

The evening also reveals that although Kelly had some intellectual pretensions in the past, he now no longer reads and finds little consolation in "ideas." Seamus, a school teacher, is genuinely dismayed to learn this about his friend. Along with Doc, now a morgue attendant, and Myles, a salesman, Kilroy's men are uniformly defeated by life. Kelly delivers a pathetic, yet poignant, rendering of a recitation of Robert Service's Yukon ballad "The Face on the Barroom Floor." The story is of the defeat of a promising painter whose muse leaves him and who dissolves in drink. The failed painter resorts to drawing the face of his former beloved on the saloon floor for the price of a drink. The depths to which he has plummeted mirror the condition of Kelly and his friends by degrees. Thus failure is one of the themes explored in *The Death and Resurrection of Mr. Roche*, but with the mention and eventual arrival of the title character, an examination of definitions of male sexuality becomes prominent thematically, too.

Thomas Kilroy, who was a director of the Field Day Theatre Company from 1988 to 1992 (the only director from the Republic of Ireland), is described in his own entry in *The Field Day Anthology of Irish Writing* as being preoccupied as a writer with "the distortions of the individual psyche in its attempts to achieve fullness within the confines of a narrow and traumatized society."[9] He contrasts in his first major play the level of self-realization achieved by Mr. Roche with the full-scale self-deception necessary for the continued maintenance of esteem in the other male characters.

From the frenetic comedy and bonhomie of Act I, which culminates with the supposed accidental death of Mr. Roche, the play proceeds to the multiple self-examination process of Act II. Kelly and Seamus, the two oldest and closest among the friends, reminisce about their humble origins and shared hometown, which now Seamus visits rarely and Kelly not at all. Thoughts of home provoke in Kelly a regret frequently expressed in modern Irish drama. As a civil servant in Dublin he is displaced from the land. Indeed, the only instances in which Kelly's bluff inarticulacy rises to poetry in the play is either in song or when he is talking about contact with the soil:

> You know, Seamus, you know when you pull a turnip from a wet drill,
> what it's like, with the roots black and wet, lovely to the touch, like silk.

Kelly must, however, also contend with a very difficult and powerful regret. He confesses to Seamus a previous homosexual encounter with Mr. Roche, a disclosure made significantly at dawn, with its illuminating implications. Seamus' hurried and stilted departure leaves the isolated Kelly alone at the end of Act II while the others try to dispose of Mr. Roche's "body." (Mr. Roche, a claustrophobe, has not died, but has lost consciousness after being locked in a crawlspace under the stairs in Kelly's flat.)

The confessional sequences of Act II have also included Seamus' monologue on his boredom with his marriage and his fundamental disaffection from his wife. Act III opens with Kelly kneeling and reciting "The Act of Contrition" (as did Francisco in Murphy's *The Sanctuary Lamp*). The reversal of the play begins with the unexpected return of Myles, who had left after the trouble began. It intensifies with the even more unexpected return of Mr. Roche in a strange, balletic entrance with the young Kevin and Doc, the character who had inaccurately pronounced Mr. Roche dead. After this denouement, *The Death and Resurrection of Mr. Roche* hastens to its inevitable close with the men shrugging off Kelly's attempts to carry the party into Sunday morning. In the final scene, Kelly, Myles, and Doc head off to early Mass at a cloistered Carmelite church nearby.

The instance of the prayer, mass-going, and the death and resurrection motifs of the play bring to the fore Kilroy's religious or quasi-religious themes. In playful or facetious mode the playwright has the "resurrected"

Mr. Roche hailed by Kelly, aghast, as "Jesus!," and there is considerable apocalyptic language in the guise of ordinary Dublin pub talk.

Although Mr. Roche is the play's title character, *The Death and Resurrection of Mr. Roche* is a play that focuses on Kelly. He is a damaged transitional figure in a changing Ireland, very unlike Mr. Roche, whose marginalized position as a homosexual has demanded that he develop as a person in order to survive. Kelly, however, is a stunted figure, emotionally, sexually, and intellectually. His belated epiphany in Act II is painful because, in part, it has been so long delayed. Kelly, then, represents Ireland in a rapidly modernizing world. Mr. Roche, Kilroy's foil character to Kelly, is an example of one of the playwright's many double characters. This exposure of a complex societal inadequacy or destructive contradiction by means of *doppelganger* characters becomes much more developed in later Kilroy plays like *Double Cross*, as its title suggests.

Matt Talbot, the title character of Kilroy's innovative *Talbot's Box* (1979), was a real person. An unskilled Dublin worker, recovering alcoholic, and mystic, Talbot has become an Irish icon. *Talbot's Box* returns playwright Kilroy to inner-city Dublin, but a Dublin quite different from the Dublin of the minor professional ranks of *The Death and Resurrection of Mr. Roche*. The play is set much earlier, at the time of the 1913 great lock-out of Dublin workers. The divergence between the public perception of Matt Talbot and the private man provides the play's fundamental tension—another form of split identity such as that which can cripple characters in much of contemporary Irish drama.

Talbot's Box returns Kilroy's audience to the Dublin morgue (mentioned but not seen in *Mr. Roche*) and also requires that the lead actor play a corpse—that of Talbot. The other focal point on stage as the play begins is the large box of the title, which is multifunctional throughout the performance. The box serves as confessional, coffin, witness stand, and functions in other imaginative capacities. The simplicity in the use of properties in the play is reinforced by the requirement that all the actors but the man playing the title role assume multiple roles. The play is visually arresting and engages in a series of trompe l'oeil; statues begin to move and speak. The dead Talbot, beyond the grave, arises and loosens the penitential and self-inflicted chains that bind his body even in death. Contrast is insisted upon, and often portrayed in the extreme—the more bound the body, the freer the soul. The smaller the earthly life, the greater the self-denial of the penitent Talbot; the greater his personal self-realization, the closer he draws to beatific insight and its limitless scope.

The dramatis personae of *Talbot's Box* consists only of Matt Talbot, First Man, Second Man, Woman, and Priest Figure, played by an actress. These actors (again, with the exception of the man who plays Talbot) are used throughout the play to represent members of Talbot's family, a chambermaid with whom he had a personal relationship, coworkers, employers, hospital orderlies, passersby, a horse, and others. The rapid switching of roles and the garrulous, haranguing quality of the speeches of many of the characters come somewhat on top of each other. They provide a vivid visual and aural contrast to the character of Matt Talbot, who is often central, static, and tense. With the exception of the two relatively long monologic speeches and more frequent exchanges toward the play's end, Talbot is much more spoken about than he speaks. This seeming imbalance in the play is, more appropriately, a theatrical means of teasing out the process by which the distinctions between the man and the myth have become blurred.

Dubliners identify strongly with local men of note, regardless of the nature of their particular contributions. They are very comfortable, if not intimate, in their talk of such historical and literary figures as Jonathan Swift, Robert Emmet, Oscar Wilde, and James Joyce, who are closely associated with their city. Stories abound about all such figures, and even when proven inaccurate, persist as a form of urban folklore. Similarly, Dubliners have identified strongly with Matt Talbot, a working-class hero who can add unalloyed piety to his qualities. *Talbot's Box* deals with the perception of Talbot as much as with Talbot himself, and although there was no cleft in Talbot between the private and public man, there is disparity in his image as perceived by others. This examination of duality, albeit superimposed and external, is one of Kilroy's continuing foci.

Because of the historical setting of the play, *Talbot's Box* also illustrates vividly, and somewhat accusatorily, the outcome of the transfer of power in Ireland into the hands of the Catholic middle class. Revolutionary Dublin is viewed as still fostering a have/have not system, with power and money often considerations as strong as emerging nationalism.

The two-act structure of *Talbot's Box* suits its theme, as does its ending of Act I with Bloody Sunday, when the events of the Dublin lock-out of 1913 peaked. The most complex of the many characters that the four supporting actors play is that of the priest, but complexity does not end here. The First Man plays a character intended to remind audiences of William Martin Murphy, the Catholic owner of many newspaper and business holdings in Dublin, who led the employers' successful attempt to crush the workers' strike. (Murphy's name is also used in the play.) The reinforcement of contrast here between the worldly-wise Murphy and the otherworldly

Talbot is made clear to the audience through Talbot's lengthy exposition of the motivation and frame of mind of the mystic. Mysticism is an experience often alien even to fundamentally religious people. The following exchange is conducted by Talbot, speaking to his sister Susan, with whom he maintained close contact all his life:

> Talbot: Go home, Susan, to your own family.
> Woman: Amn't I yer own family?
> Talbot: Sure you are 'n yer're not, Susie. The way to God was be giving up them that's nearest to me. 'Twas what Our Lord said to the fishermen, y'see. But then I discovered something strange, Susan. (She begins to move away.) Having given all up, it was all given back to me, but different, y'know what I mean. All the world and the people in the world came back to me in me own room. But everything in place. Nothing twisted 'n broken as it is in this world. Everything straight as a piece of good timber, without warp.

Talbot's wood analogy is carried throughout the play, in keeping with his respect for wood and its multiple qualities, employed in the play to represent the sole, sensual pleasure in this life.

As Act I draws to a close, Talbot's essential difference from his working colleagues is apprehended by all. Devoid of a genuine sense of politicization, Talbot breaks ranks by refusing to accept strike pay because he had performed no work for it. This is a decision that has come down through popular memory as one either of overt or covert treachery, but certainly not of solidarity.

In Act II of *Talbot's Box*, there is more of the private Talbot. It opens with his ecstatic singing of a hymn of devotional submission to the Sacred Heart of Jesus, a manifestation of the Christ figure that provides numerous metaphorical possibilities involving blood and light. (The Sacred Heart of Jesus is iconographically rendered to include an exposed heart in which a flame burns.) Talbot's turbulent family background, controlled by his violent, alcoholic father, also impinges on the character's memory and on our growing awareness. Addictive, obsessive behavior, posits Kilroy, has many faces. The flagellant, ascetic Talbot may have been merely the addictive obverse of the earlier alcoholic binger who strove to achieve oblivion in a more conventional, albeit destructive, manner.

Kilroy's second act exposes the difficult relationship that has always existed between the Church's hierarchical structure and the highly individualistic tradition of the mystic. The priest figure, who extolled Talbot's self-denial and devotion in Act I, spars with Talbot in Act II for his refusal to comply with certain devotional practices that the mystical Talbot views, ultimately, as distracting from his higher goal. The priest's pathetic attempts to use Talbot to gain insight into the nature of the true visionary, or beatific, experience are thwarted by an angry Talbot, whose aims and experiences have pushed him beyond such expectations:

> There be nuthin' to see when Gawd comes 'cause there's nothing other
> than yourself 'cause yerself is wan with what ya see so ya see nuthin'
> 'cause ya can only see what's separate from yerself, ya can only count
> what's different, not the same, not the wan, the only. . . .

Talbot's Box moves to a deft close with its recurrent timber imagery. Talbot is linked with the Holy Family, with Saint Joseph, a carpenter and Christ's father on earth, and with the crucified Christ, whose instrument of torture and death was made of wood.

Talbot's Box, which has been called Brechtian by more than one critic, has a transforming power. The playwright's aim—to represent iconoclastic behavior that conforms to the out-of-body type—provides him, simultaneously, with an opportunity to re-create such a transforming experience for the audience in the theatre. *Talbot's Box* also remains truly grounded in the recent historical past, and in the politically identifying markers that continue to resonate in Ireland today.

Recent history, political ideology, and dual manifestations of a single, contradictory, and complex personality continued to inform Kilroy's drama into the eighties. These thematic concerns also suited the aims of The Field Day Theatre Company, which first produced *Double Cross* in 1986.

The play concerns two ambivalent historical figures. William Joyce was known as Lord Haw Haw, an Irishman who broadcast radio propaganda for Hitler's Third Reich. Brendan Bracken, also an Irishman, was Joyce's contemporary and became a member of Winston Churchill's wartime cabinet. At the center of the play is the vexing question of Ireland's neutrality during World War II. This was a policy insisted upon by founding father Éamon de Valéra more in defiance of Churchill, and to guard Ireland's nascent independence, than out of any articulate sense of pacifism.

Although the dramatis personae of *Double Cross* lists 11 characters, Kilroy's stage directions indicate that the play can be performed by as few as two actors and an actress—a mechanism similar to that employed in *Talbot's Box*. Indeed, in its first production in Derry, actor and founding member of Field Day, Stephen Rea (widely known to North American audiences for his starring role in Neil Jordan's film *The Crying Game*), played both Joyce and Bracken. Such a task makes for a demanding evening for an actor, but also provides a virtuoso showcase for talent such as Rea's.

In *Double Cross*, Thomas Kilroy uses a construct already established by other contemporary playwrights. There is, as Kilroy's introduction to the play makes clear, "no evidence that Brendan Bracken and William Joyce ever met." Though historically pinned to a few years, some of the "real" occurrences and some "real" people in the play are imaginative conjectures on the part of the playwright, not a dramatic rendering of genuine meetings.[10]

Both Brendan Bracken and William Joyce denied and hid from others their national origin, and went to great lengths to do so. Kilroy chooses these men, ironically, to "dramatize the deformities of nationalism more effectively than two patriots." [11] The duality from which each man's behavior springs is rooted in deception. Such a deception is, of course, the basis of all theatrical experience. From duality to deception it is not far to go to the concept of treason—deception with political consequences, particularly in time of war. Furthermore, without highly evolved concepts of nationalism, with their concomitant requirements of allegiance, the traitorous act is an impossibility.

Anthony Roche, in his recent study *Contemporary Irish Drama*, argues that the purpose of Kilroy's central characters' "endeavour has been the choosing of an objective other identity to mediate the struggle for self-realisation."[12] *Double Cross*, with its bifurcated structure (Part I is "The Bracken Play," Part II "The Joyce Play") and with its visual projections of the face or voice of the other man throughout each of the two parts, dramatizes this struggle more completely.

Brendan Bracken's biography, which he altered to obscure his Irish and humble origins, was something in a constant state of flux. He allowed, even perpetuated, confusion about his national origins. Having spent some time in Australia, for instance, he allowed himself to be thought of and spoken of as Australian. Eventually he assumed an identity more English than the English. Bracken, in this regard, followed in the wake of real Irishmen like Oscar Wilde and fictional Irishmen like Trollope's Phineas Finn. This recurring phenomenon of the Irish man reinventing himself to great success in England requires the skill of the actor, Kilroy would argue.[13]

"The Bracken Play" uses the technology of the age to bring both men and their fractured identities together, relying mainly on the device of the radio broadcast and the one-sided telephone conversation. The role of the radio in the transmitting of essential news during the war cannot be over-emphasized, nor can the extension of telephone services. As both conveyances rely entirely on voice transmission, this is a vocal play. It calls for a demanding range and diversity on the part of the main actor. An early, lengthy telephone sequence in which Bracken wheedles an investor, a banker, a potential partner, a blacksmith, and Winston Churchill, is orchestrated by Kilroy in monologues worthy of Wilde—"Really? I'd adore meeting them anon if you can arrange it. Knew their son at Oxford, as a matter of fact. Splendid fellow." Thus is exhibited the development of social survival skills and chameleonlike adaptation at which the deft and loquacious Bracken excelled.

Bracken's next milieu in the play is equally revealing, if decidedly different. Here Kilroy explores Bracken's relationship with an entirely imaginary upper-class Englishwoman who could be based either on Lady Pamela Smith (daughter of the Earl of Birkenhead, Lord Chancellor under Churchill) or on Penelope Dudley Ward (Churchill's goddaughter), or on both. Each was said to have turned down his proposal of marriage. The "Popsie" relationship of the play exposes Bracken's sexual frailties and suggests homosexual proclivities. He is also portrayed as relying on elaborate fantasies to achieve sexual arousal.

"The Bracken Play" also includes cameo appearances by Lord Castlerosse, who exposed Bracken's heritage in the British papers (to no great consequence it should be said); Lord Beaverbrook, a New Zealand newspaper tycoon who investigated Bracken's origins; and a Fire Warden.[14] Only in conversation with the Warden does Bracken reveal his true identity, and even then it emerges only in the repressed voice of a child:

> My father, my father who is, my father was—(Low, strong Tipperary accent, boyish tone) Me father was wan of the lads, so he was, wan of the hillside men. He took the oath. He was out in the tenant's war of eighty-nine. (Shift. Heavy adult voice) Bejasus I was.

"The Bracken Play" closes with a somewhat chastened Bracken, after his slip with the Fire Warden, beginning to compose a letter to his mother. However, the final word of the play goes to Joyce, who issues an anti-Semitic tirade that severely undercuts the credibility Kilroy has built for Joyce earlier in the play.

"The Joyce Play" also begins on radio and shows the deceptive skill that Joyce exercised in his propagandistic broadcasts. That he had a personal history of traitorous behavior emerges from a boyhood memory of betraying local IRA agitators in the west of Ireland to the British officers in the garrison where his father was stationed.

The threat of treason, then, is palpable in Joyce's life. This is immediately borne out by Kilroy's construction of a scene involving a dubious English lesson conducted by Joyce's wife Margaret for Erich, an Anglophilic German and her lover. The ensuing argument between Joyce and Margaret allows the audience a glimpse of their lives as aliens and ideology-driven traitors. Joyce, we learn, is depressive and suicidal. Each accuses the other of not being strong enough in the face of defeat. Although they are also meant to be committed to free love, Joyce is shocked by Margaret's revelation that she and Erich have made love. He reacts conventionally enough by slapping her face, and continues on a full-scale abusive verbal retaliation. Margaret, earlier accused of lacking ideological fiber, responds by turning Joyce's words on him after he threatens to beat her:

> Margaret: No, William, you must listen. I insist that you recover yourself, through yourself, through your own words. We must turn our violence into energy. That's what you said. We must use that energy to master the world about us. Don't you remember? Your words, William Joyce. Personal violence is a waste. Violence controlled and directed is power. Power! Power!

"The Joyce Play" moves quickly to its conclusion with the turn of events in the war, Hitler's death, and Joyce's eventual capture. Here Kilroy telescopes the recruiting officer, to whom Joyce made the proposal to spy years before in Ireland, with the British officers who apprehended him after the war. In *Double Cross*' penultimate scene, however, Kilroy finally has Lord Beaverbrook, while visiting Joyce in prison, articulate the major thematic concern of the play. Beaverbrook has a philosophical, objectified interest in the concept of treason and in "the profound fidelities" produced by treason. This notion, of course, runs directly counter to the accepted "truth" about treason—that it is by definition an act of infidelity. A final imagined, existential, and brief meeting between Bracken and Joyce ensues. Joyce then "reads" a letter to Margaret, which makes a central focus of the Christian faith that informed Joyce's ideology.

Thomas Kilroy's dramatic corpus exhibits in its later stages, including *Talbot's Box* and *Double Cross*, a postmodern awareness of the possibilities of artificiality that underlies all theatre. Even from the time of his first dramatic success with *The Death and Resurrection of Mr. Roche* Kilroy's willingness to investigate and to expose countertruths about masculinity, and the related concepts of national identity and loyalty, has consistently shown the determination and courage of an original and distinctive voice in the Irish theatre.

Tom MacIntyre is a prolific writer who has experimented in many genres, often simultaneously. Born in 1931, in Co. Cavan, MacIntyre approaches historical subjects from a surrealistic and/or highly experimental point of view. *Eye Winker, Tom Tinker*, staged at the Peacock in 1972, deals caustically, yet imaginatively, with a nervous IRA man called Shooks. *The Bearded Lady* (1984) is an irreverent but probing play that explores the contradictory personality of Jonathan Swift through sexual means. *Rise Up Lovely Sweeney* (1985) takes up an absurdist view of the familiar tale of the king condemned to live like a bird, never lighting on the ground, as punishment for having been disrespectful to a saint. Although this myth, as has been shown in the poetry section of this book, has attracted many fine Irish writers, MacIntyre's *Sweeney* is remarkably original. (Another version of *Buile Suibhne*, or *The Madness of Sweeney*, appeared on the Dublin stage in 1997 in the form of Paula Meehan's *Mrs. Sweeney*, which approached the myth from a feminist perspective.)

Good Evening, Mr. Collins (1995), which is a play more conventionally scripted than many of MacIntyre's works, provides another idiosyncratic but highly perceptive treatment of Irish history. Rather than shining a spotlight on his subject, MacIntyre turns a strobe light on a twentieth-century Irish icon, sometimes to grotesque effect.

Michael Collins, also the subject of a recent, controversial film by Irish director Neil Jordan, was a charismatic soldier/statesman of key importance in the early days of Irish independence. Called "The Big Fella" because of his size and athleticism, Collins stood in vivid physical and psychological contrast to Éamon de Valéra, with whom he was allied in the Anglo-Irish War and against whom he fought in the Irish Civil War (1919–1923 inclusive). De Valéra, an ectomorphic mathematician, brilliantly outmaneuvered Collins, and may have been instrumental in his assassination in 1922. De Valéra himself, though he never won the fond allegiance of the people that Collins did, went on to be the prime architect of the Irish constitution. He served both as *Taoiseach* (Prime Minister) and *Uachtarán na hÉireann* (President of Ireland) and died peacefully in old age. The two men's roles in modern Irish life have always provoked heated partisan debates in life and, as now, in art.

Good Evening, Mr. Collins has three female characters, all of whom are played by one actress. The rest of the characters are male, some of the actors doubling roles as called for, especially for minor parts. The play is constructed in two acts with many short scenes in each. The sets are "minimalist," as indicated in MacIntyre's stage direction, and the pacing, as in his other plays, is fast, if not frenetic. By using rapid lighting changes, MacIntyre aims to provide the audience with cameos, glimpses, epiphanies, and bits of illumination. Thus, he crystallizes character and dominant personality traits, both positive and negative. MacIntyre wishes to exhibit complexity, but this method can also risk reinforcing simple stereotype as well.

One of Collins' lovers, Moya Llewellyn-Davies, an Anglo-Welsh socialite, appears first to engage Collins in a sexually tinged exchange. The dialogue reveals the political infighting of the day and a preoccupation with the Irish language, which was typical of the era. The political scene that follows the rather coquettish curtain raiser with Moya is markedly different, in that its dialogue is delivered in much longer and more fully developed passages. Collins is portrayed as ruthless in his avenging of sectarian deaths, and devoted to his men, who are in turn fiercely loyal to him. This sequence is then balanced with a duet between Collins and Kitty Kiernan, the Irish woman to whom he was engaged at the time of his death. Their exchanges are in part delivered as an imaginary tennis volley, which gives them a playful innocence, and undercuts the more serious aspect of their relationship.

The first prolonged exchange between de Valéra and Collins takes the significant, but comically rendered, form of a classroom lesson, with "Dev" as teacher and Collins as cheeky pupil. The ostensible subject is Macchiavelli's *The Prince*, a pragmatic text on how to rule. Here the fantasy element is quickly replaced by a realistic argument between the two men on how the new Ireland needs to be governed. This segment is then reinforced by a dialogue on fair fighting versus incipient terrorism and retaliation, conducted by Collins with Cathal Brugha, another minister in the government of the day.

Throughout *Good Evening, Mr. Collins* there are portents of Michael Collins' impending, premature death. Collins, alone on the stage, recounts a miraculous escape from death he experienced as a child. Talk of death and assassination or the threat of same is constant. Even talk of love with women is truncated and notable for its sense of being tenuous and fleeting. The character of Collins is restless throughout.

As the play continues, the insertion of surreal and fantastic episodes increases. Oddly matched couples sing and dance, lending an incongruous vaudevillian element to the proceedings. Such episodes link well with MacIntyre's representation of a historically accurate, but equally bizarre, incident that features Collins, a wanted man, dining brazenly in the Gresham Hotel among British Army officers. It is Christmas and the British have put a price on his head. Collins, reckless and secure in the knowledge of his anonymity, was noted for such acts of foolhardiness and panache. A later speech by one of the officers emphasizes and attempts to analyze this quality:

IO (Intelligence Officer): . . . curious thing Counter Intelligence—
there was that moment when I knew—and he knew—it was this thing
of shared knowledge in a hot situation—it was even sexy, don't mind
saying that, it really was—something in a phrase he used brushed me—
and there we were, knowing—and next thing I'd let him go . . . Why?
I don't know—you can't answer questions like that . . . In a riddly sort
of way, you're given leave to thus behave . . . By whom?

In Act Two Collins' military side is emphasized from the start as he
appears in his commander-in-chief uniform. Also introduced is Collins' third
lover, the beautiful Hazel Lavery, wife of painter Sir John Lavery. (Lady
Lavery, the American-born Hazel Martyn, continues to appear as the water-
mark that graces Irish bank notes.) This knowing encounter with the accomplished and socially secure Hazel Lavery contrasts with a later scene featuring
Kitty Kiernan once more. Kitty, insecure before going to bed with Collins,
models various lingerie before finding one that suits her mood, and she hopes,
his. This and other exchanges, however, always include extraneous or intermittent stage appearances. Dev plays something of a voyeuristic role, and a
British army Captain, a potential sexual rival, skirts the edges of the drama.
   Collins' distress mounts in his new thankless role as negotiator of a
treaty for Ireland with the British government. He is haunted by the recent
dead, for whose deaths he feels in part responsible. Similarly his torn
allegiances to the women in his life intensify. The innocent Kitty at home
cannot compete at times with his infatuation for Hazel, and Moya becomes
his confidante. The intensity of this part of the play is then narrowly focused
in a long debate with Dev in which the likelihood of Collins' impending
death is discussed with an element of second-sight. The exasperated and
exasperating dialogue with Dev is matched in a farewell scene with Hazel,
in what is Collins' desperate attempt to escape what he has come to view as
a fatal attraction.
   The final scene of Good Evening, Mr. Collins introduces Sir John Lavery,
here "Wee Johnny Lavery" (a reference to Lavery's small stature in reality)
as a cartoon figure of a painter. The scene also recreates briefly a cameo by
George Bernard Shaw (who dined with Collins two days before he died).
That Collins is being turned into myth even before his death is apparent,
but this is of no comfort to Collins himself. The play closes with a mixed
sequence of Collins lying in state, undercut jarringly by comic turns by Dev,
Kitty, and Wee Johnny Lavery.
   Tom MacIntyre's afterword to Good Evening, Mr. Collins discusses both
Collins and Dev as they loomed as figures in his boyhood. The former was

remembered as a mere biography on the family bookshelf; Dev a real and "cheerless tyrant." MacIntyre's illicit relationship with "the Cavalier" dead hero began as an adolescent act of rebellion, with no knowledge of Collins' reputation as a lover. Eventually the combined traits of the man would engage the playwright to undertake this work for the stage, a suitably public art for this public figure of great contradiction and perhaps unrealized potential.

Good Evening, Mr. Collins, perhaps more than MacIntyre's other dramas, is typified by fellow playwright Frank McGuinness thus:

> Behind all the diversity of MacIntyre's writing lies a terrific sense of play, an imaginative disturbance, and a darkly creative obsession with Ireland's past, . . .[15]

Eugene McCabe, who was born in Glasgow of Irish parents in 1930 and took over his family farm in the 1960s, has written novels, television plays, short stories, and stories for children. In his work, McCabe frequently favors historical subjects. His *Gale Day* (1979) is a play based on the life of 1916 patriot Patrick Pearse, his play *Pull Down a Horseman* focuses on the preliminaries to the 1916 rising, and in particular on the role of socialist James Connolly; and his recent novel *Death and Nightingales* (1992) is set in the political world of Parnellism. McCabe also assisted in the film scripting of Thomas Flanagan's sweeping historical novel, *The Year of the French*, which depicts the French invasion of Killala in Co. Mayo in 1798.

Although McCabe has written or collaborated on much dramatic work, his major achievement for the stage was *The King of the Castle* (1964), which opened at the Dublin Theatre Festival of that year. The play tells the story of Scober McAdam, a character who would not subscribe to the tenets of contemporary postcolonial critical theory—that the colonized are victims of a defeatingly self-perpetuating system, unable to break from expected modes of imposed behavior. Instead Scober McAdam is a financial and agricultural success, but a man who is loathed and jeered at by all the local men. McAdam claims it is jealousy of his wealth and plenty that prompts this ill-will, but fears the cause is his lack of an heir by his young wife, Tressa. Indeed, his lack of a son provokes much sneering, but his perceived lack of common humanity and single-minded greed has more to do with his ostracization than anything else. It is Scober's work ethic, viewed as puritanical and an indictment of his neighbors, that has alienated him from his community, and, we are led to conclude, from his countrymen. But because the role of father and the relationship to his sons serves as overriding metaphor for what being an Irishman means in the play, the focus of the male neighbors and of the play becomes and remains Scober's inability to father a son.

The presence in the play of the itinerant, bachelor thresher Matt Lynch introduces the device of surrogate father, daringly and literally portrayed. Lynch's function as surrogate in *King of the Castle* is not at all metaphorical; this is not just another man meant to help lead a male child to adulthood. Rather, Lynch's function, as Scober comes to construe it, is literally to provide a son, by impregnating Tressa. The character of Lynch is acutely uncomfortable with the genetic, moral, and religious implications of this plan. For her part, Tressa, the conduit for this experiment, remains ignorant of the scheme for most of the play. In the end, however, Lynch and Tressa make love as though fated to do so. Both have a keen sense of the way in which they and Scober are defying tradition—or tribal practice. All are infected by participation in a taboo, and by the hypocrisy of Scober's scheme:

> Tressa: To think I'd . . . have a bastard with your name tagged on, and
> you watch me grow and not pretend. . . .

Tressa McAdam recoils in shock and anger at the outrage that her husband planned to have committed upon her. Interestingly enough, however, illegitimacy, and its concomitant lack of the right to inheritance, is never mentioned in the play. Neither, of course, is the possibility that Tressa McAdam might actually conceive a daughter!

McCabe's *King of the Castle* is not merely a play about a man's fundamental urge to reproduce himself, and to have a son to inherit and work the land he has spent his life doggedly subduing. It is a play that is a consistently backhanded indictment of the New Ireland. The omnipresent mechanical thresher, relentlessly noisy and menacing in what is supposed to be an otherwise pastoral landscape, seems to place modernity, with all of its negative implications in and for modern Ireland, literally at center stage. Significantly, however, modernity in this play is also more or less taken for granted and viewed as inevitable. Only two lines in the play refer at all to the only recently abandoned time-consuming method of hand threshing. For McCabe the past is gone, tradition can be broken.

The four local small farmers who come to thresh Scober's grain, two of whose sons actually appear briefly as characters, have none of Scober's drive to defeat the inclement elements, the poor soil, and the other challenges the local farms offer. Yet the small farmers *have* reproduced, and Scober has not. McCabe's message about what it takes to prosper in a modern Ireland is, therefore, disconcerting. The play's ending has husband and wife speaking to themselves, or to each other, in disjointed phrases. The stage directions read "almost incoherently." The play's penultimate line, spoken by Tressa, "We're not yesterday people, Scober," seems cryptic unless viewed in relation to Scober's place in the New Ireland. He doesn't fit in the large house he has bought after it had been abandoned by the local gentry of the past generation. He doesn't belong with the other local farmers of his own generation either. Scober is ambitious, and like the ambitious Michael Carney of *Whistle in the Dark*, he and his type will constantly have their prosperity begrudged them. They will also be literally or figuratively emasculated.

In its cast of characters, stagecraft, and diction, *The King of the Castle* is an inhospitable and unyielding play. The character of Tressa is the only woman in the play (other than an older maid servant, Bridie), and no other woman is even referred to within the context of the play. It is as though none of the men present have wives, mothers, or daughters. Tressa, though thus very vulnerable and isolated, remains a strong and dignified character throughout.

The omnipresence of the threshing machine, already noted, implies a mechanized and traditionally male atmosphere, too. No effect at softening the effect of a working farm is made. This is not the Ireland of idyllic landscape paintings. "Bags, bales, and weighing scales on stage. Stony upland fields beyond" are indicated in McCabe's initial stage directions. The opening dialogue articulates such stage directions in its blunt, utilitarian, unadorned quality:

> Conlon: Well?! Not bad for the mountain!
> Maguire: S'alright.
> Conlon: There's a lot of it.
> Lynch: A good start

Realistic detail and systematic insistence on the deromanticizing of rural Ireland is reinforced throughout *The King of the Castle*. The play's somewhat fanciful title, suggesting a hierarchical but harmless child's game, is the sole light touch amid a weight of realistic gestures, postures, and exchanges that betray the drudgery and fatigue of backbreaking work:

> The rest of the men come offstage, palming sweat from their eyes,
> dusting their caps, and clothes, and moving across the stage slowly.

The King of the Castle, like Tom Murphy's *Whistle in the Dark*, exposes elements in Irish domestic life, especially as it is patriarchally controlled, that are disquieting and potentially destructive. Furthermore both plays implicitly link the patriarchy of Irish society to concepts of Irishness itself. Such connections between masculinity and Irishness continue in much of the work of Frank McGuinness.

Frank McGuinness, who was born in Buncrana in Co. Donegal in 1953, has continued to produce innovative, and at times startling, plays for the Irish stage since 1982. His *Observe the Sons of Ulster Marching Towards the Somme* is arguably one of the finest plays in the modern Irish repertoire. In addition to writing original plays, McGuinness has a flourishing secondary career as an interpreter of the works of other writers for the stage, having written dramatic versions of Ibsen's *Rosmersholm*, *Peer Gynt*, and *A Doll's House*, Chekhov's *Three Sisters*, Garcia Lorca's *Yerma*, and Berthold Brecht's *The Threepenny Opera* and *The Caucasian Chalk Circle*. McGuinness' dramatic work also includes television scripts that have been produced by the BBC. He has also written short stories and publishes poetry.

Considering that McGuinness has for years maintained an academic position, his creative output is prodigious. It is also uneven and highly experimental. *Factory Girls* (1982), written very quickly and first performed at the Peacock, explores the female dynamic during an industrial dispute in a Donegal shirt factory. Dealing as it does primarily with women as characters, and only with working-class characters, *Factory Girls* challenges an emerging playwright's interpretative and dramatic range, and covers territory still under-investigated in modern Irish theatre. With its earthy humor and harsh exchanges, *Factory Girls* readily conveys a world of exploitation and diminished expectations, and a spirited response to these limitations.

Three years later, the Peacock mounted another of McGuinness' plays, one that examines the female mind, but that hovers on the periphery of society, rather than on its lower socioeconomic rungs. A one-woman show, *Baglady* (1985), is in fact a monologue that exhibits all the paranoia, isolation, and pain of a woman who once was an integrated member of a society that has now discarded her. The baglady's disjointed narrative and prophetic ramblings include pieces of her family biography, which show a Yeatsian influence on the playwright (especially from Yeats' later plays such as *Purgatory*), as the baglady reveals a personal history of violence and incestuous abuse.

In *Observe the Sons of Ulster Marching Towards the Somme* (1985) McGuinness shifts to the all-male world of war—here specifically that of World War I, a war notorious for having largely killed off an entire generation of young men in Britain, including many in Ireland, north and south.

Observe the Sons of Ulster Marching Towards the Somme is a powerful and dynamic text in today's Irish dramatic canon. It examines the Unionist mind-set in Northern Ireland, although written from McGuinness' external perspective as a Donegal Catholic. The play's inarguable achievement is cast on a considerably higher, and more lasting, level than the sectarian. Frank McGuinness sets his play in a time when Unionists' pride in their unassailable Britishness was high, and the degree to which that pride would be exploited in the future was beginning to become apparent. McGuinness' introduction of homosexual characters emphasizes, as it does in so many of his plays, the fundamental human need for love. Thus McGuinness blurs conventional moral issues, especially under the extreme and horrific conditions of trench warfare.

The play, which has received much critical attention since its appearance in 1985, has been variously described as raising "unsettling questions about the extent to which Catholic nationalism has appropriated the concept of 'Irishness' in this century;"[16] and as challenging "Loyalist and Republican sentiment, north and south of the border."[17]

The dramatis personae of *Observe the Sons of Ulster* consists of nine characters who play eight men. Kenneth Pyper, the only soldier in the cast who survives the Battle of the Somme, is portrayed twice—both as an old man who narrates the beginning and end of the play, and as a young officer, who is part of the action of the play. Pyper is at first isolated among the men by his class. This isolation is then reinforced by McGuinness' pairing six of the other seven characters in boyhood friendships, or organizational and hometown ties. Two are from the Belfast shipyards, two are from Coleraine on the northern coast; the final pair forms of necessity—the clergyman Roulston from Co. Tyrone and young Crawford from Derry, whom he defends. Pyper, however, will eventually find his bond with the final character, David Craig, from Enniskillen in Co. Fermanagh.

The play is constructed in four parts. The first, very short, is called "Remembrance;" the others, "Initiation," "Pairing," and "Bonding." Most of its speeches are very short, placing heavy emphasis on dialogic and argumentative interaction. Only toward the play's end do the soldiers' speeches become longer, more poetic, and more reflective. Here, the ironic conjunctions of Ulster's sectarian history are made apparent. The Battle of the Somme, in which all but one of these men died , began on July 1, 1916, the anniversary of the Battle of the Boyne in 1690, a decisive and historic victory that guaranteed Protestant sovereignty for Britain in Ireland thereafter.[18]

The play opens with the elderly Pyper besieged by memories, many of them unwelcome. His "ghosts" eventually materialize on stage. The short introductory segment of the play ends, as the entire play will end, with the invitation or command to "dance," here urged by the Older Pyper on to the Younger Pyper.

When the audience first sees the soldiers in the 1916 time frame, it is apparent that Young Kenneth Pyper is frivolous, philosophical, and frightened. The Coleraine pair, Moore and Millan, whose personal histories are intimately intertwined, spar and bicker, but they are as close as brothers. David Craig, who is originally challenged in a discomfiting way by Pyper, is an affable man who ignores the latter's excesses and wild conversational eccentricities, and fits in well with the other pairs.

The arrival of Roulston intensifies the coincidence level and also reinforces the idea of Ulster, Protestant Ulster in particular, as a small, tightly knit, provincial place. Roulston has gone to school with Pyper and has preached in Craig's church in the past. That Roulston has also given up the cloth is significant in terms of McGuinness' plot, but his reason for this decision will not be revealed for some time. In addition, all but Pyper admit to belonging to a paramilitary organization under the guidance of Sir Edward Carson, and to their hatred and fear of Catholicism.[19] Once this fear and bigotry is introduced, however, the playwright exposes its absurdity through the telling of Pyper's wild tale that feeds on a bizarre superstition. Pyper's reports of marrying, killing, and eating his Catholic bride, who was also a whore, is total fantasy. Thematically his tale serves, however, to reinforce the androgynous or hermaphroditic, and also the homosexual references with which the play is riddled. Some Protestants even believed that Catholic women, particularly nuns, concealed a third leg which was an obvious phallic substitute. Such superstition always suggests a power base that is easily threatened.

The level of intensity in *Observe the Sons of Ulster* is raised considerably with the arrival of Anderson and McIlwaine, whose accents and volume announce their origins as Belfastmen. Their arrival also signals another fracas in that they "mistake" young Crawford for a Catholic. The "Initiation" section of the play ends, appropriately enough, when Pyper, who has indirectly defended Crawford, exhibits a self-inflicted ritualized wound to his hand. The wound becomes symbolic of the "Red Hand" of Ulster, the symbol that adorns the Ulster flag.

In "Pairings," part of the action of the play moves to Boa Island in Lough Erne in Ulster. The island is near Craig's hometown of Enniskillen, where some of the men are on leave. It is also the site of prehistoric stone carvings and a Protestant church. Crawford and Roulston are in the church, where the former issues the latter with a challenge intended to test his faith. Simultaneously, Millen and Moore are on the brink of a rope bridge at

Carrick-a-rede along the Co. Antrim coast. Here Moore, suffering from acrophobia, is issued another challenge, equally well-intentioned, by Millen. Moore, who has been severely traumatized by the war, is goaded by Millen to strengthen his resolve to re-enter the violence. In the meantime, the Belfast pair, Anderson and McIlwaine, have returned home to have an ersatz Twelfth of July celebration, although they have missed the anniversary date of the Battle of the Boyne.

Once these venues and subjects are established, McGuinness opens up the play rather operatically so that the audience hears eight male voices in conversational counterpoint with four distinct themes or leitmotifs. That between Pyper and Craig highlights the former's failed role as an artist, specifically a sculptor. His career choice was initially strongly influenced by the primitive carvings on Boa Island, to which Craig has brought him. This change of tempo and narrative format alters the cognitive terms used thus far in *Observe the Sons of Ulster* to usher in a return of the dance metaphor. However, dance no longer represents freedom, but a futile, enforced, and culturally conditioned relentless action. The shift in the play's narrative format also permits of revelation. Crawford "confesses" he is the son of a Catholic mother. Pyper reveals his French wife killed herself over him.

The closing section of *Observe the Sons of Ulster* opens with the men awaiting their orders to go "over the top." After singing a hymn to calm themselves, the nervous soldiers play a pick-up soccer match. The game, though, quickly evolves into a reenactment of a seventeenth-century Ulster battle, with men taking the roles of both horses and soldiers, one man carrying another on his shoulders. In this reenactment, however, Craig and Pyper, respectively playing William of Orange and his horse, are symbolically and ahistorically toppled. McGuinness thus foreshadows the doom of his cast of Ulster Protestant characters. This symbolism is then wed to the memories the men have of their respective regional rivers—the Erne, the Lagan, the Foyle, and the Bann. These memories, mostly olfactory, are then joined to the present smell of the River Somme.

As the play reaches its inevitable grim close, Pyper, the outsider, is presented with an Orange sash (indicating membership in a Loyal Orange Order lodge, a Loyalist and anti-Catholic fraternal organization). This precipitates a ritual exchange of sashes among men, a gesture quite profound and moving, as members have a high level of identification with their individual lodges. Thus united, the men, with the exception of Pyper, march to their deaths. Later Pyper, in his younger and older manifestations, conducts a surreal and somber conversation with himself that intones the word "Ulster" and ends with the imperative "dance."

Observe the Sons of Ulster Marching Towards the Somme is a riveting play with powerful insight into the history of a minority in Ireland (though a majority in Northern Ireland). The Loyalist population has seen itself as beleaguered and waning in power, but it is a power they have abused historically. By focusing on a great defeat for Ulster soldiers in this century, dying to defend an Empire that found them expendable, McGuinness illuminates many of the factors plaguing present-day Northern Ireland and its inability to reconcile warring traditions. The playwright's stage directions for lighting and his expressionistic sequences lend menace to the soldiers' posturing. Such techniques also give the lie to their rhetorical flights on the nature of Ulster Protestant might.

Observe the Sons of Ulster Marching Towards the Somme raises questions about Irish identity that do not allow for complacent responses from the audience. As the World War I era's soldiers' speeches resonate, with the diction and the group psychology of Loyalist Northern Ireland so familiar to us now from contemporary media exposure, we become able to access this tradition and weigh it in the balance of Ireland's future.

Plays such as *Factory Girls* and *Baglady* indirectly raise sociopolitical issues that trouble society and condemn some of its members to marginal or precarious lives. McGuinness' talents, however, are perhaps best put to use when he deals directly with historical and political realities. In *Carthaginians* (1988) he constructs an imaginative but realistic environment in which to analyze the events of Bloody Sunday in Derry in 1972.[20] The play's title refers to the Carthage of antiquity and draws parallels to the tale of Dido and Aeneas, told by Virgil in his *Aeneid*.[21] McGuinness' play, which opens with a recording of a haunting aria from Purcell's opera *Dido and Aeneas*, is cast in nine short scenes. Its dramatis personae consists of seven characters, four young men and three young women. The Dido character here is a homosexual man.

Music is an integral part of all McGuinness' drama, but he does not always draw from elevated sources like Purcell. *Carthaginians*, for instance, also features the lyrics from the cartoon program *The Flintstones* and folk lyrics, as did *Factory Girls*, and as will all his plays to follow. In *Carthaginians*, however, musical interludes add to, or emphasize, the disjointed quality of the play's surreal narrative. The three women—Maela, Gretta, and Sarah—plus the men in secondary roles, are camped in a Derry graveyard. They are awaiting a visitation from the dead, who include Maela's daughter. The dead in the play are intended to be on different planes, the dead of Bloody Sunday, and the dead who were cancer victims as a result of nuclear toxicity that affected parts of Ireland and originated at the nuclear power plant at Sellafield on England's western coast. The message, only somewhat veiled, is that overt killing is carried out by members of the British military in Northern Ireland, while quotidian and gradual threats to Irish lives are also made for political and economic reasons that favor British interests.

Each of the male characters—Paul, Seph, Hark, and Dido—seem somehow damaged by the contemporary world. Paul builds a pyramid from garbage, the detritus of modern life, while claiming to be free, unlike the slaves who built the real pyramids. His apocalyptic language, sometimes in the accent of an American evangelical preacher, grates on the sensibility of the others. Seph is mute, or chooses not to communicate verbally. Hark (Johnny Harkin) has done time in jail. Dido claims the dubious patriotic intention of seducing and/or corrupting every British soldier in Northern Ireland.

Carthaginians is a play that is fundamentally static, expectant, and tentative. McGuinness uses the venerable dramatic trope of having his characters, condemned to wait until revelation and redemption occur, engage in pursuits long associated with the ways human beings pass the time while the gods decide their fates—Maela knits, Hark plays chess.

In Scene Four *Carthaginians* moves to another plane with the enactment of a play within a play. Although this is another very traditional device, it is one used most untraditionally by McGuinness. *The Burning Balaclava* has been written by Dido; and he assigns male parts in his play to the three women and female roles to the men. Dido, the homosexual, has significantly chosen both a male *and* a female role for himself. The play spoofs such iconographic roles as the grieving mother, as represented by O'Casey's Juno, and star-crossed lovers like Maria and Tony in *West Side Story*. The play, an ironic interlude, is cathartic for all. For Seph it has the dramatic effect of releasing him from his mute state, which the audience learns is the result of his being a traumatized informer.

Throughout *Carthaginians* a modernized form of a traditional riddle sequence recurs. Dido and Maela are part of a local pub quiz team, a form of entertainment in Britain and parts of Ireland. In Scene Six this extends to all the characters, who answer trivia questions in teams. This means of exposition of major and minor themes in the play also gives a fast-paced rhythm to the dialogue in places, and helps to draw closer parallels to the beleaguered cities of Carthage and Derry, past and present.

As *Carthaginians* draws to a close McGuinness focuses more on Bloody Sunday and the recounting of realistic details of the tragedy. In Scene Eight Paul recites the names of the dead, and emphasizes their youth (all the dead were men, all but one were under 30 years old). The play closes with Dido's monologue, which affirms the survival of Derry and its inhabitants, while urging the others to be careful in their future lives.

Carthaginians is a play that deals in repressed and remembered violence but contains little overt violence itself. The redemption sought by union with the rising of the dead is never achieved by the living characters. Instead the play closes salvifically with tacit hope for the future of a city with a stoic history of suffering. However, *Carthaginians* is a play which rejects a simple polarized explanation for Ireland's past and its hopes for the future. Either/ or assertions are rejected by McGuinness in favor of his subtle use of the Dido story to "reflect the rainbow," to engage "problematics of gender and sexual orientation" as they can apply to past history and current politics.[22]

Frank McGuinness' most recent major success for the stage is *Someone Who'll Watch Over Me*, which has played since its premiere in London in 1992 in Dublin and on Broadway. The New York cast included both Stephen Rea and Alec McCowen from the original cast, and James McDaniel, familiar to North American audiences from television's *NYPD Blue*. The play is dedicated, in the Irish language, to Brian Keenan. A journalist from Northern Ireland, Keenan was one of several Westerners taken hostage in Beirut in 1985 and held for several years. *Someone Who'll Watch Over Me* is constructed in a prologue and nine scenes, and takes place entirely in one venue—a prison cell. The cast includes Edward, an Irish journalist; Adam, an American psychiatrist; and Michael, an English professor of medieval literature. As the play opens, Edward and Adam are cell mates. They are joined in Scene Two by Michael. By Scene Six, however, Adam has been executed by the terrorists, and Edward and Michael together hold the stage alone for the remainder of the play. Action and movement are at all times in this play severely limited, as the men are chained to the wall with only a few feet of chain to permit limited movement (for instance, they can do push-ups). The enforced stasis places great emphasis on the power of McGuinness' words and the vocal delivery and range of the actors. Also, because the play consists mainly of quick, sharp dialogue, occasionally relieved by poetic monologue, excellent timing is required. The portraying of interpersonal tension in a confined space and circumstance compensates for the lack of physical expansiveness.

Each of the three men is established quickly as a distinct personality and character type, and each conforms largely to preconceived notions of stereotyped national identity. The American is a strong, no-nonsense, disciplined man with seemingly little complexity. Adam insists the world is not a mystery. Edward, the Irishman, who lives in Dublin although a native of Northern Ireland, is sardonic, irreverent, witty, and poetic. For Edward the world is a mystery to which he can at times respond by poking fun. Michael, older than the other two, is a recent widower who has also lost his beloved teaching post, and had been living with his mother. His literary training can at times illuminate his understanding of the mysteries the world offers. Each man is also emphatically portrayed by McGuinness as being quite conventionally patriotic in the normative mode of his country. Adam's patriotism is aggressive and convinced; Edward's is defensive and keenly aware of historical domination; Michael's is cognizant of past imperial preeminence.

Although each man is separated from the other by his individual history and his present chained state, what they share is a common language through which they make articulate attempts to bond. The emphasis on shared language is made most pressing in the opening of Scene Two, when the newly arrived Michael, still asleep, has joined Adam and Edward:

> Edward: A bit of new company would liven the place up. I hope he speaks English.
>
> . . .
>
> Edward: Why are the Irish so religious?
> Adam: Why?
> Edward: I've asked the question.
> Adam: I suppose because they're always thanking God.
> Edward: What for?
> Adam: That they're not Belgian.
> Edward: I think your man looks a bit Belgian. . . . It would be rough for him if he couldn't speak English.

After the three men are well established as characters, they use their shared language to while away the time in captivity, and allay their fears by narrating stories. In *Someone Who'll Watch Over Me* this conceit begins early, with Edward's narrating a classic BBC radio program, *Desert Island Discs*, in which celebrities are asked which recording they would choose to take with them to another kind of imagined captivity. The process continues, as the Bible and the Koran have been left in the cell, and the inmates read the "stories" found in both seminal religious texts. In a similar vein, Edward begins to recreate movies in his mind, narrating the plots in the various artistic modes of well-known directors—Alfred Hitchcock, Sam Peckinpah, and Richard Attenborough.[23] After these imagined stories, the real stories of the men's lives emerge quite naturally, and each man feels the need to reveal some of the weaknesses and failures in his life. Adam's parents, in attempting to do good on a large scale, have ignored their son's needs; Michael's wife died in a car crash and he has been unable to write since. Edward "writes" a letter to his wife, Michael to his mother, Adam to his parents.

Scene Five includes Michael's relating a "story" central to our final understanding of *Someone Who'll Watch Over Me*. It is the story of "Sir Orfeo," which relates the Orpheus myth, but with a medieval happy ending in which Sir Orfeo is able to lead his wife back from death. Michael's insistence on the power of medieval faith sustains him and the others through their ordeal.

After the death of Adam the atmosphere of McGuinness' play hardens and becomes more somber. To compensate for this drain on the emotions of the two remaining characters and the audience, the play at times becomes more riotously funny. Michael, trying to vie in spiritedness with Edward's narrations of the "stories" of great horse races or football matches, given play-by-play with great enthusiasm, narrates the 1977 Wimbledon Ladies' Final tennis match. Edward enters into the fantasy so wholeheartedly that he assumes, at the end, the incongruous role of the Queen of England, handing out the prize at the end of the match.

Scene Eight, the penultimate, and most moving, section of *Someone Who'll Watch Over Me*, is set on Christmas Day. In celebration Michael and Edward sing Christmas carols. Most poignantly, each man relates stories of his father—Michael's a shell-shocked veteran of World War I, Edward's dying slowly in Ireland. In Michael's tale he includes another, a legacy from his damaged father, who remarked upon the seemingly effeminate habit of Spartan warriors combing each other's hair before battle. In a final flight of fancy the two prisoners, both nondrivers, imagine an escape from Lebanon via the unlikely means of a Walt Disney flying car that carries them first to England and then to Ireland. The catharsis that follows succeeds in breaking Edward's spirit for the first time. When the final scene begins, the audience is both relieved and saddened to learn that he is being released. Edward's departure will leave the quiet, brave Michael alone. In a final gesture of solidarity among warriors Edward begins to comb Michael's hair. The then solitary Michael recites "The Wanderer" in Middle English to console himself.

Someone Who'll Watch Over Me is not constructed, as it could have been, as an overtly political play. Instead McGuinness keeps as its true focus an examination of the human spirit. The men, though at times vulgar or silly, exhibit courage and faith equal to their capricious fates. The playwright thus diffuses or invalidates blame. The dilemma of the captives is that of modern man. Each has been raised in a religious tradition—Adam in the American fundamentalist church, Edward an Irish Catholic, and Michael in the Church of England (Episcopalian). Each captive has, however, somehow escaped or circumvented his religious origins to some degree. Adam's new creed is psychiatric medicine, long viewed as a postmodern religious substitute.

Edward professes journalism and serves the new god of the masses—the media. Michael clings to his tradition in the shadowy forms of his aged mother and memories of Peterborough Cathedral. Placed in a starkly realistic postmodern landscape, the comforts of traditional religious belief, though they reappear intermittently in hymns and prayers, offer insufficient true solace. A faith in themselves and in mankind must carry the men through their ordeal.

Frank McGuinness' drama targets the stress points of modern life. His characters are stripped of homes, intact families, nations, and the distractions of creature comforts. Whether living on the economic margins like Baglady, plunged into battle like his World War I soldiers, or soldiers in the post-modern world of international terrorism, his characters rise to heights of personal valor that the playwright urges us to remember we too possess.

Stewart Parker (1941–1988) is the only author represented in this volume who is no longer alive. However, Parker's premature death of cancer at the age of 47 and his unique voice in contemporary Irish theatre combine to insist upon his inclusion. Born in Belfast, where he was also educated, Parker has left a legacy of poetry and radio, television, and stage plays that are notable for their specifically musical and more broadly metatheatrical content. Parker's niece, Lynne Parker, now a noteworthy director and the cofounder of the Rough Magic Company, has done much to keep his reputation as a dramatist alive.

Parker's first major effort for the stage, *Spokesong*, was the talk of the Dublin Theatre Festival in 1975, and, since his death, has been revived in New York and in New Haven. *Spokesong*, more in the nature of musical comedy, or operetta, deals with the incongruously grim subject of the Northern Ireland crisis of recent decades. Its original score was composed by Jimmy Kennedy, a Belfast songwriter known for popular songs of the fifties. In the play, Parker introduces a mechanism he will rely on in his later play *Pentecost*—the presence of "ghosts" on stage.

Spokesong uses the bicycle as central metaphor. Frank, the play's main character, runs a bicycle shop opened in the 1890s by his grandparents in the wake of the invention of the pneumatic tire by fellow Belfastman Alfred Dunlop. This somewhat surreal and significantly circular metaphor is apt in a play that examines the lack of continuity in a city that has more or less blown up its past. The play relies heavily on visualized metaphor, as though compensating for the visual absence of missing buildings occasioned by sectarian violence in the city.

The action of the play parallels the courtship of Frank's grandparents, Francis and Kitty, a red-haired beauty and "new woman" of her era, with that of Frank and Daisy in the present of the play. The Shavian dialogue in which Francis and Kitty engage is typical of its period, with details of Oscar Wilde's trial and Frank's enlisting in the bicycle corps in World War I over Kitty's pacifist objections. They marry against her father's wishes and will eventually raise their two orphaned grandsons, Frank and his adopted brother Julian, who is now living in London. To keep their business' future assured, they bequeath its building to Julian but the business itself to Frank.

Frank cherishes fond, but sentimentalized, memories of Francis and Kitty, which Julian, who has rejected his upbringing, does his best to dispel. Frank's love of Belfast and its past prevails, however, and overrides Julian's wish to sell the building that houses his brother's meager livelihood. Similarly, Frank overcomes Daisy's restlessness and despair of Belfast's perilous state to have her stay, marry him, and agree to his buying the shop. Their final decision is an affirmation, a belief in humanity.

In his *Dramatis Personae*, a lecture delivered in Queen's University in 1986, Parker discussed the task of being a Northern Irish playwright:

> Writing about and from within this particular place and time is an enterprise full of traps and snares. The raw material of drama is over-abundant here, easy pickings. Domestic bickering, street wit, tension in the shadows, patrolling soldiers, a fight, an explosion, a shot, a tragic death: another Ulster play written. What statement has been made? That the situation is grim, that Catholics and Protestants hate each other, that it's all shocking and terribly sad, but that the human spirit is remarkably resilient to all that.[24]

Spokesong is a metatheatrical experience that engages in ingenious stage crafting, strengthened by the use of the symbol. It is a lighthearted approach to a serious subject that does not trivialize, but that leaves the audience to search for answers to the many questions it raises.

Parker's historically based trilogy of plays consists of *Northern Star* (1984), *Heavenly Bodies* (1986), and *Pentecost* (1987). *Northern Star* is set during the 1798 rebellion and has as its central character Belfastman Henry Joy McCracken, an historical figure hanged for insurgent activities and who has become folkloric in his native city. *Northern Star* was the name of the newspaper that published the views of the Ulster United Irishmen. The group, to which McCracken belonged, sought universal suffrage, but became radicalized in the wake of the French Revolution.

Heavenly Bodies moves Parker forward into the nineteenth century, with a play about Dion Boucicault, a fabulously successful Irish playwright and theatre manager of his day. The play is initially set in 1890 in New York, where Boucicault lived in later life, and where he died. It retells in imaginative and fragmented flashback the story of his controversial career. Boucicault's attraction for Parker is divulged in a line spoken by Boucicault in *Heavenly Bodies* when he is accused of lying about his past:

> I could never presume to compete with my own life for sheer inventiveness.

Pentecost, the final part of Parker's Northern Irish trilogy, was recently revived in 1996 at Dublin's Andrew's Lane Theatre, with direction by Lynne Parker, nearly a decade after its first production by Field Day in Derry. Unlike the other two plays of the trilogy, *Pentecost* centers on an historical event, not a single figure.

The timing of the play is the Ulster Workers' Council "strike" of 1974, which nearly ground the North to a halt.[25] Although this timing suggests violence, change, threats to the social order, and spiraling chaos, the setting of the play counterbalances this tendency by confining it to a cramped and condemned terraced house—the last on its street—in central Belfast. Here four young adults with ambiguous and shifting personal ties find themselves prisoners while mayhem prevails in the outside world. Marian, who wants to buy the house, despite its location and other disadvantages, used to be married to Lenny, who actually has inherited the house from his aunt. Lenny's friend Peter has returned home from Birmingham and is instantly rather sorry he has. Marian's old school friend Ruth has finally left her abusive husband, an RUC (Royal Ulster Constabulary) man. A fifth character, operating on a different plane from the others, is Lily Mathews, the ghost of the recently deceased former tenant of the house.

The testy relationship that develops between the strict and overbearing ghost of the Protestant Lily and the feisty modern Catholic Marian is the most fully articulated in the play. Lily's ghost feels reviled by Marian's presence, and particularly by Marian's interference with Lily's effects, which Marian hopes to have enshrined in a sort of urban folk museum. The spirit of Lily is also critical of Marian's having left her husband and had an abortion. Lily's fundamentalist rectitude, however, is eventually undermined and exposed in the play by revelations of her own marital infidelity.

Peter and Ruth, the two Protestant characters, emerge at ideological poles by play's end. Peter, who has traveled widely, has left much that is specifically "Ulster" behind him. Ruth identifies with Unionist efforts to save or to restore the past, however dubiously recalled. The fact that the day on which the play ends is Pentecost is only disclosed near its completion, with Catholic and Protestant characters sharing in the spirit of the occasion. Each narrates a story, perhaps the modern equivalent of the demonstration of the gift of tongues experienced by Christ's apostles as they gathered on the first Pentecost. Parker himself has described the atmosphere as the quartet unfold their tales as one of "heightened realism. This seemed most appropriate for my own generation, finally making its own scruffy way onto the stage of history. . . ." [26]

Pentecost is, finally, a redemptive play. The redemption is achieved, however, not through conventional religious experience, which Parker finds divisive in Ulster life, but in shared human experience. Parker's image of Pentecostal fire, the traditional Christian symbol associated with the feast liturgically, is life-affirming and inspirational. Pentecostal fire defeats the destructive presence of natural fire, the bomb and the blazes of sectarian violence that have rampaged through Ulster's recent past.

Anne Devlin, another Belfast playwright, bears the same name as a famous revolutionary figure from Ireland's past. (The confidant of Robert Emmet, the earlier Anne Devlin was imprisoned in the wake of Emmet's 1803 rising.) The present-day Anne Devlin is concerned, dramatically, in portraying women's contribution to revolutionary situations in contemporary Ulster, an aspect frequently ignored or cast in a different light.

Devlin's imaginative world comprises both the middle and working classes and the points at which they touch. However, that these worlds are not alike is emphasized throughout her corpus. Middle-class women theorize about the Ulster Troubles and can be affected by its violence, but it is working class women who live in its midst and whose lives are informed by violence on a daily basis.

The Long March, a 1994 BBC television play, concerns Helen, a lawyer, but an artist manqué. Her political background is pacifist, yet she takes a Republican lover. Instances of such split or confused identity in Devlin's young women recur. In *A Woman Calling*, broadcast by the BBC in the same year, the playwright moves to the affluent Co. Down coast, but her central figure in the play is Laura, the working-class friend of the daughter of the house, Sheelagh. Laura and Sheelagh are fourteen when the play opens, and only just becoming sexually aware. As a result, when Laura overhears a sexually related murder in the house, she carries this psychological fear into her own adulthood and her radicalized student days. Her later therapy with an analyst, who may or may not be the murderer from years earlier, offers

an alternate interpretation of the event which changed her life. This continued but confusing duality is offered by Devlin, without closure, as emblematic of Northern Irish life. Her insistence that there *are* at least two valid
stories to consider challenges audiences to expand their interpretations of
history, both recent and remote.

Devlin's work for the stage began a decade earlier than her radio and
television work, in 1985, with productions outside Northern Ireland, in
Liverpool and London venues intended for innovative drama by emerging
playwrights. *Ourselves Alone* is the English translation of the words Sinn
Féin, the name of the political wing of the IRA. Set mostly in Andersons-
town in West Belfast, Devlin's play features a trio of women, sisters Frieda
and Josie, and their friend, Donna, the common-law wife of their brother,
Liam. The time of the play is one of the most politically riven in Belfast's
recent history, in the wake of "the Dirty Protest" and the hunger strike that
resulted in several Republican prisoners' deaths in Long Kesh prison. It
was a protest that sought political rather than criminal status for such
prisoners.

Josie is a highly politicized activist who is the mistress of the married
head of the Provisional IRA. But by play's end, Josie is pregnant with an
Englishman's child, a man who has deceived and betrayed her and infiltrated
her cause. Frieda, like Josie, attempts an exogamous (outside the tribe)
relationship with a Protestant member of the Socialist Workers' Party, while
Donna awaits Liam's safe return from prison. All three women are dependent
upon, and in a sense quite subservient to, the men in their lives, and to the
ideologies to which the men subscribe. Flashes of independent thought are
glimpsed, however, if only through the women's subconscious desires. Josie,
for instance, relates this liberating daydream to the impressed Donna:

> Josie: Sometimes when we make love I pretend I'm somebody else.
> Donna: Who?
> Josie: Not someone I know. Someone I make up—from another cen-
> tury. Sometimes I'm not even a woman. Sometimes I'm a man—his
> warrior lover. Fighting side by side to the death. Sometimes we're not
> even on the same side.

This illuminating passage exhibits not only a sense of history, but a form of
female empowerment achieved by assuming a male persona. It also progresses to an independent level of politicization.

Frieda, the apolitical sister, suffers from an identity crisis, too, which
she expresses more conventionally, but in a similarly disempowered vein:

When did I ever get the chance to be myself? My father was interned before I was born. My brother's in the Kesh for bank robbery. You mention the name McCoy in this neighbourhood, people start walking away from you backwards.

Here, again, male political identity determines female social roles, in what Devlin suggests can be an unbreakable pattern. Graphic evidence of such female victimization by male ideology is present in the references to Frieda and Josie's Aunt Cora, who as an 18-year-old girl stored ammunition for her father and lost both her hands in a resultant explosion.

The tension in *Ourselves Alone* is a familiar one, between men whose first commitment is to country and politics, and women who want personal commitment, the love between a man and a woman. Devlin informs this play, as she does her other works, with a sympathetic view of political ideology and its exigencies. Thematically, however, she supports the primary conviction of her female characters. In this she affirms the work of Stewart Parker and other Northern Irish dramatists who seek to go beyond sectarian and ideological divisions to a wholeness dictated by human need. Although in *Ourselves Alone* all three women are left alone, their predicaments are somewhat different. In each case, though, they have begun to make decisions and remain constant in their commitment, no longer to individual men who have let them down, but to themselves and to the power of human love.

Marie Jones (b. 1951) began writing plays in the early eighties and has also written numerous television and radio scripts. She launched her career by founding the Belfast theatre cooperative, Charabanc, with four other women. Her playwriting is now an individual rather than a collective effort.

A Night in November, which was staged by Dubbeljoint in 1994 as part of the West Belfast Festival, has been described in the *London Sunday Times* as "a seriously funny play." This seeming contradiction is more in the nature of complex paradox, however, and Jones is able in her one-man play, to sustain a high degree of humor that never demeans the genuine gravity of its subject.

Jones, by choosing to fix her play in the traditionally male world of the World Cup football (soccer) final, has taken a calculated risk as a female dramatist. By exploring a nearly all-male environment, noted for condoning aggression and inculcating the sort of tribal loyalty that mimics the worst of sectarian beliefs, Jones opens up for scrutiny bigotry in its most base manifestations. Like so many other Northern Irish writers, Jones also addresses the issue of class, which complicates, and in a sense informs, sectarianism there.

Kenneth McCallister, a Protestant, is a civil servant with an upwardly mobile wife, a violently bigoted father-in-law, and irritating children. He attends a World Cup qualifying match in which the Republic of Ireland triumphs over Northern Ireland to secure a place in the finals. Kenneth is revulsed at the reaction of the Protestant fans, and by his own fear as he sings sectarian songs in order to avoid violence himself. In reaction, he undertakes a brave journey to New York to cheer on the Republic's team. This volte-face occurs only after the audience has been permitted glimpses of Kenneth's dissatisfaction with his life, and that of his class and creed. Through Jones' artful intermingling of interior and exterior monologue the audience learns Kenneth's own views, especially of a Catholic coworker, Jerry:

I cracked. . . .

Listen you stupid empty-headed bitch, I don't want Jerry to be livid, do you know that, I don't want Jerry to feel like shit, I don't want him to go home to his wife and kids knowing that I am out to get him for no other reason than he is a Catholic . . . isn't that pathetic . . . but you don't want your husband to be pathetic . . . you want your husband to be a man and stand by his beliefs like your disgusting father. . . .

But I didn't . . . I said nothing because there are thousands of Debrahs married to thousands of Kenneths and I hadn't the balls to be the Kenneth that takes on the Debrah . . . how could I blame her, how could I when I didn't even know what I believed myself. . . .

A Night in November is constructed in two acts. After an illuminating and liberating visit to Jerry's home in Act Two, Kenneth returns temporarily to his ordered and highly predictable life. Here guilt and a newly raised consciousness, which won't tolerate bigotry and smugness, cause Kenneth to expose the Protestant middle class, to which he belongs, to these charges. Finally, ostracized from his neighbors and alienated from his wife, he flees to New York and the frenetic bonhomie of the Cup final and a newly won sense of Irish identity.

A Night in November is something of a fable, offering a fairy-tale world of complete transformation where evil and human limitation do not threaten a promising future. As such it is a positive effort by playwright Jones, and (like all fairy tales) not one that is as simplistic as it may first seem. Kenneth's painful self-realization, and the courage needed to make an effective break with all with which he is familiar, are portrayed realistically and sympathet-ically, as is the uncomprehending reaction of his wife and friends. However, Jones' starkly contrasting stereotypical Protestant and Catholic characters are, finally, just that. With the sole exception of Kenneth and one minor character encountered briefly in New York at the play's end, all her charac-ters are either orderly, conventional, unimaginative, and hide-bound Prot-estants, or carefree, feckless, and fun-loving Catholics. Her ending, which emphasizes full acceptance of the former by the latter, is a fond hope, but it is also more an imaginative projection than it is in any sense realistic.

Christina Reid, born in Belfast in 1942, now lives in London. In addition to her stage plays of the eighties, including *Tea in a China Cup* (1983), *Joyriders* (1986), and *The Belle of Belfast City* (1989), Reid has written numerous radio plays, plays for television, and adaptations of the work of other creative writers for the stage and for other media. She is now writing a screenplay based on *Joyriders* and *Clowns* (1996), its sequel.

Born into Belfast's Protestant working class, Reid writes plays that concentrate on female characters from that background. Her plays "daringly interrogate issues of nationalism and colonialism."[27] *Joyriders* concerns the inadequacy of training programs and other government- sponsored mea-sures to cope with the extent of damage done to young people as a result of Northern Ireland's Troubles. It is a play that deals squarely with sectarianism and its consequences. *Joyriders* is also openly intertextual with the work of Sean O'Casey, and a scene from his *Shadow of a Gunman* is voiced over at the opening of Reid's own play. An ensemble play for young actors, *Joyriders* features a quartet of Belfast teens—Sandra, Arthur, Maureen, and Tommy, and their social worker, Kate. Sandra and Maureen are polarly described as "cynical" and "dreamy" respectively. Maureen is also responsible for a delin-quent 12-year-old brother. The teenage boys are disadvantaged; Arthur is a victim of violence, Tommy hides his mixed-race origins. Kate, separated from her charges by class and education, is committed but frustrated.

Joyriders, in two acts of four scenes each, is constructed of short exchanges of dialogue that exhibit each teenager's view of life. Reid employs their reactions to O'Casey's play, in which random violence claims an innocent female victim, to intensify our perceptions of each teenager. The resonances of O'Casey's stage violence are all too immediate in these young lives. Also, both O'Casey's and Reid's own play, although primarily about political strife, carry a strong economic message. The teenagers are all involved in petty criminal acts that they don't even feel the need to justify, given the manifest inequities of their society. Tommy, the only character who is politicized, is another feature of *Joyriders* that owes a debt to O'Casey—the young ideologue character destined for disappointment.

Joyriders is punctuated by musical or poetic choruses that are either set to popular tunes or chanted like sporting cheers. This interruption of the polemic dialogue of the play provides not only an opportunity for scene changes, but it also enlivens the verbal rhythm of the work. All the lyrics that are sung emphasize the hopelessness of Belfast's inner-city working class, and are caustic in their expression:

> First Voice
> No job, nothing to do
> No money, on the Bru
> Repeat
> Second Voice
> No job after school
> No future that's the rule
> Repeat
> All
> Unemployment. Unemployment.

The contrast provided as Act Two opens is instantly and vividly apparent. To celebrate Arthur's receiving substantial compensation for his injuries, Kate invites the teens to dinner at her very comfortable middle-class home. The young people are amazed that only two people, Kate and her widowed mother, live in such luxurious space. They sample unknown delights, such as champagne and coffee liqueur. Contrasting tempos, emotions, and experiences give pacing to the second act of *Joyriders*. Maureen reveals her pregnancy to Sandra, and narrates a childhood fable of her country grandmother, "cooped up in the flats like a battery hen," who grew a replica of a rainbow of plants on her kitchen windowsill to delight her grandchildren. The chasm between that idyllic moment and the harsh reality of Maureen's present life is starkly presented by Reid. It also presages Maureen's violent, futile death as she attempts to save her brother's life. This tragedy, bloodily and realistically presented, is followed by disjointed snatches of all the songs and anthems heard thus far in the play.

Joyriders closes inconclusively, with Tommy enduring additional surgery on his hands, broken by Catholic paramilitaries as punishment for his thievery. Arthur attempts to propose marriage to Sandra to no avail; and Kate learns after Maureen's autopsy that she was pregnant at the time of her death. The final scene, played out incongruously in an art gallery featuring an exhibit of contemporary Russian paintings, closes *Joyriders* awkwardly. This same inconclusivity and awkwardness, however, reflects the lack of closure that is a feature of the ongoing violence that typifies contemporary inner-city Belfast life. Reid's refusal to offer facile, or even partial, solutions to insurmountable problems is a sign of dramatic integrity in a corpus that does not shy away from such issues.

Billy Roche, a native of Wexford, was born in 1949, and came to writing plays after holding an assortment of jobs. Later, he turned to acting and then novel writing (*Tumbling Down* was published in 1986). *The Wexford Trilogy*, composed of three plays—*A Handful of Stars* (1988), *Poor Beast in the Rain* (1989), and *Belfry* (1991)—is his best-known work to date.

Roche's milieu is very much the same as Friel's Ballybeg in more than one sense. However, Roche, born a generation after Friel, portrays small-town Wexford life with a bleaker emphasis on the prospects it offers, especially to young men. His tone resembles more that of Tom Murphy than Friel, especially with its damning portrayal of petty class distinctions in provincial Ireland. Like Murphy's, Roche's female characters are often strong-minded, but are also exploited and marginalized. Instead of focusing on a male/female dialogue to expose the themes of his plays, Roche favors a polemic between generations. His parent figures, whether successful or not, are generally offstage forces. Men a generation older try, often with little positive result, to mold or protect teenage boys from emerging into manhood, .

Roche's characters, relentlessly working class, are quasi-rural and condemned to their situations. The first play, *A Handful of Stars*, sets the static pace of the trilogy. Although the lives of six men and one woman who appear as characters interact often and at short and predictable intervals over six weeks, the stasis of these connections is oppressive.

The Wexford Trilogy continues with *Poor Beast in the Rain*, which features a central character who could be an older version of the protagonist of *A Handful of Stars*. Danger Doyle returns to Wexford after having run away a decade earlier with another man's wife. A former local rebel, the older Doyle has been chastened by ten years of hard work in England, where he did not enjoy the flamboyant reputation he had at home.

The action of *Poor Beast in the Rain* is limited to a weekend, and features two important elements in small-town Irish life (as did *A Handful of Stars* with its snooker club). In the second part of his trilogy, Roche situates the action in the betting shop (legal in Ireland), and fixes it on the weekend of the All-Ireland hurling championship.[28]

Rumors of the return of Danger Doyle surface early in Act I, giving rise to his old friend Joe's mythologizing reminiscences:

> Joe: . . . We made fellas hop around here me and him I don't mind tellin' yeh. Me and Danger. We were the king pins in this town at the time so we were. Danger and me. Yes, the king pins we were. . . . Did I ever tell yeh about the times we used to break into this place?
> Georgie: Yeah, yeh told me about that alright.
> Joe: We used to break right into that big window there, the pair of us, . . .

Joe's need to rehearse his past glory overrides Georgie's laconic response. Playwright Roche uses this telling mechanism of inferred repetition to underscore the dead-end quality of these lives, along with indicators of the daily tedium of Stephen and Eileen, father and daughter, who run the betting shop.

The distinction between "nice fellas" and "wild boys" surfaces for the second time in *Poor Beast in the Rain*. Although Roche is careful not to portray his minor Wexford rebels in too indulgent terms, it is clear that his sympathies lie with the "wild boys", who affect men and women alike. Jimmy Brady's exploits in *A Handful of Stars*, and Danger Doyle's in this play, affect both men and women. Eileen, motherless since her mother ran away with Doyle, is now being pursued by Georgie, a "wild boy." It is Georgie who introduces again the idea of petty crime via an attempt to find her a birthday gift. Although in Roche's plays authority figures are mostly tangential to the action, and the authority of the Church is strangely absent, the enforced conformity of small-town life produces, even in conformist characters like Eileen, a restless yearning. These "wild boys" are often lionized by being paralleled to popular countercultural heroes like Butch Cassidy and the Sundance Kid and Jack Nicholson.

Act II of *Poor Beast in the Rain*, which takes place after Wexford's victory at the hurling final, turns incongruously sour rather rapidly. Molly, an older woman who works in the betting shop, taunts the returned fans, exposing indiscretions in their pasts. In a similar mood, Georgie taunts Eileen about a dubious incident from her past. Even the reputation of Danger Doyle is deconstructed to no one's gain, leaving a barren reality for all to ponder. Without artificial constructs of sexual bravado and defiance of the system, there is little to sustain this small cast of characters in this small world. The return of Danger Doyle into this chastened atmosphere occasions his likening himself to the Irish mythological hero, Oisín.[29]

Poor Beast in the Rain closes with Eileen's departure with Doyle for England to see her estranged mother. That she is "leaving people behind" links her thematically to Roche's "wild boys." However, in the wake of earlier revelations it seems that Eileen's choice of a new life is a mature decision and will be a relative success.

Belfry is the title and setting of the third part of *The Wexford Trilogy*, another closed world occupied on and off by a cast of five. But here Roche's set is split, allowing for an additional setting in the church vestry.

Belfry represents a dramatic development from the earlier plays in *The Wexford Trilogy* in that its characters are allowed greater scope to analyze their own predicaments through longer and more fluid speeches, which occasionally rise to the poetic without losing immediacy. In addition, Roche's use of direct address to the audience (a device seen in Friel's *The Loves of Cass Maguire*, among other modern Irish plays) to open up the play and to give a poignant resonance to the central character, Artie, is highly effective and well sustained.

Roche's thematic emphasis throughout *The Wexford Trilogy* is that his "wild boys," Artie, Danger Doyle, and Jimmy Brady before him, have escaped. None of Roche's "wild boys" has achieved a notable degree of success, nor great personal happiness; but each in a small, somewhat pathetic way has set himself free and achieved some minor, if dubious, distinction. More important, each of Billy Roche's young, or not-so-young, Wexford rebels has looked at society, as represented in the small world of a Wexford town, in a clear-eyed way, and assessed its shortcomings.

Sebastian Barry began publishing as a very young man, but did not settle upon drama as the genre that would best suit his talents until about a decade ago. In that short time he has produced several plays of distinction, including *The Steward of Christendom*, which seemed destined to enter the repertoire from the day it was first performed.

Barry's imaginative base is autobiographical, but by his own account these plays are more in the nature of arabesques, or perhaps fugues, on autobiographical fragments than they are in any sense historical or genealogical. Working from narrative scraps of stories, vignettes of forebears handed down by members of his family, or from his own experience, Barry takes outstanding imaginative leaps into the dramatic voice. While Barry was a young impoverished writer living in a cottage far away from Dublin, where he grew up, but close to the region from which his family came, the kindness of two elderly bachelor brothers provided him with the idea that sparked *Boss Grady's Boys*. Just the name of a forebear, Fanny Hawke, and the knowledge that she had descended from a displaced Manchester nonconformist sect, occasioned the writing of *Prayers of Sherkin*. A great-grandfather's alliance with the British imperial presence in Dublin Castle triggered what was to become *The Steward of Christendom*.

Barry's work consistently questions definitions of Irishness and demands an inclusivity denied or disparaged in past histories. Often he sets his characters at odds with prevailing belief systems. He then allows them to articulate alternative views that argue for morality, wholeness, and commitment over necessarily incomplete ideologies. Credos can be abandoned, outdated philosophies can fail to maintain our respect, and the place of heroes and authority figures is examined and reexamined.

Barry's language throughout is truly poetic. There is nostalgia, but it is tempered by personal commitment. Moral choice for his characters provides them with opportunities for fierce and poignant articulation. The temptation to rhetoric is avoided, ultimately, as it is less sustaining. The circumstance of his characters is usually strikingly simple, his plots suitably unadorned. What emerges is the emphasis on personal decision making and its consequences, the task of facing into life. The results, though often somber, are also transcendent.

Boss Grady's Boys, first performed at the Abbey's Peacock Theatre in 1988, is a play that is basically a duet for two aging bachelor brothers living on a subsistence farm on the Cork/Kerry border. Four other characters— their father and three of his contemporaries—appear only in a dream sequence card game when they are about the age the brothers are at the time of the play. Slight roles for their mother, as a young woman, and for a young girl of 18 complete the cast.

Mick and Josey are the brothers, driven into years of celibacy and isolation by their manipulative father, "Boss" Grady, now dead. Josey has always been simple (to employ the term that would have been used there and then). Now, in his seventies, Josey is becoming senile, referring at times to their father, a horse, and a much-missed dog as though they were still alive. Mick, his younger and much more competent brother, is alternately short and indulgent with Josey. Mick accepts his brother's limitations, some of which are endearing, but occasionally rails against these limitations. He continues to resent their father's frustratingly inexplicable preference for his flawed son.

Josey, usually a diminutive for a girl's name, introduces an androgynous element into the play. The brothers share their parents' "marriage" bed, and often act and speak like an aged married pair. There is occasional racy and fanciful talk of voluptuous women, fantasy creatures conjured from their past or from the films they have seen only rarely. However, the obviously repressed sexuality of their situation finds an apparent outlet in the jarring presence of the waif-like young girl who is either another fantasy figure or a ghost from the past. The sexual scenes in the play involving the girl are brutal and brutalizing for all concerned, and stand in vivid contrast to the sustained docility of the rest of the drama.

Boss Grady's Boys opens at night and soon displays two dream sequences, first for Mick, then for Josey. Mick's dream, of the card game, presents his father, Mrs. Molloy, Mrs. Swift, and Mr. Regan—neighbors who gathered habitually as each other's only company. The narratives of the dream, reveal the quartet's personal stories and the make-up of the town they live near. Their speeches are disjointed and unlike those in the realistic scenes of the play. Mick's dream also allows for a degree of release from both the sexual and religious oppression that is an obvious limitation in his waking life.

Josey's dream offers a kaleidoscopic version of a staple of father-son bonding, the fishing trip. Like many scenes in Barry's work it is lit in blues and purples that evoke the surrounding mountains and lakes. The dream explains Boss Grady's reasons for favoring Josey, who was capable only of seeing the good in his father, like a perpetual child.

The individual dream sequences are followed by one that requires miming skill from the actors as they tend a horse meant to be real, but not present on stage. Sound completes the desired effect, and is sustained for some time. That the horse is a gelding (a neutered stallion), and is referred to as "she," reinforces the earlier androgynous theme.

Act Two of this two-act play focuses more heavily on the somber reality of the brothers' lives. There has been a sudden death on a nearby farm; the brothers can't dig their own turf anymore and are reliant on neighbors; Josey is incontinent. Mick, we learn belatedly, is a tailor by trade who wanted to emigrate to America. The consequences of decision making, even if not matters of pure choice, gain in poignancy. Mick imagines the American life he might have had, had he not stayed to care for Josey and the farm:

> That I might . . . go to some glittering city with long cars in it. . . . And drink at a distant bar, after work, and go home with a confident step, and put meat on the table in a brown parcel for my wife, who would be old now but pretty with makeup like Mrs. Molloy. To think that the girl I would have met, in some park or in some street, is an old one like myself, and it was someone else she met and kissed, and was nervous talking to, and then grew stronger with. And all these years of seasons and floods, of greenery and streams and mud and whiskey nights, she has cleaned her American home, and looked out at the brisk sunlight without me.

Barry's mix of poetic flight and sad reality captures well imaginative longing made more cruel by the lessening scope of age and infirmity. Mick's poetic articulation of the road not taken is, however, counterbalanced in the play. A parallel fantasy segment features Josey playing an untuned fiddle while four large women cavort in chorus-line fashion with their backs to the audience. The jarring, near surrealist quality of the sequence artfully alters our perception of unrealized possibilities, and approaches a postmodern reading of those whom the New Ireland has left behind.

Boss Grady's Boys moves rapidly to thoughts of mortality. There are remembered conversations with their mother, although she is described as having been "silent" in life. Their father's grotesque death on the doorstep of the cottage is replayed. The play closes with the approach of another of numberless nights together in the marriage bed. This occurs after a significant reference to the sexually ambivalent Josey's imagining himself as being the victim of a sexual attack. In his dream he changes places with the young girl who has been a discordant intermittent presence in his troubled imagination.

Boss Grady's Boys was Sebastian Barry's dramatic attempt to sketch in a life for the pair of brothers whose home he never entered, but whose solicitous care of him caused him to fear for their future and the future of those like them. The play contains a reference to brothers being killed (during police interrogation); but it was inspired in part by a rash of murders of the elderly on remote farms that occurred in Ireland in the 1980s.

Prayers of Sherkin was first performed at the Peacock in November 1990, and like other of Barry's plays, featured his mother in one of the starring roles. (Barry's mother, Joan O'Hara, is an Abbey Theatre actress of considerable distinction; but the playwright claims his sole appearance upon the Abbey stage occurred while his mother was expecting his birth.)

Prayers of Sherkin relies, like *Boss Grady's Boys*, on a prevailing innocence to expose the emotion of the story. Incongruous tales of danger and death, even by misadventure, are repeated in a setting so benign as to suggest their impossibility. We are introduced to the surviving members of three families who settled on Sherkin Island, off the east coast of Co. Cork near Baltimore, to await the New Jerusalem.

The small colony on Sherkin Island consists of the widower John Hawke and his two adult children, Jesse and Fanny, his maiden sister Hannah, and maiden sister-in-law Sarah. Their lives on Sherkin are simple or "plain" in the Quaker sense. Indeed Barry uses "Quakerish" to describe their manner. The Hawke family is reasonably self-sufficient, although they do buy wax from Catholic nuns on the mainland to make candles for all of Baltimore. In addition they raise or forage for much of their own food. Though very different in their nonconformism from both their Protestant and largely Catholic neighbors, the Hawkes are liked and respected locally. They are particularly fond of the local Protestant merchant couple, Meg and Stephen Pearse. The young Meg and older Stephen, who are open and playful in their physical affection for each other, serve as vivid contrast to the Hawkes, all of whom are by necessity celibate. The vital patriarch John misses his wife Charity, who died young. There were no men remaining of the sect to marry Hannah and Sarah who, like Boss Grady's boys, have lived years yoked together, sharing the same chaste bed. As the sect shuns those who marry outside it, it is the fervent hope of the elders that, miraculously, a "brother" from Manchester will appear to marry the comely Fanny. Brother Jesse, described as a scientist because of his fascination with the natural world and astrology, is said to be emotionally and intellectually complete without a partner. In truth he suffers from a mental illness that is kindly overlooked or accommodated by his protective kin. The fate of Fanny, then, becomes the play's sole focus.

The life of the Hawkes, though certainly happy and harmonious, is a rigorous one shorn of many of the world's pleasures and distractions. Sarah chides herself for loving to go to town. She capitulates to the forbidden pleasure of running her hand through a box of colored ribbons, knowing she could only wear a black one, if any. Hannah, Sarah, and Meg hold a detailed and sensuous conversation on the quality of various cloths, as Meg tantaliz-ingly unrolls bolts of the fabric on her counter. So much of the family's sensuality and sexuality has been forbidden by the rules of the sect, or the dearth of members, that the resultant savoring of the remaining pleasures of the senses produces the type of heightened awareness often associated with people who have lost the use of one of their senses. Here the playwright's skill is remarkable. Heavily scented honeysuckle, plentiful on the island, is used over and over. Its heady perfume adorns the graves of the sect's dead. Flowers are carried in abundance by Patrick Kirwin, the unlikely, but successful, outside suitor who will eventually win Fanny's hand. References to exotic places seem to counteract the isolated nature of the islanders' lives. Fanny's prayers in Act One, which include a litany of foreign rivers—the Ganges, the Amazon, and the Orinocco—link with Stephen's strange refer-ence to Africa while in conversation with her father. These in turn link with the folkloric references of Mr. Moore, the ferryman who plies between Baltimore and Sherkin. Moore recounts the practice of sailors leaving on long journeys sending their prayers back to Cape Clear Island, very near to Sherkin, as it is the last piece of land visible in the European world. He recites prayers and songs in the Irish language that link the little island with the big world outside—specifically and exotically with Valparaiso in Chile, a major port of call for nineteenth-century merchant ships.

Prayers of Sherkin, then, provides vivid contrasts that are compelling both to hear and see. Characters savor food, or merely the idea of food; nuns glory in the magnificent aesthetic creation of an Easter candle; John develops an admiring bond with a pig. Fanny and Jesse, like some prelapsarian Eve and Adam, lie in the grass on the unspoiled island amid the sights, sounds, and smells of native flora and fauna. That this idyll is winding toward a conclusion is apparent very nearly from the play's first words. Fanny will leave the island because she must marry and have children. The imperative of the collective good is no longer as compelling as personal fulfillment, and Barry uses a deus ex machina visionary sequence to effect the required decision by Fanny in a manner that is not anathema to her beloved family. The visionary who began their sect three generations earlier becomes a vision himself and appears on the shore to Fanny in the guise of an angel. That this vision may have materialized out of Fanny's desperate need for ordinary sexual experience and a longing for motherhood hangs over the remainder of the play, but is questioned by no one within the play. The play ends poignantly with Sarah, Fanny's antecedent in many ways, and one for whom the thought of leaving her home and kin has always been a tempta-tion, making clear again that they are soulmates. Sarah asks, hypothetically, if Fanny would have taken Sarah along if she'd asked. Assured that Fanny would have done so, Sarah returns to "her own path" outside the house. Sarah, who is in fact now going blind, stands symbolically for what Fanny can expect if she stays on Sherkin. So as Fanny leaves to join Patrick Kirwin, the light on the stage (denied to Sarah) ceases to focus on Fanny's father and begins to focus, as is most natural in the life of a young woman, on the man she is to marry.

Prayers of Sherkin aims to highlight the luminous beauty of a young woman bound to be a bride—a cherished daughter, niece, and sister. The play itself also has a luminous quality—clear, uncluttered, and quintessen-tially poetic. With a few deft strokes Barry draws his individual characters—for instance, the honorable and lonely John Hawke, and his eccentric son, just as magnetic and compelling in his eccentricity as his sister is in her beauty and virtue. The fundamentally comic roles of the inhabitants of Baltimore—the Pearces, Kirwin, and Moore—provide contrast and relief to the small tragedy of their neighbors that is working toward inevitability across the water on Sherkin.

The Steward of Christendom took the London critics by surprise in 1995 and became one of the most award-winning plays of the West End that season. Its success was repeated in New York in 1997, with Dubliner Donal McCann again in the title role. It is a story of Thomas Dunne, a character based loosely on James Dunne, Barry's great-grandfather, who rose to the rank of Chief Superintendent in the Dublin Metropolitan Police. Dunne was reputed to have killed men in the Dublin Lockout of 1913, and was in charge of security for Dublin Castle, the bastion of British rule in Ireland.[30] Barry's own ambivalence about having such a branch on his family tree began as a nagging doubt and eventually resulted in Thomas Dunne, a complex and satisfying character, and a willing victim of the system he so loyally served. Left with an inadequate pension, he is shunted back home to small-town Co. Wicklow after losing his position of power and authority in Dublin. There, because of the cumulative effect of his having lost his beloved wife as a young man, and more recently a son to World War I, one daughter to emigration, and another to marriage, Dunne suffers a rather violent emotional collapse and is committed to the county mental asylum in Baltinglass.

The cast of *The Steward of Christendom* includes Dunne's four children— Willie, Annie, Maud, and Dolly—Maud's husband Matt Kirwin (Kirwin is a family name of Barry's), and Mr. Smith and Mrs. O'Dea, who now care for Thomas in the asylum. It is 1932, about a decade after the British turned over Dublin Castle to Michael Collins as representative of the Free State Government of Éire.[31]

Thomas Dunne is now 75 years old, but still sound. He is not particularly clean and is wearing only long johns. The opening passage of the play, "Da Da, Ma Ma, Ba Ba, Ba Ba," suggests an infantilism in old age, but although Dunne does tend to favor memories of his childhood not far from Baltinglass, he is by no means always incoherent.

With the introduction of Mrs. O'Dea, who acts as seamstress in the asylum, Barry introduces a complex clothing and footwear motif that richly informs the play. Thomas has given his only suit of clothes to another madman who had been a local hero. Mrs. O'Dea appears to measure him for a replacement suit of black cloth like that worn by all the inmates. But Dunne, used to years in uniform and the respect a uniform accorded him, seeks, in vain, gold trim to adorn his suit. From this point in the play the garbing of Thomas Dunne, a ritual procedure, is performed by willing female hands. In the past Annie ironed his shirts, Maud brushed his suit and brought his ceremonial sword, and Dolly polished his boots. A similar focus finds the daughters clothes shopping or discussing clothing, especially "proper" dress for certain occasions. The girls darn socks, discuss lengths of hemlines, and don or remove aprons. Thus Barry includes both male and female characters within the rubric of this complex and subtle image pattern. Authority, gender identification, and gratification are conferred by the right clothing. The labor required to maintain clothing and to show it to advantage becomes a concern and a matter of pride for *both* sexes in this play. That appearance in the play seems to bolster or reaffirm reality is apparent, and part of the playwright's purpose is to expose this connection. Thomas Dunne, a spit-and-polish officer of the law, was as clean and brisk in his work ethic, his loyalties, and his sense of duty as were his uniform and boots. He served the authority of his day, and conflicting or emerging concepts of national identity did not confuse the issue of duty for him.

The Steward of Christendom is enriched by a father-son subplot that is subtly interwoven with the play's main narrative. Thomas, confused in old age, is frightened by the daily arrival of Mr. Smith, who tends him in the asylum. Mr. Smith's unannounced appearances remind Thomas of the equally authoritarian and surprising appearances of his father, "Black Jim," who beat him and put him in the police force because he didn't excel in school. This disclosure, that Thomas Dunne had his occupation initially forced upon him, can only increase our admiration for the character's unfailing sense of honor and duty. This sense of honor is explored addition-ally in Barry's portrayal of Dunne's relationship with his own son. The long monologue that closes the play collapses three generations of male Dunnes in a turmoil of misunderstanding, love, and redemption. Old Black Jim, years earlier, had refused to kill a sheep-eating dog after he had nearly lost his young son Thomas, because of the boy's devotion to the animal. (The decision to *not* kill a dog that has killed sheep is an extraordinary one, because once a dog has killed there is no way to prevent it from happening again and again.) The terrifying Black Jim introduced earlier in the play becomes nearly fragile in his parental love. This love is, in turn, reflected in the final scene between the mad Thomas and the specter of his dead son Willie, for whose death in war Thomas feels obliquely responsible. Thomas believes that ultimately he failed to protect his son as well as Black Jim had protected him. This judgement, however, is belied by the last letter Willie sent him from the front, which is read on stage by Mr. Smith:

> . . . I wish to be a more dutiful son because, Papa, in the mire of this wasteland, you stand before my eyes as the finest man I know, and in my dreams you comfort me, and keep my spirits lifted. Your son, Willie.

The Steward of Christendom gives the reader or the audience, then, a rare glimpse into a Victorian Ireland that was expunged by warfare abroad and at home. We witness within its time frame the breakup of an old and stable social order, and the onset and eventual success of revolutionary forces. That this conflict is embodied by one aging "mad" man who can and does continue to command the respect of those in the play, and those in the audience, stands as tribute to the world he loved and tended.

Sebastian Barry has produced, in a very short time, a surprising number of major plays for the contemporary Irish repertoire. A prolific playwright who is just over 40 years old, there is more than enough reason to believe he will continue to devise more poetically satisfying and thought-provoking plays of the caliber of those already produced.

Marina Carr was born in Co. Offaly in 1964. Hers is a distinct young voice in the Irish theatre as her plays offer a female perspective, and also a rare insight into life in her Midlands home. Her first professional production, *Low in the Dark*, appeared at the Project in 1989, a "Crooked Sixpence" production. This play represented an abstract and absurdist beginning for the playwright. With characters named Curtains, Bender, Binder, Baxter, and Bones, who rarely speak more than one line of dialogue at a time, the play is decidedly Beckettian. A sample of dialogue will illustrate:

> Bender: You accuse me of screaming too much, so I had a silent birth this time.
> Binder: Did it hurt?
> Bender: After the first million you get used to it.
> Binder: Can I feed him?
> Bender: Go ahead!
> Binder: (breast-feeding and examining the baby) It's a she!
> Bender: What'll we call him?
> Binder: Alexander.
> Bender: We have an Alexander!
> Binder: There's no harm in another one!

This early disjointed style requires that the play be seen and heard, rather than just read, in order to appreciate the timing and humor with which the actors inform the dialogue. It is a style that Carr does not abandon in later plays, but that she adapts to suit her own emerging voice and thematic concerns.

In two of her recent plays, *The Mai* (1994) and *Portia Coughlan* (1996), similarities abound. Each of the title characters is a twin. Both have nearly supernatural affinities with the world of the afterlife or with those who are distant. Both plays are also obsessively fixed near water—the first overlooking

Owl Lake, the second on the banks of the Belmont River. Each play is also written in dialect, phonetically reproduced, making for difficult reading at first. *Portia Coughlan* is entirely in Midlands dialect, whereas in *The Mai* the younger characters speak standard English while the older parts are written to reflect the title character's Connemara origins. In each play the title character is well-off, Portia having married a wealthy man, The Mai having scrimped in her husband's long absence to build the house of her dreams. Each is surrounded, however, by constant familial reminders of her humble origins.

Dreams play a powerful role in Carr's work. Her title characters are haunted and verging on the clairvoyant, which is recognized, though not completely accepted, by the others. Often, the gap between what they remember or wish for stands in vivid contrast to their mundane lives in the real world represented by these others. The longing and dissatisfaction of The Mai and Portia impinge dangerously on that real world, causing them great unhappiness; but the link with the dream world is one they are unable to sever.

In *The Mai* the world of the play features absurdist flashes, with The Mai's estranged husband, Robert, materializing at the beginning of the play in ghost-like fashion. As in *Portia Coughlin*, *The Mai* uses haunting music, such as Robert's cello playing, to evoke the past for the heroine. Also as in *Portia Coughlan*, The Mai is surrounded by female relations, here a daughter, two sisters, two busybody aunts, and an eccentric granny. (Grandma Fraochlán, whose salty speech is sprinkled with Irish, is permanently accompanied by a huge oar, her sole link with her fisherman husband, now dead 60 years.) These female characters also serve to keep the heroine in what they believe is her "place," although in Carr's work this is an undertaking doomed to failure. The Mai, as the definite article that serves as an honorific conveys, is stronger in her imaginative ways than they are. And although marriage in Carr's plays is a central concern, inevitably these marriages either fail, or fail to materialize. In *The Mai* the male presence is reduced to one character. Grandma Fraochlán and Aunt Julia are widows, Aunt Agnes is a spinster, sister Beck is recently divorced, and sister Connie's local husband is offstage.

The power of the folkloric in local places surfaces in *The Mai*, mirroring the spirituality or otherness of the heroine's dream world. The play, narrated by The Mai's 30-year-old daughter Millie, 15 years after its action, contains a mythological account of Owl Lake's romantic and tragic origins, followed by this key passage:

> A tremor runs though me when I recall the legend of Owl Lake. I knew
> that story as a child. So did The Mai and Robert. But we were unaffected
> by it and in our blindness moved along with it like sleepwalkers along

a precipice and all around us gods and mortals called out for us to change our course and, not listening, we walked on and on.

The quote, which closes Act One of this two-act play, signals a shift in the play's action and mood. The mythological lovers Coillte and Bláth have foreshadowed in their tragedy the deterioration of the marriage of The Mai and Robert.[32] This doomed relationship is played out in modern terms by Carr's concentration in Act Two on Robert's ongoing marital infidelity and public humiliation of his devoted wife.

Marina Carr's drama seems to indict, finally, women like Portia Coughlan and The Mai, or to indict the society and familial structure that produce them. The coterie of family members, mostly female, that surrounds the heroine are alternately overprotective and destructive. Often they hinder the development of true communication between husband and wife or a sense of marital privacy. In addition, Carr examines women who are too much lovers to be effective mothers. In *Portia Coughlin* a woman remains in love with the ghost of her dead brother and avoids her children. The Mai remains so preoccupied in her obsessive and unrequited love for Robert that she estranges her daughter. Female behavior of this sort is both inherited and conditioned—we learn that both Grandma Fraochlán and The Mai's mother had similarly besotted love relationships and became dysfunctional mothers. Carr's idealistic young women are unfulfilled later in life. They render themselves, or are rendered, incapable of living effectively and happily in a world they find compromised and corrupt. Carr offers her central female characters, then, not as objects for admiration in their purity and elevated sensibility, but as objects for our pity. They are unable to grapple with the unpleasantness and limitations of reality. Carr's failed mothers emerge as somewhat more traditional figures than the reader would initially have assumed them to be, condemned by their families and in part by their creator. Carr's final thematic note is that women cannot really be fully independent, nonconformist, or self-fulfilled under the conditions society imposes upon them. Sympathetic as that interpretation is, it is counterbalanced by her equal insistence that female romanticization of love and obsession over men is less than truly adult behavior. Furthermore, in Carr's work women's inability to mother children is an abnegation of responsibility with sobering and repetitive consequences.

Conor McPherson is a young and very successful Irish dramatist whose reputation has spread rapidly beyond Ireland. Born in Dublin in 1971, McPherson studied philosophy at University College, Dublin, and philosophic inquiry and allusion heavily inform his work. A cofounder of The Fly by Night Theatre Company, McPherson has been one of several young Irish playwrights to be encouraged and nurtured by having been awarded a term as Writer in Residence at the experimental Bush Theatre in London.

McPherson's *A Good Thief* won a Stewart Parker Trust award in 1995, but his first major success was *This Lime Tree Bower*, which was first produced for the 1995 Dublin Theatre Festival Fringe. Since then, McPherson has gained additional fame with *The Weir* in a 1997 Royal Court production in London, and a film script, *I Went Down*, in the same year.

McPherson favors a monologic format, whether single or multiple, and a postmodern awareness of the mechanism of theatre. *St. Nicholas*, which traveled to New York in 1998, is the monologue of a theatre critic in crisis. The play gives the playwright delicious opportunity to explore layers of dramatic and critical tropes and to expose their flaws and explode their clichés. *This Lime Tree Bower* features monologues by three men who only interact as the play is nearing its close. McPherson's language, often earthy and excretory, strives to replicate unadorned "real" speech. Because more constructed in monologue than in dialogue, the language is allowed a rhetorical flow that dialogue can often check. To counter, or to hold in check, the rhetorical tendency that informs all speeches (which is what monologues are), McPherson relies on deflationary techniques to puncture the narrative on occasion. The effect is to make his characters and their narrative accounts of crucial events in their lives, or in the lives of others, very credible to audiences.

This Lime Tree Bower, its epigram and title borrowed from Coleridge's poem "This Lime-Tree Bower My Prison," is the story of interconnecting traumatic events in the lives of Joe, Frank, and Ray. Joe and Frank are brothers, a teenager and a twenty-something, respectively. Ray, an older university lecturer in philosophy, dates their sister, Carmel. Joe, Frank, and Carmel are the children of an Italian immigrant father who has lost all interest in life since the death of his wife. They run a seaside fish-and-chips shop.

Each of the men relates an incident crucial to his sense of identity. For Joe it is witnessing the rape of a girl by his friend Damien, whom he had idolized. For Ray it is his vomiting in the presence of a famous visiting philosopher and hundreds of assembled students. But Frank's "story" affects them all and overshadows the narrative of the other two men. Frank, furious with a local loan shark for his harassment of Frank's father about the repayment of a loan for his wife's funeral, robs the man's bookmakers's (bookies') shop. Both Joe and Ray are taken into Frank's confidence, thus the connection between the monologues.

McPherson constructs three male characters in *This Lime Tree Bower* who, despite similarity of background, are very different men. Joe is an innocent, a virgin who masturbates with great regularity. He has something of an adolescent crush on Damien, a companion the likes of whom cause parents to issue warnings to their offspring. Joe is something of an orphan. He was very young when his mother became ill, and was later abandoned by his grief-stricken father. Ray is the cynical polar opposite of Joe. Sexually irresponsible and jaded, he is becoming too corrupt to appreciate Carmel's very real virtue, intelligence, and grace. Ray is also professionally careless and slack, in part because of a drinking problem. His philosophical predilection gives him various means by which he can rationalize deceit, corruption, laziness, and self-loathing. Frank, much less complex than Ray but much less corrupt, becomes the "criminal" in the play, although his reasons for committing the crime are altruistic. The other crime committed in the play—Damien's rape of the girl, for which at one point Damien tries to blame Joe—is chosen by McPherson to be the one that the police pursue. A reference to the girl closes the play. McPherson thus engages the audience in a discourse on morality. He leaves us to assess degrees of criminality and corruption, and the price society should demand for such infractions. No one will ever prosecute Ray for his seduction and abandonment of his students, nor for his infidelity to Carmel. (Even her brothers countenance and are envious of Ray's ability to attract another girl to his hotel room in Cork, where the trio spend a celebratory weekend.) Ultimately, Frank gets away with his armed robbery; but so as not to be caught, he can only help his father repay the loan by emigrating to the United States and pretending to send money back from a job there. Damien is prosecuted for the rape. Although the girl is not a fully drawn character but more an offstage victim in this play, the genuine trauma inflicted upon Joe at a time of just-emerging sexuality is one of the play's many small-scale, but real, tragedies.

Although the three actors in *This Lime Tree Bower* are all on stage for the play's duration, they do not all speak to or acknowledge each other for much of the drama. This convention recalls Friel's drama, especially *Faith Healer* and *Molly Sweeney*, but in McPherson a stray remark is eventually addressed directly to the audience, thus breaking the conventional aura of performance. When Ray finally discloses that he has perhaps blighted his career by being rather floridly sick in public, a "stunned" Frank says to Ray, "I never knew that." Ray, remaining in character, but betraying the tricks of the playwriting trade, replies, "I've been saving it."

This Lime Tree Bower is punctuated with references to radio programs and personalities, touchstones that act as code to Irish people and "place" the men—their cultural tastes, their politics, their frames of reference. Although interaction on the stage or with the audience is very limited in the play, interaction of a highly artificial kind is demonstrated at times by having the male characters (including Frank and Joe's father) "talk" with players on televised sporting matches or to participants on radio talk shows instead.

The female presence in *This Lime Tree Bower* rarely emerges as more than types—the dead mother, the virtuous young woman, and the woman as whore. McPherson, however, purposely blurs some of these characteristics, too, thus making it much harder for the audience to move toward a facile judgement of the women. Carmel, though a model in many ways, is not at all virginal and treats her young brother badly. Myfanwy, the student with whom Ray sleeps, may be somewhat promiscuous, but she is not corrupt, nor is she completely corrupted by Ray. The young girl raped by Damien is nearly unconscious and incapable of making moral choices when she is assaulted.

McPherson conditions his audience to look for the gray areas of moral dilemma or moral choice in this play by having his men narrate stories, and then immediately undercut their validity with a counterstory that could equally be true. About a local mystery man, Frank says:

> Fran Ferris said he was a gunman from the North who'd escaped and they couldn't extradite him. Shamey Devereaux said he was an armed robber out on parole trying to stay out of trouble.

> This could well have been load of bollox and he might have worked in Super Value. . . .

Later, Joe constructs a similar dubious narrative with both mythic and antimythic versions about a local shipwreck:

> The story was that the ship was carrying guns for the IRA in 1920 or something and the captain was an English fellow who had fallen in love with a girl in the town. . . . That was the story the old lads in Reynolds' used to say about it.

> But Frank told me the boat belonged to a fisherman called Vinty Duggan who crashed it after drinking a bottle of Powers. . . .

Conor McPherson is a voice for the stage that is deceptively simple, but one that exhibits a growing sophistication and a speculative flair. There is obviously much more to be heard from this young voice in the future.

Martin McDonagh, like Conor McPherson, was born in 1971, but was reared in London of Irish parents. This young and prolific playwright has rocketed to fame in the British, Irish, and American theatrical worlds in only a few years. Surprisingly, this Londoner writes mainly of life in the rural west of Ireland. His two trilogies are *The Leenane Trilogy*—consisting of *The Beauty Queen of Leenane*, *The Lonesome West*, and *A Skull in Connemara;* and *The Aran Trilogy*, the first part of which, *The Cripple of Inishmaan*, was mounted by the National Theatre Company in London to great critical acclaim in 1997. Both *The Beauty Queen of Leenane* and *The Cripple of Inishmaan* were produced to critical acclaim in New York the following year. He has also written an Irish-American play, *Dead Day at Coney*, set in the old seaside amusement park at Coney Island in Brooklyn.

The Leenane Trilogy was staged at the Druid Theatre in Galway in 1997 in its entirety, and was directed by Garry Hynes. Critic Jocelyn Clarke, writing in the *Sunday Tribune*, described the experience of the audience who attended all three of the plays in one day:

> For over six hours, between the laughter and the squirming, the gasping and the nervous giggles, the audience had not only survived but also enjoyed one of the whitest knuckle roller coaster rides ever to careen across an Irish stage. . . . McDonagh deftly combines tight narrative and simple characterisation with quirky dialogue to create dramatic fairy tales which are at once knowing and naive, seductive and disturbing, charming and Grimm.[33]

McDonagh's emerging reputation is as a playwright who rings post-modern changes on the traditional Irish country-kitchen drama. Like Tom Murphy in such plays as *Bailegangaire*, McDonagh uses settings that are deceptive in that they precondition Irish audiences into believing that they may be seeing something they have seen before. There is before them, after all, in *The Beauty Queen of Leenane* (1995), "a long black range along the back wall with a box of turf beside it and a rocking chair on its right." These quintessentially Irish properties are then coyly updated, but only to 30 years ago, by a framed photo of John and Robert Kennedy. Kitsch is added in the form of a teatowel embroidered with the blessing "May you be half an hour in heaven afore the Devil knows you're dead."

The four-person cast of the play consists of Mag Folan, in her seventies; her daughter Maureen, who is forty; and two brothers, Pato and Ray Dooley, the Folan's neighbors. Pato is 40; Ray is 25. The ages of the characters are important to our understanding of their relative positions in this small society. Both Maureen and Pato have been emigrant workers, working in menial positions in Britain. Mag still very much controls her home, the play's setting, although she is somewhat infirm and hypochondriacal. Young Ray is just beginning to feel the limitations for his future in Leenane.

The dynamic of the play has a stunted predictability at its onset. Mag, from her rocker, controls Maureen's every move and is dedicated to seeing to it that her daughter is deprived of anything resembling a life. Mag is wheedling, petty, constantly demanding of small attentions, and devious.

Early in the play, however, McDonagh begins to peel away any predictable dimension, exposing truisms of Irish life to comic and ironic scrutiny. Mag's mindset is firmly colonial—thinking only in terms of young people emigrating to get jobs—although she will do her best to keep Maureen from ever leaving again. In retaliation for her mother's taunts, Maureen openly discusses a fantasy of Mag's murder.

Impatience with the aged, so deftly drawn by Synge at the beginning of the century in the tragic *Riders to the Sea* and in his other plays, is exploded in *The Beauty Queen of Leenane*. Ray, who has come to invite the women to a bon voyage party, abuses Mag roundly, using four-letter words and showing disdain for the infirmities of age. He is, he claims in exasperation, "talking with a loon." That this is not the traditional drama of Synge's west of Ireland is also underscored intermittently, but increasingly obviously, in the play by the fact that *no one* can seem to remember the local parish priest's correct name. Formerly a force to be reckoned with in Irish life, religion has become irrelevant, or at least a dubious memory. All is hopelessly out of synch in this world—Mag's liquid vitamin supplement has lumps, tea is always cold, everyone eats biscuits (cookies) they thoroughly dislike. Thus, when Maureen returns from the party to spend the night illicitly and flagrantly with Pato in her mother's house, it is not surprising that the couple don't make love.

Pato is arguably the only vital force in the play, but even that hopeful element is vitiated by circumstances and deceit. A genuinely kind man in search of a wife, Pato overlooks Maureen's shortcomings and later proposes by mail. His efforts are stymied by Mag, who is intent on not spending her final years in an old-age home.

The Beauty Queen of Leenane could still sound in this regard something of a simple update, if an irreverent one, of tradition. McDonagh's skill as an innovative dramatist, however, is demonstrated in Scene Eight of this nine-scene play, when Maureen engages in an elaborate fantasy monologue in which she is reunited with Pato just before he departs for America. That McDonagh succeeds in making the audience also believe this fantasy (because they fervently wish to) is a tour de force. Then, when the play devolves to its bleak end, the audience is shocked and devastated, instead of believing Maureen's fate to be inevitable and dictated theatrically. *The Beauty Queen of Leenane* closes, as it began, intertextual with Tom Murphy's *Bailegangaire*. A younger woman takes on characteristics of a deceased or deposed elder, embodying a bizarre form of tradition that calls into question the concept of tradition itself.

There is an uncanny vérité to McDonagh's work for the stage, an essential if the playwright undertakes to write such bare tragic tales that carry the full weight of fatalism. McDonagh's *The Cripple of Inishmaan* (1997) continues to demonstrate this skillfulness, intensified by our understanding that its plot originates in a "real" event.

In the 1930s, Aran Islander Robert Flaherty, who had gone to work in Hollywood in the film industry, returned to make the feature film *Man of Aran*. The film artistically captured the way of life of the islanders. One of Flaherty's characters is a crippled boy, and McDonagh's play also concerns a fictional orphaned and crippled boy, Billy, who is given the opportunity to travel to Hollywood for a screen test of the part in Flaherty's film. Returning to Ireland and fated to die of tuberculosis, the temporarily suicidal Billy stands as a benign contrast to an assortment of venal, cruel, and neurotic locals. Critic Robert Brustein, writing in *The New Republic*, applauds McDonagh as a dramatic voice. In an age that tends toward the examination of apathy and rarely moves beyond an existential ennui, Brustein finds that McDonagh "celebrate[s] what remains enduring and alive in human nature even in the most appalling circumstances."[34]

As in *The Beauty Queen of Leenane*, McDonagh's sensibility in *The Cripple of Inishmaan* also exhibits a nineties knowingness. In the earlier play, set in the very recent past, mention is made of priests openly fathering children by their mistresses, and in *The Cripple of Inishmaan* a priest is reported to punch boys on a regular basis. Although set 60 years ago, clerical abuse is frankly discussed in the play as it might not have been at the time. Characters in *The Cripple of Inishmaan* also mouth incongruously revisionist views of Irish historical and political icons with a sensibility which is that of today, not of yesteryear. These flaws mitigate seriously against the dramatic coherence of the play being maintained.

Finally, McDonagh's complex intertextuality with Synge declares *The Cripple of Inishmaan* one of the most acutely postmodern plays Ireland has yet produced. Billy, who is in ways a Christy Mahon figure from the earlier playwright's *Playboy of the Western World*, is, at play's end, a physical caricature of Old Mahon, complete with bandaged head. He "walks out" with the foul-mouthed Helen, whose antiromantic talk provides contrast to that of Synge's Pegeen Mike. Here McDonagh acknowledges that although "Synge and O'Casey were already pushing beyond the accepted sensitivities and sanc-timonies of Irish life, interrogating the heroes and lovable rogues of an earlier milieu," the time to replace their verities has come.[35]

It is hoped that the foregoing gives an accurate and somewhat illumi-native insight into the range and the richness of what is appearing on the Irish stage today. There is now a renaissance in Irish cultural circles, and one that has engaged the interest and imagination of many outside the country in recent years. Those outside Ireland should have much more opportunity to see Irish theatrical productions than they would have in the past. New Irish plays have found audiences not only on Broadway, but also in provincial and community theatres and on college campuses.

As drama is the most public and collaborative form of literature, it can also be the most ephemeral. Theatrical archives and the preservation of new productions on film now make it easier, both within and outside Ireland, to access elements of productions, if not the productions themselves. In addi-tion, the healthy state of Irish academic and commercial publishing makes editions of individual plays, and studies of individual dramatists or groups of dramatists, possible and likely to continue. But finally it is the talent of the playwrights, and the directors and the actors who interpret their work (and who merit a book-length study of their own in the near future), that has produced this dramatic flowering. We can only hope that it will be a perennial achievement.

CHAPTER THREE

Modern Irish Fiction —Art and Reality

There are writers living in Ireland today who have long and impressive careers to their credit, and chief among these is nonagenarian **Francis Stuart** (b. 1902). Stuart, like Molly Keane, but for very different reasons, had two writing careers. His work as a young man focused on individuals outside the normal societal parameters and who, because ostracized, seem to understand the value of suffering to achieve transcendence. Many of Stuart's novels of this sort were published in the 1930s. World War II changed much in his world, however, and Stuart, accused of broadcasting German propaganda, was imprisoned after the war. He emerged from prison to write a trilogy that again promoted the power of suffering, this time from an intensely personal perspective.

Stuart's recent work, which belongs more specifically to what is termed contemporary Irish writing, includes *Black List, Section H* (1971). An experimental novel, it investigates the psychic rather than the mystical. Stuart continues, well into old age, to write novels that are postmodern innovations that shockingly mix the sacred and the profane.

Another critic of the Irish status quo of earlier generations is **James Plunkett** (b. 1920), who writes in an accessible popular style, but with a strong historical/political level of awareness. *Strumpet City* (1969), Plunkett's best-known work, became a popular TV drama. Plunkett, too, has had a recent late-blooming, with his novel *The Circus Animals* (1990), with a title borrowed from Yeats, and set in the 1940s and 1950s. The novel tackles such controversial subjects as the church's prohibition of the use of contraceptives and the implications for Irish society of that ruling.

Yet another senior spokesman and a craftsman of fine prose is **Benedict Kiely** (b. 1919), a native of Omagh in Co. Tyrone. Kiely is a prolific writer of novels, short stories, essays, and travel literature. Noted for a consistently wry humor, Kiely is masterful in his depiction of community life at close range. Human foible interests this irrepressible writer, and though he can expose human failing with a sharp eye and a sharper pen, he is incapable, finally, of negativity or cruelty. His work is an affirmation of the human in all and at all times. Two later novels, *Proxopera* (1977) and *Nothing Happens in Carmincross* (1985), take a more sober look at the ongoing violence in Northern Ireland, which greatly distresses an author who remembers well life before the Troubles.

William Trevor was born William Trevor Cox in 1928 in Middleton, Co. Cork. A member of the Anglo-Irish bourgeoisie, Trevor is nearly unique among today's Irish writers in having had a peripatetic childhood. As his father was a bank official, it was standard procedure in Ireland in that era to move such personnel regularly. Trevor's outsider status as a Protestant in a string of Munster towns, none his hometown, provided him, from an early age, with the oblique perspective of a writer. His career as an artist, however, began as a sculptor.

In order to earn a living, Trevor eventually moved to London where his work for an advertising firm led indirectly to his beginning to write fiction. Since that time, he has continued to experiment, and to succeed, in many different types of writing, including travel writing, essays, and script-writing. Trevor's novels have attracted notice throughout the Anglophone world, and have been translated broadly. It is the short story, however, that may be his true metier.

Trevor has lived in England since he was in his late twenties, and although he has written meticulously drawn and expertly observed English characters, his subject also includes Ireland and the Irish. Like Joyce in self-imposed exile, Trevor has come to recognize that distance can be an advantage to the writer. He writes about his country from the leavening distance of both space and time, but his fiction is no less immediate because of that distance. Since the 1980s, most of his writing has either concerned Ireland or taken place in Ireland.

The title story of Trevor's 1965 collection, *The Ballroom of Romance*, is an epiphanic tale of the death of hope and the elimination of future possibilities for happiness. One of Trevor's recurring interests as a writer is to portray the varied ways in which ordinary people deal with the loss of youthful dreams. Trevor's characters, although they can be victims of large-scale tragedy, more often find themselves ignominiously sidelined by life. Such is the condition of Bridie, a 36-year-old spinster as the story begins, who has been dancing weekly at the same bleak country dance hall for the past 20 years. Because her mother has died, Bridie must continue to live at home and care for her amputee father and their farm. Hard work and deprivation have taken their toll, but Bridie remains unembittered.

In the past Bridie had been courted by a young man whom she hoped would marry her, and had fantasized their future together. Their fates, however, diverged:

> She believed he would lead her into sunshine, to the Town and the Church of Our Lady Queen of Heaven, to marriage and smiling faces. But someone else got Patrick Grady, a girl from the town who'd never danced in the wayside ballroom. She'd scooped up Patrick Grady when he didn't have a chance.

Since this disappointment, the trajectory of Bridie's limited life has brought her to contemplating marriage to a road-mender, Dano Ryan, the drummer in the Ballroom of Romance. Bridie's romantic feelings for Patrick Grady have been replaced by a practical search for a "decent man." When she intuits that Dano Ryan will marry the widow with whom he lodges, she is faced with the somber realization that she is too old to go to dances anymore. Instead, she retires to her farm to wait for Bowser Egan, a drunken ne'er-do-well bachelor who will marry her after his mother's death. Bridie knows he will need a woman to cook and care for him. With her aspirations again contracted, Bridie will even forego having a decent man so as not to be alone in old age.

Bridie's is a flawed world with limited horizons for all who dance in the Ballroom of Romance. That she is not alone in her dilemma is made clear by Trevor, who surrounds his central character with several other middle-aged people in similar circumstances, and many younger characters whose prospects look little better. The atmosphere of the ballroom, falsely alluring with its dimmed lights and rotating crystal ball suspended above the tentative dancers, is exposed at the story's end. When the harsh lights are turned on after the dance has ended, even the mirrored ball is seen to be cracked and missing some of its tiles. Significantly, although the appearance of the other dancers is minutely observed—bulging eyes, sweating brows, stumpy legs—Bridie, who is said to be "looking great" throughout the story, is never described. Nor are negative comments about her age or spinster status ever made, although catty comments, particularly about the other older women, are plentiful and, at times, cruelly funny. Thus Trevor protects the dignity of his heroine, and although her future is one characterized by pathos, it is never one with which the reader can lose sympathy.

"The Distant Past" (*Angels at the Ritz*, 1975) is a subtle study of Ireland's sectarian divide and the grip of the past on the present. The story concerns the Middletons, aging and celibate Protestant siblings—a brother and sister. The Middletons inhabit the sort of Big House that has been a feature of so much earlier Irish fiction. Ramshackle because of lack of capital, their house, Carraveagh, becomes a prison for its owners, whose own fortunes decline as their town becomes more prosperous. The New Ireland and the old, in the persons of the townspeople and the aged pair, live amicably together, sharing an amused awareness of "the distant past" of the title. Then the Troubles begin in Northern Ireland in the 1960s.

Trevor's prose maps fine degrees of ostracization within a community. In time the Middletons become the outcasts that the author is drawn inexorably to portray. At first a turned head or an unacknowledged greeting to a friend provide the warning signals. From there Trevor works toward the talismanic, as the Middletons put away treasured symbols of the past. Withdrawal to the point of death closes the story ominously and poignantly:

> Because of the distant past, they would die friendless. It was worse than being murdered in their beds.

"Death in Jerusalem" (*Lovers of Their Time*, 1978) exhibits Trevor's talent for rendering equally sympathetic portraits of Catholic and Protestant characters. This talent effectively argues for the writer's art of distancing. The story also treads gently in the volatile area of the place of religion in a secular world. The contrast is provided in the characters of a worldly Irish priest, resident many years in America, and his celibate brother, a layman, who has remained at home.

The physical differences between Father Paul and his much younger brother, Francis, are limned by Trevor in a style that the author has honed through the years. The expansive paragraph contracts to a telling closing sentence:

> His brother . . . paid the expenses when their sister Edna had gone to Canada; he'd assisted two nephews to make a start in America. In childhood Francis had not possessed his brother's healthy freckled face,

just as in middle age he didn't have his ruddy complexion and his stoutness and his ease with people. Francis was slight, his sandy hair receding, his face rather pale. His breathing was sometimes laboured because of a wheeziness in the chest. In the ironmonger's shop he wore a brown cotton coat.

Physical traits mirror character traits. The generous Father Paul plans a trip to the Holy Land for himself and Francis. The trip has been a lifelong wish of his brother's, and is blighted just after their arrival by a telegram announcing their mother's death. Father Paul's subsequent decision to withhold this information from Francis until they have had a short time to visit Jerusalem's major shrines, ends in Francis' guilt at having somehow failed his possessive mother at her hour of need. He heaps recriminations upon Father Paul for wishing to stay another day before returning for the funeral. As damaging as these recriminations are, however, Trevor delivers the final blow of the story by having patrons in the hotel bar remark on how "disgraceful" it is to see a priest, the bereft brother, drunken and slovenly in the hotel bar as the story ends.

In "Death in Jerusalem" Trevor's unnerving instinct for depicting human frailty and misunderstanding is made infinitely more complex by his deft handling of different manifestations of the religious impulse. Although Father Paul's innate holiness may never have been profound, and is now blunted by such worldly duties as fund-raising and church politicking, he is a man who is demonstrably good-hearted and generous to a fault. His guilt about his brother's being left alone to deal with their mother is palpable. Trevor's counterfoil character of Francis, whose life is blameless but severe, is portrayed with equal fairness in an unhappy family tale with no easy resolve.

Another tale in *Lovers of Their Time*, "Attracta," is, like "The Distant Past," a story that deals with sectarian strife in Northern Ireland, but this time its violence is somewhat more immediate. Like "Death in Jerusalem" the story also counterpoints sensibilities that cannot, or will not, be reconciled. Attracta, the title character, is an aging schoolteacher who had been orphaned by the political violence of the Anglo-Irish War of the earlier part of the century. She has long since been reconciled to its perpetrators, and its horror is only brought to her consciousness again by reports of a hideous series of crimes involving a young British soldier and his widow, Penelope Vade. The story's two plots, separated by more than 40 years, are fused in their demand that the reader consider the arbitrary fallout from ideologically driven violence. Attracta's parents were murdered not because they were intended victims but simply because they were in the wrong place. Penelope

Vade's nightmare only begins when vindictive terrorists mail her the disembodied head of her soldier husband.

In addition to intertwining his two plots effectively, Trevor adds Irish resonance to the story by making it intertextual with one of W. B. Yeats' late verse plays, *The Herne's Egg*, which itself turns on a postmodern interpretation of Irish mythology and folkloric belief. Similarly, both Yeats' and Trevor's work foregrounds the discomfiting manner of its heroines (both named Attracta). Each is virginal and a truth-teller who is doomed to be silenced for politically and socially expedient reasons. Trevor's Attracta, like Yeats', finds herself alone in her awareness of tragedy, surrounded by venal and uncaring characters who find her alternately irrelevant and a threat. Attracta's enforced retirement at the story's conclusion reduces her to a victim of Ireland's political violence once again.

Fools of Fortune (1983) is one of Trevor's novels dealing with the burden of history on Irish lives. Like "Attracta," the novel fuses plots from different periods, but on a larger scale more suitable to the scope of a novel. The Anglo-Irish Quinton family has a long history of intermarriage with the English Woodcombes of Dorset. In the early nineteenth century Anna Woodcombe arrives at Kilneagh, the Quinton's Co. Cork estate, as a bride. As famine strikes Ireland, Anna unflaggingly attempts to relieve the poor and starving and alert her own family and English officials to their plight. Her efforts result in her being disinherited by her enraged family. In subsequent generations the male heirs of Kilneagh continue a tradition of taking English brides. Trevor's novel moves to another traumatic era in Ireland's history, detailing the idyllic marriage of William Quinton and his wife, Evie, and their three children. Like Anna two generations earlier, William and Evie are in the minority among their class and religion in their support of popular causes, and their support of Michael Collins at the time of the Anglo-Irish War. Their tacit political activities result in the horrific conflagration at the novel's center, the burning of Kilneagh, and the deaths of William, his two daughters, and many of their servants. Evie and their son, Willie, retire to a small house in Cork city where Evie, unable to cope with the memories of the death of her husband and other children, deteriorates into alcoholism.

Much of *Fools of Fortune*, narrated through the sensibility of Willie both as a child and a young man, is an attempt to come to terms with the tragedy of Kilneagh and its far-reaching consequences for the family and the local people. In particular Willie's ill-fated romance with his English cousin, Marianne, is conditioned from the start by the events of the past. Marianne becomes pregnant while attempting to console Willie after his mother's death, and returns to Kilneagh only to learn that Willie has left the country. The remainder of the novel unravels this mysterious departure, made gradually clearer as the facts of Willie's revenge murder of the man who gave the order to burn Kilneagh are made clear. Marianne bears their child, Imelda, and continues to live in the remaining wing of the great house. She is cared for by Willie's two aunts and a defrocked priest, who is something of a family retainer. The devolutionary process of the Quinton family concludes with Imelda's eventual insanity—a victim of generations of the burden of the past. Her parents, reunited in old age, care for their afflicted daughter and, finally, draw a veil on the horrors of history.

Fools of Fortune derives its title from a favored phrase used by Willie's father as a catch-all to explain the vagaries of life. Personal choices, affairs of the heart, can make us all fools of fortune, as he himself had become. Trevor's view of history, both personal and political, partakes of the elder Quinton's conviction, but is more complex, and, finally, damning. In particular in his portrayal of the damaged female characters in the novel—the disinherited Anna, the alcoholic Evie, the abandoned Marianne, and the insane Imelda— he traces the horror that the past can inflict upon the living. In his empathy for these sensitive female survivors of tragedy, however, there is always the suggestion of the duty of human beings to shake off the strangulation of memory, and to attempt to forge a future for themselves and for the next generation. That these women are victims, and victims of decisions and actions made by men in the name of prevailing ideology, is certain. The possibility to rise above or circumvent victimhood, however, is always made equally evident. This imperative, is by association, extended to Ireland.

Fools of Fortune, with its insistent and recurring intersection of Irish and English lives, avoids the usual Irish-English dichotomy. Trevor refuses to place blame solely on past English mismanagement, neglect, or violence, all of which are acknowledged in the novel to have occurred. It is also significant that none of the women listed above are part of the Anglo-Irish minority to which Trevor belongs, and about whom he has written a great deal. The men of the novel, the Quintons, however, are Anglo-Irish, and emerge from the novel no stronger nor wiser than their English wives. In fact their unwillingness or inability to act, or act wisely, is condemned by the novelist in the vivid and lingering portraits of the women who have been affected by their choices.

Although *Fools of Fortune* is a history of prominent families and great houses, Trevor provides a more complex understanding of Irish life by including the stories of members of all classes. The jobs and perspectives of characters such as Mr. Derenzy, the faithful manager of the family's mill (and its sole source of income); Mr. Lanigan, the family solicitor, torn between the requirements of Mr. Quinton's will and the sad situation of his widow; and even Willie's various schoolmasters at boarding school, give an outside perspective on the tragedy at Kilneagh that makes few peremptory judgments. These secondary characters do, however, provide a pragmatic and therapeutic alternative to the tendency to dwell on the past. Similarly, the stories of those below the professional classes, the servants of Kilneagh and inhabitants of the nearby town, are narratives which are markedly different from that of the Quintons, because these other characters possess the ability to get on with their lives. Years after the tragedy, the return to Kilneagh of Josephine, Evie Quinton's faithful maid, is an excellent example. Josephine's own disappointment in love, destined before the fire but exacerbated by it, is marked by equanimity. She returns to visit the home of the man she had hoped to marry, meets his wife, and plays happily with their children.

Trevor's narrative in *Fools of Fortune* is not chronological, and the narrative perspective is shared by several of the characters in turn. This can initially be taxing for the reader, but is an essential element in conveying the theme. Occasionally the voice and the era of the narration fail to mesh convincingly. This is especially noticeable in the shorter late-twentieth-century segments of the novel in which there is no evidence of the passage of time in the diction and phrasing of the characters. *Fools of Fortune*, however, is a fully achieved novel that eschews simple answers to the complex and ongoing imperative of searching for a workable means of incorporating history into the Irish present and enabling its future.

The Silence of the Garden (1988) in a sense continues where Trevor left off after writing *Fools of Fortune*, in its Big House setting and its attempt to reconcile the past with the present. The more recent novel also shares the stylistic trait of using a shifting narrative perspective, and of tracing a family and its house through several generations.

Carriglas is the Rolleston family demesne, located on an island off the coast of Co. Cork. The island, where rhododendron grow in profusion, boasts substantial pre-Christian and monastic ruins—formidable standing stones, the remnants of prehistoric rites, and a ruined abbey and holy well, the site of a residual annual pilgrimage from the main land.

The Rollestons are said to have acquired Carriglas by violence, and seem to operate under a family curse. Old Mrs. Rolleston is rearing her three grandchildren, John James, Lionel, and Villana, in the Edwardian era after her daughter's early death. She must then contend with the death of their father, and the crippling of John James in World War I.

The Pollexfens, poor relatives of the Rollestons, first send their handsome and charming son, Hugh, and then their plain and retiring daughter, Sarah, to stay at Carriglas. Sarah, a governess of sorts, witnesses a hideous event when her brother and the Rolleston children, in a game got out of hand, attempt to "hunt" a local peasant child, Cornelius Downey, with a gun. The class implications of this act are recalled later in the novel during the time of the Irish Civil War that followed WWI, when Downey, attempting to kill the Rolleston offspring in the guise of a political act, kills the butler instead. In *The Silence of the Garden*, as in much of Trevor's work dealing with Irish history, violence has a ripple effect. The Rollestons' butler's murder leaves his intended bride, a maid in Carriglas, expecting a child. The tale traces a downward spiral of human attainment, vitality, and aspirations, and the accompanying decay of a Big House. Ownership of Carriglas devolves, after Mrs. Rolleston's death, to her unmarried and childless grandson, John James, who is having a seedy affair with a local, middle-aged widow. After his death, the house passes to the celibate Sarah Pollexfen, whom the equally celibate Lionel Rolleston has simply failed to ask for in marriage. Finally, Carriglas becomes the legacy of Tom, the illegitimate son of Linchy, the murdered butler and the disgraced maid, Brigid.

Although *The Silence of the Garden* is narrated mainly in flashback and largely by old Mrs. Rolleston and Sarah Pollexfen, it is also narrated in part by Tom, as a child-observer at Carriglas. Tom, an outsider in every way imaginable, believes he is nearly visibly tainted by his parents' sin. Believing that others fear to touch him lest they be contaminated, Tom develops a bond with Mrs. Rolleston, who has always felt responsible for him and secures his future.

Two subplots inform *The Silence of the Garden*. The first is the unlikely romance, wedding, and marriage of the beautiful Villana Rolleston to a local unprepossessing lawyer, Finnamore Balt. No sufficient explanation is given for this bizarre decision on Villana's part. Balt, a character who is much her senior, disappears into death unremarked as the novel progresses to its near-present-day conclusion. However, Trevor's earlier evocation of the preparations for Villana's wedding are detailed, humorous, and poignant. This is the last time that any such occasion will be hosted at Carriglas, a house that had offered hospitality to more than one of Ireland's viceroys.

Much detail in the novel is lavished on the construction of a bridge to connect the island on which Carriglas is situated with the mainland, and the controversy that inevitably surrounds this decision. The bridge, which will replace the convenient ferry service to Carriglas, is to be named for Cornelius Downey. The decision inevitably divides the town along ideological lines.

Although *The Silence of the Garden* does not emphasize female victimization to the extent that *Fools of Fortune* and "Attracta" did, it does not flinch from showing the arbitrary nature of violence. *The Silence of the Garden* also continues the earlier novel's depiction of a range of social classes living in easy and, at times, awkward proximity with each other. Trevor's cameo of the drunken Mrs. Moledy, John James' mistress, engaging the Bishop of Killaloe in conversation at Villana's wedding reception is a tour de force. But unlike *Fools of Fortune*, the classes in *The Silence of the Garden* commingle and interact to a degree unthinkable in the earlier novel. (It is the true heir to Killneagh who returns to reclaim the estate at the end of *Fools of Fortune*, not the bastard son of two servants.)

Of the two novels, *The Silence of the Garden* is the most damning in its indictment of the negative pull of Irish history on its people. The closing paragraphs of Sarah Pollexfen's diary seals the house's fate:

> Carriglas will be a place to stroll to on a summers' afternoon, . . . as we
> have strolled to the fallen abbey and the burial mound. Absence has
> gathered in the rooms, and silence in the garden.

In *The Silence of the Garden*, as in *Fools of Fortune*, Trevor excels at recapturing earlier eras and the vitality and industry of a large estate being well managed. Trevor is skillful at mapping the infinitesimal stages by which that vitality decreases with the stresses of economic realities and other factors. Again his style is less successful at conveying more recent rhythms in Irish life, speech, and mores.

When, however, Trevor takes on the task of writing a historical novel, a task that requires a broad brush, his skill is sure. It is unlikely that in generations to come there will be another writer who will be able to delineate with such care the differences and similarities of Ireland's two traditions. And, as with historical and political problems, if there are no artists who can trace the origins of the opponents and relate their histories, a resolve of such conflicts becomes more difficult.

Edna O'Brien was born in Co. Clare in 1930, and has lived much of her adult life in London. O'Brien has achieved distinction and a certain amount of notoriety in her writing career, and is something of a media celebrity both in Britain and in Ireland.

Her first novel, *The Country Girls*, was published in 1960, and was followed shortly by *The Lonely Girl* (1962, reprinted two years later as *Girl with the Green Eyes*), and *Girls in the Married Bliss* (1963). This trilogy was truly innovative at the time in providing a voice for a segment of the Irish population historically underrepresented in its fiction. O'Brien's young women, Catholic, convent-educated, and coming from small country towns to work in lowly jobs in Dublin, are a recognizable phenomenon in modern Irish life. Their predicaments often encapsulate several modern Irish dichotomies simultaneously. Marked by their religious training, their gender, their socioeconomic level, and their rural origins, O'Brien's young women are uniformly eager for experience and for love. They are equally destined to become victimized because of their ignorance and innocence.

In their vulnerability, awakening, and, especially sexual, consciousness, O'Brien's young female characters can be poignantly appealing, although at times infuriating. Their recurring, naive belief in the power of love, the love of a man, to overcome their personal lack of development, reveals human nature at its most trusting and deceived.

O'Brien's depiction of carnal desire and carnality, although always accompanied by a degree of love, was sufficiently graphic to be considered shocking nearly 40 years ago. As a result much of her work was censored in Ireland. However, unlike earlier authors for whom censorship could mean ignominy or oblivion, the censorship of Edna O'Brien's works and the introduction of television broadcasting in Ireland occurred nearly simultaneously. The author was thus allowed a vast public forum in which to plead her case.

O'Brien's heroines have tended to age with the writer. Her later fiction features unhappily married women who, out of the loneliness and isolation of unsatisfying marriages, seek lovers, as did their younger O'Brien counterparts. In *August Is a Wicked Month* (1964) the heroine is gruesomely punished by both society and the author for her infidelity, a common feature in O'Brien's novels and stories that fix on the distance between society's and women's requirements within marriage.

In addition to changing her focus from those who seek marriage to those who are or have been married, in the seventies O'Brien also experimented narratively by publishing two novels written in the second person— *A Pagan Place* (1970) and *Night* (1972). Since writing in the "you" form is considerably harder to sustain successfully than in either the preferred "I" or "she" form, these novels, while worthy experiments, are less successful than both O'Brien's earlier and subsequent work.

O'Brien's skill as a short story writer is beyond dispute, and it is arguable that her choice of theme and subject is better suited to this genre. O'Brien's small lives with their small, but moving, tragedies, fare well within the strengthening confines of the short story form.

Although Edna O'Brien's fiction captures well the prevailing mores of its time, and continues to record subtle and overt changes in those mores, it is often cast in a world that is peculiarly devoid of timely markers. Thus the reader can become disconcerted by O'Brien's characters, who often seem suspended in a world of sensation in which no one mentions a current film, no specific street names are given, and current events do not impinge—all this despite the welter of realistic detail that characterizes her style. More recent efforts have, however, taken a decidedly different turn, and O'Brien's 1994 novel, *The House of Splendid Isolation*, succeeds in combining O'Brien's scrutiny of the workings of the human heart with the greater geopolitical crisis that has informed Irish life for the past three decades.

O'Brien's first novel, *The Country Girls*, introduces most of the themes that would recur in varied form throughout her corpus. It is the story of the sensitive schoolgirl, Kate Brady, and her fearless sidekick, Baba Brennan. The bond between Kate and her mother is a powerful one, no less intense after her mother's premature death. Kate's alienation from her father is equally intense, though circumscribed. Her displacement, physical and emotional, to the convent school that becomes her home is painful but nearly complete.

The intensity of female bonding, whether familial or between friends, is marked by girls' and women's shared weaknesses, often for sensory pleasure. Kate and her mother keep candies under their pillows to savor in self-indulgent moments. But Kate's preternaturally protective mother can't sleep until she knows Kate has swallowed the candy, lest she choke. Baba's mother, Martha, whom Baba calls by her first name, discloses intimate adult details of her married life to her daughter from a very early age. These small rituals are very much stolen pleasures, kept secret from the male characters.

Indeed men are usually dealt with in O'Brien's fiction either obliquely or stealthily. O'Brien's men are powerful because of physical strength, learning, or wealth. They are manipulated, not always successfully, by the women, who operate at a disadvantage. Girls and women like Kate Brady and Baba Brennan have only sexuality to barter in their encounters with men, but usually suffer because they conflate sex with love.

Kate, or Caithleen, is conceived by O'Brien in the tradition of the fictional naïf. Even for a young girl torn from rural Ireland in the fifties, she seems peculiarly untouched by any form of corrupting experience. She thus becomes the victim of Baba's harsh tongue and capriciousness, and the gull of an older local man, ironically named Mr. Gentleman. First exposed to luxury and pleasure by Mr. Gentleman, Kate becomes his tentative lover in one of O'Brien's many unbalanced and unhealthy male-female relationships.

O'Brien's early short story, "Sister Imelda," like *The Country Girl*, scrutinizes the rhythms and idiosyncrasies of country life. Its routine, discipline, and deprivation, as they are also representative of Irish life, have a fascination for the author. O'Brien mines this seam in order to contrast the dedication and daily struggle of nuns, and the ambivalence, and at times anarchy, that characterizes their relations with their female charges.

That the convent is a world unto itself, closed off from the outside, becomes apparent as the intense personal relationships within its walls are described. The unnamed narrator, like Kate in *The Country Girl*, is the best friend and confidante of Baba, and develops a crush on the title character. Sister Imelda is distinguished in the girls' eyes from her peers in having entered the convent after attending university. She has had a personal life, the mystery of which intrigues them all, but most of all the narrator, her pet. But the ancient taboo against "special friendships" in religious enclaves, an unspoken fear of homosexuality, drives the nun and the girl apart. Finally, the relationship is shown, at the story's conclusion, to be not only just a part of the girl's maturation, but also a product of the convent's claustrophobic and outwardly ascetic atmosphere. Some of the most vivid contrasts in O'Brien's fiction are accomplished by such juxtaposition of sheltered, expectant girlhood and the liberating , but daunting, range of experience her young women undergo in the outside world as young adults.

Such experience is the subject of "The Love Object," a story of a 30-year-old woman, an older version of O'Brien's convent-bred younger heroines, but one who has suffered an unhappy marriage and is having an affair with an older married man. O'Brien maps the affair from its nervous and tentative beginnings, through its heights of passion and ineffable intimacy, to its resigned conclusion. The nameless woman, sequestered for much of the story in her flat, where most of the affair was conducted, overcomes a suicidal urge alone. Initially, not even visits home from boarding school by her two young sons can counteract her loss.

"The Love Object" returns near its ending to a familiar O'Brien trope— that of the enclosed world. As the woman acknowledges the end of the affair, she experiences an epiphany:

> That was the first time it occurred to me that all my life I had feared imprisonment, the nun's cell, the hospital bed, the places where one faced the self without distraction, without the crutches of other people.

O'Brien's heroine then willingly confines herself to a different kind of cell, one that has as its parameters love and memory, and thus succeeds in objectifying her former and also unnamed lover, as the title of the story conveys.

The House of Splendid Isolation, with its fractured narrative and plot, is something of a departure for O'Brien stylistically as well as thematically. But the chasm of sensibility between men and women that usually exists in O'Brien's work is evidenced again in this novel, although it is not its ostensible subject. After a short chapter describing the mental and physical condition of an IRA man on the run, the novel continues with a sketch of the domestic life of Garda Rory Purcell. The policeman's home life, though testy because of the pressure of his job, is loving and sustaining. This cameo in the Purcell home seems unrelated to the episodes that follow in *The House of Splendid Isolation*, until O'Brien links the lives of Purcell, the IRA man, McGreevy, and a third character, Josie O'Grady, an abused and childless survivor of a disastrous marriage.

The plot of the novel, achronological as it is, includes elements from the story of each of these characters' lives, and the arbitrary and random way they encounter each other at the novel's violent end suggests the insecurity that has become a fact of life since the start of sectarian strife in Northern Ireland 30 years ago.

Josie is a well-bred woman who marries a farmer, James, whom she considers beneath her. She becomes profoundly alienated from him because he is uncouth, particularly sexually. This alienation, and her inability or refusal to have children after an abortion, sours the marriage and indirectly causes Josie to consider an affair with a priest. After James' death, she lives reclusively, and her once-grand but now dilapidated house is chosen as a hiding place by McGreevy as he seeks to evade the gardai after he has killed a man. A strange bond develops between Josie and McGreevy, whose wife was assassinated and whose child subsequently died of illness. The damaged pair provide a strange sounding board for each other's pain, and Josie not only hides the fleeing criminal, but lies about it to the gardai. Josie's troubled reminiscences in old age, after she survives the police barrage on her house that results in McGreevy's death, are narratively imbedded by O'Brien in the middle of the novel. Their positioning, however, gives insight into the novel's outcome, and lends the novel its doomed quality of inevitability and repetition.

The House of Splendid Isolation is a highly imagistic novel. It opens and closes with references to deer—not thriving, but the victims of hunters and automobiles. Rory's wife, Sheila, doesn't know how to cook a deer shin brought home from one of his hunting trips. Significantly it is a doe that is killed by a car near the novel's end. Such animal victims, of course, mirror their human counterparts. O'Brien's novel also makes repeated use of duality, twinning, and pairing. Such duality aids in exploring the male/female dichotomy, and that of the righteous versus the damned, categories that are subject to shifting interpretation. But the pairing of characters in sibling relationships, marriages, other family pairings, or even merely by happenstance, increases the ambivalence and makes difficult any convincing resolve. Again O'Brien's novel, in this regard, seems uncomfortably to mirror life. *The House of Splendid Isolation* is representative of O'Brien's corpus at large in its insistence on chance, always a volatile and negative factor in her work.

Aidan Higgins (b. 1927) has been an influential writer in Ireland, although one who has spent much of his time outside the country. Born in Co. Kildare in 1927, he was reared in various seaside towns in south Co. Dublin and Co. Wicklow. His works include *Felo de Se* (1960), a prize-winning collection of six short stories that was republished as *Asylum and Other Stories* 11 years later. *Felo de Se* is an important collection because it contains "Killachter Meadow," a fully realized story itself, but one that also functions as a sketch for Higgins' most powerful and influential work, *Langrishe, Go Down* (1966). The latter work is a novel that tries to come to terms with the far-flung social and cultural ramifications of Ireland's troubled history since the 1880s.

"Killachter Meadow" opens with the wake of Emily Kervick, eldest of four spinster sisters living at Springfield House in Co. Kildare. The history of the house is given prominence by the author in the beginning of Part I, which follows immediately after the introductory passages concerning Emily's lying-in-state at the house. Springfield House had been purchased by the sisters' parents in the 1880s, a time when such estates passed often from Protestant to Catholic families after a series of legislative acts reduced rents to landlords and made the maintenance of such estates financially untenable. These Land Acts were thus important markers in the dissolution of the power of the Anglo-Irish class.

That the Kervick sisters' parents were also unable to make Springfield House and its lands thrive is, from the author's view, an indictment of the politically motivated legislation of the past. "Killachter Meadow" retraces the lives of Emily, Tess, Helen, and Imogen against the backdrop of twentieth-century Irish social and political history, creating an impressionistic portrait of the times. Higgins' method in this story, and in his later *Langrishe, Go Down* and *Scenes from a Receding Past* (1977), has been described as Proustian. The author employs a ruminative method that snatches recollections, objects, and people from the past in an attempt to make sense of the present. The sisters, whose lives are claustrophobically entwined in their nearly completely virginal solitude, are shown separately in their eccentric pursuits. Helen is obsessed with the care and feeding of animals, and has intellectual pretensions. Tess plays cards, gardens, and drinks alone. We are bluntly informed that she "is not in this story." Emily, a nonswimmer, bathes in the river alone and naked, though with single-minded modesty. Imogen alone has made a brief connection with the outside world—a summer romance with a German scholar who lived in a hut on the grounds of Springfield House. (Imogen's story will in large part become the focus of *Langrishe, Go Down.*) Most of "Killachter Meadow," however disjointed its seven parts, trains the readers' attention on Helen and, incidentally, on Joseph, the gardener and the only man in the tale.

Stasis, indolence, clutter, and the dust of ages cling to everything in Springfield House and to its inhabitants. Helen's musings, those of a "spinster and potential authoress" are audible:

> —And our dead ones (she was saying), our parents, do you think of them? When we were young, they were old already. And when we in turn were no longer young, why they seemed hardly to have changed. They went past us in the end, cracking like parchment.

"Killachter Meadow" closes with Emily's suicide by drowning, as she hallucinates visions of her sisters as children on the banks of the river. Higgins' use of the phrase "'presumed lost'—itself empty of expression" projects the manner in which her death will be reported. The phrase also applies to all the sisters, the house, their parents, the past, and the hope of a future.

Langrishe, Go Down was hailed as a major achievement when it was published, a postmodern take on the Big House theme in earlier Irish fiction. Seamus Deane has described the novel as one of "an almost incandescent lyricism."[1] The book is formatted in three parts, taking place successively in 1937, 1932, and 1938. Not only does this set the novel in the years of worldwide economic depression and the teething stages of Ireland's independence, but it also brings it to the edge of World War II. War as a component of modern life viewed from a distance opens the novel, as Imogen Langrishe reads of the Spanish Civil War on her homeward journey by bus. (The maiden sisters' names from "Killachter Meadow," and their preoccupations, remain the same, except that here Tess becomes Lilly, a much more fully drawn character. The surname Kervick has been replaced by Langrishe.)

At home the middle-aged sisters live in vaguely unclean conditions, shared at times with domesticated and barnyard animals. The intermittent forays outside their enclave, often by bicycle, take them past scenes not much more promising:

Poor shops, sweet shops, the black convent gates on a grey colourless
day towards the end of winter with the light gone out of everything.

Imagery associated with water and with cold pervades *Langrishe, Go
Down*, as it does much of Higgins' writing, especially about Ireland. Death
is also omnipresent, introduced by Helen's trip to the local cemetery to visit
the graves of their parents. Here too is buried Emily, whose death occurred
chronologically earlier in "Killachter Meadow." The nearby river that
claimed her death is called, less than mellifluously, the Skinkeen.

Historical references to the area's past are interlaced to thematic effect
in *Langrishe, Go Down*, especially mention of local Dutch settlers, the
Vanhomrigh family. Vanessa Vanhomrigh was one of two great unconsum-
mated loves in the life of Jonathan Swift, Ireland's great eighteenth-century
satirist and poet. The Swift connection provides the author with a centuries-
old thread of frustrated love, enforced celibacy, supposed madness, and
eccentricity, as well as with marginalized identification with mainstream
Irish life. These traits the Langrishe sisters share with Swift, the conflicted
Anglican clergyman. Thus a thematically fruitful confusion is introduced
and maintained in *Langrishe, Go Down*. The Langrishe sisters, who are
estranged from the rest of the people of the locality, are mistaken at times
for Protestants by those who don't know them. Here the legacy of their
house and its association work an illusory effect.

The love affair between Imogen Langrishe and Otto Beck is introduced by means of a parcel of love letters that Imogen rereads with care
years later. These include letters she wrote to Otto that never reached him.
Otto's presence at Springfield House had occasioned immediate fantasies in
Imogen's mind. The pair, with little in common, engaged in initial conversational forays at their infrequent early meetings, which only served to
illustrate the gap between them. He was resolutely casual in his dress and
curt in his manners. She was so much his intellectual inferior that initially
he thought she was hard of hearing:

So it went on. Star time and clock time, stellar degrees of magnitude.
Fraunhofer lines. Thermonuclear reactors. Kepler's law of planetary
motions. *Pickering's* New Selenography. For her benefit alone, she who
could make so little of it.

The gap between Otto and Imogen's worlds is made more evident
by their meeting with his bohemian friends in Dublin, whose liberal mores
and sexual conduct offend Imogen's sensibilities. Another gap, more

topical, is exposed through Imogen's ramblings, both with Otto and alone, through Dublin's streets. Evidence of the country's new independent status is constant—plaques to 1916 heroes, references to de Valéra, a trip to Glasnevin, burial place of Irish patriots. As their love affair progresses, however, the gap lessens. Higgins convincingly evokes the sexual awakening of a woman long deprived of such experience. He also realistically illustrates the differences between male and female sexuality. The experienced Otto, though involved to some extent emotionally with Imogen, maintains a distance between physical gratification and intellectual stimulus. Imogen, not capable of intellectualizing experience, is given over completely to physical sensation and loses any sense of distance between them. It is significant also that Otto, the foreigner, linguist, and scholar, is used to thematic effect by Higgins to interpret Ireland to Imogen who, though Irish, is estranged from the Irish language, the land, and its people. Otto explains origins of place-names from the Irish, pedantically corrects local lore, and identifies flora.

Throughout *Langrishe, Go Down,* Higgins uses a disjointed narrative style that employs long dialogic passages operating on a fairly realistic level, and that is interspersed with shorter paragraphs that either draw on passing incidents or local sites or events—"Barbarstown House, in ruins," followed by dialogue, followed by "The Collegiate school girls were playing lacrosse, watched by a lone attendant." These groupings, though they seem at first arbitrary, in fact begin to form a decided pattern within the novel, linking the fervid and isolated relationship of the lovers to the world outside.

A link between the dialogic and other passages is provided by Otto's two pastimes, each of which foregrounds a metaphor of thematic significance in the novel. Otto both hunts and fishes regularly (in part because he is impoverished and these provide a free source of food). Time and again, as a result, Beck is seen slaughtering small animals—game birds, squirrels, rabbits—and in and around rivers catching fish, which are also killed and gutted. The knack and sang-froid Otto displays in these acts is an indicator of his nature and his relationship to the world and to others. As the eventual and predetermined end of their relationship approaches, the slaughter and water imagery convey the dissolution of the strange bond between the pair. Ironically Otto's departure is hastened by Imogen's firing his shotgun as he bicycles away from Springfield.

Langrishe, Go Down ends, as "Killachter Meadow" began, with the death of one of the sisters. Here, Helen's funeral occasions Imogen and Otto's first meeting since his departure and the stillbirth of their child. The novel ends in isolation, despair, and stasis. The failure of the Langrishe sisters to thrive, to reproduce, or to grow remains an emblematic indictment of history. But selected passages from newspapers that appear near the novel's close, report the suicides of prominent Austrians as the Nazis take over their country. Their inclusion suggests that Ireland's shift to the modern world is not the only one that is painful or the result of violence.

Balcony of Europe (1972), considered to be Higgins' most innovative novel, begins, in a sense, where *Langrishe, Go Down* ended. Otto Beck's many interests in the earlier novel included phenomenology and the philosophy of Edmund Husserl.[2] In *Balcony of Europe* this philosophy informs the underlying structure of the novel. The use of the disjointed narrative mode of the earlier novel becomes more frequent and fragmented, but to a purpose— that is, to lessen the gap between experience and the expression of that experience. The novel concerns the love affair of Dan Ruttle, an Irishman who shares many traits with his creator, and Charlotte Bayless, an American, in Andalusia. The appearance of *Scenes from a Receding Past*, published after *Balcony of Europe*, confuses the reader, perhaps the author's intention. Its final scenes depict Dan Ruttle's marriage to Olivia, his wife of some years in *Balcony of Europe*. Chronology, the linear narrative, the autobiographical, and the fictive; all these, Higgins suggests, are arbitrary devices to be used by the writer to accomplish his individual aims. This process is continued and intensified in *Bornholm Night Ferry* (1983), which is heavily self-referent and intertextual with Higgins' work and biography. The novel uses the self-consciously archaic literary device of letters to and from lovers as its structure. Furthermore, it investigates the difficulties of the writing life (the author's writing life?) by having half the correspondence written in English by Elin, a Dane. Since she is writing in a second language, English, Elin is always groping for the right word or phrase in which to express her love for Fitz, Higgins' alter ego here.

From stories and novels about Ireland to novels that become more autobiographical, Higgins as a writer continues on a logical path to autobiography in his recent *Donkey's Years* (1995) and *Dog Days* (1997). Given the nascent popularity of autobiographical fiction at the close of the millennium, with all its evaluative cultural baggage, Aidan Higgins as writer may have been prescient in his insistence that genre boundaries be overcome to free modern Irish writing to achieve postmodern credibility.[3]

Jennifer Johnston (b. 1930) was over 40 when her first major work was published. *The Captains and the Kings* (1972) appeared to great critical acclaim and was followed in rapid succession by *The Gates* (1973) and *How Many Miles to Babylon?* (1974). This trio of Big House novels remains her best-known and most-read work, and the first and last of these share the trait, not found in her later work, of featuring male protagonists.

Johnston's oeuvre is, despite gender focus and settings that range from the period of World War I to today's Ireland, very tightly cohesive. Her plots share pulse points, her characters share traits, and through these multiple referents the novelist has been able to explore time and again similar thematic issues to resonant effect as her body of work grows.

Strictly speaking, Jennifer Johnston's world is not confined to the Big House itself, as many of her recent protagonists are not to be found in demesnes locked away from the reality of the modern world by gates which lead down long avenues of old hardwood trees. Some of Johnston's female protagonists are found, instead, in the capacious Georgian and Victorian villas that are tucked away in the affluent suburbs along the coast south of Dublin—the milieu in which Johnston herself was reared. The child of Denis Johnston, a barrister turned successful Gate Theatre playwright and director, and Sheelagh Richards, an Abbey actress, Johnston was well placed to observe a world that was not as geographically isolated as the Big House but was highly privileged. In this atmosphere Johnston examines the growth and development, or lack thereof, of young women, and the intrusion of history and politics on the choices these women make. Whereas *The Captains and the Kings* concerns the choices young men make in time of war while trying to accommodate conflicting loyalties, novels such as *The Old Jest* (1979) and *The Railway Station Man* (1984) concern choices made by women that indirectly affect the lives of the men involved in political conflict in each narrative. Frequently Johnston's protagonists, male or female, have artistic inclinations or ambitions, usually not fully realized. Alexander, the late brother of the protagonist, Charles Prendergast, in *The Captains and the Kings* (and arguably the same character as the doomed hero of *How Many Miles to Babylon*), had a musical gift and sang German *lieder* elegantly with his mother. Helen, the focal character of *The Railway Station Man*, is a painter (and the exact contemporary of her novelist/creator). Others wish to write or, if older, remember a time in which they engaged in an artistic pursuit.

Johnston uses a variation of the closed-world trope, creating a hot-house atmosphere that facilitates forcing her fiction into bloom. There is an intimate, and at times claustrophobic, atmosphere maintained by isolating characters by class, age, gender, or physical or psychological handicap. For example, Nancy in *The Old Jest* is the novel's only featured young character. In this novel, as in other instances in Johnston, there is an uncanny resemblance between her young heroines and those of Elizabeth Bowen. Each woman writer shines an illuminative beam on such young women at crucial moments of choice and change in their lives. They are expected to *do* something. Their awareness of this imperative, implied or stated, can weigh heavily on them. Older Johnston heroines, dealing with the memory of life choices imposed upon them or that they have not been strong enough to resist, can confront their fears or their oppressors from the past, i.e. *do* something. In recent novels, *The Invisible Worm* (1991) and *The Illusionist* (1995), Johnston operates within this dynamic.

The Invisible Worm shares with all of Johnston's earlier work a political context, but one that is not foregrounded. Laura Quinlan has been for many years a willing prisoner in an unfulfilling marriage to Maurice, a former protégé of her politically powerful father. However, it is her relationship with her father, not with Maurice, that consumes Laura in this book. It was their incestuous relationship that caused her mother's suicide. Memories of her father's funeral open the novel, the first stage in a process that will release her from his grasp. The plot is propelled by an outsider, Dominic O'Hara, a former seminarian with whom Laura has formed an unlikely bond. In *The Illusionist*, in which there is no initial political component, Johnston opts for what seems a completely personal crisis in which there are no sectarian or historical undertones. To do this, Johnston must move her otherwise typical Anglo-Irish heroine out of Ireland. Stella is married and living with her English husband, Martyn Glover. Her life, however, is no less claustrophobic than it would have been in a Big House. Martyn, the illusionist of the title, is a demoniacally controlling force, resentful of Stella's ambition to be a published author. Here again the plot is forwarded by a third party, her editor and friend Bill Freeman, who believes in her writing talent. The seemingly absent political element of the novel returns, however, with Martyn's death in an IRA explosion in London. The supposed randomness of this event remains an unsolved mystery, but is an ultimately liberating experience for his widow.

There is a decided chronology in Johnston's work, since the last two novels are set in contemporary, or near contemporary, Ireland and England. There is also the progression, already noted, from the male to female perspective, and to a greater concentration on the analysis of self instead of national, historical, familial, and even marital considerations. Few of Johnston's heroines are mothers, and those who are (Helen in *The Railway Station Man* and Stella in *The Illusionist*) become estranged from their children in their process of self-discovery.

A detailed examination of two of her earlier novels can yield insights into her developing thematic concerns, and inform our understanding of the imaginative world from which her characters emerge.

The Captains and the Kings has as its plot fulcrum an incipient sexual scandal that erroneously links an elderly widower, Charles Prendergast, survivor of a distinguished Anglo-Irish family, and a young local boy. The Prendergast home, like its owner, has gone to seed. Charles' relationship with his only child, Sarah, has been at best oblique, like all of Charles' interactions with people. Johnston sympathetically portrays the damage Charles' distant mother inflicted upon him, which crippled his marriage and his ability to be an effective parent. The diminished role of the Anglo-Irish in Irish life is signaled by Charles' reluctance to take up the responsibilities of managing his estate, a prospect made less appealing as his mother had sold off the surrounding land that would have made it a viable concern.

Into this atmosphere of stasis and decay is introduced Diarmuid Toorish, an untutored local boy, also the victim of an overbearing, unsympathetic mother. The unlikely bond that develops between the two unloved sons foregrounds Johnston's concerns—the gulf between classes, Irishness versus Englishness, and the constant threat of militarism, in one form or another, that can wreck lives. (The boy has been sent to Charles to work as an apprentice gardener but wishes to join the British army. He becomes fascinated by the military paraphernalia in the house that are the reminders of Charles' long-dead brother.)

Johnston's novel is framed by the presence of authority figures, representatives of Church and State, which are common icons in Irish life. Two policemen; the local Protestant vicar, a friend of Charles'; and the local Catholic priest eventually intervene to exercise damage control. Charges of pederasty against Charles have been made by Sean, Prendergast's drunken gardener, who fears for his job. The final tragedy of the novel, set into action by Sean's lies, sees Diarmuid banished to a vocational school and Charles dead.

The Captains and the Kings uses various metaphorical threads to intensify the poignancy of the situations of the old man and the boy. Charles, an accomplished pianist, makes personal and physical contact with Diarmuid, significantly, while he plays. Shortly after this contact, a touch on the shoulder, Diarmuid, starved for affection and learning, hugs the surprised man. Diarmuid, after asking to come to live with Charles, asks:

'Have I annoyed you?'
'No. No, of course not. Bemused rather.'
'Bemused,' repeated the boy, almost under his breath.
'It would merely lead to trouble.'
'I wouldn't mind.'

'I don't suppose you would. I have spent my life trying to avoid trouble.
With a certain success, I must admit.'
The boy jumped up from the floor suddenly and threw his arms around
the old man's neck.

The scene, which Johnston carefully and succinctly constructs to be
seen by the disgruntled Sean, is simplicity itself. Hers is a prose style that,
though capable of occasional poetic flight, is couched largely in a convincingly simple dialogic idiom that always rings true. Even Johnston's internal
monologues avoid the rhetorical tendency found so often in modern narratives of self-exploration. Her thinking characters, though highly literate in
some cases, are never literary.

The Captains and the Kings also features garden and floral imagery. Most
notably the wild rushes that overgrow the pond on Charles' land and are cut
back by the young Diarmuid, who represents a similarly wild or "native"
strain in the novel. Roses, on the other hand, are closely associated with
Charles' deceased "cultivated" wife, Clare. It is noteworthy that Clare is
English, not Anglo-Irish, and that the rose is a flower traditionally associated
with England, and with English beauty. Clare's roses, now jealously tended
by the bitter Sean with whom she had been somewhat close, were never cut
and brought into the house. These polar images collide when Diarmuid cuts
the roses for the house and in one instance flings them in anger on the lawn.
This shocking and desecratory act is understood by all in the novel.

In The Railway Station Man there is also a dual examination of damaged
lives. Helen Cuffe is a widow, whose husband died a mistaken victim of
sectarian violence in Derry. In an attempt to recover from her shocked state
she removes to a seaside cottage in a remote part of Donegal to paint. The
man who has bought the deserted railway station of the title is Roger
Hawthorne, a disfigured and disabled English war veteran and train buff.
These two outsiders, living on the periphery of local village life, are eventually drawn to each other in a passionate affair that is more potent than
political considerations. Helen's grown son, Jack, now a visitor in her life,
acts as Johnston's stock character who intervenes to cause events in the novel
to happen. Jack has been befriended by Damien Sweeney, who, along with
his friend Manus, is helping Roger to restore the station. All three young
men become involved in IRA activities, and accidentally cause Roger's death,
in a random explosion of stored armaments.

The Railway Station Man, though a more dynamic and violent version
of Johnston's thematic preoccupations, resembles her other novels in its

exposition of humane possibilities dashed by venality, misinformation, and chance. Most importantly, however, the novel features peripheral characters whose historical baggage and political commitment threaten the lives of those who are her focus.

Damien's conversation with Jack encapsulates the dilemma from the nationalist perspective as seen by the author. Quoting his grandfather, he says:

> And he'd talk about Ireland. You'll have to shoot them out, he used to say. . . . They'll never go any other way. . . . They simply don't understand the need that people have for freedom. People would rather be poor and suffer and be free. . . .
> 'He didn't think it was right. He thought it was inevitable. . . . like an operation without an anaesthetic, painful and possibly maiming.

An alternate reading of recent history and its consequences is spoken by Helen, in a view that is perhaps closer to Johnston's own view. Speaking to Roger of his bitterness about his English past in terms that could apply easily to the recent Irish past, Helen says,

> . . . Those are images of the past. . . . It's all over now. Stop conjuring up nightmares. Leave the past alone. That will be your freedom.

In many of Johnston's novels her female characters struggle to achieve freedom, either from oppressive male characters, especially husbands or fathers, or from familial and societal constraints placed upon them. In *The Railway Station Man* Helen has already freed herself, and has also in a sense been freed from such constraints. Helen is the only developed female character in a novel in which there are four men who, in varying degrees, make attempts to curtail her recently achieved freedom. Her son is shocked and revolted to learn Helen has taken Roger as a lover. Roger tries to convince her to marry him when she wishes to prioritize her work. Even the secondary characters, Damien and Manus, pass judgment on her. Damien observes her swimming naked, another minor defiance of convention by a middle-aged mother. Manus makes a pointed comparative reference to his own mother:

> 'Of course I have a mother. . . . just a straightforward, run-of-the-mill mother. No mysteries.'

That Johnston has Helen remain somewhat above or beyond the control of these men is an achievement for which the reader is urged to admire her. It also represents a progression from the situation of other Johnston heroines. But the novelist also emphasizes throughout the book the heroine's vagueness and lack of commitment. Living on the periphery may not be the answer. By cruelly depriving Helen of the prospect of happiness with Roger at the novel's end, Johnston may be indicating that such emotional detachment or carelessness as that which Helen habitually exercises has a price too.

Jennifer Johnston, a Dubliner now living in Northern Ireland, a woman, and a member of Ireland's Protestant minority, is accomplished at detailing the difficulties of Irish people who are not part of the mainstream face, and who find it hard to maintain autonomy and a sense of self. Theirs is not, however, a self-indulgent search for personal fulfillment. Rather Johnston's central characters struggle to survive despite challenges that are often cruel, senseless, and casually accidental. Her imaginative world is a dangerous place under its posh surface, and her characters develop surprising degrees of resilience to overcome the dangers they face. Johnston opts for the human spirit in all cases, but her thematic conclusions are far from naive.

Novelist **John McGahern** was born in 1934 in Co. Leitrim near where he now lives, after many years in Dublin and outside Ireland. McGahern was educated at University College, Dublin, and became a national (primary) school teacher. This autobiographical marker, like many in his life, appears in his fiction. His second novel, *The Dark* (1965), catapulted the young writer into national controversy when the book was banned. It was also discovered that McGahern had married his first wife, a Finnish woman, outside the Church. These combined elements, viewed as scandalous at the time, caused him not only to be fired from his position, but also prohibited from teaching in the archdiocese of Dublin by the formidable Archbishop John Charles McQuaid. The story, which became the subject of newspaper articles and heated national debate, resulted in McGahern's abandoning Ireland for a decade to travel widely.

McGahern's first novel, *The Barracks* (1963), had set the existential tone, however, for all his writing to follow. In the novel the detailed examination undertaken of the life and slow death of a married woman, a former nurse, is based loosely on his mother's life. The novel is a frank, and at times bleak, study of doubt. Its protagonist finally rejects the comforts of the faith in which she has been educated throughout her life. The barracks of the title are married quarters for the widowed gardai sergeant she married, and his children. It is a world that author McGahern also knew intimately from his sad childhood, and transforms into the next venue, a farmhouse, for the following controversial work.

The Dark, which opens with a horrific scene of a father beating, or threatening to beat, his naked son, takes as its starting point all the tensions and suffering of *The Barracks*, but is less relieved by the rare moments of fleeting love and humor of the earlier work. In *The Dark* the brutalized children and grieving and beset widower become undeclared enemies in an atmosphere of cruelty and distrust that the children learn to use in their defense.

Mahoney, the father in *The Dark*, is a farmer disgruntled, but proud in time, because his son wins a scholarship to secondary school and thence to a university. The son, as protagonist, contends with every impediment that can be placed in the path of his success—poverty, intimidation, the loss of his mother, the vexations of the onset of sexual awareness, and the need to contribute to the brutally hard seasonal farmwork. But none of these privations or troubles is as anything to the burden of his father. Mahoney, a malevolent but mercurial force from the novel's first page, is at times hideous. But he is often poignant in his loneliness and futile bouts of anger.

The Dark articulates crucial societal truths about modern Ireland. Freedom from rural poverty and deprivation came to boys through two means. The first was academic achievement; the second, related, was through religious vocation. A farmer's son, able to excel in round after round of state examinations, could proceed to higher-level education or to a job in the civil service, or in one of Ireland's several semi-state bodies (including the gas and electric companies, the telephone service, etc.) Bright boys were also reminded that they could proceed to seminary. In *The Dark*, as in Joyce's *A Portrait of the Artist as a Young Man*, the attraction of the priesthood is seen first in terms of the niceties missing in each protagonist's life—order, privacy, and a degree of privilege. Each young hero is tempted by the lure of the status accorded the priesthood; but each is also haunted by sexual and other sterility that is a feature of the celibate life, and is therefore fearful of a lifetime of loneliness.

The young man in *The Dark* who goes off to the university is unlike Joyce's Stephen Dedalus, however, in that he finds most of his teachers uninspiring, and fails to connect with the life of the mind. Eschewing the chance of obtaining a degree, he accepts in his confusion a secure lower-level pensionable job in Dublin to escape the pressure to excel. His abusive upbringing has failed to prepare him to succeed. In *The Dark* a heritage of deprivation, of both the emotional and the tangible sort, overpowers natural talent and enthusiasm, leaving its dread mark for life. The protagonist's sole hope is that, freed from family and all it entails, he may find in life the love and the female companionship he was denied as a child. However, McGahern's tortuous scenes near the end of *The Dark*, of the boy being unable to bring himself to enter his first dance, suggest that his road in the future will not be an easy one either.

Parallels between *The Dark* and *A Portrait of the Artist*, raised earlier in reference to the rejection of a vocation, are more varied than that particular thematic concurrence might suggest. That Stephen Dedalus' mother is a waning figure in *A Portrait*, and dead when Dedalus reappears in *Ulysses*, is mirrored by the dying mother in *The Barracks* and the dead mother in *The Dark*. Each protagonist also has a horde of unidentified siblings. Similarly the acrimonious Oedipal defeat of each father provides most of the structuring principle of both novels, and sets in motion the compulsion of each son to escape.

McGahern's style in *The Dark*, in particular his use of person, may at first seem random but is, in fact, highly structured. Segments of the novel are constructed in the first, second, and third persons in order to change perspective and to vary the subjective and objective reactions to young Mahoney's experience. The use of secondary characters also helps to open up the claustrophobic battle between father and son. Father Gerald, a family member, represents both the hope and the fear of a vocation. As young Mahoney nears the end of his secondary schooling, he is taken to Father Gerald's world, instead of undergoing the intermittent intrusion that the priest's visits to his own world have occasioned. Here the boy is given a glimpse of his possible future as a priest. The subservient character of Joseph, the priest's unlikely 16-year-old houseboy, provides an uncomfortable contrast. Joseph, who would never be considered suitable for the seminary, refers to young Mahoney as "Mr. Mahoney" and calls him "sir." This mark of respect for his potential achievement does not, however, produce the desired effect. Young Mahoney, instead, identifies strongly with Joseph's servile station, especially as it mirrors that of Mahoney's sister, Joan, in unhappy domestic servitude in another house in the town.

The Dark illuminates aspects of sexual behavior among the adults in the novel that cast Irish rural and small-town life and Irish Catholicism in a dubious and unsavory light, part of the reason for the negative reception of the book. Mahoney's father, seeking sexual solace, fondles his son in bed. Years later the boy is similarly tortured by Father Gerald's nocturnal intimacy at the rectory. Joan is sexually abused by her employer. The young man's dual decisive actions, taken simultaneously, to reject the priesthood and to bring his sister back to the relative safety of their family home, are evidence of growth and measurable change on his part. These decisions also give credence to his ability at novel's end to reject university life in favor of the anonymity of Dublin and the perceived freedom of a paycheck. In the final pages of the book, father and adult son are forced by circumstances to share a bed for the night in Galway. They do so perhaps not as equals, but with a hard-won degree of respect and love largely achieved by the son's persistent efforts to understand and forgive.

McGahern's next novel, *The Leavetaking*, has a most unusual publishing history. First published in 1974, it was rejected publicly by the author and reissued in substantially revised form a decade later. Part of the reinforced structure of the novel is its degree of emphasis on the day—a day—as a unit of time. The "extraordinary ordinary day" provides a rhythm in human life that the novelist uses artfully to give a similarly palpable rhythm to his fiction. The day's beginning, progression, and inevitable and unfluctuating end shape reality and provide time for reflection and evaluation. So too the novel's circular structure, a feature of all of McGahern's work, is rhythmic while never belying the complexity of life or of the work.

In McGahern's most recent and most acclaimed novel, *Amongst Women* (1990), these structuring principles continue. His intense focus here is life at Great Meadow, the Moran family farm. Using the same family name as he did in *The Leavetaking*, McGahern binds his narratives, and recreates variations on a by now familiar family dynamic. Old Moran, like Reegan in *The Barracks*, has been widowed and remarried. Rose, his second wife, is not the mother of the nearly grown children of the novel. Like Elizabeth Reegan, she serves to provide a female perspective that is intimate without being in the first instance maternal. As its title suggests, *Amongst Women* substitutes the stifling relationship between father and son for that between father and daughters. Maggie, Mona, and Sheila all lead adult lives outside Great Meadow. Their frequent returns, portrayed as essential to both father and daughters, underscore their preordained familial roles. Moran's oldest son, Luke (a version of young Mahoney from *The Dark*), has rejected this construct and refuses to return home from London. The younger son, Michael, has been given over to his older sisters to rear and remains for some time outside his father's range of interest.

In McGahern it is family, not the narrower individual nor the broader community, from which one gains definition. Moran has mesmerizing power over all at Great Meadow, mixes infrequently with the townspeople, and discourages his children from doing so. The girls are at times confused by this type of distinction imposed upon them. Rose, Moran's new bride, although to a degree powerless against him, continues to be friendly and affable, greeting people and visiting her own family regularly. This very ordinary behavior strikes Moran's daughters as being common; their father sees it as betrayal.

In all of McGahern's fiction the claustrophobic, behind-closed-doors world of family life is intense and psychologically both complex and volatile. It is also both isolated and self-isolating, whether it be the garda barracks or Great Meadow. Part of the tension of this fiction is again provided by the ubiquitous rendering of the Irish secondary-school examination processes. In *Amongst Women* both Mona and Sheila torture themselves and the others as they prepare for school-leaving exams. Sheila's excellent results and defeated acceptance of a job in the Department of Finance, instead of a coveted place in a university to study medicine, repeats young Mahoney's fate from the earlier novel.

As Moran's daughters leave, and Maggie and Sheila marry, McGahern reinforces an established pattern—neither husband is accepted. One is considered irreverent about Moran family pieties and violates established customs; the other is considered weak and unaccomplished. Only young Michael's wife, an accomplished young woman, but one who is reverential to tradition, is accepted by Moran—another woman to control. His grandchildren, living in Dublin and London, however, are too far away for him to influence. As a result, Moran exhibits little interest in them, although a wary Sheila guards against his contaminating the spiritedness of her own children when they do visit.

Amongst Women is a study of dominance, cast as a gender battle rather than the generational and/or Oedipal battle of McGahern's earlier work. As such, it is very much a novel of its time, although McGahern convincingly asserts the timelessness of such struggles within families. The strong, often destructive father is again his chief interest. Perhaps more intriguing for the reader, however, is the process of watching the etiolated results of such paternal control. The characters who are the victims of such control are touching and admirable in the resourceful methods they devise in order to survive and to find definition in their lives. That they do so, in McGahern's fiction as in life, without wholesale rejection of misguided but loving fathers, stands as a testament to the author's subtle understanding of the multifaceted dynamic of the family.

Julia O'Faolain (b. 1932), daughter of the noted writer Sean O'Faolain, has lived in Los Angeles and Rome, and now resides in London. A linguist by training, O'Faolain has published six novels and four collections of short stories, many of which are set in continental Europe. She has recently returned to writing short stories after more than a decade-long publishing hiatus, and describes the short story form as "a tricky genre which should be able to condense enough light to burn through to the essence of things."[4]

O'Faolain has set her writing in a variety of eras and venues, from sixth-century Gaul to Rome in the 1970s. Her world is often the world of women, and her earlier work features convents and boarding schools. Conventional religion and religious practices, beliefs, and rituals are also frequently explored, but the author's attitude toward religion is not conventional.

Not all of O'Faolain's work portrays sequestered environments, however, and in two of her best-known novels, No Country for Young Men (1980) and The Irish Signorina (1984), the author expands her focus to meet the demands of the novel and the worldly arena of international politics, modern terrorism, and the complexities of male/female relationships. Such complexities in O'Faolain can include cross-generational affairs, adultery, and incest. Traditional in format—female characters in O'Faolain's novels are usually stationary and domiciled, whereas male characters are usually peripatetic or nomadic—No Country for Young Men does experiment with a split narrative that tells two intertwining stories that occur a half-century apart.

O'Faolain's traditional trappings, like her use of religious settings, can be misleading. For instance, the heroines of both the novels are homebodies, but in each case they are reluctant and ambivalent about their roles. Grainne O'Malley in No Country for Young Men is a poor housekeeper, an ignored wife, and an ineffectual mother. Anne Ryan in The Irish Signorina, a sheltered only child, has remained at home to nurse a dying mother, more because she is not strong enough to defy the conventional demand that she must, rather than out of any genuine sense of conviction or love.

In each of these novels the male characters share a high degree of involvement in the official or marginal political culture of their day and respective countries. In keeping with these dual feminine and masculine worlds established early on by O'Faolain, characters in No Country for Young Men are also divided into the parallel plots taking place in the 1920s and 1970s. The link between the plots is the involvement of Grainne's male relatives and her lover in IRA-related activities. In the novel's present, Grainne's uncle and son are among those engaged in factional politics and violence. All the men are highly mobile. Uncle Owen Roe O'Malley turns up at inopportune moments, whereas her son's extended absences are a worry. Grainne's husband, Michael, disappears to drink. He is a fastidious musician and her distant cousin, and for these reasons, and also because he is not political, he is given an emasculated role in the novel. James Duffy, Grainne's American lover, begins the novel politically naive, but as his involvement increases and he becomes more savvy, he becomes more powerful and more peripatetic. But the most potent character in the novel is Owen Roe, who was also Grainne's former incestuous lover, and who is a political manipulator—groomed by the characters in the earlier plot.

The volatile 1920s in Ireland is conveyed in part in *No Country for Young Men* through the fractured consciousness of the elderly Sister Judith Clancy, Grainne's aunt who figures in both plots. Sister Judith, forced into wandering from the home of one relative to another, is an aberrant female character. A victim of a 1970s trend toward "relevance," she has been traumatized by being sent into the world after the closure of the convent she called her home for decades. But Sister Judith had been traumatized much earlier by murderous events in the family in her youth. She was sent into the convent as part of a Machiavellian plan on the part of her father and brothers to silence a secret that begins to absorb the interest of the 1970s characters. Thus are the two plots inextricably linked.

In *The Irish Signorina*, Anne Ryan is transplanted after her mother's death to the Tuscan villa in which the mother had been an au pair a generation earlier. Here Anne soon becomes the secret lover of Guido and Neri Cavalcanti, who are father and son. But it is Guido's mother, the Marchesa Niccolosa, who is the powerful center of life at the villa. Guido and Neri are at opposite ends of the Italian political spectrum. Guido is a prominent lawyer defending a cabinet minister's son against terrorist charges. Neri is, ironically, also a terrorist. O'Faolain's penchant for illustrating the alienating effects of political involvement on domestic life has the wandering Guido "spotted" in unlikely places throughout the novel. Neri, who has been forbidden entrance to the villa by his grandmother because of his politics, lurks around its periphery and that of the lives of all the characters who come and go from his former home.

The choreography already described in both novels focuses the reader's attention on the plight of nonpolitical women who run households that restrict their free movement, and of the politically propelled men who return to these homes only when the stress or danger implicit in their commitment becomes too real. In both novels the heroines become gradually more politicized themselves, but not in the pattern that this choreography may at first suggest. They do not, either of them, leave home in any literal or figurative sense to espouse the political causes of one of the men in their lives. Instead they become politicized in the broader sense, coming finally to know themselves and their individual potential. They will not have their futures dictated to them, as their pasts had been, by men. In each novel, furthermore, it is the example of the older woman that guides the heroine's decisions. Sister Judith's life acts as a cautionary tale for Grainne. The dutiful daughter, now an elderly outcast, accepted the politics of the men in the family and became the victim. Anne, in *The Irish Signorina*, has a stronger role model in the Marchesa, who has a lifetime of wealth and beauty behind her. These are powerful weapons that the Marchesa uses effectively to retain control throughout the novel. Although Anne has neither wealth nor beauty at her disposal, she has learned from the dowager's independence. Each of O'Faolain's young heroines also absorbs a knowledge of the power that women with secrets can wield. (Judith retains the secret of an earlier murder; the Marchesa knows that Guido's former union with Anne's mother resulted in Anne's illegitimate birth.) As Grainne and Anne progress to maturity in the novels, they will carry their own powerful secrets with them, too.[5]

Much contemporary Irish fiction explores overtly or surreptitiously the subtle connections between the formation of personality in the young and the process of politicization. These allied themes have also begun to surface in Ireland in art forms other than literature.

John Banville was born in 1945 in the town of Wexford. He is in the minority of Irish writers in that he is not university educated, and has been employed most of his life in capacities in Irish newspapers. He now serves as literary editor of the *Irish Times*. Banville wrote an early collection of short stories (*Long Lankin*, 1970), but has worked specifically within the form of the novel since then. *Nightspawn* (1971) is a political thriller set in Greece. *Birchwood* (1973) is Banville's acclaimed contribution to the Big House genre. A tetralogy of sorts followed, which plumbs the biographies of great scientists and questions the methods and parameters of scientific inquiry. *Dr. Copernicus* appeared in 1976, followed by *Kepler* (1981), *The Newton Letter* (1982), and *Mefisto* (1986). The last book in the tetralogy uses a mathematician, possibly Einstein, as its model. In each of these four novels, however, Banville argues a case for scientist as artist, which adds complexity and innovation to the undertaking.

Banville's next three novels have a very different focus, however, concentrating on criminality and guilt, although their central character was at one time a mathematician. *The Book of Evidence* (1989) begins Banville's exploration of this thematic seam, and is loosely based on a real murder. *Ghosts* (1993) and *Athena* (1995) return the reader to the precincts of murderer Freddie Montgomery's deranged mind. The latter novel questions the nature of a love affair after guilt and recrimination have been thoroughly dissected in the two earlier works.

Banville's fiction is the most highly allusive and self-consciously literary that is being written in Ireland today. It is also simultaneously the most poetic and the most spare. The economy employed in his sentence structure can be highly evocative. A sentence describing one of a pair of lovers in *The Newton Letter* provides an effective example: "Hers was the brave brightness of all big awkward girls." Similarly, an early passage in *Birchwood* describes the kitchen of the house: "In the kitchen the stove squats in a hot sulk after its labours, the air is dense with the smoke of burnt fat." Here, as in many instances in Banville's writing, prose passages comprised wholly or nearly wholly of monosyllabic words heighten clarity of emotion and remembered experience. And not only are these early works notable for pared sentences and paragraphs, the novels themselves are economical. *Birchwood* is 175 pages long, and *The Newton Letter* is only 92. Banville, who is on record railing against the publishing industry's dicta on length and other technical restrictions for novels, exhibited early in his career an independence of style and format that separated him immediately from popular novelists. His smaller readership is the price paid for such artistic integrity. Although Banville made an early reputation in Britain and Canada, it has been slow to spread to the United States. His work is translated into a range of European languages, but it attracts only a select, loyal readership outside Ireland.

Birchwood lays the foundation for an understanding of Banville's corpus. Gabriel Godkin, its narrator, after a short introductory chapter from an adult perspective, begins to tell the story of Birchwood and his family remembered from childhood. Memory is shifting and unreliable, and Gabriel is aware of this variable from the outset. In time both he and the reader are made aware that even elements that should be known or constant are not. He is not his mother's son, but the product of an incestuous relationship between his father and aunt. The woman whom he fondly remembers as his fragile mother is a Lawless, and her family lost Birchwood to the Godkins in an earlier generation. The phantom sister whom Gabriel seeks throughout much of the novel does not exist, but a male cousin turns out to be his twin, and rival as heir to the house and demesne. Such tampering with bloodlines indicates a decadence that pervades other aspects of the novel. Duplicity in the literal and figurative sense manifests in a host of dual or twinned characters and even in the second family he acquires as he joins a traveling circus to avoid being sent away to school.

Gabriel believes the circus troupe of grotesques are presided over by a character named Prospero, who also fails to materialize. The grotesquerie and incipient magic of his circus experience has, however, been presaged in the novel by characters who make up their own families. Granny Godkin is a gabbling, garrulous, miscreant presence who conveniently dies of spontaneous combustion. Ineffectual Grandpa Godkin experiences supernatural visions before being found dead on the grounds with his dentures imbedded in a nearby tree. Each has significantly left Birchwood to die outside, an indication of their interloper status as Godkins.

Gabriel's story is told against the backdrop of nineteenth-century famine. At first he is sequestered in the relative security of Birchwood, and then within the strange, otherworldly atmosphere of the circus troupe, but the famine and its inexorably progressive suffering gradually impinges. Although told from a purposely oblique perspective, Gabriel's awareness of the famine's implications serves to recreate a valid contemporary perspective untainted by the historical cataclysmic view that informs most fictional and nonfictional accounts of the period. Imperceptibly the extent of the horror becomes clear. So too does the menacing reality of a world on the brink of anarchy. Roving bands of soldiers and bandits murder and rape. The vaga-bonds who make up the circus live cunningly on the edge of a deteriorating society that had previously provided them with their meager livelihood. Throughout his travels and despite setbacks, Gabriel searches for a greater sense of understanding for "the whatness of things." He remembers coming upon his parents making love in a deserted cottage on Birchwood's grounds (again, *outside* the home itself): "a woman's pale hands clutched and loosed in langorous spasms a pale white arse bare below a hiked-up shirt-tail." Gabriel does not believe he has discovered love. Instead he claims, "all I had found was the notion of—I shall call it harmony." There is an ordering principle in the world, but this harmony can only be glimpsed in isolated moments when we are receptive to or are able to absorb its grand scale.

Significantly Gabriel returns to Birchwood at the end of the novel to write his story. In this regard he is like the narrators of the tetralogy. *Doctor Copernicus* relates the scientist's crisis as he discovers that his writing is a *fiction*. In *Kepler*, like *Doctor Copernicus* narrated by a scientist, Kepler publishes his discoveries. The nameless would-be biographer of Isaac Newton in *The Newton Letter* suffers writer's block, or loss of faith in the undertaking. Instead he narrates letters that relate the details of his life and the novel. These are addressed to Clio, the Muse of History. The letter of the title is an historical document, a second letter is not, but a fictional composite of his and/or of Banville's. In *Mefisto*, Gabriel Swan writes of his downfall in a black book. In each of these novels, then, there is a sustained, self-conscious awareness of the act of writing within a fiction. This mechanism, of course, calls into question the validity of the creative act, and the degree to which it approaches but never quite achieves the desired "harmony" it too seeks.

The Newton Letter, like *Birchwood*, is set in Ireland. Fern House, located near the coast south of Dublin, is its venue. Its narrator takes up residence in the gate lodge and becomes the lover of Ottilie Lawless. Ottilie has borne a son as a result of a relationship with a farmhand. Her Uncle Edward, a former gardener on the estate, has married Charlotte Grainger, the daughter of his employer. As in *Birchwood*, incest and the displacement of local gentry by the lower classes signal inevitable decay. The narrator, though Ottilie's lover, becomes obsessed by Charlotte. His obsession, however, is based on a consistent misreading of people and events at Fern House. He initially mistakes the boy, naturally enough, for Charlotte's son. Later he believes Edward to be the boy's father. He mistakes the Catholic family for Protestants, and dismisses Edward, who is terminally ill and in great pain, as a drunk. Charlotte, who *is* permanently under the influence of drugs, he finds simply charmingly vague. Finally the narrator must face the truth, the reality, of his situation and theirs, and admit his entire imaginative construct to be a fiction. He has grappled earlier in the novel, however, with a similar problem in his work. He has lost faith in the purpose of writing and "the poignancy of text." He has also allowed reality to overtake his studies, or reality has impinged to such a degree as to make academic study and writing impossible. In his dilemma the narrator resembles Isaac Newton, who suffered a similar crisis. Each tried to fit reality into an unworkable theory of his own construction. (In Newton's case, he tried in his *Principia* to posit that space, time, and motion were absolutes, a theory refuted by John Locke.)

The opening chapter of *The Newton Letter* discloses the outcome of the narrator's stay at Fern House and his blighted affair with Ottilie. He has taken a teaching position in a remote, unnamed Nordic university, and maintains contact with Ottilie by letter. His final resolve is to return to Fern House, in part because Ottilie is pregnant with his child. This intrusion of reality serves as another counter to his former fantasizing of a relationship with Charlotte. He will reenter Fern House but on a different plane—"become a nurseryman and wear tweeds, talk about the weather, stand around chewing a straw." In this decision, which smacks suspiciously of his assuming the persona of the dead Edward, a subversion of reality is yet again threatened.

The Newton Letter was made into a film shortly after it appeared. The film, entitled *Reflections*, provided the narrator with a name—Willie Master. This allusion to Goethe's *Willheim Meister* makes obvious Banville's debt in this, and in most of his fiction, to the works of the great German writer. But *The Newton Letter*, like all of Banville's writing, is multiply allusive, weaving direct and indirect references not only to the major scientific and mathematical minds of earlier centuries, but also to such diverse writers as Henry James, W. B. Yeats, and Jean-Paul Sartre.

The Book of Evidence marks a decided turn in Banville's writing and one that persists to the present. As he explored the scientific mind in his earlier work, he dissects in his later work what would be conventionally (realistically?) termed the critical mind. What seems thematic divergence, however, becomes thematic continuum in that each is allied in a sense to art. Scientific inquiry is initially an imaginative act. So is writing. Freddie Montgomery, the monstrous murderer at the center of *The Book of Evidence,* blames his crime on "a failure of imagination." The imaginative leap required on the part of the reader to believe Freddie's view is aided by Banville's having Freddie kill, ostensibly, in the name of art. He is obsessed by a painting, a seventeenth-century Dutch interior that seems to resemble a Vermeer. Observed in the act of stealing the painting, he bludgeons a hapless servant girl to death, another instance of reality forcing itself upon illusion in the form of both the work of art (an artifice) and Freddie's fantasy of his owning or controlling it.

The Book of Evidence takes its title from a legal term under British and Irish law. Here it takes the form of a prison notebook kept by Freddie that is intended to explain, but not condone, his crime. Freddie is thus another of Banville's writers creating a fiction within a fiction. In his analysis Freddie opts for a form of reality that rejects the legal in favor of the more mundane reality of the life of the girl and the real world. He castigates himself for being absorbed with the world of the painting rather than, or to the exclusion of, the real world that it represents and by which it was inspired.

Freddie Montgomery, by no coincidence in Banville's fictional world, is a former mathematician who finally rejects the rational, quantitative world of figures and the legal world of facts and of the law that has found him guilty, but, he argues, for the wrong reasons. The real world, which he begins to celebrate for its defiant irrationality, has now claimed him.

In *The Book of Evidence* John Banville tests his readers. The central act of the murder is unspeakably brutal and Freddie shows a chilling lack of remorse for his crime. The reader, anticipating a defense that would force him to judge the criminal on the basis of his dedication to art, is forcefully told by the perpetrator himself to reject that defense. By continuing to use Freddie, a fundamentally hateful but endlessly fascinating protagonist, Banville continues to make demands on his readers in both *Ghosts* and in *Athena.*

Banville's most recent novel, *The Untouchable* (1997), seems to take yet another, but related, thematic direction. The novel is based loosely on the real espionage tale of Guy Burgess, Kim Philby, Donald MacLean, and Anthony Blunt, who were conscripted out of Cambridge University to become Soviet KGB counteragents. (However, Banville takes some liberties. The Blunt/Maskell character has several biographical interstices with poet Louis MacNeice, who was a secondary-school roommate of Blunt's. Banville also creates a vile character, Querell, to represent novelist Graham Greene, with whom he had a personal quarrel.) Since Anthony Blunt, on whom the central character is based, was one of the world's most prominent art historians and curators, the reader finds himself again in the realm of art, with another central character who is possessed by a particular painting. This novel is perhaps simply what one reviewer has termed an exercise in "prodigal aesthetic pleasure."[6]

John Banville is a unique voice in fiction in Ireland today. One very important distinguishing trait between his work and that of his contemporaries is that although his work is sometimes set in Ireland , it is not really about Ireland. Questions of national identity do not engage this author, nor do timely social or political issues (historically the stuff of certain types of novels). Banville is interested in posing large, philosophical, and timeless questions, and in attempting to provide a response that can be valid for readers in this age. He is also one of the few novelists in Ireland today who exhibits continually within his texts a postmodern awareness of the arbitrary nature of the task of attempting to express his ideas in the novel form, after the deconstructing work of Joyce and Beckett. Those earlier Irish writers' antinovels should make the novelist's enterprise a questionable, skeptical undertaking, but their deconstructive projects seem not to have impinged on the consciousness of most prose writers in Ireland today. These distinctions of Banville's may explain why in the words of his most perceptive critic, Rüdiger Imhof, "Banville has so far managed to remain a moving target for his critics."[7]

Bernard MacLaverty was born in Belfast in 1942 and attended Queen's University there as a mature student. He has taught in Scotland, where he also lived both in Glasgow and on the Isle of Islay in the Hebrides.

MacLaverty's writing is Northern Irish–based. His early novel *Cal* (1983), the story of a Catholic widow of a Protestant who takes a young Catholic boy as a lover, is made more complex and poignant by the boy's having been instrumental in her husband's death. Such intricacy, which reflects the permutations of life, is a feature of MacLaverty's fiction. Both *Cal* and *Lamb* (1980), his first novel, have been made into films that have enjoyed considerable popular success. *Lamb*, an even more audacious and sensitive story than *Cal*, concerns a religious brother who risks being considered a child molester rather than allow an abused and ignored child to be maltreated by family and religious institutions any longer.

MacLaverty's books of short stories, *Secrets and Other Stories* (1977), *A Time to Dance* (1982), *The Great Profundo* (1987), and *Walking the Dog* (1994), were followed by his recent novel *Grace Notes* (1997), which was received with acclaim. "My Dear Palestrina," a story published in *A Time to Dance*, introduces characters and themes that MacLaverty would develop years later in *Grace Notes*. Both stories are ostensibly about the growth and development of a musician. The earlier story concerns Danny McErlane, a young working-class boy whose mother forces him to begin piano lessons after the family acquires a piano. Danny's innate talent is recognized and nurtured by Miss Schwartz, a Polish émigré with a local reputation for being an exotic. In the contrasting local-vs.-foreign dichotomy between pupil and teacher, and the story's musical ambiance, "My Dear Palestrina" is intertextual with Carson McCullers' well-known story "Wunderkind." (The word "wunderkind" appears in MacLaverty's story.) Each of the stories also locates the onset of pubescent awareness of adult sexuality, and delicately examines the fear and reluctance experienced when a young person must leave childhood behind. In "My Dear Palestrina" Danny is tutored in the ways of the world not only by Miss Schwartz, but also by a local farrier, whose occupation marks him as the virility principle in the story. As the story ends, Danny, deprived of Miss Schwartz's cosmopolitan world overview and of the world of music, is ominously urged by his mother to "join us." This threatened return to the provincial and culturally deprived world of the McErlanes is portrayed by MacLaverty as tragic. The artistic or the ordinary choice remains for the author a central concern, returning again as it does as the focus of *Grace Notes*. Like Joyce's, MacLaverty's artists and would-be artists know their choice will require sacrifice, but that any hardship they suffer for their art is worth the pain it causes them or others.

The choice to make difficult or unorthodox decisions forms the crux of much of MacLaverty's writing, and nowhere with such dire consequences as it does in *Cal*. The title character is a young man, unemployed and living with his widowed father. There is constant tension in their lives as they are the only remaining Catholics in a Protestant neighborhood and are frequent victims of threats. Through a series of flashback passages, MacLaverty has Cal reconstruct the horror of the crime in which he has unwillingly participated to repay IRA protection of himself and his father.

Drawn inexplicably to the young widow of his victim, Marcella, Cal gets a job on her in-laws' farm and eventually begins to live in an abandoned cottage on the grounds. Thoughts of sins and guilt plague Cal, along with fear of being apprehended for his crime. He and his father have been burned out of their home, and Cal's insecurities mount, causing him in his confusion to believe he can expiate his guilt by serving Marcella in some way. When she reveals to him her loneliness since her husband's death and her dislike of living with his parents, the two become illicit lovers. The relationship, doomed from the start, ends abruptly, as does the novel, with Cal's arrest.

He hopes that his guilt will be assuaged by the punishment meted out to him by the authorities. His suppression of his rage against and resentment of the paramilitaries, who have destroyed both his and his father's lives, is an acknowledgment that his crime was in some ways his own doing. Regardless of the circumstances, it was a decision he made and for which he will pay.

In *Cal*, as in all of his other fiction, MacLaverty explores the tension between societal and political pressure and the individual conscience. The ideologue, whether religious, political, or cultural, has suppressed his or her innate humanity to serve that ideology. In MacLaverty's work it is the unenviable task of those who have not lost touch with that humanity to act in accordance with their personal beliefs and to treat others as individuals— not as the enemy or the other. If they fail, they fail themselves.

Neil Jordan, best known outside Ireland as a film director (*Mona Lisa* [1986], *The Crying Game* [1992], and *Michael Collins* [1996] are among his best-known films), was born in Sligo in 1950. Long before Jordan concentrated his artistic efforts on film, however, he had authored poems and stories. His writing also includes four novels, including an impressive first effort, *The Past* (1980), which deals sensitively, but probingly, with the negative effects of social and personal repression. Jordan's recent *Sunrise with Sea Monster* (1995, published in the U.S. as *Nightlines*) returns to the exploration of a father-son relationship, one of Jordan's constant thematic quests, often with national or international implications. His earlier *The Dream of a Beast* (1983) has been described as ". . . a fever dream of a book that took Joyce's Dublin and handed it over to Kafka."[8] It is a hallucinatory nightmare exercise, featuring endless doors (indicating endless choices), and a bestiary that recalls *Alice in Wonderland* in structure and intent, but which is considerably more macabre. Jordan, who worked with the writer Angela Carter to turn one of her fabulist tales into his film *The Company of Wolves* (1984), has been described as having a talent that is "baffling and disturbing but never essentially pessimistic."[9]

Many of Jordan's works have a seaside setting that often contrasts the purity of sea and strand (or beach) with the tackiness of seaside resorts. The placidity of a bay in Northern Ireland is contrasted with the honky-tonk atmosphere of an adjacent amusement park in the sinister kidnapping scene that opens *The Crying Game*. Significantly, the sea is similarly featured from the time of Jordan's earliest work.

The author's sole collection of short stories, *Night in Tunisia and Other Stories* (1976), is a surprisingly deft effort considering it is Jordan's first published prose work. *Night in Tunisia* was published by the Irish Writers' Co-operative, an excellent small publisher of the time, which Jordan helped to found.

The title story is a superb piece of modern fiction that entered the Irish pantheon with its inclusion in *The Field Day Anthology*. Set along Ireland's eastern coast, north of Dublin, "Night in Tunisia" is a coming-of-age story of a motherless boy, 14 as the story begins, who is spending the summer at the seaside with his musician father and pubescent sister. Joined to his father by his natural talent as a saxophonist, the boy spends much of the story neglecting the talent that the father envies. Instead, he is fixated on a local girl of dubious reputation and falls in with bad company. Thus he squanders his musical talent to gain entry into a clique and to compensate for his being relatively young and sexually untried. Jordan contrasts the girl's knowing-ness and experience and the boy's straining innocence in a passage that issues from the boy's consciousness. He observes the girl playing tennis with an older man who then takes her away in his car:

> He felt there was something wrong, the obedient ball, the running man. What had she lost to gain that ease, he wondered. He thought of all the jokes he had heard and of the act behind the jokes that none of those who told the jokes experienced. The innuendos and the charged words like the notes his father played, like the melodies his father willed him to play.

Here and elsewhere in his oeuvre, Jordan dares to openly mix the powerful combination of music with sexuality (as he does in his films, especially *The Crying Game*). However, in "Night in Tunisia" the blend is both more potent and more subtle, as the reader has already noted the boy's repeated reluctance to speak to the girl or to play his father's music. Maturation, sexual and otherwise, comes at one's own pace.

"Night in Tunisia," Dizzy Gillespie's well-known jazz piece, which his father wills him to play, becomes a metaphor for experience, and one that the boy eventually comes to understand intellectually and emotionally. His mastery of the piece eventually separates him from the world of boys, which is represented as being at a significant distance from the girls and women they study and desire. On a raft offshore, the boys scrutinize and make juvenile innuendos about women displayed in bathing suits on the beach. The scene recalls bathing sequences in other innocence-to-experience fiction, from Joyce's *A Portrait of the Artist* to F. Scott Fitzgerald's "Winters Dreams, " a similar summer romance and coming-of-age story. "Night in

Tunisia" thus examines a teenage boy's desire to know and, more importantly, to understand women, their bodies, and the mysterious differences
between the sexes. Indeed Jordan's story owes much to Joyce, not just in this
particular, but in its subtleties of exposition. The tension between the
adolescent's outward aloofness but fervid dedication to sensual and sexual
discovery is also Joycean, as is Jordan's experimental style, which features
typographically isolated paragraphs that can consist of a single sentence.

Other stories in *Night in Tunisia*, including "Skin," "Her Soul," "Outpa-
tient," and "Free," examine as fully the female psyche as did "Night in Tunisia"
the male perspective. "Skin," a nearly eventless sketch of an unnamed,
middle-aged housewife, uses the domestic metaphor of peeling an onion to
describe the aging process, and exhibits an empathy surprising in a writer
so young:

> And in her the need for the secret inner life still bloomed. It would
> come to the fore in odd moments. A fragment of a song, hummed for
> a bar or two, then broken off. A daydream. She would slide into it like
> a suicide eases himself into an unruffled canal.

Linking as he does middle-aged longing with death, Jordan as author
travels well beyond the consciousness of the woman and anticipates the
story's anticlimactic close. The woman takes a final plunge into the sea,
exposing her aging figure. Her failure to excite a man on the beach makes
a knowing intertextual statement on Joyce's famous seaside encounter
between a young Gertie McDowell and a middle-aged Leopold Bloom in
Ulysses where the reverse gender dynamic results in Bloom's arousal.

The final story in the collection, "A Love," begins with the funeral of
Éamon de Valéra, who died shortly before *Night in Tunisia* was published. De
Valéra and Michael Collins, opposing figures in the founding of the Irish
State, loom large in Jordan's imagination, as they do in that of many living
Irish writers. "A Love" charts the unlikely coming of age of the young male
protagonist, named Neil like the author, who is sexually initiated by a
woman much older than he. Their meeting years later begins in Dublin
during de Valéra's funeral and marks the end of another era, that of their
illicit love. The couple travels across Ireland to Lisdoonvarna in Co. Clare,
a spa and matchmaking center for older bachelors and spinsters. There they
make love a final time, she an aging woman, he a young man now. In the
West of Ireland, the epicenter of the nation's founding myth, the final
changes are wrung on a relationship that is anathema to the public virtues
encouraged in the formative years of the country. This love, however, is

manifestly more genuine than the repressive, idealized virtue that was meant to denote neotraditional Irishness. Again, Jordan details a poignant affection for the older female form. The reader focuses, perhaps more artfully than in "Skin," on the transience of both love and life. The phrase "we've changed" is repeated in the story. Its meaning extends beyond the recognition artic- ulated by the lovers, to the transitional state of Ireland, as it begins a new chapter after the death of its founding father. As with all parental deaths, real or metaphorical, there is sorrow but also release.

Neil Jordan's stories, like his novels, examine change and growth, and so are never static, despite an atmosphere of hesitancy and contemplation. Plotting in Jordan serves only as a backdrop for detailed thematic explora- tion, which is in turn served by judicious use of imagery and metaphor. Secondary characters, such as Neil's father in "A Love," and even the boy's father in "Night in Tunisia," are lightly sketched and severely subservient to the protagonist. This latter feature is one that is also consistent with Jordan's directorial aims in film.

Neil Jordan's creative work forms an arc that encompasses contempo- rary Irish experience and looks toward the future. At the end of "A Love" Neil anticipates that future in a minor but significant act:

> . . . I crossed the square and bought a paper and read more about the
> President who had died, but in small print now.

Patrick McCabe, born in Co. Monaghan in 1955, has published four novels—*Music on Clinton Street* (1986), *Carn* (1989), *The Butcher Boy* (1992), and *The Dead School* (1995). He has been a teacher in London and now lives in Dublin.

The Butcher Boy brought McCabe to public attention and has since been made into a stage play, *Frank Pig Says Hello* (1992), and an award-winning film (directed also by Neil Jordan) that returns to the original title. Like much of McCabe's fiction, the novel features a child's world, from the child's perspec- tive, and one that is comprised of father, mother, and an only son. McCabe often constructs his fiction on a dual level—offering parallel plots, parallel lives that will eventually intersect. Often, the interstices between characters' lives become flash points that can occasion horror and violence. Such a connection provides the crux of the early *Carn* as the female protagonists— young Sadie Rooney and aging Josie Keenan—meet. In *The Butcher Boy*, Francie Brady, the offspring of one unfortunate family, attaches himself to the dubi- ously attractive Nugent family with dire consequences. In *The Dead School*, McCabe uses both these plot structures to advantage when generations meet, and the blessed meet the accursed in the characters of the saintly, disciplined Raphael Bell and the anarchic, slovenly Malachy Dudgeon.

McCabe's fictional world is usually small-town and borderland. Here country meets city and political entities meet at the border. These liminal places can spark violence that erupts to the surface after years of resentment and abuse. The author also uses duality, and the friction it can cause, to explore the unspoken hierarchical demands of small-town Irish society, especially in earlier decades. Often in McCabe's fiction volatility is occasioned by sons or daughters being confined to or defined by the status of their parents. In places where everyone knows everyone else's business it is difficult for these young characters to escape the drawbacks of having a father who is a drunkard or a mother who is an adulteress. Given that the local wisdom was often that such shortcomings tended to be familial traits, the stigma that attaches, or seems to attach, to some of McCabe's characters can be quite strong.

In *The Dead School* McCabe combines his examination of small worlds, childhood trauma, and clashes of generation with the broader theme of Ireland's rapid modernization. Perhaps more than any other fiction writer today, he exposes the tears in the fabric of a society that is expanding its perspective at a reckless pace. Raphael Bell, the exemplary, if at time stuffy and self-righteous, protagonist of *The Dead School,* is one of McCabe's men who watches in horror as his time, his mores, his faith, and his work ethic become anachronistic in what seems a flash. He is a classic hero born of a tragedy in part his own making. That his personal biography coincides with the founding of the country—his father is killed by Black and Tans in his presence—makes Raphael's story the story of the Ireland of his time. His purity of devotion and selfless dedication to his widowed mother, to his church, and to the teaching profession that he considers to be a sacred trust, is flawless and unswerving. Raphael is the man who has always done the right thing. The author, however, by altering his narrative stance toward the characters, succeeds in making the reader at times wary or skeptical of Raphael's apparent virtue. The charming scenes of his innocent and virginal courtship of his wife Nessa, who is equally pure, are genuinely touching as they recapture a simpler age. As Raphael becomes affected by the religious fervor that overtook the whole nation when Ireland hosted the Eucharistic Congress in 1932, however, McCabe urges the reader to examine some of the more naive or conformist elements of the society of the day. Then, when McCabe introduces the contrasting milieu from which Malachy Dudgeon emerges a generation later, the whole of Raphael's structured life is debunked and called into question. Malachy, unworthy in almost every sense to follow

Raphael into the teaching profession, is shallow, lazy, and limited. The victim of a marred childhood, like Raphael, Malachy's response has been to cheat and cut corners. This trait McCabe fairly presents as one that impoverishes alike Malachy and those with whom he tries to bond. His passionate but precarious affair with Marion is one that he is ill-equipped to nourish. His ability to achieve gravitas as a young teacher is hampered by his history of not having applied himself while in training college. Malachy's genuine attempts at self-improvement, sometime poignant when they are fleetingly successful, ultimately come to naught.

Malachy Dudgeon's ineptitude and lack of moral fiber might simply be considered sad, except that in McCabe's fiction consequences for actions, or for failures to act, always resonate. Malachy's ineffectuality as a teacher helps to destroy the excellent reputation of the school Raphael has built, and ends in the tragic death of one of the boys.

The Dead School is in many ways a dual character study. McCabe illuminates Malachy's aspirations and gentle qualities through the use of Marion as a subsidiary character. Similarly, he provides Father Desmond Stokes as a means of exhibiting Raphael's bonhomie and old-fashioned manliness. Stokes and Bell are contemporaries and friends of many years; but Father Stokes has weathered the struggles during the years of managing the school by a Darwinian process of adaptation. Stokes stands in stark contrast in this regard to Raphael Bell's unflinching rigor. This difference in perspective will eventually drive a wedge between the old friends.

McCabe also traces changing cultural trends throughout the novel by the deft use of the introduction of modern media into Irish life. The radio, in particular a program that features traditional folk music, waltzes, and sentimental ballads, is Raphael's favorite, shared by Father Stokes. Television, especially in the form of a popular talk show with a relentlessly hip host, threatens the values espoused by the outmoded radio program. The affront to Raphael, and by extension to his generation, is made palpable in the following excerpt:

> The topic tonight was ladies underwear. The sort they wear for their boyfriends or husbands. It was the word "bra" that rooted Raphael to the spot. He felt as if someone had slapped him right across the face. . . . Just the sound of the word made needlepoints of sweat break out all over Raphael's back. Terry Krash might as well have been shouting "Are you listening out there, Mr. Bell? Did you hear it? You didn't? Then very well, I'll say it again, just for you. Haha! Come on now everyone. Bra! That's it! Bra!

The easy humor of submitting a middle-aged man to the broadcasting of a word associated with intimacy is carefully balanced in McCabe's passage by an acute sense of a cultural affront that is immediate. As Terry Krash continues in his career to interview women who have had abortions and who espouse, and talk about, premarital sex, Raphael Bell has reason to wonder what the world, *his* world, is coming to.

The unraveling of one value system in the novel is set against another. McCabe maps the disintegrative process Malachy undergoes after being fired from his teaching job and moving to England. The fate of the emigrant in Thatcher's Britain is graphically portrayed, as Malachy shifts from one menial job to the next, and eventually enters into a twilight world of drug-induced despair. Depraved as it is, this world is then matched in squalor and degeneracy by the bizarre world of "The Dead School." This fantasy school, devised by Bell after his resignation from his job and his wife's death, is his sole consolation.

Patrick McCabe's fictional world, like that of Roddy Doyle and Dermot Bolger, studies of whose work follow, is one in which incipient brutality is the end product of social stress. As novelists try to track the socioeconomic atmosphere of marginalized areas, created only recently by the upheavals of Ireland's modernization process, they are creating a new fictional world for their country. Although this world seems, at times, glaringly postmodern, the process used by McCabe and his contemporaries is traditional for novelists, especially those with a social conscience. McCabe's Raphael Bell and Malachy Dudgeon, though vivid characters in their own right, are additionally valuable in literary terms as they help to define their milieu and the social ills of their country and their age.

Roddy Doyle was born in 1958 on the north side of Dublin, not far from the "Barrytown" of his fiction. Doyle, who worked as a primary school teacher for many years, published his first novel, *The Commitments*, in 1989 to broad acclaim. He then rocketed to fame when the novel was filmed by award-winning director Alan Parker. Two more novels, *The Snapper* (1990) and *The Van* (1991), completed what is now called Doyle's *Barrytown Trilogy*.

Doyle's work gives voice to yet another previously unheard segment of the Irish population. The Dublin working-class poor has, of course, been the subject of O'Casey's great tragicomedies and the novels and plays of Brendan Behan, but each of these authors wrote at a time when Dublin's urban poor were truly urban. Doyle's subjects suffer the dual disadvantage of being not only deprived economically and socially, but also being displaced from their tightly knit urban tenements to the new suburban wastelands like Kilbarrack (the real-life name for Barrytown).

Doyle's trilogy, unlike his more recent fiction, focused on the positive traits of this segment of Irish society. This focus was not exclusive nor was it artificial or hagiographic. Doyle's Barrytown contains not a single place to which a tourist to Ireland might choose to go. His world is visually bereft, scarred by lack of money and lack of opportunity, and beyond the viability of economic betterment schemes. Yet Barrytown thrives because of inbred humor of a self-deprecating and good natured, but withering, kind. It is also a place where dreams die hard, and fleeting attempts at the entrepreneurial erupt periodically. When hope springs eternal in a Barrytown heart, neighbors, friends, and family might scoff, but a certain solidarity can always be expected. Doyle's concentration on Dublin wit and resourcefulness can sometimes act as a refreshing antidote to years of rural Irish pieties. However, the eroding effects of poverty and deprivation begin to emerge in his work with *Paddy Clarke Ha Ha Ha* (1993). This novel, which won Doyle the prestigious Booker Prize, inhabits a world that is the flip side of that in *The Commitments*. The chronic unemployment and alcoholism that are acknowledged in *The Barrytown Trilogy* are scrutinized in *Paddy Clarke Ha Ha Ha*, along with the related social evils of domestic violence and neglect. This tendency in Doyle's fiction continues with *The Woman Who Walked into Doors* (1996), the title of which ironically suggests the socially accepted explanation for spousal abuse. It is clear that Doyle's position as a teacher of young children allowed him to observe not only the humor and resilience of the families of his charges, but also the stress under which many of those families were forced to function.

The Commitments is the story of the emergence of an unlikely Irish "soul" band composed of a motley group of Dublin's disenfanchised youth, and the brainchild of manager Jimmy Rabbitte. The Rabbitte family's members will also form the core of the plots of *The Snapper* and *The Van*. Jimmy is filled with fantasies of rock 'n roll fame. Privacy, however, is something of a rare commodity in the Rabbitte household, and his dreams are punctured regularly by his parents' reality checks and the teasing of his siblings.

Approached by his friends, Outspan and Derek, to help provide a new image for their amateur band, Jimmy eliminates outworn local ideas, proclaims that soul music is their future, and rechristens the band "The Commitments." Soon they are joined by Deco, a vocalist, and James on keyboard. Matters take a bizarre but promising twist when, in answer to an ad for musicians, an older man, Joey "the Lips" Fagan, appears. He is a trumpet player who claims to have played with great soul musicians in the past. Joey, who has acquired a strong religious impulse in the process, is a strange mix of the sacred and the profane. Billy Mooney on drums and

Dean Fay on saxophone complete the band, which will be joined by three girls who serve as backup singers.

The girls, Imelda, Natalie, and Bernie, and some of the weaker members of the band, are coached in the refinements of soul music by the patient Joey the Lips, and the impatient Jimmy. The novel then charts the fledgling careers from embarrassing false starts and church hall gigs to the point of their being promised a record contract. The high point in the short lifespan of The Commitments is the night they give a wildly successful concert and are offered a contract by the aptly-names Eegit Records. Soon, however, disappointment, distrust, and anger swell among the members of the group who are already suffering from growing pains and growing egos.

Doyle's strength in the novel, which is vulgar and extremely funny, is in creating individual portraits of young men and women who have started from very little, and through work and enthusiasm have managed to make something of themselves. Although The Commitments, like so many rock bands, is destined to split up after a relatively short period of success, its members have profited from the experience and grown as people and musicians in ways that will help to mold their future lives. Success can be had, even if you come from Barrytown.

Doyle's signature as an emerging novelist was his flawless recreation of working-class Dublin speech. Nearly all *The Commitments* is written in dialogue, a demanding undertaking for a prose writer. But dialogue is the key to the novel's breakneck pace. There are few speeches and most exchanges are very short and pithy. The style is not only suitable, but necessary, to recreate the quick wit, the put-downs, and the parenthetical asides that comprise the verbal facility that marks the Dubliner, and differentiates him in ways from the rest of his or her compatriots. Not all of this dialogue is sparkling—this is not Oscar Wilde's world of studied and learned repartee. Doyle recreates faithfully the overreliance on four-letter words. He also marries this world, and its speech rhythms, to that of "soul." With a shared sense of limited horizons combined with aspirations, the characters each produce a discourse that is defined by a poignant longing for something better.

Paddy Clarke Ha Ha Ha represented a major shift in perspective for Roddy Doyle. The Paddy Clarke of the title is a ten-year-old boy in 1968 as the novel begins. Written from a child's perspective, the book is true to its hero, and avoids the natural tendency of adults to sentimentalize the world of children, here very much the world of boys. Paddy is a genuine kid. He comes saddled with a little brother, Francis, outrageously nicknamed

Sinbad, whom Paddy both loves and loathes. Paddy's days, on one level, are filled with dreamy aspirations of the priesthood, and maybe sainthood, but also with "nicking" (stealing, or in this case, shoplifting), and a preoccupation with the correct time to pick the perpetual scabs on his knees. He is victimized by the local bully, sometimes does well in school, and loves his parents. Paddy is, however, disturbed and confused by his parents' faltering relationship. Like all children, he just wishes they would always be nice to each other and to him and Sinbad. Moments of familial joy and tenderness alternate uncomfortably with eruptions of temper, and anything having to do with sexuality remains a mystery to Paddy.

A family outing in the car his father is nervously learning to drive conveys the family dynamic. The memory of similar outings in the past impinges:

> Even when Dad was taking pictures of us Sinbad wouldn't smile . . .
> he'd tell us to move a bit and then he'd take ages looking down into the
> camera and then up at us, and then he'd notice that Sinbad wasn't
> smiling. . . . All the photographs were the same, me and Ma smiling
> like mad and Sinbad looking down at the ground. We held the smile
> for so long, they weren't really smiles anymore.
> There were no photographs this day.

The Clarke household expands, with babies arriving regularly. Little sisters are added to Paddy's world, but they rarely impinge. However, his father's drinking and increasing physical abuse of his mother does. Doyle's deftness at conveying the violence from a child's half-comprehending perspective is convincing and horrifying. Paddy begins falling asleep in school and crying with no provocation, and in each case he genuinely doesn't understand why. The boy's frustration at his inability to do anything to stop his parents' fighting leads him to imagine himself a referee:

> I was like the ref they didn't know about. Deaf and dumb. Invisible as
> well.

In *Paddy Clarke Ha Ha Ha* Roddy Doyle keeps visible at all times the effects of poverty, unemployment, and drink on the children in failing marriages. In his subsequent novel, *The Woman Who Walked into Walls*, he shifts his focus to the wife and mother in his fictional family, with the same degree of insight.

Doyle's Barrytown and the world of Dermot Bolger's fiction intersect geographically and socioeconomically, but they are significantly different. Doyle's outer suburban world is fundamentally a domesticated place, and his primary interest is in portraying families and community life. His characters are not loners. They may not like their neighbors, but they chat with them regularly, and know all their children's names, ages, and faults. Bolger's world is much more that of young men who have perhaps left such homes and no have no fixed address. Bolger's Dublin is also more sinister, drug-infested, and anonymous. In this distinction Doyle's fiction conveys a unique perspective and one that combines a traditional Ireland and a contemporary one in a troubled but loving "marriage" similar to those he has created.

In the last decade **Dermot Bolger** (b. 1959) has worked equally in drama and in prose, producing six novels—*Night Shift* (1985), *The Woman's Daughter* (1987, rev. 1991), *The Journey Home* (1990), *Emily's Shoes* (1992), *A Second Life* (1994), and *Father's Music* (1997).

Bolger's Dublin is an environment more familiar to North American readers through the work of Roddy Doyle, but his Finglas is not favored with the same degree of leavening humor. Bolger is more overtly ideological, condemning the new have/have not society that has emerged in Ireland in the last two decades as a result of changes in economic policy and Ireland's entry into the European Union.

Bolger's fiction is often centered on the portrayal of marginalized lives—in addition to his young nomadic men, he writes of the elderly and those without intact families. Often the young men and women whom Bolger creates show initial promise—a desire for success and some ambition. They are distinguished from their contemporaries by a faith in themselves or in the system, a faith that is eventually eroded after a series of misfortunes or betrayals. Bolger's talent is shown to best advantage as he traces this type of disintegrative process in the young or old. The decay of hope and the onset of despair and resignation is conveyed convincingly through such means of exposition as his description of the draining quality of hard labor, unsocial working hours, and insalubrious working conditions. His characters' uniformly hand-to-mouth existence is made more precarious by the unspoken fear of the working poor everywhere—that they are one paycheck away from the streets.

Exhaustion, poverty, and no promise of a future is a potent mix, and Bolger accurately and vividly maps their combined effects to an inevitability of substance abuse and violence. His world is largely male, but the female figures who appear in either primary or secondary roles are often poignant in their beauty and innocence—a poignancy made more painful by Bolger's implication that these qualities are doomed to be short-lived.

Night Shift is a slight but affecting early novel or novella. In this first full-length prose work Bolger etches in his world. Donal Flynn, the 18-year-old protagonist, has recently married Elizabeth, his schoolgirl lover. Elizabeth is pregnant and the newlyweds are living in a caravan (trailer) in her parents' garden. Neither is prepared for the responsibilities of marriage or parenthood, but Donal has outwardly assumed an adult role by taking a factory job on the night shift of the title. Their budding lives are developed by the novelist in contrast to the waning existence of Dan, an elderly, religious factory hand whose diminished and pathetic existence comes to a violent end.

Much of Bolger's narrative is constructed in a veil of confusion. Donal and Elizabeth have extended family, but after their having insisted upon and organized the wedding of the young couple, they seem to have abandoned them in their barely adult state to face the rigors of a new life together. Confusion in Donal is also induced by drink, drugs, and fatigue. Elizabeth exists in a torpor that is the result of pregnancy and enforced inactivity. Donal wanders the streets aimlessly at odd hours, Elizabeth lies in bed, also at odd hours, waiting. She awaits her husband's return; she awaits motherhood. Their infrequent outings and splurges begin festively enough—grooming, dressing up, exchanging greetings with others ready for a night on the town. Time and time again, however, Bolger's narrative unwinds remorselessly. Scenes are played out against a backdrop of Dublin's down-and-outs, and all promise deteriorates. That this new marriage is doomed is foretold thematically and imagistically from the start.

In addition to Donal's relationship with Elizabeth, his place in the world of men and work is detailed. His childhood friend Frankie leads a life that only belatedly becomes a cautionary tale to Donal. He escapes the factory floor by securing an office job in the factory, but the dust, grime, and failure of those he has left behind seem to cling to him.

The structure of the novel is progressive, despite the stasis and confusion of the lives portrayed. It is an inevitable downward spiral, relieved only by brief moments of minor success and self-understanding. In this first novel, which defines Bolger's terms of reference, secondary characters are often simply functional. The factory villain, "Duckarse," remains, for instance, something of a cardboard figure. His lack of human feeling is told, not shown. Elizabeth's mother is humanized heartrendingly in a scene with Donal after Elizabeth's self-inflicted miscarriage, which brings the novel to its sad close. But she is not given any three-dimensional characteristics before this scene. Even Frankie, lionized by Donal since childhood, exhibits little of the panache for which we are told he is admired.

Bolger, then, eschews all such development in an attempt to insist the reader enter into the plights of Donal, Elizabeth, and the aging Dan. A bizarre and frightening incident of the mutilation and killing of a horse by local boys is one of the few unsettling connections between Dan and Donal's life. The other is Donal's knowledge of Dan's pornography collection. The two sordid incidents, however, do combine to alert the reader to the urban and societal degradation to which both aspiring men succumb.

Night Shift is the first of Bolger's prose indictments of the New Ireland that has created a feared and despised underclass. His office workers fail to understand factory labor disputes. Only Donal, credentialed by the system with a Leaving Certificate (high-school diploma) can ever hope to get out of the ranks of the underprivileged. The nighttime world of this class exists unwitnessed by the daytime world of the comfortable, secure, and upwardly mobile. Bolger, who has himself bridged the gap between these worlds, is able to inhabit the netherworld in his fiction and to give it voice in the greater world beyond.

The Journey Home (1990) features a pair of young men similar in their background to Donal and Frankie in *Night Shift*. Hano and Shay in *The Journey Home* are "the children of Limbo," whose families were displaced, in the former instance from their country origins and in the latter from close-knit inner-city communities, to suburban tenement wastelands. Hano, like Donal again, in possession of a Leaving Certificate, eventually finds work in a stultifying civil-service job. In the aimlessness that results he also finds Shay.

The Journey Home operates on several levels. Thematically it is intended to examine the rural/urban split in Irish society. The brutality of a political power structure that is controlled by a rural elite is exposed. Contradictorily Bolger also seems to affirm the comfort and security of the rural tradition from which, until quite recently, most Irish people have come. This novel, like *Night Shift*, also exposes shortcomings and omissions in the programs for economic prosperity and growth that now inform Irish life. Surprisingly, on another level the novel harkens to a variant of an older trope from Irish fiction. Hano and Katie, who was Shay's girlfriend, return after Shay's death to a decrepit Big House, the home of one of Hano's few friends. She is described in the text only as "the old Protestant lady." The young people return there after the murder of an abusive politician who has the characteristics of the "gombeen man" of the Irish past.[10] After having been freed in a sense from the grip of this avaricious and malevolent representative of the Catholic bourgeoisie, Hano and Katie (whose name in a rural setting transmutes in the narrative to the Irish form Cait) assume quasi-servant roles in this Big House, sleeping "downstairs." Rather than a sense of their subservience, the novel conveys the idea that they have acquired, at least temporarily, the security, the home they have sought throughout the novel.[11]

Bolger's fiction, it has been noted, does not flinch from detailing the violence that can be found in contemporary Irish life. This violence was, with the exception of the killing of the horse and the injury inflicted on Dan mentioned above, kept largely under wraps in *Night Shift*. But it erupts in numerous ways in *The Journey Home.* Hano is violently assaulted in a homosexual attack. Katie was beaten and abused by her uncle after the death of her parents. Shay lives in threatening and subhuman conditions as a migrant worker in Germany. In none of these cases, we are conditioned to believe by Bolger, does society protect the young or the disenfranchised. Bolger's characters are victims, to be sure, and are perhaps too quick or too willing to think of themselves as such. On the positive side, though, rarely do his victims become brutalized to such an extent that they in turn victimize others. This crucial thematic line is not crossed and allows for the substantial degree of redemption achieved in all of Bolger's fiction.

Dermot Bolger often creates unlikable or unlovable characters. He probes into areas of human behavior that are unsavory, and to some, repellent (Dan's pornography collection in *Night Shift*; the violent homoeroticism of Patrick Plunkett in *The Journey Home*; the fetishism indicated by the title *Emily's Shoes*). But there is maintained consistently in the narrative an understanding of human failings and limitations. Similarly, although Bolger's world is mostly male, his insight into the female psyche, especially in *The Woman's Daughter*, produces memorably clarifying moments. Differences of gender are exposed while the author explores simultaneously the shared experience of the human race. Often this double or multiple perspective is facilitated by a multilinear narrative format. The reader can access the minds of more than one character in a contrapuntal fashion. In addition, Bolger's fragmented narrative underscores the jagged, disjointed lives under scrutiny and the rough poetry that can be articulated in attempts to find continuity in broken lives. In *The Journey Home*, Hano (whose real name is the much more mundane and countrified Francis, or Francey, Hanrahan) ponders his position in Irish society as it reflects his position in his own family:

> I didn't understand it then, but I grew up in perpetual exile; from my
> parents when on the streets, from my own world when at home. . . . At
> fourteen I tried to bridge the gap by journeying out into my father's
> unchartered countryside. . . . I arrived home with reports he couldn't

comprehend: long-haired Germans in battered vans picking up hikers;
skinheads battling outside chip shops in Athlone.

Here the Germans and the skinheads, foreign in every sense, provide an
incongruous link between the Kerry countryside of Hano's father's memory
and the Dublin of the present. Modernity, somehow always overwhelming
and strange in Bolger, has an exotic fascination, but it is never a lasting one.

As the twenty-first century approaches, Irishness, so rapidly redefin-
ing itself in the past three decades, will continue to evolve. Fiction that takes
as its subject matter the economic and social problems plaguing the Western
industrialized world, fiction such as Dermot Bolger has written, will continue
to fill a cultural need. That Bolger's fiction is able to do so in a literate and
innovative manner is part of his impressive achievement.

Dermot Healy was born in 1947 in Co. Westmeath and now lives near Sligo
town. He has participated in many collaborative and community-based arts
undertakings. In addition to publishing award-winning collections of short
stories and poems, Healy has written plays and worked in other capacities
in the theatre, and has also edited arts magazines. Major recognition,
however, finally came to this writer on the publication of his lyrical novel
A Goat's Song in 1994, a work in part anticipated by an early story, "Banished
Misfortune."

Taking his title from the etymological source for the word tragedy,
Healy begins with the primitive and folkloric, or even perhaps the mythological. In ancient Greece goats were herded by gender onto different
islands. As goats are unable to swim, when the nanny goats came into heat
and their scents reached the billy goats, the male could only send up a
mournful cry—a goat's song. Healy's protagonist, Jack Ferris, a playwright,
both begins and ends this novel in metaphorical terms by sending up a
mournful song for his lost love, Catherine Adams. The novelist interlaces
his text with multiple references to Jack and Catherine's being separated by
divides that cannot be traversed, often bodies of water. Jack intermittently
earns a livelihood by fishing off the remote Belmullet Peninsula in Co. Mayo,
where they met. He speaks or cries out to Catherine over a ship-to-shore
radio and by phone. Late in the novel their affair disintegrates as she holidays
alone on Cyprus, another distant island.

However, the gap between these lovers is not always not simply
geographic. Catherine Adams is from Co. Fermanagh in Northern Ireland
and is a Protestant. Jack, originally from Co. Leitrim in the Republic, is a
Catholic. Healy's novel, largely set in Belfast, Belmullet, and Dublin,

operates in supposedly neutral territory where their lives intersect, but that is home to neither of them.

Perhaps *A Goat's Song*'s most vividly and perceptively drawn character, however, is Jonathan Adams, Catherine's father. He is dead as the novel begins (and chronology in the novel is complex), but predominates in much of the book's flashback narrative. Adams, a failed clergyman, becomes a member of the Royal Ulster Constabulary (RUC) in order to give structure and some sense of purpose to his life. A man of rigid conscience and religious belief, he marries a Methodist woman from Co. Limerick, in the Republic. They have a happy, secure marriage and two daughters, Sara and Catherine.

Healy's narrative and his focus on Adams' career and beliefs move inexorably toward the traumatic events of Bloody Sunday in January of 1973, in Derry. On that day Sergeant Adams participated in the riot and was then forced to assess his actions while watching the violence replayed on television. Adams sees himself on the tape, and comes face to face with his bigotry and hatred. Ever after a scorned figure, since he has been recognized by all his neighbors and coworkers, he retreats to the confines of his home and family. The sole outsider with whom Adams communicates is a local Catholic handyman named Matti Bonner, who had been responsible for Adams meeting his wife, Maisie.

From this point, Healy as novelist seems to focus his thematic concerns on the effects of ostracization, isolation, and loneliness on the human spirit. Adams, seen by many as an ogre, keeps a low profile as sectarian violence in Ulster escalates, and his fears of retaliation grow. Matti Bonner maintains his friendship with the RUC man and pays a terrible price for the loyalty. His eventual suicide by hanging, in a public place between both local churches is an indictment of all.

The Adams' gradual move to austere and windblown Belmullet augers a new beginning. Co. Mayo, with its Catholic religious feasts, Irish-speaking enclaves, and less stringent upkeep of property in the face of inclement weather, is a foreign experience for the Adamses. Sara and Catherine seek the freedom from regulation the local habits seem to allow. They are seen by the locals to be both beautiful and exotic, and in time they acquire a reputation, deservedly or not, for precociousness and promiscuity. Healy's exposition of the girls' sexual awakening is artful and recreates life's experiences deftly. First, the two speak of sexual matters only between themselves and exchange misinformation about men. Later, through the device of having two men lodge in turn with the family while giving Irish-language lessons, Healy begins to reveal the girls' developing sexuality. Initially the sisters, in a sense, share Jack Ferris, who is at first attracted to Sara. Both sisters, accomplished at an early age at role playing because of their marginalized position in society on both sides of the border, become actresses. That Catherine's career should take off, finally, in a play written for her by Jack but mounted after their love affair is over, brings Healy's novel full circle.

Communication in *A Goat's Song* is the key to happiness, the end to isolation and marginalization. Too often, however, communication fails or is incomplete. When Jonathan Adams dies in Belmullet, his body is accompanied back to Fermanagh by several of the locals, all Catholics. In Healy's representation of Adams' Protestant brother, Willy, trying desperately to communicate with the visitors, the ill-ease across sectarian lines is tangible:

> "So you were friends of Jonathan," said Willy, with a brisk smile.
>
> "I wouldn't say that." Bernie felt the back of his neck and bared his teeth.
>
> He looked uneasily at Joe Love.
>
> "I am his brother, you see," continued Willy.
>
> "Ahhh! I've got you."
>
> "You look like him, too," nodded Joe.
>
> "The eyes," said Bernie.
>
> "And the chin."
>
> "He has him round the eyes."
>
> "I was not aware that I looked like Jonathan."

The writer's talent for dialogue is multifaceted, juggling as he does in one novel raunchy conversations between fishermen; pub talk between people in the advanced stages of drunkenness; the formal, gentlemanly conversations between Jonathan and Matti Bonner; snatches of dialogue in a mental asylum, and talk among theatre people. Since the novel also wanders throughout Ireland, Healy takes the opportunity to use dialectic idiom without lapsing into cliché. His knack for capturing varied speeches is allied to his ability to portray place, especially the coastal area of Mayo that has featured in contemporary poetry, but rarely in fiction. Here the power of the elements and the fragility of lives render secondary religious and political questions of identity. People are what they do, and Healy's protagonist, Jack Ferris, the ostensible writer, fails or succeeds on that basis.

A Goat's Song is a record of a love affair between two damaged people. Catherine, traumatized by Northern violence and her father's death, seeks redemption in her love for Jack. The love flounders as a result of their increasing dependency on alcohol, and his inability to write for long periods. The novelist, linking Jack's stasis indirectly to the North and its troubles, has dealt artistically and innovatively with the fundamental trauma in modern Irish life. He has also done so in a style that is perhaps ultimately more effective than that of writers who take the Northern troubles as their sole focus and venue. In *A Goat's Song* there are no effective borders, and geopolitical divides are not powerful enough to prevent tragedy from striking anywhere on the island. His somber conclusion, with Jack and Catherine permanently estranged through lack of communication in the form of letters that go astray, suggests little hope in the immediate future for a reconciliation in their country.

Colm Tóibín, born in Wexford in 1955, gained acclaim as a journalist and travel writer before publishing his award-winning novels, *The South* in 1990 and *The Heather Blazing* in 1992. His most recent novel, *The Story of the Night*, appeared in 1997.

Tóibín writes an economical prose that scrupulously avoids the temptation to the rhetorical or the sentimental. Instead, complexity and nuance are vested in characters, moral dilemmas, and eerily emphatic landscapes. The latter, always delicately and precisely evoked, along with the people who inhabit those landscapes, displays Tóibín's gift as a travel writer to advantage, too.

Tóibín's characters, always seeking self-illumination as a preliminary step in the painful process of connecting with other human beings, have love as their ultimate goal. They are often post-Christian, Europeanized wanderers, common figures in recent Irish writing. Tóibín's deracinated Katherine Proctor in *The South,* and his half English, half Argentine Richard Garay in *The Story of the Night*, are each in part or temporarily far from their emotional and cultural origins. As a result they are continually forced into self-reflective postures. In *The Heather Blazing,* Tóibín's only major work set in Ireland, primary alienation does not originate in exile in the geographic sense. Instead its protagonist, Eamon Redmond, engages in a lifelong practice of emotional displacement from family and loved ones, as removed as if he had been living on a different continent.

The South, written in a realistic mode, is composed of two parts that are in turn divided into short chapters or segments. Many of the individual segments are in the form of diary entries or letters, which are dated. The conscious use of this format "dates" the fiction in another sense in an attempt to recreate the strictures of life in 1950s Barcelona under Franco's dictatorship.[12]

The novel's beginning is a study in isolation made more complete by loss of language. Katherine Proctor has only begun to learn Spanish before arriving in Barcelona, after leaving an emotionally incomplete marriage. She has left behind her husband, Tom, her ten-year-old son, Richard, and her claims to her land. She is a somewhat willing prisoner in her *pension*, venturing out at first only to eat. Since Barcelona's first language is Catalan, not Spanish, she is baffled in her infrequent attempts to communicate. Throughout the novel, the extent of Katherine's traumatization is recorded by long periods of sleep and withdrawal. She has also undergone an initial menacing sexual encounter on the train that brought her to Spain. Her intense personal struggle is, however, something she faces directly:

> I am absorbed in myself most of the time. Sometimes I don't see things around me. I think about myself all the time. What I'm going to do now; how in God's name I'm going to survive.

Katherine's gradual reclamation process begins with her taking a Catalan lover, Miguel, an artist who is the antithesis of her husband. Miguel, an anti-Franco Republican in Spain's Civil War, has survived prison but remains damaged by the experience. Their relationship is a dual healing process, and eventuates in their leaving Barcelona to live in a remote Pyrenean village. There Katherine unwillingly bears their daughter, Isona. Her sexual relationship with Miguel, at first illuminating in its satisfaction and warmth, deteriorates along with Miguel's mental health.

A pivotal figure in *The South* from its earliest pages is Michael Graves. He is an Irishman, also from Enniscorthy in Co. Wexford, the place that Katherine has just left. Graves, like Katherine and Miguel, is an artist; but he is a natural artist and has taught himself to be a fine draughtsman. His insistence that drawing skill is a prerequisite for painting places him at odds with Miguel artistically. He thus influences the malleable Katherine, whose views on art are as yet unformed. This artistic triangle, plus the nexus of Spanish and Catalan artists whom they encounter, gives Tóibín an opportunity in the novel to examine tenets of modern painting. Graves' presence in the novel also provides an opening for examining the negative effect of class in Ireland. This inequity has set in motion Katherine's decision to leave Enniscorthy as, the reader learns, her mother did before her.

Katherine's mother, another pivotal and intermittent character in *The South*, is a memorable fictional achievement. It is she who has provided the chillingly antimaternal and isolated example that her daughter seems doomed to follow. *The South* is notable for such structural parallels and a high level of coincidence. Miguel, too, takes a preordained, disintegrative path by following in the footsteps of Carlos Puig, an old Republican prisoner who dies, disoriented, at their mountain home. All the Proctor children are abandoned. First Katherine is left behind as her mother retreats from Irish Republican violence in the 1920s. Then Richard, Katherine's son, is abandoned when she leaves Enniscorthy too. Isona is also abandoned by her mother, in a sense, to her unstable father's care. Michael Graves and Carlos Puig, each insistent figures, remind Katherine and Miguel uncomfortably of their respective pasts. Both secondary characters are always referred to in the novel by both their first and surnames, a feature that emphasizes their iconographic functions.

Part II of *The South* begins five years after Miguel's and Isona's deaths. Katherine is reconciled with her son, now married with a daughter of his own, and living in Enniscorthy, as is Michael Graves. Eventually these old friends, who become lovers, move to Dublin, where Katherine experiences the rewards of her first major exhibition. The novel has charted the gradual and painful process of development of a person and an artist. Katherine, a young wife and mother and fledgling artist, grows and changes as a woman into a somewhat reconciled, but fulfilling, middle-age. Tóibín's focus on Katherine's sexuality in youth, maturity, and middle-age reflects development in other areas of her life. She grows in her work and in her ability to form satisfactory relationships with family and friends. Her final sexual relationship with Michael Graves, long delayed, lacks the frigidity she experienced with her husband, but does not feature Miguel's passion. It does, however, offer an ease and security that she has also newly found in her bond with her son and his family.

Colm Tóibín's narrative and metaphoric skill is restrained, formal, and often minimalist. Part II of the novel, for instance, opens with a section "spoken" by Katherine to the dead Miguel. This method, though written as if it were oral, is similar to the letter format used in Part I. Tóibín's characters' individual stories, their personal histories of pain and change, are slipped into other narratives. Michael Graves' incarceration in a tuberculosis sanatorium parallels Miguel's stays in prison. Miguel's confession of setting a policeman's house on fire intersects the story of Katherine's mother's departure from Ireland after the blaze that destroyed their home. When Miguel tells the story of his crime to Katherine, it

> . . . stayed with her for days, as though she had eaten something strange
> and strong, but vaguely familiar.

Tóibín's fusion of the power of memory with the equally powerful experience of the sensory, here taste, to linger through years of disparate experience, marks him as a prose writer of sure skill and delicate imagination.

Éilís Ní Dhuibhne lives in Dublin, where she was born in 1954. She has worked for many years as a curator in the National Library of Ireland and is trained as a folklorist. Ní Dhuibhne's writing is varied—ranging from children's literature to television scripts—but her recent novels and short stories have brought her a wide readership.

The Bray House (1990) is a fascinating postnuclear novel, a slightly futurist fantasy with allegorical implications. Ní Dhuibhne creates a Swedish archeological expedition, consisting of three women and a man who journey to a devastated Ireland. They have been sent to record the effects of the disaster in the hope of preserving the world from more like it. Robin Lagerlöf, the leader of the group, has lived previously in Ireland with her Irish husband, Michael, now dead.

The crew chooses the seaside resort town of Bray in Co. Wicklow for the site of their dig, a place that Robin and Michael had visited years earlier. Thus Ní Dhuibhne sets up the mechanism for self-exploration that vies for prominence in this innovative novel. *The Bray House* also functions as a study of the destruction not only of a part of a civilization and an entire country, but also of a marriage.

Ní Dhuibhne chooses midway into the narrative of the novel to switch from the rather blunt, naive, but quasi-omniscient voice of Robin to a pseudodocumentary style. The narrative thus takes on the authority of an investigative or academic report. The life of the inhabitants of the Bray house is recorded, artifacts are listed room by room, and supporting documents, such as newspapers, are used to fill in the life that once existed there.

The Bray House ends with its one male character dead, murdered by Robin, and one female survivor of the Irish nuclear holocaust being taken back to Sweden. In keeping with the desolate subject matter and setting of the novel, *The Bray House* ends on a bereft and ignominious note—Robin's suicide after no interest has been shown in her research.

Ní Dhuibhne's novel enlists a combination of unsatisfactory sexual encounters among its characters, truncated interpersonal relationships among the crew members, and details of Robin's unusual upbringing to support the thematic horror at its center. A peculiarly cold and disaffected narrative voice helps to fuse plot, characters, and imagery in a chilling cautionary tale.

As can be seen, then, Ní Dhuibhne's fictional world does have a domestic element, and her perspective is decidedly female. Yet for all her artful ordering and recording of the minutiae of household life—its colors, textures, smells, and spaces, hers is not at all a conventional voice. The quotidian meets the irrational in Ní Dhuibhne's fiction, and it is a provocative and fruitful mix. The panic of a hostess attempting to prepare a Christmas lunch in the title story of *Eating Women is Not Recommended* (1991) results in near-comic memory loss. The heroine, Lennie, struggles to remember who her guests are and why she has invited them. The story finally erupts into full-scale resentment of the imposition of traditional female roles. The strictures imposed upon married women and the expectations society has of them are questioned and cast in an unsettling light. "Needlework" opens with a charming description of a determined little boy teaching himself to knit. His mother cannot knit or sew, the source of much humiliation in her girlhood, but also the source of a furtive bond with her non-knitting mother. (Irish girls are still taught sewing and knitting as part of a required primary school curriculum.)

Ní Dhuibhne's investigation of the nonconventional can lead to the fantastic and the whimsical. "The Wife of Bath" concerns an unlikely and imaginative meeting between a twentieth-century incarnation of Chaucer's character from *The Canterbury Tales* and a disaffected modern wife on holiday in the spa resort of the title. Alisoun, the wife of Bath of Ní Dhuibhne's story, sets the record straight on medieval sexuality and marriage. She is dismissive of the nineteenth-century author Jane Austen, also associated with Bath, but a woman who never married. The story ends with a surreal sequence in which Chaucer's character and Ní Dhuibhne's character metaphorically melt away in the spa waters. As is true in much of this writer's fiction, liberation from petty responsibility and the dictates of society can become, if only fleetingly, available to women who are seeking it.

In "The Mermaid Legend" Ní Dhuibhne makes use of the silkie legend that has had an appeal for so many of Ireland's women writers. Ní Dhuibhne has the tale told by an unnamed female narrator sitting in an English pub. The author then uses water imagery as a backdrop to another divide—that between Irish and English modes of living. The narrator has abandoned her Irish husband and her two daughters in his home village of Spiddal in coastal Co. Galway. Unable to cope with the privations of the isolated life there, and with continuing differences with her husband, she has returned across the sea. Like the unfortunate mermaid, though, the woman is destined not to be at ease in either place, and pines for the children she left behind.

The Inland Ice and Other Stories (1997) is an ambitious collection that alternates independent but thematically linked stories with a narrative, "The Search for the Lost Husband," that is broken into 14 sections. The effect of the broken narrative, which replicates nightly story telling, is to give an authentically folkloric ring to this tale. A young woman becomes enchanted by a goat who magically transforms into a man and fathers human children.

He leads the mortal woman on a merry chase through an underworld filled with witches, curses, and magical objects. The alternation between Ní Dhuibhne's more contemporary and topical tales, which frequently feature professional women who find themselves far from home for career reasons (France, Perugia, Denmark, Sweden), and the simplicity of "The Search for the Lost Husband," suggests a day-and-night rhythm. The latter, interrupted tale is thus placed in the *seanachaí* tradition of fireside stories, often told serially at night.

Éilís Ní Dhuibhne's voice is a distinctive one in today's Ireland. Her trenchant social commentary is delivered with humor and a sprinkle of magic, and can be devastatingly on target. It is a sustained and highly imaginative voice that is all the more distinctive in that, while answering a feminist imperative, it is not constrained by contemporary feminist fashion or critical *dicta*.

Colum McCann, born in Dublin in 1965, now lives in New York. The acclaim that greeted his first novel, *Songdogs* (1995), occasioned a reprinting in the United States of his first published work, a volume of short stories, *Fishing the Sloe-Black River* (1996). McCann's writing is influenced by Jack Kerouac, whose novels his journalist-father would bring back from the States. His style is perhaps even more influenced by the type of magic realism now most closely associated with Latin American writers. Irish writers Desmond Hogan and Neil Jordan have also written in this mode, but for McCann it seems to be becoming a signature. Such a style lends itself to his postmodernist view of Ireland and the world beyond Ireland, to which his protagonists often travel.

Fishing the Sloe-Black River is a collection of a dozen stories that dissect the Irish trope of exile, often presented as a form of displacement. Exile in McCann can be real in the geographic sense, or imagined. All the protagonists seek either a way "home" or a way to escape home. The title story uses a magic realist construct to address the very real phenomenon of the deserted Irish townland. (Beginning in the 70s towns experiencing large-scale emigration were described as not having enough men left to field a football team.) In McCann's imagined townland, exhausted middle-aged farmers futilely continue to play football while their distraught wives "fish" the local river for their émigré sons. The women symbolically number 26, one for each county in the Republic.

The story links these lost sons with the greater world in a conversation between a central pair who imaginatively connect their river with "the Thames or the Darling or the Hudson or the Loire or even the Rhine itself, where their own three sons were working in a car factory." These rivers are found in the areas of the world (England, Australia, the United States, France, and Germany) to which the Irish continue to emigrate in search of employment. Such an emigrant is Padraic Keegan in "Stolen Child," who is a social worker in New York. The adjustment to a new country is traumatic for Padraic, although he is fortunate to have emigrated with his Irish wife, Orla. Padraic's culture shock is, however, more profound because he works with the outcasts of American society—crack children.

One of Padraic's charges, who demands the greatest share of his care and attention, is Dana, a 16-year-old African American girl who is blind. Her name, that of Ireland's pre-Christian sun goddess, occasions Padraic's recounting the myth of the Tuatha de Danaan (the followers of Dana) to the girl. Padraic hopes the storytelling will calm Dana and increase her attention span and periods of rational thought. Although the girl is impressed by these tales, Padraic feels he has failed her. He is also appalled by her plans to marry a homeless Vietnam veteran who is an amputee and twice her age. Only at Dana's rather bizarre wedding, attended by an assortment of misfits from her care facility and the groom's group of alienated friends, does Padraic belatedly realize that Will, the wheelchair-bound veteran, has reached Dana in a way Padraic can't. As bride and groom leave the church, Dana steers Will's wheelchair, becoming in effect his legs, as he guides her with his eyes.

"Stolen Child," which takes its name from a Yeats poem quoted in part in the story, is only one of several intertextual passages in McCann's work. "Cathal's Lake" is a hidden lake with many swans adrift on its surface on a winter morning as the story opens. Cathal, a farmer, keeps a tally of the sectarian deaths in Northern Ireland, vividly imagining the lives of murderers and victims alike. We learn that he is cursed in this regard: each time a person is killed in Northern Ireland, they become surrealistically interred on his property. He must dig up each corpse, which is transformed into the body of a living swan. Cathal then liberates the swan from the earth to the freedom of the lake, where it joins the souls of that year's violence. With a Sisyphus-like repetition and predictability, the swan-souls depart the lake annually to make room for more victims, and Cathal continues to dig to free them all.

McCann's artful combination of swan and water imagery with earth, digging, and burial imagery, makes idiosyncratic use of Irish tropes to produce chilling results. However postmodern McCann's intertextual takes on the Children of Lir myth,[13] or on Yeats' swans, or indeed on Heaney's digging, his magical world is never entirely nightmarish. Like Padraic in

"Stolen Child," Cathal in "Cathal's Lake" has no reason to be optimistic about the future, given the somber present in which he lives. However, as each swan is released to its natural element, order is temporarily restored and hope returns, if only fleetingly.

Songdogs takes its title from the Native American name for coyotes, each of which was believed to have its own song. The novel opens in a territory McCann has made his own in his earlier volume—a deserted Irish waterside landscape. Here the protagonist, Conor Lyons, after extensive wandering in Mexico in search of his mother, returns to visit his elderly father, Michael, a farmer in Co. Mayo. Juanita was a Mexican woman who had years earlier abandoned them both, unable to adjust to life in Ireland. The river and the fish in it are Michael's preoccupation, although McCann makes it clear to the reader from the start that these are not halcyon days:

> Not even the river itself knew it was a river anymore. Wide and brown,
> with a few plastic bags sitting in the reeds, it no longer made a noise at
> its curves.

The story of Conor's parents' meeting and romance forms the basis of the plot of *Songdogs*. Michael, a self-taught and obsessive photographer, twice orphaned, fought in the Spanish Civil War and from there traveled to Mexico where he met his wife. McCann's evocation of Mexican village life in the 1940s and later is highly textured. The fiction is also populated with eccentric characters who, like Michael, indulge their singular obsessions. Juanita's widowed mother skins and sells rabbits and is the village midwife, credited with curative powers. Juanita favors chickens as obsessively as her mother does rabbits. Vividly drawn local characters intersect their lives.

In this novel of wandering by two generations of Irishmen, McCann's venues shift rapidly, father's and son's adventures alternating or dovetailing. Conor's parents venture to San Francisco, where they take up with Cici Hinkle, one of the few people from his parents' world whom Conor will meet on *his* trip to the New World. Cici, he recalls,

> sang to me like a wren, on and on, memories of startling lucidity,
> incidents pouring from her, a threnody of nostalgia, . . .

Both in reality and in his imagination, Conor retraces his parents' steps. A sojourn in the Bronx is conjured by an old photograph of a street scene. From it he creates a life for the people in the photo, a timeless emigrants' tale. As McCann later brings the narrative of the past up to his parents' return to the west of Ireland and the time of his own birth, the present-day narrative reveals that Michael is dying.

McCann's *Songdogs* is a palimpsest of images—the images his father created around the world in his photographs, and in particular the sensuous and loving photographs he took of his wife. That Juanita burned those images and his darkroom one day in a rage immediately before leaving him gives credence to a maxim mouthed by Cici early in the novel and repeated frequently at its end—"Memory is three parts imagination and the rest pure lies."

Conor reconstructs his identity from the fragmentary knowledge he has gleaned from the past. His search is complicated by the fact that he has ostensibly gone on a real search for his mother in a foreign country, which although it has a claim on him is not in any sense his own. But his metaphorical search for identity can, in the end, only be found by reconnecting with his father and with Ireland.

The character of Juanita, while representing the exotic, is also important in the novel for our understanding of the protagonist. Like his mother, whom he resembles, Conor is given to dreaminess and an urge to leave places abruptly. Like his mother, he also fails on his return to Mayo to fit in with the locals, whose connection with his past seems tenuous. Mrs. O'Leary, the publican and his mother's only fast friend in the village, has died in his absence. A young waitress and former schoolfriend is dimly remembered and objectified—he recalls at first only her family name. Finally, she is avoided. Even the appearance of another schoolmate, now the local postman, causes him to hide.

Songdogs develops in part like a traditional bildungsroman in that McCann allows the reader to know that there are societal structures in place that could have led to forming Conor as a person. These structures—village life, formal education, and religion—are rejected in favor of a personal, and lonely, search for truth and meaning. Conor's guides in his search—Cici, an old Indian woman named Eliza, her son Kutch, a Mexican man from his mother's village, even his father—are all unreliable. He must leave them all in turn to continue alone.

The global wandering of Conor Lyons in *Songdogs* is a variation on a theme pursued by many young Irish writers. In McCann's novel this journeying is given resonance by particulars of Conor's parentage, Mexican and Irish, which are those of Irish founding-father Éamon de Valéra. Finally, although his return to Ireland and partially achieved reconciliation with his father also follow a predetermined path in this type of contemporary fiction, McCann leaves his ending unresolved. That Conor will leave Ireland again is nearly a certainty. His destiny and his fate will lie, the author determines, elsewhere.

Emma Donoghue (b. 1969) is a very prolific young writer who grew up in Dublin, but now lives in Cambridge, England, where she was educated. Donoghue has published scholarly work and edited an anthology (*Passions Between Women: British Lesbian Culture 1668 – 1801* [1993] and *What Sappho Would Have Said: Four Centuries of Love Poems Between Women* [1997], respectively). She has also rewritten the Brothers Grimm in *Kissing the Witch* (1997), a collection of feminist fairy tales. She is best known thus far, however, as a lesbian novelist. *Stir-Fry* (1994) appeared to critical enthusiasm and was followed quickly by *Hood* (1995) .

Stir-Fry is divided into eight aptly named chapters that recreate the steps required to achieve culinary perfection in cooking the title dish ("Mixing," "Cutting," "Stirring," and "Serving," for example.) This is the story of Maria, a freshman in university in Dublin, who comes to realize that the two older women with whom she is sharing a flat, Ruth and Jael, are lesbians. *Stir-Fry* is, then, a novel that concerns a young woman's coming-of-age simultaneously with her coming out. Donoghue, well-versed in English literature and its history, can and does draw from the tradition of the lesbian novel in English. It is a type, however, with little precedent in modern Irish literature, except in the work of Kate O'Brien.

One of the many accomplishments of *Stir-Fry* is Donoghue's stylistic expansion throughout the novel, which mirrors young Maria's growing ease with Jael and Ruth's homosexuality. Donoghue's prose, at first stiff and contracted, conveys the freshman's complete lack of ease in all areas of life— in her studies, finding her way in a new city, with the young men in her classes, and in making female friends. Maria's world has been very sheltered. As the eldest in a secure, conventional country family, with a houseful of younger brothers, her limited experience must expand rapidly to include the temperamentality of the university dramatic-society members, the pseudo sophistication of Dublin's club scene, and the brutality of Dublin's lower-end working class. The latter group she encounters as a cleaning woman working nights in downtown office blocks.

O'Donoghue's women's world is sketched simply, but with a humor and an eye and ear to detail to which we must attune our senses. Matters of dress, posture, and speech are shorn of gender-based expectation, causing us to shake off complacency as readers. *Stir-Fry*, issued by Penguin and obviously geared toward a wide readership, is not, therefore, the stuff of small women's or alternative presses. Donoghue instead presents what is believed to be an accessible and acceptable face of lesbianism for the 1990s. The novel does, however, suffer the fate of a pioneering effort in the sense that a good deal of its self-deprecating humor can fail after repetition. Similarly, some of its dialogue, obviously meant to demythologize lesbianism, can read like speeches from diversity-education films.

Hood is a more metaphorical and subtle novel. It also deals, at times more squarely, with the kind of prejudice and heartbreak that still very much go with being homosexual in a society such as Ireland's, which is only beginning to openly discuss sexuality, let alone understand alternative sexual preference.

In *Hood,* the character Pen suffers the fate usually reserved in fiction for "the other woman." When her lover Cara dies in an automobile accident, she is not permitted the role of first mourner, but suffers being marginalized in her grief by the dead woman's family, to whom she had not come out. This novel, using the hooded metaphor of the title, deals in dreams and the evocation of memory and loss, before coming to a satisfactory revelatory end for a brave heroine. Pen emerges as a woman who is much more real and sustaining than the insipid models of ideal girlhood with which she had to content herself in her youth.

Robert McLiam Wilson (b. 1964) is a Belfast writer who was educated for a time at Cambridge, which he left to take a number of odd jobs and to write. The author of three novels to date—*Ripley Bogle* (1989), *Manfred's Pain* (1992), and *Eureka Street* (1997)—Wilson has something of the prodigy's reputation. *Ripley Bogle* appeared to a flurry of critical praise both in and out of Ireland, and garnered prizes for the fledgling writer.

The novel takes place over the course of four days, Thursday to Sunday—a long weekend, or lost weekend, in the life of the eponymous hero who has recently become down and out in London. A narrative that illuminates in sometimes excruciatingly realistic detail the daily routine of a homeless man, *Ripley Bogle* also incorporates a genealogical and biographical thread. It is reminiscent of Lawrence Sterne's *Tristram Shandy*, especially in its preoccupation with the protagonist's conception, birth, grotesque family, and early years. In this regard McLiam Wilson can also claim Flann O'Brien as an influence. Bogle's Northern Irish Catholic roots, like his creator's, are exposed to cold scrutiny, made more complex by the fictive father's Welsh origin (and unusual name.) Ripley is, in the time-honored tradition of fictional heroes, the eldest son, and presumptive Bogle heir. Unlike his literary forebears, he is not at all promising, but a manifestly unattractive child presumed by family and teachers to be somewhat dimwitted. A transformation occurs, however, and the ugly duckling is transformed, not into a swan, but into something of a peacock. Bounding over the intellects of his peers, he begins to gobble major authors at an impressive rate, changes schools accordingly, and becomes so handsome as to be irresistible to young girls. The history of this positive turnabout solaces to some extent the now-vagrant Bogle in his present dire condition, but his acerbic self-analysis keeps some of his vanity at bay.

Wilson's style, part Beckett, part psychobabble, part drama, and part social commentary verging on outrage, struggles to make the inequity of a materialist culture a stark reality for the reader. That Ripley is aware that certain actions and decisions made in his life are responsible for his down-ward slide is made clear; that society is responsible is also emphasized. He began life woefully disadvantaged and abused by limited and beleaguered parents. He tried, succeeded, failed, tried again, and finally has failed to fit in. Blame in the novel abounds, but it is apportioned.

On the first day of the time frame of the novel much of Bogle's past and present is given. The narrative widens on Friday to include an encounter with Perry, another homeless man. Perry, unlike Bogle, is a veteran of homelessness, and quite old. Perry's life gives Bogle a frightening view of his potential future. This is followed by Saturday's events, which include a knife fight that leaves the hero with a chest wound. As Bogle's predicament goes from bad to worse he learns on Sunday of Perry's death. He steals money from the dead man's ramshackle shack, but unconvincingly throws it away to preserve the last shreds of his ersatz dignity.

Interspersed with these timely events in his life, Ripley narrates the sad story of the two women in his life who got away. Deirdre, the first, a respectable Protestant girl from Belfast, became pregnant—something, he claims, not of his doing. When an abortion nearly killed her, he was banished from her sight. Later, after he (like his creator) has become a student at Cambridge, he claims the English Laura succumbed to his charms, but rejected him when he was forced to leave the university. Wilson's use of these two female icons, who never rise to the condition of full-fledged characters, is illuminative, especially in light of the novel's final disclosures. In truth Bogle did father Deirdre's child; in fact, he never seduced Laura. Bogle's ruminative reconstruction of his past—in part for the reader's benefit, in part for his own—is a sham or an exercise in wishful thinking after the fact. The reader becomes conditioned to accept the parallel deceit of his account of the sectarian death of a friend, Maurice, in Belfast. Unlike his first account of the tragedy, the revised version at the novel's end discloses Bogle's cowardly role in that death as an IRA informer.

Ripley Bogle ends philosophically, but inconclusively, with the ever-resourceful and self-deceptive hero proclaiming:

> The world did me wrong by making me an Irishman. I've kicked hard
> but Micksville packs a boot like a donkey. When you think about it,
> I'm practically faultless—a victim of circumstances, timing and nation-
> hood. It's Ireland's fault, not mine.

With this dubious reading of postcolonial theory, Bogle, but not Wilson, extricates himself from his dilemma.

Ripley Bogle maintains as one of its minor narrative preoccupations the hero's disgusted and incredulous rejection of his real father, and subsequent search for a suitable replacement. Bogle names various movie actors and writers in the vain search. This strain in Wilson's writing takes something of an ill-considered turn in *Eureka Street*, in which he sets to lampooning various Irish literary forebears, especially Seamus Heaney. Heaney's prominence as a Nobel laureate makes him a target for such debunking attempts by younger writers, as we have seen in the work of Paul Durcan and Paul Muldoon. Wilson, who is on record as rejecting the rural Ireland of nearly a half-century ago, which is often Heaney's imaginative landscape, denies the validity of such an Ireland even for those for whom it was a reality. *Eureka Street*, on the other hand, is an urban work of art, a contemporary paean for a city the author loves:

> . . . The city is a repository of narratives, of stories. Present tense, past
> tense, or future. The city is a novel.

Wilson's very urban talent, so well-exhibited in both *Ripley Bogle* and *Eureka Street*, not only makes excellent use of the urban history of great novels, but also carves an innovative place for itself. Treading a fine line between cockiness and genuine literary surefootedness, Wilson's writing validates the urban experience. It is regrettable, especially in the latter novel, that the author, in his urgent need to explain to readers the Ireland of his young manhood, feels compelled to deny the validity of such a literary undertaking in the work of writers a generation older. Perhaps the years of sectarian strife in Northern Ireland make it impossible for its youth (Wilson is more or less as old as the Troubles) to think in any other terms than "us and them." Finally, Wilson's Oedipal struggle with Ireland's writers degenerates at times into a mere series of potshots.

Robert McLiam Wilson is a talented and promising young novelist with a distinctive narrative gift, and a genuine feeling for the plight of the victims of contemporary society's greed and indifference. His documentary of 1992, *The Dispossessed*, is also written in the voice of his time, a voice that needs to be heard.

◆ ◆ ◆

In the last decade or two in Ireland there has been a notable trend in the publication of volumes of autobiographical prose. Some are written and intended to be read as nonfiction; others are set in a fictional frame. Some authors intentionally or unintentionally have fudged the distinction between nonfiction and fiction. Modern critical reading methods, of course, encourage, or indeed demand, that such differences either be blurred or abolished. If all narrative is fiction, then the conflating of fiction with autobiography must be accepted as the challenge it is.

Many of the writers represented in this volume have penned memoirs, often in the form of an essay/reminiscence, such as Michael Longley's *Tuppeny Stung* (1994). Memoirs like *Drink to the Bird* (1992) by Ben Kiely are not unusual, and are in fact expected and welcomed from older writers. But this newer form of Irish memoir, nearly exclusively male, is unusual in that it is very much connected with the current cultural debate on identity. Four such examples of autobiography will serve to illustrate the range today's reader can expect, and also the recurring motifs that identify this genre. This is not just the autobiographical essay or sketch, nor is it the summing up of advanced age. Rather these works are probings of self and country by men middle-aged or younger who wish to illuminate their caste, religion, or region and to, by extension, define national characteristics. All such exercises are, of course, apparently and in the first instance inclusivist, defining who "we" are by means of shared traits. They must also be seen as equally exclusivist. Where there is a "we," there must be a "they." The "us" and "them" in these narratives does not always divide predictably at the religious border one would expect, either. Sometimes the "other" in the narratives is the equally predictable divide of the English versus the Irish. Sometimes it is the less predictable female/male gap that also figures indirectly in defining national identity, since that process is almost exclusively connected with maleness. Finally, these narratives can find the male protagonist or narrator defining himself against the "other" of his father's generation, for whom national identity was defined in colonial or premodern terms.

Warrenpoint (1991) by Denis Donoghue takes its title from the town in which this prominent Irish literary critic was reared. Donoghue, for many years now the Henry James Professor of English and American Letters at New York University, was the son of a Catholic sergeant in the RUC (Royal

Ulster Constabulary) in that seaside town just north of the border. *Warren-point*, intended to be read as nonfiction, explores Donoghue's boyhood with particular reference to his father's somewhat anomalous situation in life. The children of the sergeant are of necessity estranged not only from the Protestant community in the town, but also from other Catholics. This estrangement, this difference or "otherness," the reader is urged to believe, may have strengthened the author's predisposition to solitary study and to self-examination. The Northern Ireland in which Donoghue grew up was not, however, the place of sustained political tension it is now. The author is thus free to begin and to fix this memoir in a detailed survey of the town, its amenities, and its denizens. It is the intact and ordered existence of such a town and such a time, underscored by the disciplined life of Donoghue's policeman father, that is assessed here in minute and often loving detail, as it informs the growth and development of his youngest son.

The town, the book, and Donoghue's worldview are resoundingly hierarchical. Even his choice of the term "town," as opposed to "village," is carefully and convincingly explained in the opening pages of *Warrenpoint*. (Although there are official distinctions for the same in Ireland, Donoghue's definition is both more poetic and quite practical. Warrenpoint is a town because it is not there merely to serve the surrounding farming community; and unlike Tullow, Co. Carlow where he was born, in Warrenpoint you "cannot smell cows when you stand in the Main Street.")

Irish people reared in towns or villages, and not on farms or in cities, make up a large proportion of the population; they also embody elements of the rural/urban divide that defines identity in their country. Like Brian Friel's characters from Ballybeg, Donoghue and those who formed the world in which he grew up lived in a community. They did not have a primal attachment to the land, but were all the same quite firmly identified with their place of origin. (Donoghue and his father cycled 126 miles to Tullow twice a year to visit his father's birthplace.) The regional, rather than the national, is therefore an important factor in identity; in the years after Donoghue's birth, the early years of the Irish state, notions of Irishness were solidifying rapidly, particularly north of the border.

Fathers occupy pride of place in all the autobiographical prose under consideration here, and indeed in all of this genre, especially as written by the first generation of the New Ireland. In their middle age, in the 1980s and 1990s, change in Irish society accelerated and looked to be irrevocable. Thus the imperative to capture and to define modes of Irishness before they disappeared entirely became compelling. There is, of course, in Irish writing a healthy tradition, in both Irish and English, of writing one's life in terms of, or against the backdrop of, one's father's life. (Examples of such writing include Tomás Ó Crohan's *The Islandman*, Maurice O'Sullivan's *Twenty Years A-Growing*, Joyce's *A Portrait of the Artist as a Young Man* and *Ulysses*, and Yeats' *Autobiographies*. Joyce and Yeats provide detailed portraits of the authors' *father's* friends as much as they do their own.) This preoccupation with fathers extends to a related thematic concern, and that is education. School days, school rooms, school masters, and schoolmates are worked into the hierarchy of the autobiographies, in particular as they are formative in the development of the author.

In *Warrenpoint*, Donoghue locates the points at which these elements fuse. Of his father he writes:

> He was grimly related to the present tense and determined to gain a better future for his children, so he hadn't much time for nostalgia. He seemed to consider his life merely a preparation for someone else's; mine, to be specific.

William Trevor's *Excursions in the Real World* (1993) is a series of essays, only some of which deal with familial and childhood memories. Contained within is a comparably vivid portrait of Irish town life—the world of the author's father in the early days of the State, of formative educational experiences, and of a hierarchical society. Trevor etches the details of town life of the period for the Protestant Irish as Donoghue does for the Catholics (both authors were born in the same year, 1928). For those who mistakenly take to heart Brendan Behan's jocular definition of a member of the Anglo-Irish metacaste as "a Protestant with a horse," Trevor reminds the reader that Protestant boys like him would, if lucky, have only been invited to serve as ball boys at the tennis parties featured in Big House novels like those written by Elizabeth Bowen. Never would people like his parents—his father was a bank manager—have been invited to be guests at such parties.

Of his banker father, Trevor begins his description with a paragraph that again seeks to tie together the contraries of Irish life—the country and the city—and to do so in a way that both emphasizes and bridges the gap between them:

> My father was a big, healthy-looking man with a brown bald head and brown tobacco fingers. He liked to tell stories rather than jokes— stories about people or events that amused him. . . . As he advanced in his career as a bank official he became skilled at guessing which farmers to lend money to. He was popular with the townspeople he lived among, popular with the country people because he understood them.

That the worlds of *Warrenpoint* and *Excursions in the Real World* intersect becomes a certainty as the young William Trevor Cox embarks on *his* educational journey through adolescence and into adulthood as a writer. The boy, glumly returning to boarding school by bus, crosses the road cycled by Donoghue and his father:

> By the time we reached Bunclody the odor of long-boiled cabbage that hung about the school's kitchen and dining room was beginning to mingle with the bus's exhaust fumes. By Kildavin, the noise of the play-yard echoed; by Tullow, Monsieur Bertain was striking the blackboard in a fury. In Rathvilly the sarcastic science master was in full flow.

Recent autobiographical prose takes care to place sons in relation to the waning worlds of the fathers, to relive the expansive, if fraught, experience of education, and to define Irishness. In addition , however, religion as cultural identifier is an omnipresent factor. Another element subsidiary to the search for national identity is a strong underlying sense of place. *Warrenpoint* proclaims this element in its title, and Seamus Deane's *Reading in the Dark* (1996) is very much a Derry book. George O'Brien's *The Village of Longing* (1987), the first volume of his autobiographical trilogy, is the Lismore, Co. Waterford of his childhood. Trevor's *Excursions in the Real World* may seem the exception, as the author's family moved regularly and he was not reared in one place, but Cork and the Southeast are very identifiably Trevor territory.

Reading in the Dark, in form like neither Donoghue's memoirs or Trevor's essays, is a novel which won the prestigious Guardian Prize for fiction. Seamus Deane presents Derry beginning in 1945, at the end of World War II, when he was five years old. The reader becomes sensitive to the enforced intimacy of working-class life and of the rapid, acerbic wit that characterizes the Derryman. Even the topography of the city emerges, with details of the city's walls, the River Foyle, and the undeveloped hills outside the walls where prehistoric remains provided space for play and for hiding. Also Derry's long history as a city of sectarian loyalties is reflected in the young boy's consciousness, struggling to understand his position in a Catholic city and a Protestant province. The mood in *Reading in the Dark* hovers as a result on the edge of the dangerous and the sinister, providing a sharp contrast to Donoghue's seemingly benign *Warrenpoint*.

In *Reading in the Dark* preoccupation with the father is sidelined into a search for a mysterious missing uncle. Deane populates his novel with a range of family members, including his father, his perceptive mother, a sister who died in childhood, and many uncles and aunts who are vivid presences in his protagonist's life. However, the young boy (who represents Deane) intermittently seeks Uncle Eddie, who was reputedly on the run. Eddie's association with the IRA makes him both a romantic and an outlaw figure, and one who shapes the family's identity in the city. An incident that took place in 1949, when Deane was nine years old, grimly underscores the family's position. ". . . [s]ince we had cousins in gaol for being in the IRA, we were a marked family and had to be careful." The boy's playing in public with a German pistol, a memento from the war, results in he, his brother, and their father being taken into police custody and beaten. The trauma that remains with the boy in the aftermath of this event, and his father's resentment of their treatment, continues to inform the family's allegiances throughout the novel. Uncle Eddie, both the man and the myth that has sprung up around him, functions doubly in the novel. He not only provides identity markers for the protagonist, he is also the family secret.

Each of the autobiographical narratives here features such secrets. They involve familial no-go areas, subjects that are not discussed, or perhaps not discussed fully or honestly. The child protagonist, in piecing together information about the family secrets (often simply a painful death over which the veil of silence has been drawn), finds his place in that family, and by association, in his country. In *Warrenpoint* the death of an elder brother helps to define the younger brother's role. In *Excursions in the Real World* the unhappy marriage of parents and frequent family moves bring siblings closer together and help make education a refuge. *The Village of Longing* is the story of a motherless child who, though reared by a doting family, seeks to unravel the secret of his father living in far-off Dublin.

George O'Brien's autobiographical trilogy consists of *The Village of Longing*, which details childhood in his Co. Waterford home; *Dancehall Days*, a record of his time in Dublin before his emigration to London in 1965, and *Out of Our Minds*, which recounts the exploits of young adulthood in that city. O'Brien's books, if for no other reason than their sheer size, represent the most minutely observed autobiography to emerge from his generation in Ireland. A similar aim has been partially achieved in John Waters' *Jiving at the Crossroads* (1991), which attempts to disabuse the notion of Ireland's provincial towns in the fifties and sixties as being places where nothing happened and time stood still.

O'Brien's books, however, and *The Village of Longing* in particular, are, in their unobtrusively recorded completeness, fascinating narratives of quotidian Irish provincial life beginning three decades after Irish independence. O'Brien is a village dweller, unlike Trevor and Donoghue in their towns, and

Deane in Derry City. He can more easily, perhaps, encompass *all* that was Lismore, even though his social status did not afford him entry into all levels of Lismore society. (Lismore Castle was owned by the wealthy and powerful Dukes of Devonshire, resident for a part of the year in the castle during O'Brien's youth.) Lismore's ordinary citizens, however, are presented, and their minor class distinctions carefully examined as though they were subspecies of exotic flora and fauna, now extinct. Their tribal practices and arcane rituals are lovingly recorded with the keen eye of a native who assumes the guise of an anthropologist who has fallen in love with his subjects. There are the poor lads who live in the lanes and in Chapel Street, a notch below the author; there is Willy, one of the few men whom the boy knew who didn't wear work clothes and had actually retired. Other older men were simply "too old and sore for work."

But O'Brien's autobiography, unlike the other examples of the genre given here, is notable for its fatherless gap. Given as a child to be reared by his paternal grandmother and aunt after the death of his mother, George (or Seoirse, as he was sometimes called in the Irish version of his name) only saw his father when work in Dublin permitted them visits. *The Village of Longing* ends with such a visit to his father in Dublin, and illustrates well how, through the use of recurring themes, such autobiographies can serve to inform each other. The boy's loyalty to his Uncle George in Lismore, an avid hurling enthusiast, is tested by his filial allegiance. His father takes him to the movies instead of to the final match of the Gaelic game being played in Dublin, against his Waterford home team. Since the sport is so closely linked with Irish identity, the Irish language, and patriotism, the child's choosing to be silent about the missed matched out of a desire to be alone with his father places him in the first of a series of oblique situations that question conflicting loyalties. His father's being at odds with national imperatives, or appearing to be, is not, of course, unique, nor a simple matter. It mirrors the position of Donoghue's RUC father, and Trevor's Protestant bourgeois father.

There is historically a strong tendency toward a flowering of autobiographical literature at the end of any era, especially a millennium. The 1890s is a case in point. In Ireland at the end of the nineteenth century the proclivity to sum up one's age was intensified by the traumatic death of Parnell and dashed hopes of Home Rule. In the 1990s there is the usual millennial imperative overlaid with an urgent sense of rapid societal change, and the resultant breakdown of institutions and certainties that initially informed the development of today's Irish writers. Those who wish to better understand the creative work being produced in Ireland today are well

advised to pore over such personal memoirs. Therein is illuminated the world
that produced the poetry, plays, and novels that are being written simultaneously, and in some cases by the same authors.

Novelists and other prose writers in Ireland today tend to favor traditional
forms and genres associated with Irish writing in past eras. The modern Irish
novel, with rare exceptions, is markedly noninnovative in structure. Irish
writers, who have always found the short story a felicitous genre, continue to
do so. Fiction and putative nonfiction that is autobiographical in intent not
only emerges from, or merges with, the tradition of such writing in Irish, but
has also gained predictably in popularity as the century ends.

Contemporary prose, however, differs substantially from earlier
efforts. There are more city dwellers, and their urban dilemmas vie with
stories of small-town and country people. Family life continues a strong
focus, but there is a greater willingness in today's authors to address the
dysfunctional elements of families. The authoritarian grasp of religion and
the hierarchy has given way in part to analysis of the dissolution of the
Church's power. In some cases writers create characters and fictive worlds
far removed from the religious past.

Local history and politics are still very much with the Irish writer, but
global awareness and worldwide travel have kept that focus from being
exclusivist. Exile continues to be a fact of life and a staple of fiction, but Irish
emigrants in books, as in reality, now show up in unlikely places, and are
rarely forced to remain there against their will indefinitely. Poverty, too,
remains, but education and the expectation and affluence that result from
education can present a different range of problems. Each can be alienating.
Sexuality in its various forms is no longer a taboo subject, but love is still
ephemeral or goes unrequited at times. Parents still love children, and
children their parents, but the channels of that love are convoluted by pain
and misunderstanding.

Perhaps the greatest innovation in contemporary Irish prose is the
readiness of its writers to explore the potential for human violence and to
try to shed light on the darker side of human emotion. Humor is still a mighty
factor, but it has a harsher edge. In short, Irish fiction, using traditional forms,
and exploring well-worn tropes, has kept pace with modern Irish life. The
repression of the past was corrosive, but the self-regulating mechanism of
shared values and hierarchical structures did protect some who may be cast
adrift now. In all ages and societies such shifts occur, but in Ireland the
intensity of societal change has often been so violent as to be palpable to
all. Such intensity has been captured best in recent prose writing.

In addition, a healthy publishing industry in Ireland has made possible a constant flow of Irish prose that need not conform to an outside view of Irish life. This development alone has fostered an atmosphere in which Irish novelists, short story writers, and memoirists can interrogate definitions of their own national identity unburdened by the internal strictures of the past or conflicting external preferences or requirements of what Irishness should be.

Notes

INTRODUCTION

1. Patricia Haberstroh, *Women Creating Women: Contemporary Irish Women Poets* (Syracuse: Syracuse University Press, 1996), p. 57.
2. The German name for a type of novel that charts the growth and development, traditionally of a young man, to intellectual and aesthetic maturity.

CHAPTER ONE

1. The Williamite or Jacobite War was waged from 1689 to 1691 between the supporters of the deposed Catholic King of England, James II, and the Protestant supporters of William III, who reigned with Mary, James' daughter.
2. Mountjoy, Lord Deputy of Ireland at the beginning of the seventeenth century, who accepted the surrender of Hugh O'Neill, Earl of Tyrone, at the end of the Nine Years War (1594–1603). This defeat occasions the Flight of the Earls. See also Thomas Kilroy's play *The O'Neill*.
3. The parish is a legal, not just an ecclesiastical, term in Ireland. It is similar to that used in Louisiana in the United States. A parish consists of one or more townlands, which are independent of village structure.
4. A ford is shallow place in a river where it is easily crossed, thus a place of strategic value.
5. Durrow is an ancient monastic site associated with learning, which produced some of the finest illuminated bibles of earlier medieval times.
6. Maurice Harmon, *The Poetry of Thomas Kinsella* (Dublin: Wolfhound, 1974), p.15.
7. Thomas H. Jackson, *The Whole Matter: The Poetic Evolution of Thomas Kinsella* (Syracuse: Syracuse University Press, 1995), p. xi.
8. Brian John, *Reading the Ground: The Poetry of Thomas Kinsella* (Washington, D.C.: The Catholic University of America Press, 1996), p. 246–247.
9. "Butcher's Dozen" is an ironic variant of "baker's dozen," or 13, a phrase that originated from the practice of bakers including an extra item for those who bought a dozen.
10. In January 1998 a decision was made by the British government to begin another inquiry into the events of Bloody Sunday.

11. Robert Emmet, a revolutionary who mounted the unsuccessful rising in 1803, was executed on the spot where Lord Kilwarden was assassinated.

12. Fintan O'Toole, "Out at the Edge of Things," *The Irish Times*, "Weekend," October 7, 1995, p.1.

13. The Lough Derg pilgrimage is still undertaken annually by thousands of believing Irish people, and some European and North American pilgrims. Historically, penitents make the pilgrimage barefoot. Frequently, the inclement Irish weather makes the undertaking more difficult or more penitential.

14. *The Annals of the Four Masters*, an early chronicle of Irish history, written in Latin, records this vision at the beautiful monastery on the River Shannon. Clonmacnoise is preserved in ruin and can be visited.

15. Nicolas Jenkins, "Walking on Air: Travel and Release in Seamus Heaney," *Times Literary Supplement*, July 5, 1996, p. 10.

16. Sally M. Gall and M. L. Rosenthal, *The Modern Poetic Sequence: The Genius of Modern Poetry* (New York: Oxford University Press, 1983).

17. In terms of literary inheritance, Howth Head is the spectacular promontory at the end of Dublin Bay that is the scene of Molly Bloom's courtship, which she remembers in the soliloquy that closes Joyce's *Ulysses*.

18. Yaddo is the name of an artists' retreat in New York state, which peaked in popularity in the 1940's when writers like Robert Lowell, Theodore Roethke, and other prominent, or soon-to-be prominent, authors exchanged ideas there.

19. Brendan Kennelly, *Selected Poems* (Dublin: Figgis, 1996), p.viii.

20. Tomás Ó Crohan, *The Islandman* (New York: Oxford University Press, 1982). This classic Irish language text was first published in Irish in 1929, and in English in 1934.

21. Eavan Boland, *Object Lessons: The Life of the Woman and the Poet in our Time*, (Manchester: Carcanet Press, 1994), p. 236.

22. A Jungian analyst and concentration camp survivor, Bettelheim espoused the belief that realistic tales and stories for children satisfied their needs more fully than those with contrived happy endings.

23. Sir Edward Carson, whose statue with uplifted hand stands outside Stormont, the site of the erstwhile Parliament of Northern Ireland, was a dedicated Unionist.

24. The fishing rights for most rivers in Ireland have been private and inherited.

25. Jonathan Allison, "Poetry from the Irish," *Irish Literary Supplement* (Spring 1994), p. 14.

26. Patricia Boyle Habertsroh, "An Interview with Eiléan Ní Chuilleanáin," *The Canadian Journal of Irish Studies*, vol. II, no. 2 (December 1994): 62–74.

27. Lawrence Norfolk, "The Abundant Braes of Yarrow," *Times Literary Supplement*, October 7, 1994, pp. 32–33.

28. *Madoc* is also the name of a long poem by Robert Southey, which is based on the Welsh traditional tale of Madoq Ab Owain Gwynedd, who flees the strife of his fatherland in search of a better place where such things as murder and war are unknown, and discovers America. See Robert Southey, *Madoc* (Boston:

Monroe and Francis, 1806), 2 vols. Also, the poets Coleridge and Southey were part of a plan to start an ideal economic community in America, on the banks of the Susquehanna River in Pennsylvania. It was an experiment that failed.

29. My thanks to Janet McIver of the Northern Ireland Bureau, British Embassy, Washington, D.C., a native of Moy, where the Muldoon family farmed.

30. Brucephalos was the name of Alexander the Great's beloved horse, for whom the conqueror was to name a kingdom.

31. MacNeice's play, *The Mad Islands*, was first broadcast on radio on the BBC in 1962.

32. A familiar Hiberno-English word for rabbit, based on the Irish *coinín*, and related to the Latin *cunnicula*. "Coney" is also a form found in archaic English and appears in Shakespeare.

33. Kevin McEneaney, "Flower Masters and Winter Works," *Irish Literary Supplement* (Fall 1983): 40.

34. Kathleen McCracken, "An Attitude of Compassion," *Irish Literary Supplement* (Fall 1990): 20.

35. Medbh McGuckian and Nuala Ní Dhomhnaill, "*Comhrá*," with a foreword and afterward by Laura O'Connor, *The Southern Review*, xxxi (July 1995): 3, 581–614.

36. "Querencia," a bull-fighting term, means a place of greatest strength—the bull's turf, inside of which the matador may inflict no harm upon him. (*Comhrá*, p. 588). Interestingly, this term is defined in the conversation not by McGuckian but by Ní Dhomhnaill.

37. Guglielmo Marconi (1874–1937) was an Italian national with an Irish mother who was the acknowledged inventor of radio.

38. Kate Newmann, "All Sorts of Untils," *The Irish Review* (Spring/Summer 1992): 173–74.

39. Fred Johnston, "Surprised by Familiarity," *Books Ireland* (December 1995), p. 323.

40. See *Comhrá*, cited above.

41. The occasion was a conference, "Women in Contemporary Ireland," held at the Catholic University of America, Washington, D.C., in April 1986.

CHAPTER TWO

1. Marie Hubert Kealy, "Spirit of Place: A Context for Social Criticism in John B. Keane's *The Field* and *Big Maggie*," *Irish University Review* 19, 2 (Autumn 1989): 287-301.

2. Bernard Farrell, interview by Jocelyn Clarke, in "The Tribune Magazine," *The Sunday Tribune*, Dublin, August 17, 1997, p. 2.

3. Canon is a Roman Catholic honorific conferred on a priest, similar to that of Monsignor. It is no longer in use.

4. Hedge schools, though private and fee-paying, were themselves a response to an elitist educational system. The schools varied greatly in quality, according to the qualifications of their masters. There was a strong emphasis on classics and mathematics, and classes were taught in the Irish language. Hedge schools also usually served as a means of providing religious education.

5. For the best material explaining these ideological conflicts, see Tom Dunne, "New Histories: Beyond Revisionism" in *Irish Review* 12 (1992): 1-12; Luke Gibbon's essay "Challenging the Canon: Revisionism and Cultural Criticism," in volume III of Seamus Deane, ed., *The Field Day Anthology of Irish Writing*, (Derry: Field Day Publications, 1991), pp. 561–568; Ciaran Brady, ed., *Interpreting Irish History: The Debate on Historical Revisionism, 1938–1994* (Dublin: Irish Academic Press, 1994); and Nancy J. Curtin, "'Varieties of Irishness': Historical Revisionism, Irish Style," *Journal of British Studies* 35, 2 (April 1996): 195–219.

6. Quoted in Fintan O'Toole, *The Politics of Magic: The Work and Times of Tom Murphy* (Dublin: New Island Books, 1994), p. 9.

7. O'Toole, p. 144. See also O'Toole's analysis of the parallels of this play to Greek tragedy, in particular to *The Oresteia* of Aeschylus.

8. 'Tho' from earth thou'st flown before me." This aria has been described as "a passage of mournful beauty, which has few equals in Italian opera." (The Earl of Harewood, ed., *Kobbé's Complete Opera Book*, 9th ed. [London: Putnam, 1976], p. 461.)

9. Seamus Deane, ed., *The Field Day Anthology of Irish Writing*, vol. III (Derry: Field Day Publications, 1991), p. 1307.

10. In this the play markedly resembles Tom Stoppard's *Travesties*, in which the Zurich of the early stages of World War I and of alien residents James Joyce, Tristan Tzara (the founder of the artistic Dadaist movement), and Lenin are brought together with a traveling production of Oscar Wilde's *The Importance of Being Earnest*. There is equally little evidence any of these people, like Kilroy's Joyce and Bracken, ever met.

11. Thomas Kilroy, *Double Cross* (Oldcastle, Co. Meath: Gallery Press, 1994), p. 11.

12. Anthony Roche, *Contemporary Irish Drama* (Dublin: Gill and Macmillan, 1994), p. 206.

13. A compelling and provocative analysis of the phenomenon is presented by Irish historian R. F. Foster, "Marginal Men and Micks on the Make: The Uses of Irish Exile, c. 1840–1922," in *Paddy and Mr. Punch* (London: Allen Lane, 1993), pp. 262–280.

14. The fire warden rose to urban folkloric eminence in the London bombing raids during the war, and continues in literature to resonate of T. S. Eliot's great blitz poem "Little Gidding," written while Eliot himself was taking his turn as local fire warden. The figure came to represent ordinary Britishness, or a certain end-of-empire grit in the face of continuing destruction and danger.

15. Frank McGuinness, *The Dazzling Dark: New Irish Plays* (London: Faber & Faber, 1994), xi.

16. Roche, *Contemporary Irish Drama*, p. 266.

17. Michael Etherton, *Contemporary Irish Dramatists* (London: Macmillan, 1989), p. 49.

18. The Battle of the Boyne is now celebrated, of course, on the twelfth of July; but the western calendar changed from the Julian to the Gregorian in 1752 in Britain and its American colonies. Eleven days were suppressed to move forward the vernal equinox to accommodate new scientific knowledge.

19. See discussion of Ciaran Carson's poem "The Brain of Sir Edward Carson" in the poetry chapter.

20. See discussion of Thomas Kinsella's poem "Butcher's Dozen" in the poetry chapter.

21. Dido, daughter of the King of Tyre, escaped after the murder of her husband by her brother to found Carthage (in present-day Libya). There she was wooed by Aeneas, who had been shipwrecked on the Carthaginian coast, until the gods required that he continue on his journey. Aeneas' departure results in Dido's despair and self-immolation on a funeral pyre.

22. See Elizabeth Butler Cullingford's "British and Irish Carthaginians: Anticolonial Metaphor in Heaney, Friel, and McGuinness," *PMLA* iii, 2 (March 1996): 228. "Reflect the rainbow" is McGuinness' phrase, which appears in "The Arts and Ideology: Jennifer Fitzgerald talks to Seamus Deane, Joan Fowler, and Frank McGuinness," *Crane Bag* 2 (1985): 60–69.

23. This was a technique used effectively in another play about imprisonment, based on Manuel Puig's novel, *The Kiss of the Spider Woman*, in which one cellmate narrates old films from memory to amuse himself and the other man, who is drawn reluctantly into the recreated fantasies.

24. John Malone Memorial Lecture. In Claudia W. Harris, "From Partness to Wholeness: Stewart Parker's Reinventing Theatre," *Colby Quarterly*, xxvii, 4 (December 1991): 223–241.

25. The strike was the result of a Unionist rejection of the Northern Ireland Executive power-sharing agreement reached at Sunningdale. The agreement provided for Catholic participation in the region's government.

26. Stewart Parker, Introduction, *Three Plays for Ireland* (London: Oberon, 1989), p. 10.

27. Maria M. Delgado, "'Beyond the Troubles': The Political Drama of Christina Reid," introduction to *Christina Reid: Plays I* (London: Methuen, 1997), p. viii.

28. Hurling, a native sport with strong Irish-language and rural ties, attracts huge crowds in Ireland.

29. Oisín was condemned never to return to earth from Tír na n'Óg (the Celtic afterlife, literally the land of youth) under threat of turning instantly into an aged man. Doyle's return to Wexford threatens the same metaphorical fate.

30. See discussion of Thomas Kilroy's play *Talbot's Box* earlier in this chapter.

31. Collins is a recurring figure in Barry's work. His visits to the locality are mentioned more than once by Mick in *Boss Grady's Boys*.

32. In the myth Coillte, Bláth's spring and summer lover, must surrender Bláth to a witch in autumn and winter because he is under her curse. Coillte cries a

lake of tears (Owl Lake) and the witch drowns her in the lake. When Bláth emerges in spring from the curse, he learns of his beloved's death.

33.   Jocelyn Clarke, "Trilogy Eulogy for Prodigy," *The Tribune Magazine*, June 29, 1997, p. 33.

34.   Robert Brustein, "The Rebirth of Irish Drama," *The New Republic* vol. 216, no. 14, Issue No. 4290 (April 7, 1997): 28–29.

35.   C. L. Dallat, "From the Outside," *Times Literary Supplement* (January 17, 1997), Issue No. 4894: 14–15.

CHAPTER THREE

1.   Seamus Deane, *A Short History of Irish Literature* (London: Hutchinson, 1986), p. 225.

2.   Phenomenology is a philosophical system based on scientific principles that has as its aim an evolutionary development of the mind. Edmund Husserl (1859–1938), a German philosopher, was a committed phenomenologist.

3.   The most comprehensive essay on Higgins' career is by Rüdiger Imhof, "The Prose Works of Aidan Higgins: Fiction, Fictionalized Autobiography, Travelogue," *Anglia*, Band 114, Heft 1, 1996, pp. 57–90, to which this assessment is indebted.

4.   Quoted in *Contemporary Novelists*, fourth ed., Lesley Henderson, ed. (London: St. James Press, 1991), pp. 77–79.

5.   Part of this analysis of Julia O'Faolain's fiction appeared in Theo D'haen and José Lanters, eds., *Troubled Histories, Troubled Fictions: Twentieth-Century Anglo-Irish Prose*, vol. 4, *Proceedings of the Leiden IASAIL Conference: The Literature of Politics, the Politics of Literature*, Costerus New Series, 101 (Amsterdam: Editions Rodopi B.V., 1995), pp. 151–158.

6.   Maggie Gee, "Inside the Insider," *Times Literary Supplement*, May 9, 1997, p. 20.

7.   In *John Banville: A Critical Introduction* (Dublin: Wolfhound Press, 1989), p. 13.

8.   Tom Shone, "Civil Wars," review of *Nightlines*, by Neil Jordan. *The New York Times Book Review*, October 15, 1995, p. 13.

9.   Judy Cooke, "Neil Jordan," *Contemporary Novelists*, fourth ed., Lesley Henderson, ed. (London: St. James Press, 1991), pp. 509–510.

10.   The gombeen man was a money-lender, opportunist, and middle-man who took advantage most often of the poor. The character recurs as a homegrown villain in Irish drama and fiction.

11.   See Cormac MacCarthy, "Ideology and Geography in Dermot Bolger's *The Journey Home*," *Irish University Review* 27, 1 (Spring–Summer, 1997): 98–110.

12.   Francisco Franco was a Spanish general who led a Fascist revolt against the Spanish Republic, commonly known as the Spanish Civil War (1936–1939). He ruled as dictator over Spain until his death in 1975.

13.   The children of Lir—in Irish mythology the children of the ocean-god were turned into swans by their step-mother, Aoife, in a jealous rage after their mother, Aobh (Aoife's sister) dies in childbirth.

SELECTED BIBLIOGRAPHY

The following bibliography lists all living writers mentioned in the text, plus the late Stewart Parker. Dates given in text represent first publication or first production in the case of plays. In the bibliography more recent and U.S. editions and dates are listed where available. Please note later editions may be revised.

POETRY

Boland, Eavan. *New Territory*. Dublin: Allen, Figgis, 1967.

———. *In Her Own Image*. Dublin: Arlen House, 1982.

———. *Night Feed*. Dublin: Arlen House, 1982.

———. *The Journey*. Manchester: Carcanet, 1987.

———. *Outside History*. New York: Norton, 1990.

———. *In A Time of Violence*. New York: Norton, 1994.

———. *An Origin Like Water*. New York: Norton, 1996.

Carson, Ciaran. *The New Estate*. Oldcastle, Co. Meath: Gallery, 1976.

———. *The Irish For No*. Winston-Salem, NC: Wake Forest University Press, 1987.

———. *Belfast Confetti*. Winston-Salem, NC: Wake Forest University Press, 1989.

———. *First Language*. Winston-Salem, NC: Wake Forest University Press, 1994.

———. *Opera et Cetera*. Winston-Salem, NC: Wake Forest University Press, 1996.

Ní Chuilleanáin, Eiléan. *Acts and Monuments*. Oldcastle, Co. Meath: Gallery, 1972.

———. *Sites of Ambush*. Oldcastle, Co. Meath: Gallery, 1975.

———. *The Rose Geranium*. Oldcastle, Co. Meath: Gallery, 1981.

———. *The Second Voyage*. Winston-Salem, NC: Wake Forest University Press, 1991.

———. *The Magdalene Sermon and Earlier Poems*. Winston-Salem, NC: Wake Forest University Press, 1991.

———. *The Brazen Serpent*. Winston-Salem, NC: Wake Forest University Press, 1995.

Cronin, Anthony. *The End of the Modern World*. Dublin: Raven Arts, 1989.

———. *Relationships*. Dublin: New Island, 1994.

Dawe, Gerald. *Sheltering Places*. Belfast: Blackstaff, 1978.

———. *The Lundy Letter*. Oldcastle, Co. Meath: Gallery, 1985.

———. *A Real Life Elsewhere*. Belfast: Lagan, 1993.

———. *Against Piety*. Belfast: Blackstaff, 1994.

Deane, John F. *High Sacrifice*. Portlaoise: Dolmen, 1981.

———. *Thistledown*. Dublin: Dedalus, 1990.

———. *The Stylized City*. Dublin: Dedalus, 1990.

———. *Far Country*. Dublin: Dedalus, 1992.

———. *Free Range*. Dublin: Wolfhound, 1994.

Deane, Seamus. *Selected Poems*. Oldcastle, Co. Meath: Gallery, 1988.

Ní Dhomhnaill, Nuala. *Selected Poems: Rogha Danta*. Dublin: Raven Arts, 1988.

———. *Pharaoh's Daughter*. Winston-Salem, NC: Wake Forest University Press, 1993.

———. *The Astrakhan Cloak*. In Irish, with translations by Paul Muldoon. Winston-Salem, NC: Wake Forest University Press, 1993.

Dorgan, Theo. *The Ordinary House of Love*. Galway: Salmon, 1990.

———. *Rosa Mundi*. Galway: Salmon, 1995.

Durcan, Paul. *Teresa's Bar*. Oldcastle, Co. Meath: Gallery, 1976, 1986.

———. *The Berlin Wall Café*. Belfast: Blackstaff, 1985.

———. *Going Home To Russia*. Belfast: Blackstaff, 1987.

———. *Daddy, Daddy*. Belfast: Blackstaff, 1990.

———. *Crazy About Women*. Dublin: National Gallery of Ireland, 1991.

———. *Snail in My Prime*. London: Harper Collins, 1993.

———. *Give Me Your Hand*. London: MacMillan, 1994.

Egan, Desmond. *Collected Poems*. Orono, ME: National Poetry Foundation, 1983.

Ennis, John. *Dolmen Hill*. Oldcastle, Co. Meath: Gallery, 1977.

———. *A Drink of Spring*. Oldcastle, Co. Meath: Gallery, 1979.

———. *The Burren Days*. Oldcastle, Co. Meath: Gallery, 1985.

———. *Telling the Bees*. Dublin: Dedalus, 1995.

Fallon, Peter. *The Speaking Stones*. Oldcastle, Co. Meath: Gallery, 1978.

———. *Winter Work*. Oldcastle, Co. Meath: Gallery, 1983.

———. *News and Weather*. Oldcastle, Co. Meath: Gallery, 1987.

———. *News of the World: Selected Poems*. Winston-Salem, NC: Wake Forest University Press, 1993.

Greacen, Robert. *Collected Poems, 1944-1994*. Belfast: Lagan, 1995.

Grennan, Eamon. *Wildly For Days*. Oldcastle, Co. Meath: Gallery, 1983.

———. *What Light There Is*. San Francisco: North Point Press, 1989.

———. *As If It Matters*. St. Paul, MN: Graywolf Press, 1992.

Hartnett, Michael. *Selected Poems*. Dublin: New Writers, 1970.

———. *A Farewell to English*. Oldcastle, Co. Meath: Gallery, 1978.

———. *Collected Poems*. Dublin: Raven Arts, 1985.

———. *A Necklace of Wrens*. Oldcastle, Co. Meath: Gallery, 1987.

———. *Poems To Younger Women*. Oldcastle, Co. Meath: Gallery, 1988.

———. *The Killing of Dreams*. Oldcastle, Co. Meath: Gallery, 1992.

———. *Selected and New Poems*. Winston-Salem, NC: Wake Forest University Press, 1994.

Heaney, Seamus. *Death of a Naturalist*. Boston: Faber & Faber, 1969.

———. *Door into the Dark*. New York: Oxford, 1969.

———. *Wintering Out*. New York: Oxford, 1972.

———. *North*. New York: Oxford, 1975.

———. *Field Work*. Boston: Faber & Faber, 1979.

———. *Poems 1965–1975*. New York: Farrar, Straus, Giroux, 1980.

———. *Sweeney Astray*. New York: Farrar, Straus, Giroux, 1984.

———. *Station Island*. Boston: Faber & Faber, 1984.

———. *The Haw Lantern*. Boston: Faber & Faber, 1987.

———. *New Selected Poems 1966–1987*. Boston: Faber & Faber, 1990.

———. *Seeing Things*. London: Faber & Faber, 1991.

———. *The Spirit Level*. New York: Farrar, Straus, Giroux, 1996.

Hutchinson, Pearse. *Selected Poems*. Oldcastle, Co. Meath: Gallery, 1982.

———. *Barnsley Night Seam*. Oldcastle, Co. Meath: Gallery, 1995.

Kennelly, Brendan. *Dream of a Black Fox*. Dublin: Allen Figgis, 1968.

———. *Selected Poems*. New York: Dutton, 1972.

———. *New and Selected Poems*. Oldcastle, Co. Meath: Gallery, 1976.

———. *A Small Light*. Oldcastle, Co. Meath: Gallery, 1980.

———. *Moloney Up and At It*. Dublin: Mercier, 1984.

———. *Cromwell: A Poem*. Newcastle upon Tyne: Bloodaxe, 1987.

———. *Poetry my arse*. Newcastle upon Tyne: Bloodaxe, 1995.

Kinsella, Thomas. *Nightwalker and Other Poems*. New York: Knopf, 1968.

———. *Notes From the Land of the Dead*. New York: Knopf, 1973.

———. *One and Other Poems*. Dublin: Dolmen, 1979.

———. *Peppercanister Poems 1972–1978*. Winston-Salem, NC: Wake Forest University Press, 1979.

———. *Poems 1956–1973*. Winston-Salem, NC: Wake Forest University Press, 1979.

———. *St. Catherine's Clock*. Dublin: Peppercanister, 1987.

———. *Blood and Family*. London: Oxford, 1988.

———. *Collected Poems, 1956–1994*. London: Oxford, 1996.

Liddy, James. *Collected Poems*. Omaha: Creighton University, 1994.

Longley, Michael. *No Continuing City*. London: Macmillan, 1969.

———. *An Exploded View, Poems 1968–1972*. London, Gollancz, 1973.

———. *Man Lying On A Wall*. London: Gollancz, 1976.

———. *The Echo Gate*. London, Secker & Warburg, 1979.

———. *Selected Poems 1963–1980*. Winston-Salem, NC: Wake Forest University Press, 1981.

———. *Poems 1963–1983*. Oldcastle, Co. Meath: Gallery, 1987.

———. *Gorse Fires*. Winston-Salem, NC: Wake Forest University Press, 1991.

———. *The Ghost Orchid*. Winston-Salem, NC: Wake Forest University Press, 1995.

Mahon, Derek. *Night-Crossings*. London: Oxford, 1968.

———. *Beyond Howth Head*. Dublin: Dolmen, 1970.

———. *The Snow Party*. London: Oxford, 1975.

———. *Selected Poems 1962–1978*. London: Oxford, 1979.

———. *The Hunt by Night*. Winston-Salem, NC: Wake Forest University Press, 1995.

———. *Selected Poems*. New York: Penguin, 1992.

———. *The Yaddo Letter*. Oldcastle, Co. Meath: Gallery, 1992.

———. *The Hudson Letter*. Winston-Salem: Wake Forest University Press, 1995.

McFadden, Roy. *Collected Poems, 1943–1995*. Belfast: Lagan, 1996.

McGuckian, Medbh. *The Flower Master*. London: Oxford, 1982.

———. *Venus and the Rain*. London: Oxford, 1984.

———. *On Ballycastle Beach*. Winston-Salem, NC: Wake Forest University Press, 1988.

———. *Marconi's Cottage*. Winston-Salem, NC: Wake Forest University Press, 1992.

———. *Captain Lavender*. Winston-Salem, NC: Wake Forest University Press, 1995.

———. *Selected Poems*. Winston-Salem, NC: Wake Forest University Press, 1997.

Meehan, Paula. *Return and No Blame*. Dublin: Beaver Row, 1984.

———. *Reading the Sky*. Dublin: Beaver Row, 1986.

———. *The Man Who Was Marked by Winter*. Dublin: Gallery, 1991.

———. *Pillow Talk*. Oldcastle, Co. Meath: Gallery, 1994.

Montague, John. *Forms of Exile*. Dublin: Dolmen, 1958.

———. *Poisoned Lands*. London: MacGibbon & Kee, 1961.

———. *A Chosen Light*. London: MacGibbon & Kee, 1967.

————. *Tides*. Dublin: Dolmen, 1970.

————. *Selected Poems*. Dublin: Dolmen, 1982.

————. *The Rough Field*. Winston-Salem, NC: Wake Forest University Press, 1989.

————. *New Selected Poems*. Oldcastle, Co. Meath: Gallery, 1989.

————. *Collected Poems*. Winston-Salem, NC: Wake Forest University Press, 1995.

Montague, John and John Hewitt. *The Planter and the Gael*. Belfast: Northern Ireland Arts Council, 1970.

Muldoon, Paul. *New Weather*. London: Faber & Faber, 1973.

————. *Mules and Other Poems*. Winston-Salem, NC: Wake Forest University Press, 1985.

————. *Why Brownlee Left*. Boston: Faber & Faber, 1985.

————. *Quoof*. Winston-Salem, NC: Wake Forest University Press, 1983.

————. *Selected Poems, 1968–1983*. New York: Echo, 1987.

————. *Meeting the British*. Winston-Salem, NC: Wake Forest University Press, 1987.

————. *Madoc: A Mystery*. New York: Farrar, Straus, Giroux, 1990.

————. *The Astrakhan Cloak*. Translations with original poems by Nuala Ní Dhomhnaill. Winston-Salem, NC: Wake Forest University Press, 1993.

————. *The Annals of Chile*. Boston: Faber & Faber, 1994.

————. *The Prince of the Quotidian*. Winston-Salem, NC: Wake Forest University Press, 1994.

Murphy, Richard. *Sailing to an Island*. London: Faber & Faber, 1963.

————. *The Battle of Aughrim*. London: Faber & Faber, 1968.

————. *High Island*. New York: Harper & Row, 1974.

————. *Selected Poems*. Boston: Faber & Faber, 1979.

————. *The Mirror Wall*. Winston-Salem, NC: Wake Forest University Press, 1989.

————. *The Price of Stone and Earlier Poems*. Winston-Salem, NC: Wake Forest University Press, 1990.

O'Driscoll, Dennis. *Hidden Extras*. London: Anvil, 1987.

————. *Long Story Short*. Dublin: Dedalus, 1993.

————. *The Bottom Line*. Dublin: Dedalus, 1994.

O'Grady, Desmond. *The Dying Gaul*. London: MacGibbon & Kee, 1968.

————. *A Limerick Rake*. Oldcastle, Co. Meath: Gallery, 1978.

————. *My Fields This Springtime*. Belfast: Lapwing, 1993.

O'Siadhail, Micheal. *The Image Wheel*. Dublin: Bluett, 1985.

————. *The Chosen Garden*. Dublin: Dedalus, 1990.

————. *Hail! Madam Jazz*. Newcastle upon Tyne: Bloodaxe, 1992.

————. *A Fragile City*. Newcastle upon Tyne: Bloodaxe, 1995.

Paulin, Tom. *The Book of Juniper*. London: Farrar, Straus, Giroux, 1981.

————. *Selected Poems, 1972–1990*. Boston: Farrar, Straus, Giroux, 1993.

————. *Walking a Line*. Boston: Farrar, Straus, Giroux, 1994.

Simmons, James. *Poems, 1956–1986*. ed. Edna Longley. Dublin: Gallery, 1986.

Sirr, Peter. *Talk, Talk*. Oldcastle, Co. Meath: Gallery, 1987.

————. *Ways of Falling*. Oldcastle, Co. Meath: Gallery, 1991.

————. *The Ledger of Fruitful Exchange*. Oldcastle, Co. Meath: Gallery, 1995.

Strong, Eithne. *Sarah, in Passing*. Dublin: Dolmen, 1974.

————. *Patterns*. Dublin: Poolbeg, 1981.

————. *The Love Riddle*. Dublin: Attic, 1993.

————. *Flesh*. Dublin: Attic, 1993.

DRAMA

Barry, Sebastian. *Prayers of Sherkin and Boss Grady's Boys*. London: Methuen, 1991.

————. *The Only True History of Lizzy Finn; The Steward of Christendom; White Woman Street*. London: Methuen, 1995.

Carr, Marina. *Low in the Dark*, in *A Crack in the Emerald: New Irish Plays*, sel. and intro. David Grant. London: Nick Hern, 1994.

————. *The Mai*. Oldcastle, Co. Meath: Gallery, 1995.

————. *Portia Coughlan*. London: Faber & Faber, 1996.

Devlin, Anne. *Ourselves Alone; A Woman Calling; The Long March*. London: Faber & Faber, 1986.

Farrell, Bernard. *The Plays of Bernard Farrell*. Dublin: Co-op, 1982.

————. *I Do Not Like Thee, Doctor Fell*. Dublin: Brophy, 1988.

Friel, Brian. *Selected Plays*. Washington: Catholic University of America, 1986.

————. *Dancing at Lughnasa*. London: S. French, 1990.

————. *Wonderful Tennessee*. Oldcastle, Co. Meath: Gallery, 1993.

————. *Molly Sweeney*. New York: Penguin, 1995.

Jones, Marie. *A Night in November*. Dublin: New Island Books, 1995.

Keane, John B. *The Field*. Cork: Mercier, 1966.

————. *Big Maggie*. Dublin: Mercier, 1969.

————. *Three Plays*. Dublin: Mercier, 1990.

Kilroy, Thomas. *The Death and Resurrection of Mr. Roche*. London: Faber & Faber, 1969.

————. *Talbot's Box*. Oldcastle, Co. Meath: Gallery, 1979.

———. *Double Cross*. Boston: Faber & Faber, 1986.

———. *The O'Neill*. Oldcastle, Co. Meath, Gallery, 1995.

———. *The Secret Fall of Constance Wilde*. Dublin: Gallery, 1997.

Leonard, Hugh. *The Patrick Pearse Motel*. New York: S. French, 1972.

———. *Da*. New York: Atheneum, 1978.

———. *Selected Plays of Hugh Leonard*. Washington: Catholic University of America, 1992.

McCabe, Eugene. *The King of the Castle*. Oldcastle, Co. Meath: Gallery, 1978.

McDonagh, Martin. *The Beauty Queen of Leenane*. London: Methuen, 1996.

———. *The Leenane Trilogy*. London: Methuen, 1997.

———. *The Cripple of Inishmaan*. London: Methuen, 1997.

McGuinness, Frank. *Observe the Sons of Ulster Marching Towards the Somme*. London: Faber & Faber, 1985.

———. *Plays*. London: Faber & Faber, 1996.

MacIntyre, Tom. *The Great Hunger: Poem into Play*. Dublin: Lilliput, 1988.

———. *Good Evening, Mr. Collins*, in *The Dazzling Dark: New Irish Plays*, sel. and intro. Frank McGuinness. London/Boston: Faber & Faber, 1996.

McPherson, Conor. *This Lime Tree Bower*. London: Nick Hern, 1996.

———. *St. Nicholas and the Weir*. London: Nick Hern, 1997.

Murphy, Tom. *A Whistle in the Dark*. New York: S. French, 1984.

———. *The Gigli Concert*. Oldcastle, Co. Meath: Gallery, 1984.

———. *The Sanctuary Lamp*. Oldcastle, Co. Meath: Gallery, 1984.

———. *Bailegangaire*. Oldcastle, Co. Meath: Gallery, 1986.

———. *Plays: One*. London: Methuen, 1992.

O'Kelly, Donal. *Asylum! Asylum!*, in *New Plays from the Abbey Theatre*, ed. C. Fitz-Simon and S. Sternlicht. Syracuse: Syracuse University Press, 1996.

———. *Catalpa*. London: Nick Hern, 1997.

Parker, Stewart. *Spokesong*. New York: S. French, 1980.

———. *Three Plays for Ireland*. London: Oberon, 1989.

Reid, Christina. *Plays: 1*. London: Methuen, 1997.

Roche, Billy. *The Wexford Trilogy*. London: Nick Hern, 1992.

———. *The Cavalcaders*. London: Nick Hern, 1995.

Woods, Vincent. *At the Pig's Dyke*, in *Far from the Land: Contemporary Irish Plays*, ed. John Fairleigh. London: Methuen, 1997.

FICTION

Banville, John. *Birchwood*. New York: Norton, 1973.

———. *Doctor Copernicus*. New York: Norton, 1976.

———. *Kepler: A Novel*. Boston: Godine, 1983.

———. *Mefisto*. New York: Warner , 1986.

———. *The Newton Letter*. Boston: Godine, 1987.

———. *The Book of Evidence*. New York: Warner, 1991.

———. *Ghosts*. New York: Random House, 1993.

———. *Athena*. New York: Random House, 1995.

———. *The Untouchable*. New York: Knopf, 1997.

Bolger, Dermot. *A Second Life*. New York: Viking, 1994.

———. *The Woman's Daughter*. London: Penguin, 1995.

———. *The Journey Home*. London: Penguin, 1995.

———. *Emily's Shoes*. London: Penguin, 1995.

———. *Night Shift*. London: Penguin, 1995.

Deane, Seamus. *Reading in the Dark*. New York: Knopf, 1997.

Ní Dhuibhne, Eilís. *The Bray House*. Dublin: Attic Press, 1990.

———. *Eating Women is Not Recommended*. Dublin: Attic, 1991.

———. *The Inland Ice and Other Stories*. Belfast, Blackstaff, 1997.

Donoghue, Denis. *Warrenpoint*. New York: Knopf, 1990.

Donoghue, Emma. *Stir-Fry*. New York: Harper Collins, 1994.

———. *Hood*. New York: HarperCollins, 1995.

Dorcey, Mary. *The River that Carries Me*. Galway: Salmon, 1995.

———. *A Noise from the Woodshed*. London: Onlywoman, 1996.

———. *The Biography of Desire*. Dublin: Poolbeg, 1997.

Doyle, Roddy. *The Barrytown Trilogy*. New York: Penguin, 1995.

———. *Paddy Clarke Ha Ha Ha*. New York: Viking, 1994.

———. *The Woman Who Walked into Doors*. New York: Viking, 1996.

Hamilton, Hugo. *The Last Shot*. New York: Farrar, Straus, Giroux, 1992.

———. *Dublin Where the Palm Trees Grow*. London: Faber & Faber, 1996.

———. *Head Banger*. London: Secker & Warburg, 1997.

Healy, Dermot. *Banished Misfortune*. New York: Allison & Busby, 1982.

———. *Fighting with Shadows*. New York: Allison & Busby, 1986.

———. *A Goat's Song*. New York: Flamingo, 1994.

Higgins, Aidan. *Felo de Se*. London: Calder, 1960.

————. *Killachter Meadow*. New York: Grove Press, 1961.

————. *Langrishe, Go Down*. New York: Grove, 1966.

————. *Balcony of Europe*. New York: Delacorte, 1972.

————. *Scenes from a Receding Past*. London: Calder, 1977.

————. *Donkey's Years*. London: Secker & Warburg, 1995.

————. *Dog Days*. London: Secker & Warburg, 1997.

Hogan, Desmond. *The Ikon Maker*. Dublin: Irish Writers' Co-operative, 1976.

————. *The Diamonds at the Bottom of the Sea*. New York: Braziller, 1979.

————. *Children of Lir*. New York: Braziller, 1981.

————. *A Curious Street*. New York: Braziller, 1984.

Johnston, Jennifer. *The Captains and the Kings*. London: Hamish Hamilton, 1972.

————. *The Gates*. London: Hamish Hamilton, 1973.

————. *How Many Miles to Babylon?* New York: Doubleday, 1974.

————. *Shadows on Our Skin*. New York: Doubleday, 1978.

————. *The Old Jest*. New York: Doubleday, 1980.

————. *The Christmas Tree*. New York: Morrow, 1982.

————. *The Railway Station Man*. New York: Viking, 1988.

————. *Fool's Sanctuary*. New York: Viking, 1988.

————. *The Invisible Worm*. New York: Carroll & Graf, 1993.

————. *The Illusionist*. London: Sinclair-Stevenson, 1995.

Jordan, Neil. *Night in Tunisia and Other Stories*. Dublin: Irish Writers' Co-operative, 1976.

————. *The Past*. London: Cape, 1980.

————. *The Dream of a Beast*. New York: Random House, 1989.

————. *Sunrise with Sea Monster*. New York: Random House, 1995.

Kiely, Benedict. *A Ball of Malt and Madame Butterfly*. New York: Penguin, 1976.

————. *Nothing Happens in Carmincross*. Boston: Godine, 1985.

————. *Proxopera*. Boston: Godine, 1987.

————. *Drink to the Bird*. London, Methuen, 1991.

Kilroy, Thomas. *The Big Chapel*. London: Faber & Faber, 1971.

McCabe, Patrick. *The Butcher Boy*. New York: Fromm International, 1993.

————. *The Dead School*. New York: Dial, 1995.

————. *Carn*. New York: Delta, 1997.

McCann, Colum. *Songdogs*. New York: Picador, 1996.

————. *Fishing the Sloe-Back River*. New York: Metropolitan, 1996.

————. *This Side of Brightness*. London: Phoenix House, 1998.

McGahern, John. *The Barracks*. New York: Macmillan, 1964.

———. *The Leavetaking*. Boston: Little, Brown, 1975.

———. *Getting Through*. New York: Harper and Row, 1980

———. *The Dark*. New York: Penguin, rpt.1983.

———. *The Pornographer*. New York: Penguin, 1983.

———. *Amongst Women*. New York: Viking, 1990.

———. *The Collected Stories*. New York: Random House, 1993.

MacLaverty, Bernard. *Lamb*. London: Cape, 1980.

———. *A Time to Dance*. London: Cape, 1982.

———. *Cal*. London: Cape, 1983.

———. *The Great Profundo*. London: Cape, 1987.

———. *Grace Notes*. London, Cape: 1997.

McNamee, Eoin. *Resurrection Man*. New York: Picador, 1994.

———. *The Last of Deeds & Love in History*. New York: Picador, 1996.

Moore, Brian.*The Lonely Passion of Judith Hearne*. New York: Little, Brown, 1956.

———. *The Feast of Lupercal*. New York: Little, Brown, 1957.

———. *The Luck of Ginger Coffey*. New York: Little, Brown, 1960.

O'Brien, Edna. *The Country Girls Trilogy*. New York: Penguin, 1980.

———. *A Fanatic Heart*. New York: Farrar, Straus, Giroux, 1984.

———. *Lantern Slides*. New York: Farrar, Straus, Giroux, 1990.

———. *House of Splendid Isolation*. New York: Farrar, Straus, Giroux, 1994.

O'Brien, George. *The Village of Longing and Dancehill Days*. London: Penguin, 1990.

———. *Out of our Minds*. Belfast: Blackstaff, 1994.

O'Connor, Joseph. *Cowboys and Indians*. London: Flamingo, 1992.

———. *Desperadoes*. London: Flamingo, 1994.

———. *The Salesman*. London: Secker & Warburg, 1997.

O'Faolain, Julia. *We Might See Sights!* London: Faber & Faber, 1968.

———. *Melancholy Baby and Other Stories*. Dublin: Poolbeg, 1978.

———. *The Irish Signorina*. London: Viking, 1984.

———. *No Country for Young Men*. New York: Carroll and Graf, 1987.

———. *The Judas Cloth*. London: Minerva, 1993.

Patterson, Glenn. *Fat Lad*. London: Chatto & Windus, 1988.

———. *Burning Your Own*. London: Chatto & Windus, 1992.

———. *Black Night at Big Thunder Mountain*. London: Chatto and Windus, 1995.

Plunkett, James. *Strumpet City*. London: Hutchinson, 1969.

————. *Collected Short Stories of James Plunkett*. Dublin: Poolbeg, 1977.

————. *The Risen People*. Dublin: Irish Writers' Co-operative, 1978.

Stuart, Francis. *Black List Section H*. Carbondale: Southern Illinois University Press, 1971; rpt. New York: Penguin, 1996.

————. *A Hole in the Head*. London: Brian & O'Keefe, 1977.

————. *The High Consistory*. London: Brian & O'Keefe, 1981.

Tóibín, Colm. *The South*. New York: Penguin, 1992.

————. *The Heather Blazing*. London: Penguin, 1992.

————. *The Story of the Night*. New York: Henry Holt, 1997.

Trevor, William. *Mrs. Eckdorf in O'Neill's Hotel*. New York: Viking, 1970.

————. *Angels at the Ritz and Other Stories*. New York: Viking, 1976.

————. *Beyond the Pale and Other Stories*. New York: Viking, 1981.

————. *Fools of Fortune*. New York: Viking, 1983.

————. *The News from Ireland and Other Stories*. New York: Viking, 1986.

————. *The Silence of the Garden*. New York: Penguin, 1990.

————. *Collected Stories*. New York: Viking, 1992.

————. *Excursions in the Real World*. London: Hutchinson, 1993.

————. *Felicia's Journey*. New York: Viking, 1995.

Wilson, Robert McLiam. *Ripley Bogle*. Belfast: Blackstaff, 1989.

————. *Manfred's Pain*. London: Picador, 1993.

————. *Eureka Street*. New York: Arcade, 1997.

INDEX